600

D0810194

STAYING CURRENT

A Proficiency Guide for Serious Pilots

by DAN MANNINGHAM
and the Editors of *Business and Commercial Aviation*

Ziff-Davis Publishing Company/New York

Contents

CONTENTS

V   WEATHER   207

VI   FUEL   279

VII   PROBLEMS   317

CONTENTS

Preface

Human knowledge is accumulating at an extraordinary rate. Historians believe that a few hundred years ago all knowledge could have been contained in three or four volumes. The Library of Congress now has tabs on nearly 10,000,000 titles.

Between 1800 and 1900 total knowledge approximately doubled. In the next fifty years it doubled again. In this decade knowledge will likely double every two or three years. Nowhere is that more evident than in aviation.

Every serious pilot is faced with the constant need to remain informed. Surprisingly, there have been precious few volumes devoted to the real challenges of professional aviation. This volume is intended to fill the gap in existing aviation literature between the basic flight instruction manuals and the advanced engineering texts on testing and design. In short, this volume is for *all those* who take their flying seriously.

Business and Commercial Aviation magazine is the largest publication in the world devoted to the particular needs of commercial flight crews and the businessman pilot. Over the years, B/CA has covered many vital subjects in the field of commercial aviation, often with award-winning expertise. This volume, *Staying Current,* is an anthology of the best and most instructive articles on pilot proficiency from *Business and Commercial Aviation.*

Between these covers you will find 51 challenging, thought-provoking selections. Each has been carefully selected for its lasting value. You will not learn how to fly in this book, but you will learn how to fly more safely, efficiently and wisely.

Dan Manningham

Mansfield, Ohio
April 1980

PEOPLE

I

The single most important element in aviation is people, operating individually and in combination. Pilots, mechanics, air traffic controllers, and those fragile units we know as passengers are all subject to physiological and emotional problems that can seriously compromise the safety or comfort of a flight.

Yet people are at once the most critical and least studied elements in all of aviation, even though their physiological reactions to a demanding environment, their mental attitudes and limitations and their personal health maintenance are vital safety factors.

Several catastrophic accidents have been ascribed to the physical incapacitation of the pilot in control. Passenger problems can seriously complicate a flight. Crew fatigue has been studied and measured, debated and regulated with great heat and only moderate light being generated. The human influence is everywhere, always important and sadly neglected.

This section is devoted to those very special human problems.

The Inoperative Pilot 1

by Dan Manningham

Item: Captain, age 38, died or collapsed due to heart failure associated with coronary artery disease at critical point during night IFR approach. Copilot unable to recover aircraft from loss of control. Fatal to all occupants.

Item: Captain, age 45, collapsed after coronary occlusion shortly after takeoff. Aircraft crashed into ocean: 56 fatalities, eight survivors.

Item: Copilot executed a particularly smooth landing and reversed all engines. Airplane drifted toward runway edge and captain corrected back to centerline. Copilot slumped to the left as if still reaching for the throttles and did not regain consciousness.

Physical incapacitation has been a potential hazard since man first left the ground. Great progress has been made in many areas of aviation medicine but inflight pilot dysfunction continues to pose a very real threat.

Pilots are quite rightly concerned about engine fires, hydraulic failures and rapid decompression. We practice, study, discuss and drill. But until recently, little has been said about the practical, on-line problems posed by the inoperative pilot, even though that problem is far more common than many of those covered in flight manuals.

Aviation medical specialists divide incapacitation into two broad categories, obvious and subtle. Let's look at them both.

Obvious inflight incapacitation is that sudden functional loss you would expect from massive heart failure or gross cerebral stroke. Your flying partner simply collapses and slumps unconscious with little or no warning and you are abruptly faced with the problems of flying the airplane, removing the interference caused by his inert form and executing a safe landing.

Your biggest problem may be in regaining control of the airplane in light of the interference caused during and after your partner's collapse. You will, however, have the advantage of immediately recognizing such sudden and obvious collapse. Once control is regained, the immediate problem shrinks to an elementary abnormal situation.

Let's not overlook the possibility that obvious incapacitation can be something far less dramatic than a crewmember slumping over the controls. We at B/CA have witnessed this happening due to a speck of dust in a crewman's eye, to glasses being knocked off, to a sneezing fit and even to an excruciating need to go potty. All of those possibilities and more must be kept in mind.

A far more insidious predicament is created by the pilot who inconspicuously passes into a condition of dysfunction with no warning and little or no indication. Subtle or partial incapacitation is that situation in which a pilot appears to be functioning but is mentally disengaged from his immediate responsibilities and surroundings. He may sit with eyes open and hands on controls, looking perfectly normal to his fellow crewmembers, while his cerebral cortex (that portion of the brain responsible for thought and analysis) has ceased to function. He is conscious but, as the doctor says, he is not cerebrating.

Subtle dysfunction is a treacherous condition which poses several challenges for the remaining crewmembers. It can be very difficult to recognize due to the indistinct nature of the symptoms. In fact, it may only involve a transient reduction of cerebral function which remains undetected because it occurs during some relatively safe phase of flight.

When a pilot does become subtly disabled during some critical maneuver, the unimpaired crewmembers may have difficulty detecting the lack of function due to high workloads associated with the more demanding phase of flight. The human potential for non-performance, without warning or indication, is a serious threat to flight safety.

There are several potential causes of partial loss of function, but two bear marked interest for the line pilot: hypoglycemia and cerebral dysfunction.

Hypoglycemia: You may recognize hypoglycemia by the more familiar term "low blood sugar." When the equilibrium mechanism that controls blood-sugar levels malfunctions, the brain can be deprived of its only nutrient, glucose, and several things may happen: sweating, weakness, hunger, tremors, mental confusion, irritability, headache and even convulsions. In fact, by starving the brain, hypoglycemia can mimic any neurologic or psychiatric disorder.

Cerebral Dysfunction: The cerebral cortex is that fine outer layer of grey matter over the brain which is responsible for what we might call human intelligence. This organ generates those intricate mental processes that allow such complex psychomotor activities as flying.

Mild cortical defects are not uncommon and may go undetected indefinitely if the central nervous system is not stressed beyond routine levels. The natural processes of compensation and rationalization will obscure such defects from the individual and his associates.

If critical stress is first encountered during some pivotal flight maneuver, that pilot may cease to function effectively at the worst possible moment with little or no warning to other crewmembers.

There are several possible causes of hypoglycemia, but the easiest to correct is poor diet.

When you awake in the morning your blood glucose level will have dropped during that long period at night without food intake. If you start the day with coffee and a sweet roll, you are a setup for reactive hypoglycemia two to three hours later.

It works like this: When that sweet roll hits bottom, your system converts the refined sugar and starches into glucose so rapidly that your blood sugar level rises at an abnormal rate. When the homeostatic system, which balances glucose levels, senses the sharp rate and rise, it signals the pancreas to release insulin proportionately. In this case the rate is abrupt and will only be sustained over the very brief time it takes for your body to convert the refined carbohydrates to glucose. As a result, too much insulin is triggered to the bloodstream so that glucose volume is driven well below the fasting level.

That doughnut for breakfast will give you an initial shot of blood glucose within 30 minutes, but two to three hours later your system may sag far below acceptable levels. The 10:00 o'clock "sinking spell" can be triggered by your inadequate 7:00 o'clock breakfast. But there is an easy defense.

Proteins are processed by the body at a much more steady rate so that your homeostat detects a gradual but sustained rise in blood sugar. In that case appropriate quantities of insulin are metered out to stabilize glucose levels at the optimum point. Since the reduction and conversion of protein continues for several hours, you avoid the peaks and rebounds brought on by a pure carbohydrate intake.

Fruit or unsweetened fruit juice are excellent snack foods because fruit sugars are absorbed more evenly by the intestinal tract and do not overstimulate the pancreas for insulin release. After fruit ingestion, blood sugar rises quickly to normal levels and then tapers gradually without rebound. Four simple dietary practices will obviate reactive hypoglycemia even for those who are particularly susceptible.

(1) Avoid refined carbohydrate (sugar and all refined starches) at all times. Limit the amount of carbohydrate in your diet to 25 percent.

(2) Eat protein rich meals every four hours, especially when on flight duty.

(3) Use fruit or protein snacks (cheese, nuts, etc.) for odd duty times.

(4) Substitute milk or fruit juice for coffee and soft drinks.

There is also a simple medical test that can determine your susceptibility to reactive hypoglycemia. It is the glucose tolerance test used to detect the high blood sugar (hyperglycemia) of early diabetes mellitus. One major airline administered this glucose tolerance test to a group of 175 pilots age 40 and older, and found that 25 percent indicated a rebound hypoglycemia. In each case, by simple adjustments to diet, these pilots were able to avoid these dangerous glycemic cycles.

Check your eating habits. Talk to your doctor. Hypoglycemia is a very real, but manageable, potential hazard.

Symptoms can be as mild as the erosion of previous proficiency levels and some change in disposition over a considerable period of time. Proper diagnosis often requires a fusion of professional and medical data.

When a responsible and experienced pilot demonstrates obvious proficiency problems, he may be suffering from some form of transient or altered cerebral dysfunction. In such cases, professional evaluation must be supplemented with appropriate medical information. So therefore, accurate records are vital since they establish the baseline against which deviation can be measured.

Hypoglycemia and cerebral dysfunction are distinct but not exclusive causes of subtle inflight incapacitation. Brain tumor, epilepsy and even simple psychological stress can trigger serious mental lapses. Before you warn your best pilot to pull himself together, let the flight surgeon have a thorough look. Close rapport between operations, training and medical counsel, along with good records, can save lives and careers.

Perhaps no one has contributed more to an understanding of the operational problems and potential of inflight incapacitation than Doctors Kidera and Harper, of United Airlines. Besides co-authoring several medical papers on the subject, these two doctors were the first to recognize the value of a controlled operational study regarding inflight incapacitation. This study took place at the UA Flight Training Center and included both obvious and subtle dysfunctions.

Qualified DC-8 and Boeing 737 line crews were utilized while flying the respective simulators. Sound movie film was used to record the mock incapacitations and subsequent events. Aircraft attitude, airspeed, altitude and course deviation were spliced in at the frame bottoms from movies made of flight instruments in the simulator control room. Three-man crews were used in the DC-8 and two-man crews in the 737.

Obvious Incapacitation: Obvious incapacitation was simulated by the collapse of one crewmember at some pre-designated cue, for which only he had been briefed. All but a few episodes took place below 1700 feet and several below 200. No instructions were given to the crew on how to handle the emergency.

Although there were no "crashes" during this study of obvious dysfunction, Kidera and Harper noted some interesting aspects.

The surviving pilot was often so startled by the abrupt and obvious collapse of his fellow crewmember that he failed to handle the total problem satisfactorily. Situation analysis and aircraft control were generally adequate but command ability frequently suffered. Faced with a completely unfamiliar situation, pilots tended to fixate on something less than the total problem, at the expense of flight safety.

There is nothing new about this "startle reaction." It is the very reason that pilots are trained and drilled in emergency procedures. Repeated exposure to proper remedial actions minimizes the adverse effects of surprise. Gross incapacitation is just one more serious emergency for which business pilots must prepare to react automatically. United has developed the procedure and we'll look at it in a moment.

Interference from the unconscious body was found to be a significant problem in the UA study. Standard inertia-reel harnesses allow an unconscious body to fall from the sitting position to almost any portion in the control area. Two-pilot crews are particularly vulnerable to this hazard. Three-man crews have a real advantage since the third member is normally available to restrain the unconscious body from interfering with controls and switches.

In light of this problem, the 737 simulator cockpit was equipped with an experimental restraint system for preliminary evaluation. This device consisted of a motorized unit, energized by a guarded switch available to the opposite pilot, which:

· Retracts the shoulder harness firmly back into the seat.
· Drives the seat to the full aft position.
· Alerts the cabin attendants to come to the flight deck.

Brief initial tests indicated the usefulness and desirability of a restraint system, particularly in two-pilot aircraft. Even simple military-type, hand-locked harnesses are sufficiently confining when the lock is engaged.

Cockpit communication is the essential element in counteracting the hazards of subtle incapacitation. Good crew interaction provides a desirable matrix for early detection of inconspicuous psychomotor failure.

In order to establish baseline information on crew communication, UA line pilots were observed by simulator instructors as they handled routine instrument or systems failures. Detection/reaction times were recorded in 50 separate incidents. Results were measured as a range of time and a mean time from the failure to the point where that information was communicated to the other pilot(s). Four specific failures were employed.

(1) Failure of primary radio navigation display of pilot making VOR approach for landing: range—0.5 seconds to 28.0 seconds; mean—10.0 seconds.

(2) Yaw damper failure during steep turns: range—0.5 seconds to one hour; mean—10.6 minutes.

(3) Flaps split during an engine-out backcourse ILS approach: range—1.5 seconds to 40.0 seconds; mean—16 seconds.

(4) Failure of HSI of pilot making ADF approach from information displayed on RMI: range—0.5 seconds to 15.0 seconds; mean—5.2 seconds.

In general, crews communicated well when faced with such common failures. In 95 percent of the cases, recognition and communication were essentially simultaneous.

The next step was to expose these crews to subtle human failure with no preparation or training. The captain was briefed privately to cease functioning somewhere inside the outer marker. He was told not to appear incapacitated but only to refrain from making any control inputs or communication.

Twenty-five per cent of the "flights" crashed. Of those that did not crash, mean detection/reaction time was 1.5 minutes. Several copilots were reluctant to take over the controls even though they felt sure that the captain was not functioning properly. The basic fundamental of crew concept tended to break down in the presence of a totally unfamiliar emergency.

In the final stage, test crews received a short presentation on the possibility and hazards of subtle pilot dysfunction. Emphasis was placed on the need for total crew involvement and the use of communication as a tool in detecting human failure. No crashes or unsafe flight parameters developed from the series of simulated subtle incapacitation incidents that followed this briefing. This is a highly significant finding: *a knowledge of, and preplanning for, subtle incapacitation reduces the risk to near zero.*

The results of this UA study are clear. In the case of subtle incapacitation, early detection is crucial and United has developed what they call the "two-communication rule." It works like this. Each pilot passively monitors the other in the process of routine cockpit communications. A high index of suspicion is warranted whenever your partner does not respond appropriately to:

(1) Two verbal communication attempts, or

(2) The first verbal communication attempt associated with any significant deviation from standard flight profiles.

Standardized operating procedures are essential to the success of this "two-communication rule" because these procedures create a familiar sequence of events. This pattern then becomes the structured background against which irrational behavior can be detected. When cockpit routine is irregular or undisciplined, irrational behavior is effectively clouded by that unstable environment.

Standardize your procedures. Be aware of your flying partner's actions and attitudes. And be especially alert to assume control anytime the two-com rule is broken.

Once the incapacitation is detected, your worst problem is over. The rest of the drill involves simple but necessary cleanup procedures that will allow the remaining crew to land the aircraft and secure medical aid.

The first procedural step is so elementary there is a danger it may be overlooked. *Assume control of the airplane* and (if necessary) climb to a safe altitude. We know that sounds obvious, but your startle reaction may prompt you to exert undue attention to your crew mate as he clutches his chest and grimaces with intense pain. Avoid that temptation and just fly the airplane. Carefully, even methodically, check the position of essential controls and switches because your partner's behavior just prior to his failure may have been irrational. A thorough cockpit inventory will further serve to nullify your own emotional response.

When you are satisfied that the airplane is safely configured (fuel, hydraulics, generators, anti-ice, autopilot, radios) ask ATC for a holding vector and consider declaring an emergency. Right then you'll need all the help you can get and the NTSB is going to require a written report anyway because of the incapacitation.

When flight conditions are stabilized you will need to restrain and remove the sick pilot for his own good as well as to reduce the distraction and possible interference he will create. It takes at least two people to handle the dead weight of an unconscious body without risk of interference to controls and switches, so you will need help from another crewmember or passenger. Delegate the first aid to someone else so you can concentrate on your responsibilities as sole pilot.

After you are alone, reorganize the cockpit for a landing as soon as practicable. You may want a cabin attendant or passenger in the empty seat to read checklists and reach out-of-the-way controls, but he must be carefully briefed on the narrow limits of his activities.

Your primary burden is still to fly the airplane, but when time allows, call ahead for medical help. The really essential element is an ambulance. Doctors are helpful, but your patient will very likely require treatment that is available only in a hospital. If you have time, give a brief factual summary of the patient's symptoms and condition, but don't overload yourself or delay the landing.

After the landing is completed, your responsibility shifts to the patient's care. When he has been properly cared for, notify your company and arrange for your passengers' needs.

The incapacitation procedure is logical and brief:

(1) Assume control and fly the airplane to a safe situation.

(2) Restrain and/or remove the incapacitated pilot.

(3) Reorganize the cockpit and prepare for a landing.

(4) Arrange for an ambulance to meet the airplane.

You can minimize your exposure to inflight incapacitation with two simple precautions:

(1) Establish a professional liaison between your flight department and a flight surgeon. Arrange for him to fly in your cockpits periodically, and be sure he knows each pilot in the operation.

Coordinate your training, operational and medical records so as to recognize significant behavioral changes. When everyone is alert, the chances of early detection increase substantially.

One regional United Airline medical office undertook a daily working relationship with the flight training and flight operations departments with significant results. In five years, 20 serious problems were detected including brain tumor, hypoglycemia and psychiatric disorder. Fourteen of these 20 were having noticeable proficiency problems with no apparent medical aspect. Several of these pilots were failing to meet even minimum standards and seven of them were about to be fired for incompetence. When proficiency records were augmented by sound medical monitoring, noticeable patterns emerged. Once the physical problem was diagnosed, medical treatment and counseling removed the operational hazard and softened the letdown for those unable to continue flying.

(2) Arrange for realistic incapacitation training for each pilot on a non-scheduled basis. Basic simulator drills based on the "two-communication rule" and the four-step incapacitation procedure can readily prepare pilots to cope with that problem as routinely as any other emergency or abnormal situation.

Business pilots bear some unique responsibilities. As the primary command/control system in the aircraft, we are constrained to conscientiously monitor ourselves as well as our peers. There are times when we must be candid if not brutally frank with each other and especially with ourselves. The corporate pilot who considers himself too healthy, too tough, too competent, to become a detriment in the cockpit sets the stage for disaster.

Passenger Problems 2

by Dan Manningham

When you think of it, flying an airplane is a simple job. The whole act is laid out in the aircraft's flight manual. All the pilot has to do is learn his part. The problems come from other participants in the act who may miss a line or make a mistake. Other pilots, air traffic controllers, mechanics and passengers are all linked elements in that weak human chain that complicates flying far beyond simple mechanical problems.

One element, largely ignored, is the area of passenger problems. Passengers present several possible challenges to the professional operation of a trip. As pilot-in-command, you should be familiar with at least the following potential problems:

Drunks—Intoxicated passengers are difficult on any aircraft, but in corporate aviation the problem is often compounded by the very delicate relationship that exists between crew and passengers. Airlines are forbidden by law to accept intoxicated passengers; you may not enjoy that luxury. When you do have a drunk, try to appease him and keep him seated. Consider leaving the seat-belt sign on while setting the cabin altitude at the maximum permissible level and perhaps he will fall asleep. It works quite often.

Upset and angry passengers—This one's a toughie. You cannot allow the passenger to interfere with your judgment or your operation of the aircraft, but his anger definitely needs some attention. The real threat with an angry passenger is that someone will provoke his anger into outright belligerence or irrational behavior. If you can swallow your pride long enough to let him blow off some steam, the problem usually will resolve itself in short order. The primary thing is to avoid a physical confrontation inflight no matter how much pride you must swallow. If the situation continues to heat up, land.

Problem passengers can complicate a trip even more than many mechanical or operational difficulties. As with most challenges, a small amount of anticipation and planning can turn an otherwise unpleasant experience into a happy—and safe—trip for everyone.

Children and infants—Really small infants are best carried in a bassinet. If possible, position the bassinet against a rear-facing bulkhead during takeoffs, landings and emergencies to protect the child from being tossed about by turbulence or a crash.

The mother will prefer to hold the child in her lap, but the bassinet/bulkhead combination is far safer.

Children often have trouble clearing their ears during climb and descent so it is reasonable to expect that they will cry and complain of a headache or sore ears. Fortunately, crying is one of the best remedies for otitis (inflammation of the ear). When the child begins to cry, he will probably experience some relief. Chewing gum or drinking something may be enough to prevent a serious problem if given at the first sign of discomfort.

If you have children of your own, you know how restless they can get. Simple diversions such as playing cards, pencils, pads of paper and balloons are usually enough to satisfy most children.

Elderly passengers—This may be the most relative term of all. Some people are "old" at 60; others are informed, inquisitive and agile in their 80s.

It is probably fair to say that older people are likely to be somewhat more apprehensive about new experiences than their more youthful counterparts. They will also prefer that you avoid aviation jargon and picayune details in favor of simple, direct explanations.

Blind passengers—There are several definitions of the word "blind," but in all cases, these people lack the vision necessary to function normally. I have carried many blind people over the years and have found them to be interesting, confident and resourceful. All they seem to ask for is a fair shake.

Offer only as much help as the blind passenger desires when boarding and leaving the aircraft. It is too easy to smother him or her with physical maneuvering when simple verbal instructions about steps and doors and seat locations are sufficient.

When seated, describe the cabin layout in simple terms including exits, bathrooms, life vests, air vents, ashtrays, reclining seats, refreshment holders, folding tables and call buttons if they are available. Allow the blind passenger to operate the seat-belt and emergency oxygen equipment by himself so he can be independent during the actual flight. When serving a meal, describe the tray layout by the clock method, alerting the passenger to hot items.

Many blind passengers travel with seeing-eye dogs and this should not present a problem. Don't pat the dog because he will be trained to receive affection only from his owner. Do allow the dog to remain with the passenger if at all possible. On high-altitude flights arrange the seating so there will be a separate oxygen mask available for the dog.

Deaf passengers—Deafness is a relative term. Experts say there is no such thing as an absolute lack of sensation to all sound. Even those with so-called total deafness can perceive some extreme frequencies through direct nerve and bone detection. Consequently, deaf passengers will be far more comfortable during the trip if you explain, beforehand, the most obvious changes in vibrations such as takeoff power, landing-gear movements, speed-brake deployment and reverse thrust.

Take time to point out all items of emergency equipment, including the emergency equipment card. It's also nice to explain, with maps, notes or lip reading, the route of flight and other items of interest because your deaf passengers will not hear any inflight announcements.

Fatigue in the Safety Equation

3

by Nancy R. Day

At about 0126 hours on May 10, 1975, a Piper Aztec crashed 3.3 nm short of Runway 5R while making a night VFR approach to Cleveland-Hopkins International Airport. The pilot was killed on impact; his 14-year-old son, the only passenger, was saved by being thrown clear of the wreckage, but was seriously injured.

The NTSB found no evidence of adverse weather conditions, malfunction in the aircraft, aircraft systems or navigational aids, and no sign of pilot incapacitation. The Board determined that the probable cause of the accident was "the pilot's failure to arrest the aircraft's descent during a landing approach. . . ."

Although the official report states that the reasons for this failure could not be determined, the Board said since the pilot took 22 seconds to acknowledge the approach controller's last transmission, that the autopilot appears to have been on and that there was a "relaxed atmosphere" and light work load in the cockpit "suggests that the pilot was not aware of the aircraft's progress and flight path *because he was asleep.*" (Emphasis ours.)

The pilot, age 36, had 6705 hours, 862 in type. He flew five nights a week until well past midnight, Monday through Friday for a scheduled air taxi courier service, over a route from Rochester, New York to Cleveland via Buffalo, Pittsburgh and Columbus. He had told another pilot who often accompanied him that he became progressively more tired toward the end of each week; in fact, this pilot stated that the deceased occasionally dozed off and awoke to his call sign on the radio. On this trip, he had brought his son with him for company, but the boy was sleeping at the time of the crash. The accident occurred on the last day of his week.

Unfortunately, this classic example of an accident caused by pilot fatigue is far from unique. In the five years from 1970 to 1974, NTSB figures show 183 accidents in which pilot fatigue was either a cause or a factor,

77 of which involved fatalities. Here are a few selected cases:

· At 2100 hours, a 51-year-old private, instrument-rated pilot with 12,500 total hours, who was flying on business, crashed due to an uncontrolled descent in a Piper Twin Comanche over Eliasville, Texas. The NTSB found evidence that he was both impaired by alcohol and asleep at the time of the accident. The pilot, the only occupant of the plane, was killed.

· An air taxi cargo pilot, age 26, with 1446 total hours, crashed in a Cessna 310P near Antwerp, Ohio, at 0540 hours. After 18+40 on duty, in violation of FAR Part 135.136(b) flight time limitation rules, he "failed to follow approved procedures and directives." The accident was fatal.

· On final approach to Madison, Alabama at 0404 hours, a Cessna 210A on a business mission, flown by a pilot, age 41, collided with trees, killing the pilot and two passengers. The pilot, who had flown 10 hours in the last 24, had become lost on the previous leg. The causes of the accident were improper IFR operation and failure to read instruments properly; fatigue was listed as a factor.

· While landing at North Bend, Oregon at 0935 hours, a 31-year-old corporate pilot with 3380 hours, 451 in type, overshot, colliding with electronic towers. The plane, a Piper Pressurized Navajo, was damaged substantially, and the pilot was seriously injured. The weather was rainy and the runway was wet, but the pilot "selected [the] wrong runway relative to existing wind, misjudged distance and speed, [and] delayed in initiating a go-around." Fatigue was determined to be a factor.

Fatigue-related accidents appear to have several things in common. For one, the vast majority occur during the night and early morning (between 1800 and 0600 hours), despite the fact that there are fewer aircraft movements at these times. Many of the accidents involve confusion, disorganization or inattention on the part of the pilot. These accidents are more likely to occur when the weather is bad. Also, a disproportionate number of fatigue-related accidents occur during the landing phase of flight, which is the most demanding on the pilot and comes at the end of his duty time.

According to Dr. Stanley Mohler, the FAA's chief of aeromedical applications and an expert on fatigue, there are 10 more accidents in which fatigue was involved for each one the NTSB conclusively proves to be fatigue-related. Fatigue is often dismissed as a cause or factor in favor of a more concrete reason but, Mohler said, "I think it is the most common factor," as it influences a pilot's thinking, judgment and actions, and drops low proficiency even lower. Although fatigue should not be used as a convenient excuse for pilot error, it should be recognized and dealt with as an important and real threat to safety.

Dr. Kenneth G. Bergin, author of a textbook on aviation medicine, observes, "Statistics, as always, are notoriously unreliable, but pilot error is commonly quoted as the cause of an accident. . . . No doubt in my mind that there is a very real relationship between fatigue, pilot error and accident rates. . . . It is often very difficult to identify fatigue as a cause of an accident for the simple reason that all facts are not known, and many near-accidents are not reported. . . . Fatigue is difficult to quantify but can be clearly identified by clinical observation by a doctor experienced in civil aviation medicine."

Most experts on fatigue would agree with Dr. Douglas Busby of the FAA's Civil Aeromedical Institute that "one of the greatest problems we have is defining fatigue."

Fatigue is all too often defined in terms of what it does rather than what it is. It is assumed that fatigue causes a performance decrement; therefore, that performance decrement is synonymous with fatigue. This leads to the circular reasoning inherent in the joke about the Air Force pilot who asks, "Why am I missing the target?" "Because you're tired," his commander replies. "How do I know I'm tired?" the pilot asks. "Because you're missing the target," is the answer.

Mohler defines fatigue in terms of what it isn't. A person who is in good health, is physically fit and has had—and usually gets—a good night's sleep shows an absence of fatigue. Such an individual would demonstrate the ability to think, learn and remember with ease. He would have a flowing movement and would report a general feeling of well-being.

S. Howard Bartley, a psychology professor and a leading authority on fatigue, feels that even this distinction is not very useful. He has made the following observations about the nature of fatigue:

· Tiredness comes and goes during the day.

· We can wake up from a full night's sleep and feel more tired than when we went to sleep.

· Doing an unpleasant task makes us feel more tired than doing a pleasant one.

· We can be tired by one task, but switch to another that may require more energy and soon feel less tired. (For instance, after a hard day at the office, we can feel like a million dollars behind the lawn mower.)

· We can go without rest for long periods when we're having a good time.

· We make the most mistakes when we're tired, making us more tired.

· When we're tired, we aren't likely to be enthusiastic about anything, but if we are enthusiastic, we rarely feel fatigued.

· We can't always say why we are tired.

Since fatigue can come and go rapidly, Bartley concludes it cannot be the result of lactic acid build-up from muscular activity as it was once thought, since it takes some time for these chemicals to disappear. Instead, he sees fatigue not as an objective measure of an individual's energy resources, but as "a personal experience . . . a self-assessment of an individual's feelings of aversion to, and/or inadequacy for, carrying on in a responsible way."

15

Mohler states that the most common cause of pilot fatigue is not getting enough sleep. Obviously, a pilot should plan to get ample sleep before flying if he possibly can. However, what may be adequate sleep for one person may not be for another. Seven to eight hours generally fulfills average sleep requirements, but as little as four hours or as much as 13 hours a night can be normal for some individuals. Too little sleep slows a person's reaction time, impairs his judgment and makes his reactions erratic. However, too much sleep can also be detrimental, as the basal metabolism drops so low that the individual is sluggish upon awakening.

Not only the quantity but also the *quality* of sleep is important. Sleeping quarters should be selected so that the temperature, humidity and ventilation are comfortable and noise is minimal. A sleeper makes four or five cycles a night from REM (rapid eye movement) sleep to deep sleep and back to REM, and detrimental effects are noted when too much of either *type* of sleep is lost.

Insomnia, the inability to fall asleep and stay asleep throughout the night, is a widespread problem in this country. Inability to fall asleep can result from pain, stress, anxiety or eating a heavy meal just before retiring. Many people have the habit of thinking far into the night, which consumes a lot of energy unproductively. There are several possible medical reasons for waking up during the night—anticipation of an exciting event the next day, depression or drinking quantities of coffee, tea or alcohol in the evening.

Pilots who must fly at night and sleep during the day have some sleep problems built into their schedule. First, day sleep is seldom as refreshing as night sleep; it is hard to block out the sunlight and the noises of everyday living, especially at home if there are children.

Such a reverse schedule not only puts a pilot out of phase with the world, but with his own biological rhythms as well. The human body operates on a circadian rhythm (from the Latin "circa dies," meaning "about a day"), which is synchronized by the earth's cycle of darkness and light. There is a daily pattern to mood, blood pressure, pulse, respiration, blood sugar levels and ability to metabolize drugs and, as a result, in reaction time, keenness of sensory perception and performance efficiency in various types of tasks.

There is a wide variation in individual body rhythms—we all know "morning" people who are "early to bed and early to rise" and "night" people, who like to get up at noon and work or party into the night. Despite individual differences, very few people are truly nocturnal, so a pilot who will be assigned to continuous night duty must be selected with great care.

Wiley Post was the first to recognize the detrimental effects of traversing several time zones on the sleeping and eating patterns of air travelers. When, at the destination, a traveler finds himself on a different dark-light cycle, it takes some time (usually from one to three days) for his own biological clock to readjust. Again, there is much individual variation in the time it takes to adjust; for instance, younger pilots adapt more quickly than older ones. It is also harder to travel from west to east than from east to west. This is because most people have a daily cycle that is from one to three hours longer than 24 hours. Thus, we are normally under some pressure to compress our daily cycle. In traveling from west to east, the day is shortened and the pressure to compress the cycle is increased. There is also less time left to rest before the next day's activities. East to west flights also disrupt circadian rhythms but at least provide additional time for rest.

According to Mohler, the second most common cause of pilot fatigue is obesity. Very heavy people require more energy to move their bulk. Obesity is definitely associated with fatigue, but it should also be mentioned that crash dieting produces fatigue as well.

Obesity is closely linked with the next most common cause of fatigue— lack of physical fitness. Pilots are, unfortunately, among the most sedentary of professionals, and it is hard for them to fit a regular fitness program into their irregular schedules. Yet the job of flying demands physical fitness to cope with split-second responses and such rigors as multiple takeoffs and landings.

Eating right is also important in staving off fatigue. You have to eat enough, or you will become tired and irritable. But you also have to watch *what* you eat. Candy bars, danish pastry and pizza provide quick energy, but won't get you through the day. Protein foods, such as meat and cheese and fruits will give you more energy in the long run. A pilot should never eat a heavy meal before or during flight since the digestive process directs blood away from the brain and makes a person sluggish and sleepy.

Visual problems are also integrally related to fatigue. We all know the feeling of our eyes being dry and scratchy when we are tired. After about 16 hours of wakefulness, they become scratchy as "sand" or "sleep" begins to form. Eye scratchiness increases with excessive smoking or conditions of low humidity, common in pressurized planes. Scratchy eyes are both a result of being tired and a cause of an individual reporting he feels tired. The only way to ease the condition is to get a good night's sleep.

Eye strain is also a common problem among pilots who must constantly switch from reading charts to reading the panel to looking outside the aircraft. The older a pilot is and the more paperwork he does, the more likely it is he needs correction for farsightedness to read the panel properly. Many pilots let this slide, but the problem can become acute, particularly in night conditions and when the person is already fatigued. Pilots' eyes are also subjected to very bright light, especially on top of clouds, which in the absence of sunglasses is tiring to the eyes.

17

A number of operational factors have a bearing on fatigue, among them the number of takeoffs and landings, schedules and routes, traffic density, weather, type of aircraft, powerplant reliability, fellow crewmembers and crew rest facilities. Experts have attempted to quantify the contribution to fatigue of these factors; those results will be discussed a bit later.

The cockpit environment itself provides a number of factors that give rise to fatigue. First, a cabin altitude of 5000 feet or more can create a condition of mild hypoxia, a known fatigue-producer. High and low temperatures, or a wide variation in temperature, are also fatiguing. Vibration and turbulence force you to use your muscles to continually move back to the position you wish to remain in. Noise is not only irritating, but forces you to listen harder and speak louder. According to the EPA, a steady exposure to noise of 90 dB or more increases muscle tension and decreases response time in decision-making.

Cockpit design factors are also starting to be recognized for their part in reducing or promoting fatigue. Pilots' seats should be centered and fully adjustable, forward, backward, up and down. A seat that is too high or low can give the pilot a backache. Restraint systems and oxygen masks should also be as comfortable as possible. The least tiring way to sit for a period of time is with both feet resting on the floor and with the back supported by the seat back cushioning.

A cramped cockpit in which the pilot cannot stretch or move in any direction promotes fatigue. In many cockpits, there is no place to put the required documents, maps and charts, forcing the pilot to reach down, behind or under his feet, and that reaching is fatiguing.

The layout of the instrument panel is important, too; nothing should be hard to reach, read or differentiate. Night lighting that is neither too dim nor too bright enhances readability. On some instrument panels, each instrument and the figures on it are about the same size, or there are long lines of look-alike switches. This situation makes it easy for a tired pilot to misread an instrument or flip the wrong switch. If switches are in a line, the "off" or "stop" mode for all of them should at least be in the same direction.

Fatigue problems are also complicated by the effects of aging. For example, reaction times of a 60-year-old pilot are likely to be twice as long as those of a 40-year-old pilot. However, it is important to differentiate between chronological age and arterial age, since two pilots the same age can be in very different states of physical fitness. Also, older pilots have the advantage of experience and the resultant economy of effort.

Stress is an important factor in pilot fatigue and pilots are exposed to stress from a multitude of sources. For one, they are constantly on the move, having to adapt to new surroundings. Sitting alone in the cockpit with nothing much to look at outside the aircraft can produce boredom and a sense of isolation. Just one hour of boredom can consume more nervous energy than an entire day of work.

Flying is a routine, but it is punctuated by demands for split-second decision-making under pressure, and the faster, higher and farther aircraft are built to go, the more this is true. This last type of stress can be exciting and challenging, so is not necessarily negative, but it does steadily drain a pilot's ability to perform.

Less pleasant job stresses that pilots face are worries about losing their medical certificate or being phased out by a younger man. Pilots are also subject to stresses common to many other jobs, such as conflict with co-workers, too much to do in too short a time, or worries about not being paid enough or given adequate recognition.

A pilot's job also creates pressures on his life outside his job. Most pilots, because they are away so often and live on such an irregular schedule, can't keep many social engagements. They tend to have relatively few friends and interests outside of aviation, thus missing the chance to pursue a hobby that gives them a real break from their work. In addition, marital problems and divorces are common since it is hard for pilots' spouses to adjust to their mate's irregular lifestyle.

How can you tell when a pilot is too tired for flying duties? David Beaty, author of *The Human Factor in Aircraft Accidents*, observes, "It would be invaluable . . . if only there was some sort of gauge like a thermometer that could be popped into the mouth and a reading of fatigue taken." Failing this, we must look for other measures.

As we mentioned earlier, performance decrement is the most visible effect of fatigue, as well as the effect most relevant to aviation safety. It has been substantially proved that performance becomes poorer during an extended period of work, and prior sleep loss compounds this effect. Common symptoms of this type of acute fatigue are disruptions in timing, loss of fine motor control, erratic performance and lowered standards. There is some speculation that part of this performance decrement might be due to an increased incidence of lapses of attention lasting only a few seconds, called "blocks," the longer one works without sleep. These blocks, during which all mental functions momentarily cease, go unnoticed by the individual involved.

Being fatigued produces different effects on different types of tasks. Vigilance is the function most affected by acute fatigue, so it is difficult for a tired pilot to monitor the instrument panel effectively or watch for other traffic. However, a sudden change in conditions or an emergency can restore efficiency for short spurts.

But such a spurt rarely continues beyond 20 minutes and it takes longer to reach peak efficiency. As one would expect with decreased vigilance, tasks based on large, discrete cues are easier than tasks based on small cues. Concentration is also reduced, so it is hard to accomplish tasks that are lengthy and complex. It has furthermore been noted that fatigued persons are slow to move from one task to another.

In accordance with reduced powers of concentration, a pilot is likely to focus on one individual instrument reading instead of looking at the total picture. His attention narrows and his thinking becomes inflexible so that, faced with two alternatives, he may only be able to see one, the one he has the most experience with.

A fatigued pilot is apt to become nervous and anxious about his ability to perform his flying tasks, which in turn will make him more fatigued; thus, a vicious cycle is set in motion.

The phenomenon of the "end spurt" has been discovered in some fatigue studies; that is, the subjects' performance improves when the end is in sight. But usually just the reverse is true, the landing is the time of poorest performance.

A doctor trained in aviation medicine can usually spot pilots who *are* suffering from fatigue, especially since fatigue has several medical manifestations. Still, it is far more important for the individual to recognize his own fatigue.

There are several symptoms of fatigue that a pilot can look for in himself. A primary symptom is irritability, evidenced by a tendency toward short temper, increased arguments with other crewmembers, ground crew, controllers or spouse, and a tendency to "make a mountain out of a mole hill." You may also notice loss of motivation and morale.

A second warning signal is difficulty with short-term memory, that is, forgetting something you may have just heard.

A third symptom to watch for is making mistakes—forgetting to do something or doing it wrong. You may notice you are having trouble doing simple mathematical calculations correctly. Or you may be more vulnerable to visual illusions. Also, loss of accuracy and timing goes with fatigue. First evidence of this is doing the right thing at slightly the wrong time; eventually gross errors are produced.

In addition, a tired pilot is likely to accept a wider margin of error in his performance than he would normally. If he is aware of this tendency, he generally thinks it doesn't really matter. Beware of such an attitude—it is easy to fall into and it is obviously extremely dangerous when you are operating an aircraft.

Physically, fatigue makes you more susceptible to colds and other infectious diseases, so you should be aware of the possibility of cumulative fatigue if you have had more than your share of those ailments. If you are a victim of acute fatigue from sleep loss the previous night, you will probably be aware that you are fatigued, but you should avoid flying an aircraft if you are experiencing sleep loss symptoms like burning eyes, nausea, poor coordination, muscle weakness and foolish speech or laughter.

Over the longer term, warning signs of cumulative fatigue include increased use of alcohol, tobacco or drugs, withdrawal from social activities and hobbies outside of aviation, and a general feeling that coping with everyday demands is an effort.

If you suspect you are suffering from fatigue, see your doctor immediately. He can help you pinpoint the problem and suggest remedies. Remember that once you recognize the problem, it can be solved.

In preventing fatigue, you can be your own best line of defense. The first step is self-analysis of your living patterns to determine where your problem areas lie. You can determine the highs and lows of your own body clock by asking yourself questions like these:

· When you wake up, do you jump out of bed energetically and wind down the remainder of the day, or do you wake up gradually as you go along?

· What time do you go to bed and get up on vacations or weekends?

· What time of day are you happiest and when do you feel lowest?

When do you eat your biggest meal? Once you understand your cycle, you can try to schedule your most demanding activities during your high points.

Perhaps you should be going to bed earlier and getting up earlier or planning to get unpleasant chores out of the way early in the day. Of course, a pilot's work schedule is obviously not completely in his own hands.

Keeping physically fit is excellent insurance against fatigue. Despite all the travel and irregular hours, there are ways for pilots to keep fit.

Try to schedule physical activities you enjoy. Such activity is not only more fun, but also more beneficial, as it relaxes you and reduces tensions by taking your mind off your problems. Taking up an absorbing outside hobby would have much the same results.

The simplest and most convenient exercise, as well as one of the best, is brisk walking. It brings every muscle into play, stimulates circulation, can be done anywhere and even gets you where you want to go. If you walk an extra mile (about 20 minutes) each day for a year, you can lose 10 pounds with the same eating habits.

Your eating habits may need a change too. Try to eat natural foods instead of artificial ones as much as possible, and balance your diet to include foods from each of the four basic food groups. Go easy on desserts, fatty meats, beer, sweet wines, hard liquor and soft drinks with sugar, and avoid eating "on the run." Some fruit or juice every day is good. Whether you eat breakfast, or what kind you eat if you do, is largely up to your own needs and preference, but breakfast does not have to be limited to typical breakfast foods. For extra protein in the morning, you could try meat, cheese or leftovers from dinner. It has not been proved whether vitamins are helpful, but you might take one a day against skipped meals.

But what can you do if you recognize the symptoms of fatigue while in the cockpit? What you need is a "second wind," and there are several ways to help bring it on. Even mild exercise will pump blood to the brain and dispel boredom, so walking around is beneficial if it is possible. If not, you can exercise some muscles by pulling up in your seat and stretching your arms, shoulders, legs and torso. If someone else is with you, try to keep talking, particularly about flight aspects or your destination so your mind will not wander from the job at hand. If you are alone, think about a pleasant event that is coming up. It also might help to blow cool air in your face, or to put cool water on both your eyes and forehead.

There are pros and cons about turning on the autopilot when you know you are fatigued. It could have a beneficial effect by causing a nervous, tense and consequently tired pilot to relax. However, the reduced workload may make a tired pilot drowsy and encourage him to drop off to sleep.

Dr. Bergin states a conviction that "the management/pilot relationship is one of the most important factors in the physical and mental health of pilots, and indirectly of flight safety, and all must share some responsibility and blame in these matters." He recommends that management develop a closer understanding of pilot problems by becoming more aware of areas of discontent, frustration or lowered morale. In this regard, Dr. Mohler of the FAA recommends that some sort of monitoring system be established to pinpoint fatigue- and stress-producing situations *as they arise.* This might be done by having pilots fill out subjective fatigue questionnaires periodically or, better yet, by designating one person to monitor the "fatigue pulse" of flight crews and keep a log of crew observations of apparent fatigue-producing situations associated with flight department equipment, schedules or routes.

When management first becomes aware of a fatigue problem in one of its pilots, it should make sure that the pilot has a checkup to discover any medical causes. If this possibility is eliminated, a change in flight assignments or motivation for the pilot might be indicated.

How can management determine when a man is or is not fit to fly? Unfortunately, there is no magic formula that covers every individual and every eventuality. Flight time limitations represent an effort to protect a pilot's physical, mental and psychological well-being while keeping the economic considerations of management in mind.

However, as A.N.J. Blain points out in his book, *Pilots and Management,* "It is possible to conform to all legal instructions and yet fly pilots to a point of mental and physical exhaustion where the lives of passengers —and crew—are endangered."

Mohler stresses the need for pilots to retain a "physiologic reserve" to enable them to cope with the stresses of delays, disruptions, unforeseen operational problems and inflight emergencies and has developed a formula to help management make sure this is done.

He found that there are three major fatiguing factors in long-distance flight: the number of time zones traversed, multiple night flights in close sequence and 24-hour layovers after a night arrival. In addition there are several moderately fatiguing factors, including the first day of any pattern, multiple transits, day sleep, flight toward the east and patterns of more than seven days.

Crewmembers can recover fairly well after a flight segment involving any one of the major factors, but will find it harder to recover if another major factor or two or more moderate factors are involved. Each of these factors was weighted to produce a physiological index that indicates how hard a particular pattern, and each segment of that pattern, will be on a pilot. Mohler suggests that, where travel through time zones is involved, scheduling should be as individualized as possible so that those pilots who adjust to circadian disruptions most easily are assigned the most potentially disruptive flights.

Another method that can be helpful to flight department management is a formula developed by the International Civil Aviation Organization (ICAO) to determine appropriate rest periods after flight traversing time zones. The formula gives more weight to late departure times to compensate for the effects of sleep loss; it also weights early arrival times more to compensate for disruptions experienced during early morning flights and the effects of arriving at the beginning of a working day when circadian rhythms are out of phase.

It is vital that company executives understand a pilot's need for adequate rest. Flight time limitations such as the type outlined here should be devised and written into the flight operations manual. And even then, as much as possible, a pilot should be allowed to retain authority over when he will or will not fly. If both pilots and management understand the phenomenon of fatigue and utilize this understanding in flight operations, countless accidents can be avoided.

For the businessman pilot the problem is usually much more difficult to resolve. Normally, the businessman is his own management and that makes it all but impossible to set and hold to flight duty time. Moreover, almost by definition, the businessman pilot is a tired, often distracted pilot. Therefore, it is doubly important that he eat properly and get away periodically to catch up on his rest.

It is also doubly important that he train often and hone his flight skills to a high level of proficiency. He needs a high level of proficiency, perhaps even more than that of the professional, because the best defense he can have against a fatigue-induced accident is excess capability. In that regard, a businessman pilot who often flies late in the day should be especially selective in equipment. The simpler the better. An airplane with more speed, retractable gear, more gadgets, might get him home 10 minutes sooner, but his risk of accident may go up an unacceptable amount due to the narrower gap between his excess capability to handle the flight situation and the actual capability needed.

In summary, pilots should avoid fatigue. That being impossible, they must be students of the results of fatigue. Know which skills decrease as fatigue increases and monitor yourself, and fellow crewmembers if you have them, for the most likely, fatigue induced errors.

Oxygen Roulette

4

by Dan Manningham

Quick now, what is the least used system in your airplane? If your operation is like most, the oxygen system probably ranks close to the bottom of the list. In most cases that green bottle just sits there, month after month, with no more action than an occasional check for pressure.

Aircraft oxygen systems are simple to understand and easy to operate. Oxygen utilization by the human body is not so easily comprehended. Vision, thought, judgment and consciousness itself demand an adequate and uninterrupted supply of oxygen to the red blood corpuscles. Aircraft oxygen systems are designed to insure that supply when it is not available from the prevailing environment.

At sea level, we breathe in air under atmospheric pressure equivalent to a column of mercury 760 mm high. That air is approximately 21 percent oxygen and 79 percent nitrogen by volume. The Law of Partial Pressures states that the pressure exerted by each component is in proportion to the volume of each component present. In the case of dry, sea level air, oxygen exerts a partial pressure of 21 percent of 760 mm or 160 mm.

Inhaled air passes into the trachea where it is fully saturated with water vapor, which prevents damage to the delicate lung tissues. This water vapor exerts its own partial pressure which slightly alters the arithmetic:

Tracheal air (S.L.)	760 mm
Water vapor partial pressure	−47 mm.
	713 mm

Once the inspired air has been saturated in the trachea, 47 mm of the total pressure is exerted by water vapor. Oxygen and nitrogen together are now responsible for only 713 mm of pressure so that those partial pressures are reduced to:

Oxygen —21% of 713 mm=150 mm
Nitrogen—79% of 713 mm=563 mm

From the trachea, air flows into the lungs, which retain a constant residue of carbon dioxide. Total pressure in the lungs at sea level is still 760 mm but the CO_2 assumes its own partial pressure which effectively reduces oxygen pressure by 40 mm. When you add it all up, pulmonary air pressures break down like this:

Oxygen	(14.3%)	109 mm
Water vapor	(6.2%)	47 mm
CO_2	(5.3%)	40 mm
Nitrogen	(74.2%)	564 mm
Total	(100.0%)	760 mm

In the lungs, at sea level, 109 mm of pressure is available to diffuse the oxygen through permeable membranes directly into the red blood corpuscles. The rate of diffusion is in direct proportion to that partial pressure of oxygen in the lungs. That pressure and that rate are the very focal points of human oxygen requirements at altitude.

As altitude increases, total air pressure diminishes so that oxygen partial pressure, and therefore oxygen diffusion, is reduced. When that partial pressure is reduced below about 100 mm, the blood can no longer take on a full load of oxygen.

Notice that while oxygen pressure decreases on a straight line basis with increasing altitude, the ability of the blood to hold oxygen follows a much different curve (see Figure 1). This characteristic is called the "oxygen dissociation curve" and it bears heavily on oxygen requirements at altitude.

As blood saturation drops, essential life functions are progressively disturbed. From 93 percent saturation, where some visual problems are encountered, there is a steep deterioration to unconsciousness.

Let's look at the hypoxic effects an average person can expect at increasing altitudes. Hypoxia is an insidious, almost undetectable, condition in which you progressively lapse into incompetence while maintaining absolute faith in your own ability. Unless you've been through an altitude chamber or some actual hypoxic situation, you must assume that you will not recognize hypoxia in yourself, even to the point of unconsciousness.

· *5000 feet.* The retina of the eye is more demanding of adequate oxygen than any other organ. At 93 percent saturation, this little extension of the brain will begin to function somewhere below maximum so that night vision may be diminished.

During night flight at this altitude, instruments and maps are more easily misread and ground features may be misinterpreted. This level of hypoxia is insidious, and you must consider it to be a real threat. Extra attention to charts and instruments will normally suffice to compensate for these real, but minor, night vision deficiencies.

· *10,000 feet.* When blood saturation drops to 90 percent, the brain is receiving an absolute minimum supply of oxygen. This is the highest altitude at which you can trust your own performance. Your discrimination

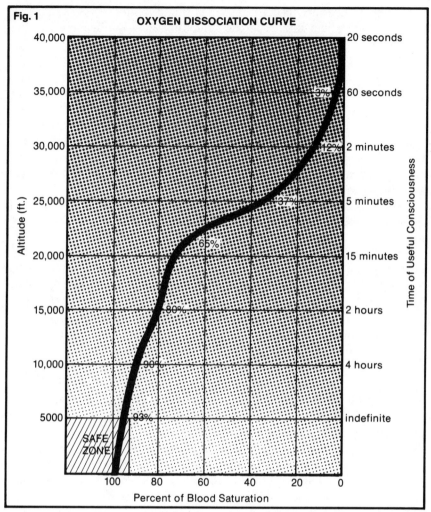

Fig. 1

OXYGEN DISSOCIATION CURVE

Altitude (ft.)

Time of Useful Consciousness

Percent of Blood Saturation

The curve in this graph shows that the ability of blood to hold oxygen diminishes rapidly with increasing altitude. Without supplemental oxygen, unconsciousness will occur in about 10 minutes at 23,000 feet where the blood saturation level is 65 percent. To maintain a sea level equivalent at this altitude, 35 percent of supplemental oxygen is required.

and judgment will definitely be impaired, although you may not feel any differently. Proceed with care, caution and vigilance. Above 10,000 feet, saturation and performance fall off the deep end. Hypoxic symptoms may not become apparent for up to four hours.

· *14,000 feet.* Here, where saturation is down to 84 percent, you will be appreciably handicapped. Your vision will dim. Your hands may shake. And you will experience serious degradation of thought, memory and judgment, otherwise feeling just fine. Hypoxic symptoms may not become apparent for up to two hours.

· *16,000 feet.* Your blood is now only 79 percent saturated, and you are considerably handicapped. You will probably be disorientated, belligerent, euphoric or all three. This level of hypoxia is very similar to a full load of martinis. Your judgment will be decidedly irrational and unreliable. As a pilot or other crewmember, you are positively dangerous.

· *18,000 feet.* With 71 percent blood saturation, you are seriously handicapped and incapable of functioning in any useful fashion. At first you may feel great, even better than normal, but time of useful consciousness (the time it takes to pass out) is about 30 minutes.

· *20,000 feet.* You are on the brink of imminent collapse, if not already unconscious. Prolonged exposure may cause death. TUC is five to 15 minutes.

· *25,000 feet.* Above this altitude *and* with a sudden decompression, you may suffer from aeroembolism, more commonly known as "the bends." When ambient pressure drops too rapidly, nitrogen in the blood and tissues bubbles out. Pain is usually detected first in the joints, then in the chest, abdomen and along nerve trunks. Only increased ambient pressure can reverse the process. Supplemental oxygen cannot correct this decompression sickness once it has begun. TUC is three to six minutes.

If you smoke, subtract 2000 to 3000 feet from all altitudes, so that, for instance, you may collapse into unconsciousness as low as 17,000 feet. Alcohol and all depressant drugs, even in small doses, will markedly increase the effects of altitude. Just being tired is enough to substantially reduce your altitude tolerance.

Smoking, fatigue and depressants all function to reduce the diffusion rate to the red corpuscles so that higher partial pressures are necessary for saturation. A fatigued smoker with alcohol in his blood may require a 50 percent or more increase in partial pressures to attain a given level of saturation. He may well be hypoxic at sea level.

Aircraft oxygen equipment is designed for one purpose: to increase the percentage of oxygen in inspired air so that oxygen partial pressure in the lungs is sustained at desirable levels.

Look at the situation at 21,000 feet. At that level, ambient air is totally inadequate as you can see:

Ambient pressure at 21,000	335 mm
Water vapor partial pressure	−47 mm
	288 mm

21 percent $\times$ 288 mm = Oxygen partial pressure—60 mm. When you subtract 40 mm for the CO_2 partial pressure in the lungs, there remains only 20 mm to push that life-giving oxygen through the membranes. You need 100 mm. If you wear a mask which supplements ambient oxygen, raising the proportion from 21 percent to 50 at 21,000 feet, the numbers change significantly in your favor:

Ambient pressure at
21,000   335 mm
Water vapor partial
pressure $\underline{-47\text{ mm}}$
                                288 mm

50 percent $\times$ 288 mm = Oxygen partial pressure—144 mm.

When the 40 mm is subtracted for CO_2, there is still 104 mm of oxygen partial pressure which is more than adequate for 100 percent blood saturation.

Even at 34,000 feet, where ambient pressure is only 188 mm, supplemental oxygen delivered at 100 percent will supply pulmonary partial pressure of 100 mm after allowance is made for 87 mm of water vapor and CO_2.

Above 35,000 feet, pressure breathing must be employed so that oxygen is delivered to the lungs at pressures greater than ambient to assure adequate oxygen partial pressure.

Aircraft designers are faced with two specific challenges in regard to oxygen system design: (1) They must provide adequate oxygen to sustain passengers and crew during planned flights above 10,000 feet cabin altitude; (2) They must provide adequate oxygen to sustain passengers and crew in the event of decompression in pressurized aircraft.

Several different types of oxygen equipment are available but they all fall into three broad categories: continuous flow, demand and pressure.

Continuous Flow. These systems deliver a constant flow of oxygen to the mask. In its simplest form, continuous flow oxygen can be merely a tube supplying oxygen directly to the mouth, although that would be less comfortable and efficient than some form of a regulated mask.

Continuous flow oxygen is delivered through a face mask which dilutes the oxygen with ambient air drawn through ports incorporated for that purpose. The volume of diluting air entering the mask is determined by the rate of oxygen flow and the breathing rate of the user. The flow of oxygen is at a constant, arbitrary rate for any given altitude. No provision is made for adjusting oxygen flow to individual requirements.

More sophisticated constant flow masks incorporate a reservoir or re-breather bag for three reasons.

(1) Efficiency is markedly improved by the reservoir action of the bag

which retains a fraction of the expired air from each breath. This first slug of exhaled air is rich in oxygen because it only filled the mouth and trachea when you inhaled, and never reached the lungs. By preserving this oxygen-rich portion, the bag becomes an economizer circuit to maximize available oxygen. The mixing of incoming oxygen with the previously expired breath also moisturizes and warms the next intake to make the use of the supplemental supply more comfortable.

(2) Dilution by ambient air drawn through the ports is delayed until the reservoir is empty. This conserves oxygen and assures that the richest mixture will go deep into the lungs.

(3) The bag provides an accumulator action which efficiently supplies the cyclic demands of respiration with a fixed flow of oxygen.

Most passenger systems are continuous flow, with oxygen flow rates regulated for cabin altitude. These systems are reliable, inexpensive, light-weight and easy to maintain. They offer reasonable safety for very brief periods up to pressure altitudes as high as 40,000 feet. Prolonged operations above 25,000 feet are not recommended without more advanced mask and regulator designs.

Demand Flow Systems. Demand systems are distinguished by a control valve in the mask or regulator that responds to the pressure reversals of the breathing cycle. When you breathe in, the valve opens to permit oxygen flow until the end of that inspiration. When exhalation begins, the valve closes to conserve oxygen until you breathe in again.

Demand systems deliver oxygen at a rate proportional to the user's respiration. Unlike constant flow systems, demand oxygen adjusts automatically to the user's level of physical exertion. No matter how fast you breathe, there is always more oxygen ready for the next gasp. This system will normally have a diluter function governed by cabin altitude so that oxygen is conserved by delivering only that percentage necessary for adequate partial pressure in the lungs.

Dilution is regulated to decrease with altitude so that the mask receives 100 percent oxygen above some predetermined level around 30,000 feet. Demand oxygen is acceptable up to 35,000 feet and for brief periods between 35,000 and 40,000. Above that level, even 100 percent oxygen will not provide enough partial pressure for adequate blood saturation.

Pressure Systems. At 35,000 feet, pure oxygen will produce the same effect as breathing ambient air at 5000 feet. At 40,000 feet, barometric pressure is 141 mm so that 100 percent oxygen allows only 54 mm partial pressure in the lungs. That's about what you get normally at 12,000 feet and far below acceptable levels for flight crews.

Pressure breathing systems are the only way (aside from pressurization) to maintain oxygen partial pressures above 35,000 feet. One-hundred percent oxygen is delivered to the face mask under positive pressure to raise the pressure in the lungs above that of the surrounding atmosphere. This supercharging is effective up to a maximum of about 50,000 feet where the pressures required to maintain adequate blood saturation place increasingly unbearable internal pressures on the chest. Above 50,000 feet, pressure suits are required to reduce that differential and prevent physical damage to the individual.

There are other problems with pressure breathing. The high pressure differential in the chest cavity reduces cardiac output. Just plain breathing requires extra effort because you must forcibly expel the air from your lungs after every breath. There is a certain uncoordination in this reversed respiration cycle which produces discomfort and anxiety. Pressure breathing may keep you alive and functioning, but your performance will certainly deteriorate with any prolonged use of this method.

Pilots operating aircraft above 10,000 feet (Part 135.2) or 12,500 feet (Part 91) must insure adequate oxygen supplies for all occupants in accordance with the applicable FARs. Naturally these are minimum requirements and may not be adequate for some corporate operations.

Piston and turboprop airplanes are normally operated over route segments and at altitudes that are not overly critical. Specific flights over very high terrain may require extra oxygen in the event of pressurization failure. In general, however, propeller equipment is not exposed to any substantial risks.

Jets are different. They demand careful attention to oxygen planning, especially for long over water trips. When you do flight plan over water, and fuel for optimum burnout altitude, you may be betting the whole airplane (and your life) on the pressurization system. Let's look at the numbers.

The most oxygen-critical route for any airplane is a maximum range, over-water route with no enroute alternates.

Consider a G-II, flight planned from Los Angeles to Honolulu, against average winter winds of 90 knots. For the sake of this example, we'll assume a crew of two with eight passengers in back. Cruise is planned at 43,000 feet for fuel conservation.

The climb to 41,000 feet requires no oxygen but above that level the FARs require one pilot to wear and use oxygen, and for good reason. Sudden decompression above that level leaves so few seconds of TUC that even the best pilot may not survive without his mask in place, delivering oxygen prior to the decompression.

One pilot begins using oxygen as the plane climbs through 41,000 and continues to use it for the next 222 minutes as the plane proceeds to the Point of Equal Time (PET). By selecting the diluter demand-function on his regulator, oxygen consumption is held to 2.4 liters per minute at the cabin altitude of 8000 feet. At PET, say pressurization fails for some reason and emergency descent is executed to 25,000 feet, the maximum reasonable altitude for passenger subsistence and comfort.

Cruise is resumed at 25,000 with all occupants on oxygen, crewmembers using the diluter function. Final descent is delayed as long as possible in the interest of conserving fuel and all occupants discontinue oxygen use as the airplane descends through 12,000 feet. Total oxygen required for this profile is 6473.6 liters or 227.1 cubic feet. If we assume the aircraft is carrying a standard installation of two 48-cubic-foot bottles, there is a net *deficit* of 131.1 feet or 3737.6 liters of oxygen to complete the profile. Clearly, these people are not going to reach Honolulu.

When you do flight plan this sort of trip, there are three ways to cover the worst case of depressurization. They are as follows:

(1) Take enough additional oxygen to supply all occupants at 25,000 feet from the PET.

(2) Carry enough fuel to complete the trip from PET at 10,000 to 12,000 feet maximum.

(3) Reduce the passenger load to the point where installed oxygen will suffice.

Several business jets are now available in versions which allow long-range flights.

When you do use that capability, take a hard look at the oxygen supply. Those old green bottles will become your most critical components when you lose that vital cabin pressure.

Memory and Recall   5

by Nancy R. Day

A White Plains, New York based corporate pilot sheepishly recalls the time in his fledgling days when he forgot to include Canadian charts in his kit for a flight to Canada. Luckily the other pilot, a veteran, had a "photographic memory" and was able to provide the necessary numbers.

Most corporate pilots are too professional to neglect something as crucial as charts. But even among the pros, memory lapses occasionally occur, and often there's no alert second crewmember—or Lady Luck—present to come to the rescue.

Like any other faculty, memory is a tool that the corporate pilot should develop and utilize. It can help avert the disaster the White Plains pilot invited as well as the embarrassment he suffered. It can buy the pilot a few seconds in his busy cockpit routine and in general make his job easier.

Memory is vital to all mental activity. It helps us make decisions, solve problems, follow instructions, find our way around, keep track of things, learn, plan, read and calculate. Without it ideas would not spread and experience would be useless.

Memory has been variously defined as a faculty for recalling facts and past experiences, a capacity for remembering, a storehouse of all that is remembered and a habit formation. Donald and Eleanor Laird state in their book, *Techniques for Efficient Remembering,* that remembering is a function—something we do rather than a tangible entity called "memory" found somewhere in our cerebrum. Maryse Metcalfe in *Aspects of Learning and Memory* states that "the mechanism by which we recall the past is frequently a process of matching a present image with a past image."

This does not mean that remembering is non-physiological. In fact, the simplest recollection involves biochemical changes in thousands of nerve cells in many parts of the brain, and the rate of electrical waves from the brain is related directly to an individual's ability to remember.

How about its opposite—forgetfulness? Forgetting is often defined as "loss of memory strength over time." However, it is impossible to prove that time alone is responsible because no experimenter has yet devised a way for a subject to do absolutely nothing, block out everything and thus establish a control over other factors and interfering thoughts.

Interference consists of competitive thoughts which are introduced before, during or after the thought or thoughts one wishes to remember. We have eight to 12 thoughts a minute, so competition can be fierce.

In flying, of course, interference is another word for distraction. According to New York Region NTSB safety investigator Michael Kuzenko, a number of accidents have occurred when the pilot "didn't do something because he was busy doing something else."

One school of thought, subscribed to by such luminaries as William James and Sigmund Freud, holds that memory is permanent. This means we may have memory traces, or closely linked mental impressions, of everything to which we have been exposed. These memory traces can be inhibited or distorted, but they cannot be destroyed, according to the memory permanence advocates. A modern memory expert, Harry Lorayne, stresses the concept of *original awareness:*

"Anything of which you are originally aware *cannot* be forgotten," Lorayne says. The theory of memory permanence, however, is hard to prove scientifically. The idea that memory can be separated into short-term and long-term compartments originated with educators and philosophers like John Stuart Mill and William James in the 19th century. James noted the difference between thoughts held currently in consciousness and those that could be brought to consciousness after a mental search.

Short-term memory is a continuous process in which the mind receives new impressions and calls on relevant information from long-term memory for problem solving. It is the long-term memory that holds the vast store of what one knows. Thoughts are moved from short-term to long-term memory through practice, or rehearsal, and fixed by a chemical process in the brain.

The short-term memory holds only five to nine pieces of unrelated information after a brief exposure. Unless this information is continuously rehearsed, it is usually gone in less than a minute. A typical example of short-term memory is remembering a new telephone number just long enough to dial it. Long-term memory is retaining information for many years without any conscious effort. It is long-term memory that helps us remember faces and the meaning of words.

Short-term and long-term memory seem to obey different laws. For instance, subjects in a short-term memory experiment were shown lists of letters and rehearsed them aloud or silently. When they were asked to recall the letters, they tended to confuse the ones they had seen with ones that *sounded* similar (s for f but not q for g). This indicates that short-term memory storage is more auditory than visual. Thus, acoustic interference apparently is more likely to empty short-term memory than will other types of interference.

Confusion in long-term memory, on the other hand, appears to be caused by things with similar meanings. Long-term storage is, therefore, assumed to be semantic in form. One's vocabulary is thought to be arranged more like a thesaurus than a dictionary. Semantic arrangement allows us to recognize a novel situation by searching through our memory and not finding a situation in our memory bank similar to the one at hand.

All modern information processing machines use the short-term/long-term memory process because computer designers have found that approach works best. Like its human counterpart, the machine uses its short-term memory to draw on long-term memory for data to solve a problem. A machine's short-term memory may be faster and more efficient than a human's, but a machine's long-term memory doesn't compare to its human counterpart in terms of capacity and flexibility of retrieval. Most machine memory is held in numbered address boxes; human memory is "addressable by content," to use computerese.

Some people are able to recall images better and in more detail than the expected norm. The "eidetic" photographic memory phenomenon is extremely rare and is found more often in children, since older people tend to rely more heavily on their verbal skills.

Unfortunately, photographic memory can't be taught. Usually, we have to be content with our innate capacity, but a lot of that often goes untapped.

Memory capacity differs with intelligence and age. Despite the absent-minded-professor stereotype, the greater one's intelligence, the greater one's memory capacity tends to be.

Humans naturally lose some of their memory capacity as they grow older, partly because with advancing age individual brain cells are lost, or not replaced, and so pathways between them grow less firm. Thus, people in their 60s recall about 40 percent less of something they just read than do people in their 20s.

Imagination and willpower have also been found to be closely related to memory capacity. Imagination helps an individual visualize something he wants to remember and create associations between it and what he already knows. It is basically an innate gift, but it can be stretched by frequent use. Willpower, too, is partly innate and partly created and helps one focus attention on the task at hand.

Basically, memory is unlike muscles, which can be exercised to peak condition. Practice is less important than learning the rules for utilizing full memory capacity.

The Lairds have devised the following five rules which they claim will double the efficiency of your everyday memory if they are applied until they become second nature.

(1) *Try* to remember the experience accurately at the time of exposure.

(2) React *actively* to it; look, listen, talk and think about it when it occurs.

(3) *Refresh* your memory of it at strategic times.

(4) Concentrate on the *meanings* of the things you intentionally store.

(5) *Write* it down.

Try to remember—Dr. James J. Moore conducted a study in which his subjects remembered seven times more facts from a story when admonished beforehand to try to remember as much as they could. The significance is that you should decide at the time whether you need to remember something for a short time, a long time or forever—and why.

Motivation helps strengthen an individual's memory.

Point out to yourself how remembering the information you are trying to learn will make you a more professional pilot or could save your life.

React actively——It helps to react using as many senses as you can. Dr. Wilse Webb found that training conducted both visually and aurally was remembered better than training stimulating just one sense. If you see a new word or hear a new name, say it. Write it down several times. As you read instructions, go through the motions or actually do it.

Above all, make yourself an active participant rather than a passive observer. Reaction is most likely to help you remember when it is done several ways over a long period with strong personal interest.

Diseases, even colds, lower reactivity—and thus memory. So do lowered body temperature and insufficient vitamin B (but vitamin B doesn't help unless you have a deficiency in the first place). On the other side of the coin, good physical health and conditioning increase reactivity and memory power.

Loss of sleep, even a few hours, also lowers reactivity and remembering. Fatigue has the same effect; after one or two hours of steady mental application, you will need a short break.

What you eat and drink play a part in memory as well. In one experiment, children who had a glass of milk daily scored higher on memory tests than those who did not. Even moderate amounts of alcohol result in poor retention. Moderate amounts of coffee, tea and cola stimulate activity for one to four hours, but large amounts tend to interfere with remembering. In small doses, prescription pep pills (amphetamines and benzedrine, for example) also improve reactivity and remembering, but produce mental confusion in larger doses. Aspirin doesn't affect reactivity, but does keep mild pain from interfering with work.

Reactivity is naturally lowered with age, which accounts for the loss of *recent* memory in older people. Many find it easier to recall something that happened to them as a child than something that happened yesterday.

Embarrassment and frustration lower reactivity while interest, even feigned, increases it.

Thus, you can control your reactivity level by staying in good health, sticking to a balanced diet, avoiding fatigue and sleep loss, using mild stimulants when circumstances warrant and fostering a positive attitude. Improved memory should be the result.

Refresh your memory——The time to start refreshing your memory is a few minutes after a trace is first established. If you wait longer, you may recall it incorrectly. Bedtime that night is the next strategic time. Brush up often in the next two weeks, tapering off after that.

Keep referring to the original for accuracy—the average person is wrong about half the details recalled the same day the trace originated because people tend to distort details in line with their own beliefs and other facts. Keep in mind that the first memory account, even if it lacks detail, is usually the most accurate. Understand your prejudices and biases and look for their interference in what *you think you remember.*

Concentrate on the meaning——When something has meaning for us, we can memorize it more quickly and retain it longer. Conversely, it's difficult to remember something we don't understand in the first place. Think about the significance of a new fact or experience. Ask yourself why and how it works, how can it be applied to other problems and situations in the future?

Write it down—Even the smartest people forget more than they remember. Details register better when you write them down. So, if the situation allows, write down what you must remember—immediately, completely and systematically.

Bruno Furst, director of the School of Memory and Concentration, explains the two goals of his memory system in his book, *Stop Forgetting.* First, he says, "You must strengthen your powers of observation, concentration and classification so your memory will retain things without much effort." Second, he presents methods of memorization you can apply to almost any situation.

We will look at some helpful organizational methods—his as well as those of Harry Lorayne, Dr. Joyce Brothers and others—in relation to specific types of memory problems pilots are apt to face.

Emergency checklists—There are few things as important for a pilot to remember as emergency procedure checklists. In order to remember them, you must learn them well. This requires an effective approach to study.

First, read through the checklist carefully and understand it and the logic behind it. Then recite it aloud five to 10 times. This is one of the best ways to achieve memory permanency and also helps to pinpoint your weak spots. Repetition with one's own voice increases remembering from 25 to 100 percent. Unfortunately, it is not practical to read aloud since it takes twice as long as silent reading. But it helps to read silently and periodically review aloud. Experiments have shown that subjects recall four times as much when they use a third of their reading time for oral recitation.

It helps to repeat the procedures you are learning three times during the first day, then once a day for the next five days and periodically thereafter. If you can remember something for two weeks, you have a fair chance of retaining it—especially if periodic recitation continues.

Check yourself after each recitation so you don't commit mistakes to memory. Practice *more* than you think you need to. This is called over-memorizing or overlearning and is good insurance when you run into an emergency.

The important thing is to spread your practice out—practicing five times in one day is *not* as effective as one time a day for five days. The longer and more difficult the material, the greater space you should leave between practice sessions, but be sure to review at least once a day. Massed learning can give you a false feeling that you know something when really you don't. For instance, you can be fooled by "memory echo." We've all had the experience of not listening to what someone is saying, but "hearing" it a moment later when pressed for a response. Through this process, we may be able to repeat what we just read and delude ourselves that we actually remember it.

The best time for initial study is usually in the morning. Memory span appears to become shorter as the day progresses. If you are a night person, afternoon or evening may be better.

Sleep helps—Refreshing your memory is most effective just before you go to bed at night. This makes up for the interference of other activities subsequent to the learning session earlier in the day. Sleep does not interfere; in fact, dreaming (REM sleep) helps set the material in the mind because memory, along with the subconscious, continues to work when we are asleep. It is thought that during REM sleep we are actually processing the day's visual information input, and that dreaming consolidates newly learned material into long-term memory.

Research indicates that people remember unfinished tasks that they wanted very much to finish 50 percent better than completed ones. Each time we near a goal, our efficiency increases. Therefore, if you must interrupt your study, break *before* you reach the end of a chapter or section.

Researchers have also found that subjects tend to remember best what they are exposed to last (recency effect) and first (primary effect). This means the middle portion is most easily forgotten, so study and practice that part the hardest.

If you can't recall an item, pressing your memory may only produce the wrong item (which you may falsely identify as correct). Instead, warm up your mnemonic faculties by concentrating on the whole situation you're trying to recall. Try to put yourself back into the scene where you first learned it. Imagine the action, your posture and your mood at that time as thoroughly as possible. Think intently about the original situation, then wait and let your thoughts flow as they will. This same method of recall is useful in locating misplaced articles.

To further integrate a set of procedures into your memory structure rewrite the information in the most useful form. When memorizing a checklist, you might simplify it with headings that will remind you of details in the manual. The act of organizing and writing the material down will chisel it into your memory.

Another approach is to integrate what you are learning into conversations. Your friends and family may think it's strange that you're babbling about emergency procedures, but it works.

Use your strengths—Some people remember best what they see, some what they hear, some what they do. An "eye-minded" person, as described by Furst, profits most from reading books, remembers where a number was printed on a page and recalls actions and incidents from a movie. An "ear-minded" person gets more from lectures and may be able to repeat a conversation even though he can't remember who had it. A "motor-minded" individual remembers things connected with motions made or observed as well as movements involving touch, smell and taste.

You may immediately recognize one set of skills as being predominant in you. If not, try this test: Read the first half of a page silently and write down what you remember. Then have a friend read the second half of the page to you and again write down what you remember. Copy down the next half page and, without looking, write down what you remember. Whichever method gives you greatest recall is probably best for you.

Of course, no one is 100 percent one type. Everyone benefits from varied approaches, but you can learn most quickly if you know and use your own best tool.

Organization—A library may have every book in print yet be virtually useless because there is no classification system for finding particular books. Likewise, organization is the key to memory files. Dr. Joyce Brothers parallels the human brain to a "series of file cabinets into which every single thing that you see, hear and read is immediately categorized, filed and stored."

The trick is to file it in a way that it can be recalled when you want it.

Most mnemonic systems taught in memory schools and used by memory performers are really associative devices that put new facts into existing categories. Furst says we must connect a new idea to an existing one, like a mason cements two bricks with mortar. Harry Lorayne's basic memory rule is, "You can remember any new piece of information if it is associated to something you already know or remember."

Carl Jung distinguished modes of association as being based on logic, emotion or imagination. An association by imagination is the strongest.

Lorayne uses imaginative association as the basic of his chain link memory system. He suggests making and visualizing ridiculous and bizarre associations between two items. Such associations force you to concentrate and stretch your imagination. In conjuring up mental images, he urges the use of substitutions. Say you are linking "airplane" with "tree." Instead of seeing an airplane tangled in a tree, imagine a tree flying like an airplane. Conjure a picture out of proportion. (You might see a 1000-foot tree or create a whole squadron of flying trees.) And try to activate the image (flying, in this example).

If you are trying to associate an abstract word, find a tangible word or phrase as a substitute to jog your memory. For instance, "Minnesota" might become "mini soda."

All this becomes second nature if you do it often enough. Significantly, optometrists have discovered little physiological difference between signals activated by sight and those activated by the mind's eye (imagination). So once you "see" a ridiculous image, you should remember it as long as it is useful to you.

Lists——To remember lists in correct order, associate the subject or title with the first item, the first item with the second, and so on, like a linked chain. If you forget the first link, you can start anywhere and work backwards to the beginning. Learning elements in serial order can be accomplished by rote practice, but association is easier and more effective. It is most useful in learning otherwise unrelated material.

Early Greek and Roman orators used the "locus" system to remember key oratorical issues. They associated each major point with a room in either their own home or a familiar public building so that the speech proceeded as a mental walk through familiar space. This is how the expression "in the first place" was coined.

Although mnemonic devices are often thought of as "tricks," there is no denying that they are effective. (Who forgets, "East is least and west is best?") One study found that remembering through such devices yielded 12 times the efficiency of rote learning, provided the device itself was correctly recalled. Here's the catch: If the device is not remembered correctly, you may have no way of recalling the correct response directly.

If you have to learn a number of similar verbal lists, your recall job is going to be difficult. The variety of overlapping emergency procedures pilots need to know is made easier in part by the fact that you do not do all your learning by memorizing lists; you also have to learn what to do physically. Reinforcement of motor skill learning makes recalling emergency procedures easier.

Learned motor responses fall into two categories: continuous and discrete. The first is a paced activity that requires continuous error nulling, like driving a car on a narrow road, riding a bike or routinely keeping an aircraft on course. The second is a self-paced series of tasks. Following an emergency procedure would be a discrete motor response.

Unfortunately, discrete motor tasks are more subject to forgetting than are continuous motor tasks. For instance, you may never forget how to ride a bicycle, but you may forget whether the lever on the right handle bar is to the front brake or the rear one. Discrete tasks are behaviorally more complex and seem to have a verbal component. (For instance, a person may remember an action as an instruction to himself to "flip that black switch to the left.")

Since these skills are more subject to forgetting and are not routine in a pilot's job, pilot training must include overlearning and periodic practice of every procedure involving a discrete task. Simulators are invaluable in allowing pilots to gain experience in emergency handling of an aircraft without risking their lives.

The very fact that we are talking about *emergency* procedures here suggests a special memory problem for the pilot—he must be able to remember these procedures in a panic situation.

According to Roland Fischer, the brain processes and stores information differently at different levels of arousal. Each bit of knowledge is tied to, and most easily retrieved at, the level of arousal at which it was learned. A panic state is a very different level of arousal than the normal, calm, contemplative state in which the pilot may have learned the procedure. As a result, it is more difficult to recall a procedure during an actual crisis than it was during training.

What can be done? It would seem a good idea to advise pilots to remain calm in emergencies. This is not always possible to achieve. Therefore, we suggest that emergency procedures be practiced in the panic state. Mere repetition is not enough. Most corporate jet pilots have access to flight simulators during training. Although they know they are not in an actual flight situation and their lives are not in danger, they are so intent on performing well that they often think and react as if they were thousands of feet above the ground. Instructors should take advantage of this phenomenon and create a panic state by giving the pilot two or three simulated emergency situations to deal with simultaneously. This is realistic since one actual emergency often sets off others.

There are many occasions in flying when short-term memory of numbers is either helpful or essential. For instance, a busy controller may sound off heading, altitude, altimeter setting and several frequencies and codes all in one breath. How can a pilot help himself remember this barrage of numbers, especially if his shorthand is slow?

At first, the task seems formidable. As we said earlier, short-term memory can usually hold only five to nine items. Each individual has his own limit (or memory span) which is more or less innate. It can be stretched through effort but additional stretching hinders recall. The fact that we can't concentrate on two things at once is what limits memory span. Remember, too, that short-term memory deteriorates with fatigue and work overload.

Numbers are often considered the hardest material to remember because they are abstract. Luckily, most numbers a pilot works with have associative meaning. Visualizing that meaning is one key to remembering them.

For instance, try to visualize the meaning of the heading and altitude numbers as the controller gives them to you. Think of "heading 080" as a direction rather than as a number. Imagine your present position and that to which you have been cleared in three dimensions. Listen to what the controller tells other traffic and plot this information into your image.

The last point can be important because controllers are also subject to human error. One B/CA editor reported being cleared to cross a fix at 5000 feet. Luckily for him and a load of airline passengers, he remembered hearing the controller tell another flight to continue holding at the same fix at 5000 feet.

Frequencies, transponder codes and altimeter settings are harder to visualize. As the controller issues them, you might make a mental picture of yourself setting the dials or imagine how the numbers would look written down.

Some pilots jot down categories for frequencies, transponder codes, altimeter settings, headings and altitudes. If you're making mental notes, do the same thing. Have a fixed order for those categories in your own mind and associate each number with the proper category as you hear it.

You may have room in your short-term memory for only seven unrelated items, but these can be more than single digits. If you have five categories, you should be able to remember five numbers to fill them. This is the principle of chunking or clustering.

After a pilot receives instructions from ATC, it is to his advantage to adjust his instruments and radios accordingly as soon as possible. Researchers have found that subjects recall more items from a list when they set down the last few items first and then go back to the initial ones. The first items are remembered better than the middle ones, so middle items should be set down second.

Using this procedure, you may have to ask ATC to repeat a couple of the first items, but if you attempt to remember the entire string in sequence, chances are your memory will be blocked by the middle ones. Consequently you'll forget the last as well. Therefore, if a pilot receives five instructions in rapid succession, an appropriate order of recall would be 4-5-3-1-2. Uneven remembering can be somewhat equalized by spending the same amount of attention on each item as it is presented.

In the corporate pilot's function of ferrying VIPs, it is also advantageous if he remembers names and faces well. Many people seem to have trouble in this area.

When you meet a new person, observe his or her face carefully and categorize it by style and color of hair, glasses or no glasses and so forth. Note any outstanding features. Draw the face mentally. You can practice this on pictures in a magazine or on faces of people around you in restaurants and other public places until you can do it without seeming to stare.

Since the face is generally easier to remember than the name, Lorayne advises making the face tell you the name. If the name has no inherent meaning, find a substitute word that does and associate it with the outstanding feature of the face.

Furst suggests that you concentrate on the name when you are first introduced, not on the witty response you ought to make next. Always repeat the name to be sure you have it right. Studies have shown that people remember names 34 percent better when they repeat them during the introduction. If it's a foreign name, you might ask what it means and how it is spelled; this will make an additional impression on your mind. Later on, write it down and review it.

If, in addition to the face and name, you wish to remember some other characteristics, such as what the executive likes to drink, you can associate that characteristic with the name or substitute the word for the name. Of course, a card file is more effective in the long run, but this memory method will serve to record the characteristics you wish to remember until it is convenient to jot them down.

One word of caution: Don't become so enthusiastic about developing and using your memory that you foreswear checklists, charts, plates and pencils. Only a computer can rely totally on its brain.

Memory is a vital tool in the conduct of a safe, efficient flight. But it is not the only one.

The Booze News

6

by Dan Manningham

It ain't good. The booze news, that is—at least as it relates to aviation. General aviation fatalities in the United States over the past 10 years indicate an alarming incidence of alcohol involvement, and these statistics only refer to the positive presence of alcohol in the pilot's body as revealed by an autopsy. Unfortunately, no one knows the real extent of alcohol's effect on aviation safety because of the insidious nature of the problem.

Alcohol is a drug that acts as a depressant on the central nervous system. As such, it markedly alters the activating and inhibiting functions of the brain. The results are well-known—lowered blood pressure, increased reaction time, slurred speech, loss of coordination and modified behavior.

Alcohol is metabolized by the liver at a fixed and constant rate, equal to about 0.015 percent each hour. It doesn't matter how much alcohol is in your bloodstream, how much you exercise or how much coffee you consume afterwards. The metabolic rate is a steady, plodding, 0.015 percent per hour, and you cannot change it with aspirin, oxygen, coffee or a "hair of the dog."

Suppose you stop in for a toddy on the way home and drop two martinis in the first hour. Your blood alcohol will approach 0.10 percent, the level set by many states as the limit for drunk driving. Two more martinis in the next hour and you head home for nine hours sleep in preparation for tomorrow's trip. Your blood alcohol will likely be in the 0.20 percent category.

Nine hours of sleep, shower, shave and coffee and you feel like a million bucks. Well, at least you look like a million bucks and your blood alcohol is well below that legal limit of 0.10 percent. Remember, however, that that definition of impairment is pertinent to motor vehicle operation and bears little relation to flying.

One study of the effects of alcohol on experienced pilots utilized single-engine aircraft under simulated instrument landing approach conditions. Some of the subjects had distinct difficulty at a blood alcohol level of 0.02 percent. None were consistently able to perform the required tasks with blood alcohols between 0.04 and 0.05 percent. There just is no acceptable level of blood alcohol compatible with flight.

If you went to bed at 2300 hours with an alcohol level of 0.20 percent, it will still be 0.06 percent as you brush the fuzz off your teeth at 0800. When you rotate that great silver bird at 1000 hours, your blood alcohol will be sufficiently high to cause some measurable impairment of the very skills on which your passengers' lives now depend. You have satisfied every legal requirement, and yet those toddies from the previous evening are very effectively reducing your performance. Even when all the alcohol is metabolized, the hangover effect will getcha for several more hours. Hangovers not only feel bad, they are a very real medical phenomenon. In fact, several physiological mechanisms contribute to the blah sensation that follows excessive drinking like a shadow.

One major effect of alcohol is a temporary alteration of the fluid balance. In short, the sauce dehydrates your body. It accomplishes this by stimulating the kidneys to produce a large quantity of diluted urine, so that the body loses more liquid than it takes in. This dehydration produces a concentration of all those solutes normally found in bodily fluids, and that chemical concentration causes weakness, fatigue and irritability.

Another major element in hangover production is the assortment of organic impurities found in all alcoholic beverages. These aldehydes, ketones and so on are metabolized in complex ways and may remain in the bloodstream long after the alcohol is gone. While present, they produce fatigue and the blahs of their own making.

You can minimize your intake of these impurities by drinking only clear beverages such as gin and vodka, but you cannot eliminate them altogether. There is a real germ of truth in that old invitation to "name your poison."

Just when you need extra rest to compensate for these deleterious effects on the old bod, the alcohol itself will have degraded the quality of your sleep. Specifically, alcohol in the blood reduces the proportion of sleep spent in the dream state. This reduced dream sleep has been shown to induce fatigue, anxiety and impaired concentration.

Finally, the minute residual alcohol level in your blood will markedly affect the vestibular organs that control balance and spatial orientation. Your adaptive resistance to motion sickness and disorientation may be compromised sufficiently to cause mild nausea and discomfort. Vision may be impaired, especially under low illumination levels found at night or in clouds. Both of these problems can be induced or aggravated by rotational and G forces for periods as long as 20 to 36 hours after drinking.

What about a cure for the hangover? The very best one is to allow a maximum amount of time for sleep and recuperation between drinking and flying. Aside from time, there is no magic medicine, but you can minimize the more obvious effects and maximize your performance with a few simple remedies:

· Stick to vodka or gin to reduce your intake of impurities.

· Reduce dehydration by drinking several glasses of water before going to bed and several more when you awake.

· Try some coffee or tea. The caffeine is a stimulant and will tend to counteract the depressant effects of alcohol. Your liver will not metabolize any faster, but at the very least you will be a wide-awake drunk.

· Eat some fresh fruit or honey, or drink some fruit juice. The fructose sugar in fruit and honey is believed to help the body eliminate alcohol. Besides that, you need to eat something even if you don't feel hungry.

Bear in mind that none of these remedies will cure the hangover. At best you can hope to mask the more unpleasant effects of overdrinking.

Don't kid yourself about those martinis. They will have a specific and measurable effect on your performance for much longer than most of us would care to admit.

Once Around the Pattern, Double Time

7

by Arnold Lewis

Hey Mr. Corporate Pilot, here are some additions to your equipment checklist:

(1) Tennis shoes (sneakers), two each.

(2) Sweat socks, two each.

(3) Athletic supporter, one each.

(4) Gym shorts (or sweat pants), one each.

(5) Sweat shirt, one each.

Sounds sort of silly, doesn't it? Can't you picture yourself jogging a mile around the Page Airways tiedown area during a three-hour layover at Washington National? May not be as funny as it sounds, however. And the added equipment is sure to have a minimum effect on weight and balance.

Considerable time and money are spent annually developing and pursuing preventive-maintenance programs for airplanes, but how many preventive-maintenance programs have you seen for the pilot lately? Even the FAA will admit that its medical requirements for pilots are the bare minimum—just sufficient to make relatively sure that the pilot is reasonably safe from incapacitation for the period of the medical certificate, and no more.

As a group, professional pilots are a pretty healthy lot. Only 0.49 percent of the aeronautically-active Class I population for the three-year 1964-to-1966 period were denied medical certificates for known medical causes, according to an FAA survey.

However, "Most corporate pilots are not active enough," says Dr. Robert L. Wick Jr., professor of aerospace medicine at Ohio State University. In addition to establishing a formal medical examination program, over and above that required by the FAA, he advises: "Get off your can and get exercise. Quit smoking. Watch your diet and particularly watch your weight. If you're doing these things, you're loading up for a long and healthy corporate-aviation career."

Dr. Wick is no novice in the business of looking after the health and welfare of professional pilots. In fact, he specializes in helping pilots either retain or regain their medical certificates when he's not involved with teaching and research in aerospace medicine. An ATR, qualified in the DC-3, B-25 and P-38, Dr. Wick is the only certified instrument flight instructor/physician with an exemption from the FAA to fly with pilots who occupy the left seat while under the influence of alcohol or drugs. But that's a story in itself. He also is immediate past president of the Civil Aviation Medical Association and was flight surgeon to the civilian crew of the X-15. He is not alone in the belief that professional pilots spend too much time on their collective "can."

"Perhaps in the U.S. we are a little slower in encouraging pilots to involve themselves in exercise programs," said Dr. Gordon K. Norwood, FAA's chief of aeromedical standards. "Some think that Americans are not oriented toward exercise as a group. There are probably quite a few pilots who are concerned and do have programs—different types of programs to be sure. And many take pride in the fact that, as a group, they're pretty healthy. There's the human-nature factor, however," Dr. Norwood added. Many airline physicians tend to "low key" physical-fitness programs because they feel that if their pilots are pushed, they may tend to resist it.

What Drs. Norwood and Wick are driving at is hardly protection of the professional pilot image—flat stomach, puffed-out chest and a whiz with the girls. They're hitting at the medical Achilles' heel of the professional pilot—coronary heart disease.

Dr. Wick and a number of OSU associates in aerospace medicine conducted a study a number of years ago for the Air Line Pilots Association on in-flight airline-pilot incapacitation. A result of the study was the discovery that under age 40, the pilot's major health hazard is the aircraft accident. Over 40, however, it's heart and cardiovascular disease. "My personal experience tells me that the exact same thing applies to corporate and business pilots," Dr. Wick said. "If we can do something about heart and cardiovascular disease, we can keep a guy on flying status."

The starting place is a good formal medical program for the corporate flight department (Dr. Wick conducts such programs for Executive Jet Aviation and a number of corporate operators).

"Philosophically," says Dr. Wick, "pilots have problems with their [medical] examiners. Mostly, the examiner represents a hazard to the pilot," unlike the military, where there generally exists a close relationship between flight surgeon and pilot. There are some examiners "who feel pilots should be supermen. The challenge for me is to take a man with something wrong and get him flying again.

"There's no answer to the question of what constitutes a good physical examination. So the FAA says, 'What are the minimum requirements?' A

Class I physical is no better than a Class III physical from the standpoint of pilot longevity. Much of the examination is identical with Class III, but the requirements are higher. The primary question in establishing a formal medical program for the corporate flight department is simply a matter of economics—how much do you want to invest in a medical program for the pilots?"

A basic program, according to Dr. Wick, should include two physicals a year—the bare six-month Class I and the second Class I plus a number of other tests designed to establish a good solid base line of information on the individual pilot.

Additional tests should include blood sugar, cholesterol, chest X-ray, pulmonary lung function, sigmoidoscopy and an electrocardiogram. Even though the FAA does not require electrocardiograms for Class I pilots until age 35, and only annually after age 40, Dr. Wick believes they should be started at an earlier age to create a record in case abnormalities should arise at a later age.

"We're looking for early indications of, first, cardiovascular disease, but also diabetes, possible lung tumors and so on," he said. "The challenge is to see what we can spot that might get a guy into trouble two, three, five or 10 years down the road. If you can spot these things early and talk turkey, you can keep him flying 15 or 20 years hence—that is where the challenge lies."

There also is the safety aspect. "Airplanes don't crash because of physical handicaps. They crash because pilots make mistakes. There are safety aspects a flight surgeon can work with—problems at home, financial problems, the pilot who can't get along with co-workers—these are the guys who are going to have an accident. Their minds are outside the cockpit."

A one-shot examination won't tell the story. It's important for the examiner to see the pilot at least on an annual basis. "It's impossible to predict what's going to happen, but from the standpoint of odds, the guy who's 'clean' will have 10 times the chance of making it to age 60 and still be flying."

By "clean," Dr. Wick refers to a person's ability to control certain "risk factors" that play an important role in determining longevity—weight, smoking habits, inactivity and diet. Singularly, these factors may not pose a particular health threat. Combine two or more, however, and the potential for a problem becomes real.

"If you smoke a pack (of cigarettes) a day, you've got three or four times the chance of developing lung disease. If you smoke two packs, you have 10 to 11 times the chance. If you're overweight, a heavy smoker and have a family background of cardiovascular disease, well . . . Abnormal blood sugar usually goes hand in hand with excess weight. Knock off the excess weight and the blood sugar goes down."

49

Cholesterol is an area of some controversy as to its exact significance concerning cardiovascular disease, but it is generally thought to be a definite contributing factor, and it can be controlled through diet and exercise. Eliminating high cholesterol food from the diet—eating lean meat, fish, skim milk, margarine—will knock the cholesterol level down, but it will still be high. Dr. Wick said physical activity is the more important. "The more physical activity, the more the cholesterol level will be reduced."

So you come down to the question: "Just where in the hell do I go for exercise during transient layovers?" Surprise! At least one FBO already has thought of that. About two years ago, two pilots from Burlington Mills walked up to Hank Esposito, manager of ground services at Atlantic Aviation at Teterboro and said, "Hank, how about a nearby tennis club?" That got the ball rolling and now, during stopovers at Teterboro, you have a choice of indoor tennis, swimming, or a health club complete with running track, hand ball, exercise room, whirlpool, steam and sauna baths, sun and snooze rooms.

"It's an incentive to have people come to our base," Esposito said. And it has matured to the extent at Teterboro that Pan Am, which operates the airport, began assisting with and promoting the program. You simply pick up the "activity phone" at Atlantic and Michelle (on the other end of the line at Pan Am) will make all the arrangements. Courtesy transportation is provided. The health club ($3 per visit) is five minutes away by car and the tennis club ($7 per hour for four persons) is 15 minutes away. Golf, horseback riding or fishing are also available, if you prefer. Acceptance has been good. "If more pilots know these activities are available here, perhaps other FBOs will follow suit."

"I'd recommend such facilities at all major airports, so the corporate pilot can get exercise. Perhaps it's not economically feasible, but it's an interesting thought," Dr. Wick said.

Choice of exercise is up to the individual. "I'd rather have a guy do what he likes to do because he's more likely to do it. Running is as good as anything and better than most. Swimming comes close. Golf is great relaxation, but I don't recommend it for exercise. Tennis and handball are good.

"Any structure in the body gets strong when it's stressed, and if you get the heart rate up to 140 to 150 per minute, then you've stressed it." Once the individual gradually works himself into shape (it's best to check with a physician before launching such a program), he need not work out more than three or four days a week. "That," Dr. Wick said, "will preserve the longevity of the corporate pilot more than anything else. But it's hard work."

AIRPORTS

II

At first glance, it may seem extreme to think in terms of airport survival. In fact, many pilots may even consider operating at ground terminals to be inconvenient interruptions of the "real business" of aerial navigation, but airports do demand their own special considerations. After all, nearly 30 percent of all serious business aviation accidents occur on or around airports.

No airport is inherently safe, nor is it inevitable that a particular airport will be dangerous. Each one has particular characteristics that need to be analyzed and understood by the pilot in command. Airport survival begins with knowledge and mental attitudes that are established on the ground. This chapter is meant to enhance that knowledge and encourage healthy attitudes about handling the problems that the airport environment can impose. It has been said, in fact, that it is the airport environment that demands the most scrupulous discipline from the pilot.

In a sense, airports are a limiting element to aviation, because they constitute the most congested part of the system. In another sense, they are the foundation of the system, the points of departure and the vital destinations that make air transportation possible and profitable. They are at once a blessing and a curse.

Every pilot needs to view aviation real estate with a shaped and cautious perspective, taking nothing for granted and demanding no more than the particular facility can provide with safety. That is the point of this chapter. It is impossible to provide all the answers to operations at all of the many kinds of airports there are, but we can offer many and seek to insure that pilots know what the real questions about airports are.

Surviving the Airport   8

by Richard N. Aarons

A while back, an aviation insurance broker told us that several major companies were planning significant increases in premiums for light-twin coverage. The losses, he said, are getting out of hand.

A month later we ran into an insurance company executive who acknowledged the rate increases and added that his company was thinking of getting out of the light-twin insurance business altogether. Those light twins, he said, are eating us up.

Frankly, our first reaction to these reports was that, as an industry, we'd best get cracking on a light-twin safety program. Perhaps, we thought, light twins don't provide the safety margin that their higher capital costs and operating expenses would seem to imply.

We went to the NTSB for the answer. The NTSB, of course, determines probable causes of all serious general aviation accidents. We obtained reports for a three-year period and culled them in hopes of finding exactly what was wrong with the light twins. Specifically, we were trying to find out if there was a safety problem inherent in these machines.

What we found surprised us. Light twins fall victim to the same accident causal factors that plague the high-performance singles.

Why then are the insurance companies so upset? The answer is simple. When a pilot forgets to lower the undercarriage of a light twin, the resulting hull damage amounts to significantly larger repair bills than the same offense in a high-performance single.

A second consideration is that by virtue of the fact that he can afford a light twin in the first place, the death of an owner-pilot of a light twin is liable to mean higher outlays by insurance companies.

Finally, the light twin is admittedly more flexible than the single-engine aircraft and is therefore pressed into service when the single-engine airplane is left on the ground.

It is our conclusion that the light twins are not involved in more accidents than they should be statistically, but rather that light-twin accidents are more costly to the insurance companies and therefore the companies are more sensitive to these mishaps.

This is not to say that the light-twin safety record—and, for that matter, the high-performance-single safety record—could not be improved.

Accident reports indicate that we've simply got to get back to basics. Rarely do exotic environmental conditions combine with unpredictable design flaws to produce a serious accident.

From the accident investigator's viewpoint, most business aviation mishaps are dull. We land short or hard and wipe out the gear. We fly into the ground while breaking minimums. We run out of fuel. We stall on initial climb. We lose directional control on rollout. We catch wing tips in gusty crosswinds. We use flaps when we shouldn't, and don't when we should.

No wonder accident investigators and insurance underwriters throw up their arms in despair. If as an industry we could limit hull and people losses to those hopeless-case pilots who insist on trying to maintain VFR in IFR conditions or fly into known severe icing conditions without proper equipment or fly into the teeth of fierce squall lines, our insurance problems wouldn't be too bad.

But even if you do everything right, the numbers may still combine to get you. Take the case of the Cessna 340 pilot who began a routine approach to the airport at Griffith, Indiana. Just prior to landing, he glanced down and saw that his landing-gear safe lights were out. He elected to go around, but the left engine wouldn't develop power. So he retracted the gear and flaps and landed straight ahead on a sodded portion of the airport. All went well until the fuel tanks ruptured and the aircraft caught fire. Happily, there were no injuries; unhappily, a minor incident had compounded itself into the loss of an aircraft.

More often, however, the accident report reads like this: "Instrument-rated pilot with 6900 hours, 365 in type, landed a Cessna 421 at Republic Airport, Long Island, on a dry runway and failed to maintain directional control during rollout. The left main gear failed when it hit a taxiway lip. No injuries, but the aircraft suffered substantial damage."

Or like this (taken from the same page of a recent issue of the NTSB's accident briefs): "A commercial pilot with 282 total hours, 15 in type, attempted to land his Cessna 182 on a slushy runway in a crosswind. He (1) improperly compensated for crosswinds, (2) failed to make a proper recovery from a bounced landing, (3) failed thereafter to maintain directional control and (4) demolished the aircraft. There were no injuries."

We're not picking on Cessna. We could compile the same list for Piper, Beech, Mitsubishi, Lear or Grumman. The point we *are* trying to make is that most accidents are dumb. They happen when pilots forget basics.

A research team recently culled NTSB accident reports for three successive years. We were looking for the chink in business aviation's safety armor, and it wasn't hard to find. *Over 50 percent of our accidents occur on or around the airport.*

These airport accidents fall into three major categories—hard landings, loss of directional control during rollout and takeoff run, and stall/spin on short final or initial climb.

Hard landings aren't difficult to figure out. They occur when the vertical descent rate at touchdown induces loads that exceed the structural integrity of the undercarriage.

We should pause here for a moment and think about the term "landing gear." The *landing gear* is inclusive of those structures designed to take up the stresses of landing. Does that include the nose gear? Of course not. The nosewheel is a balancing and, in most airplanes, a steering device. However, accident records seem to indicate there is some confusion over this point—at least when it comes to businessmen-pilot operators of high-performance singles and light twins.

Spread the word, lest the confusion continue. If you fly with a guy who puts the nosewheel on before the mains, point fingers at him and hold him up to public ridicule. Ostracize him from the Friday night drinking sessions because, surer than hell, he's going to contribute to a hull rate increase someday.

It could well be that your nosewheel-barbarian friend was led astray during his early training by well-meaning—but misinformed—flight instructors. How many experienced pilots to this day can still hear their instructors shouting: "Control airspeed with the stick and altitude with the throttle."

Of course, that advice is wrong. It was wrong when first offered and wrong now. Obviously, whenever thrust *can* be varied, throttle controls airspeed and the stick controls altitude.

You need proof? Consider an ILS approach. Coming across the outer marker, you ball-park the power to produce an airspeed and rate of descent appropriate to the approach. Thereafter, you meet glideslope excursions with movements of elevator and you make speed adjustments with the throttle.

The autopilot makers have always been aware that altitude is controlled with the stick and airspeed with the throttle. When an autopilot wants to change aircraft altitude, it changes pitch attitude. The crew must then adjust airspeed with the throttles . . . unless the aircraft is equipped with an autothrottle system. How about an autothrottle system? Its sole purpose is to move the throttles to maintain programmed airspeeds. Some instructors argue that defining what controls what in the approach isn't really very important because a pilot intuitively controls airspeed with the throttle and altitude with the stick no matter what he's been told.

Accident statistics indicate that that argument is not valid. Let's look at what happens when airspeed is controlled with the stick and altitude with the throttle.

Our pilot is a believer in the old saw that a good landing is preceded by a good approach, so he attempts to stabilize the aircraft visually on a three-degree glidepath with a long, comfortable final. As his aiming point moves in the windscreen, he attempts to correct small altitude excursions with throttle. But there's a lag between throttle application and aircraft acceleration, so it takes a while before the lift vector changes. If gusty conditions are causing rapid changes in his perception of the aiming point, his throttle jockeying will completely destabilize the approach in short order.

Somehow he manages to continue the approach to short final despite the throttle jockeying. He notices that airspeed is falling off so he responds with a slight nose-down elevator movement. The wing dumps lift at this reduced angle of attack and vertical speed increases immediately in response. But his speed is where he wants it, and he's in no danger of undershooting the runway, so he simply sits there waiting to arrive at his flare point. He is now only seconds from wiping out the nose gear because the elevator does not have enough power to overcome the excessive rate of descent generated by the nose-down maneuver used to pick up lagging airspeed.

You think this scenario is too pat? Unfortunately it's not. This type accident happens several times a day around the country, causing tens of thousands of dollars worth of damage to training aircraft, high-performance singles and light twins.

We've talked about how to do it incorrectly. Now we'll look at the right way to stabilize an approach. Remember, this is the right way for *any* trainer, high-performance single or light twin. A *stabilized* approach is stabilized in two modes—airspeed and vertical rate. The combination of the two produces a stabilized glidepath. So the first thing you must do is select an aircraft configuration and airspeed appropriate to the ambient conditions.

Pilots still argue over what a *normal* approach configuration is for light aircraft. However, aircraft designers stopped arguing about this years ago. So let's set the record straight right now. A *normal* approach is conducted with *power on, with flaps deployed* and at an airspeed not greater than *1.4 times the stalling speed* for the existing configuration. Over-the-fence speed should be 1.3 times the stall. Any other approach configuration is *abnormal* for routine light-aircraft operations.

We'll look at these elements individually.

Power on—The businessman pilot rarely gets to an airport where traffic is such that he can cut the power at a "key" position and drift down in a power-off approach. Even if he could, he wouldn't want to. Most high-performance singles and light twins develop descent rates of 1000 fpm or more in this configuration, leaving no room for misjudgment in the flare maneuver.

It used to be that students were warned to make all pattern turns within power-off gliding distance of the runway. When this rule came into vogue, aircraft engines were so unreliable that *all* flying, in or out of the pattern, was done within gliding distance of some surface that could serve as a runway.

In short, a power-on approach *is* normal for today's light aircraft in today's airport environments.

Flaps—Full flaps are normally used for the final portion of an approach. Flaps change the airfoil shape to increase lift to allow lower touchdown speeds, and they also increase drag to facilitate slaving the aircraft to those lower touchdown speeds. There are many old wives' tales floating around about the use and misuse of flaps. Your owner's manual or aircraft flight manual is the only valid place to find flap limitations appropriate for your aircraft. However, these general rules apply in all cases. Use flaps for final approach when the crosswind component is relatively low, even in gusting conditions. Use flaps in crosswinds unless your operator's manual or aircraft flight manual specifically warns against their use in slips or crosswinds.

Remember, a no-flap landing is an *abnormal* operation.

Speed—You'll never make consistently good, consistently safe landings unless you nail down airspeeds. (And remember that airspeed control is accomplished with the throttle.) All certification work is done with an over-the-fence speed of 1.3 times stall in the landing configuration. This speed is slow enough to prevent float and fast enough to maintain a healthy margin over stall. Any speed in excess of 1.3 times the stall speed coming over the fence (unless necessary to compensate for severe gusting which we'll look at in a moment) is undesirable. High touchdown speeds prevent a proper flare and touchdown on the main wheels, and usually lead to a nosewheel landing, which can quickly lead to wheelbarrowing.

If you ever get a chance to thumb through an issue of the NTSB's accident briefs, you'll be surprised at the number of airplanes wrecked when the pilot loses control during *rollout*. The main contributing causal factor to these rollout accidents is hot touchdown. Avoid it. An extra 10 knots for the wife and kids can be damn dangerous.

In very light FAR Part 23 airplanes, one landing speed is all you need to remember. However, too many pilots of high-performance singles and light twins forget the fact that landing speeds for their aircraft depend on approach weight. Unless you've got an angle-of-attack indicator onboard, the fence speed must be adjusted to account for existing weight. The Cessna 421, for example, has an over-the-fence speed of 103 knots at 7200 pounds decreasing to 87 knots at 5200 pounds. (That's with 45-degree flaps.) If you attempt to flare a 5200-pound 421 at 103 knots, the airplane will begin to balloon. Most pilots remedy this by releasing a bit of back pressure, which allows the nosewheel to hit first. Then they're whizzing down the runway in a wheelbarrow configuration.

This presents several problems. First, the nosewheel simply isn't designed to take the stresses of landing impact. Second, the nosewheel and rudder are usually interconnected. If the mains are off the ground (or light) and the nosewheel is on solid, aerodynamic steering help from the rudder is not available. (If you move the rudder pedals far enough to displace the rudder into the slipstream, the nosewheel will turn and you'll be heading for the boondocks.) Finally, in a wheelbarrowing situation the pivot point of the airplane is way up front at the nosewheel, but the force that causes the airplane to pivot (ground loop) is crosswind on the fin and rudder, which are way aft. That long arm—from nose to tail—often results in a harsh lesson in applied physics as the airplane weathervanes off the runway.

In most Part 23 airplanes, you don't have to go back to the owner's manual for speeds during each approach. Simply work up a rule of thumb. In the case of the Cessna 421, obstacle speed decreases 16 knots as landing weight decreases 2000 pounds, or four knots for each 500-pound decrease from maximum landing weight. Therefore, if the airplane on a given approach weighs 6400 pounds, the pilot would mentally subtract 6400 from 7200 to get his weight change factor—800 pounds in this case. If a 500-pound decrease from 7200 pounds requires a four-knot speed reduction, an 800-pound decrease requires a six-knot reduction. (You're right. The numbers aren't exact, but nobody can hold a half knot anyway.)

To this point, we've been talking about the last mile of the final approach. In that last mile, the aircraft should be stabilized with full flaps at 1.4 times the stall speed. Coming over the fence, speed should be reduced to 1.3 times the stall. Touchdown must be on the mains.

But speed control starts long before you fly the last mile. You need a plan tailored to your airplane's performance to get to the threshold window. Some guys arrive in the pattern at 200 knots on one day and 120 knots the next. They have no scheme for speed reduction; no fixed place when they think about gear or flaps. Their approaches are rarely stabilized because they have no starting point, and this situation busts airplanes.

Part 23 owner's manuals usually tell you what you can't do with your airplane, but they rarely tell you what you should do. You'll have to work out some things for yourself, including a speed-reduction schedule for approaches. When you settle on a schedule, stick to it unless ATC forces you to do something else.

B/CA pilots worked out an approach schedule for our company Cessna 310. We'll share with you the thinking that went into it.

Basically, we worked the problem backwards. We knew we wanted to cross the fence at 1.3 times stall *for our weight* and that we wanted to be stabilized with full flaps at 1.3 times stall plus 10 at least a mile out on final.

However, we didn't want full landing flaps before that one-mile point because, quite frankly, our 310Q has very poor go-around characteristics, especially in high ambients.

On the positive side, we wanted plenty of maneuvering speed early in the approach, and we wanted the capability to accelerate to best single-engine rate-of-climb speed until we were committed to a landing.

With a pocket computer and the owner's manual, we were able to develop appropriate speeds for various positions in the approach. Here's the way we worked it. On downwind in VFR conditions, or anywhere on the approach course in IFR conditions, we wanted to be stabilized with wheels down, 15 degrees of flaps and an indicated airspeed of 115 knots.

Our initial approach speed of 115 knots is equivalent to the stall speed in approach configuration with a 60-degree bank . . . plus 10 knots for mom. This speed gives us plenty of maneuvering capability, and it's comfortably above the best single-engine rate-of-climb speed of 107 knots. Of course, these speeds are not exact since they must be adjusted for weight.

We carry 115 knots in this configuration to a one-mile final, then we add full flaps and decelerate to 105 knots—that's obstacle speed plus 10. Coming over the fence, we reduce speed to 95 knots for flare and touchdown.

Your own schedule, of course, must be designed around the numbers for your airplane, but keep these points in mind. For airport maneuvering, you want a comfortably slow speed, but one fast enough so that a sudden traffic-evasion maneuver won't drop you into an accelerated stall. If your airplane has a strong pitch-up tendency when initial flaps are lowered—such is the case with late-model Cessna 310s and Piper Aztecs—get initial flaps down *before* entering the pattern (VFR) or establishing the aircraft on the approach course (IFR). Unless your aircraft is overpowered (and few light planes are), don't use full flaps until you're on relatively short final and landing is assured. However, remember that full flaps should be used in almost all circumstances once you've made the decision to land.

There are a number of formulas to adjust approach speed to compensate for gusts. Keep it simple and add half the gust factor to your programmed speeds. For example, if the wind is 20 gusting to 30, add five knots to the final approach speeds. Don't get carried away with this, however. Any compensation more than 10 knots is probably too much and will lead to porpoising and a nosewheel landing.

The example we used here produced an approach speed profile for a light twin. However, the same logic can be used to construct an approach profile for a single-engine aircraft. The only difference is that you won't have to worry about single-engine speeds or single-engine go-arounds.

This discussion started in search for ways to avoid hard landings. As we've seen, the prevention of hard landings begins long before you ever leave the ground, when you sit down to work out an approach speed/configuration schedule. Let's list the high points once more:

· Work out a descent/approach speed profile that you'll follow.

· Remember, altitude is controlled by the stick; airspeed is controlled by the throttle.

· *Normal* approaches and landings involve the use of power and full flaps.

· Monitor descent rate coming over the fence. Anything over 500 fpm should scare hell out of you.

· Use appropriate landing speeds.

· Land on the *landing gear,* not the *nosewheel.*

· Remember to put the wheels down.

If you accomplish the seven exercises listed above, you will not be involved in a hard-landing mishap, nor will you land short, nor will you land wheels-up. Remember, 50 percent of all accidents happen in the traffic pattern or on the runway. If you follow these seven tips, you'll be able to avoid well over half of that 50 percent.

What about the other half? We said earlier that airport accidents comprise over 50 percent of the total accidents involving business and executive aircraft. The three major categories, we cited, were hard landings, loss of directional control during rollout and takeoff run, and stall/spin in final or initial climb.

If you maintain an intelligent approach speed profile and if you keep all turns coordinated, you won't spin out on final. It's as simple as that. We've seen that if you land on the main gear at a speed slightly above stall, you'll avoid wheelbarrowing and thus avoid loss of directional control on rollout. So the major airport accident categories left are loss of control on takeoff run and stall/spin during initial climb.

Perhaps too much has been written over the years about takeoff planning for light twins, at least as far as discussions of V_{MCA} and V_{YSE} are concerned. Maybe we're just muddying the waters. Two B/CA staffers, who regularly conduct pilot proficiency checks, are beginning to think we've taken too sophisticated an approach to light-twin training. Instead of a small red line on the airspeed indicator marking theoretical V_{MCA}, perhaps we should have a skull and crossbones. Instead of involved explanations of asymmetric thrust, torque and rudder power, we should merely warn people that to allow a light twin to decelerate below the skull-and-crossbones mark under any circumstances will lead to an abrupt and grisly end to their flying careers. So we're going to limit our discussion of V_{MCA} to that thought. However, we do want to pass along one comment on the subject of light-twin safety that we overheard recently at the FAA Academy at Oklahoma City: "Light twins have two engines because they won't fly on one."

Sure that's an oversimplification. Light twins, under some circumstances, will fly well and far with but one engine running. That's why we buy them. So to be fair to the light-twin class, we ought to change that comment to this: "Light twins have two engines because they need two for takeoff and climb to maneuvering altitude . . . and for most other sustained flight." If you apply thought to light-twin takeoff planning, V_{MCA} won't kill you. So let's leave that subject and look at some of the less spectacular ways guys wreck airplanes on takeoff and climbout.

Loss of directional control during takeoff and landing takes a surprisingly high toll in damaged and destroyed high-performance singles and light twins. Part of the problem must be that these aircraft accelerate rapidly and their pilots simply get behind them, especially when gusty crosswinds combine with torque effects to displace the aircraft from the runway.

Here are three tips that, if followed, will go a long way toward keeping you out of the boondocks:

· *Abort the takeoff early if a directional control problem develops.* One B/CA editor watched a friend die in a totally avoidable takeoff accident several years ago. As in all accidents, there's a lesson to be learned from this one. The friend was flying left seat in a Curtiss C-46, which was taking off lightly loaded from a relatively narrow, paved runway. The crew forgot to lock the tailwheel because they forgot to use a checklist. It was apparent to witnesses that the crew was having directional problems as soon as the takeoff roll started; the aircraft was making small swings back and forth across the centerline. As the aircraft accelerated, the swings became larger and a main gear slipped off the runway. By this time the tail was up and, incredibly, the crew hauled back on the stick, probably theorizing that they could regain control in the air. The aircraft stalled at 100 feet and did a half-turn spin before impacting in a ravine.

The accident could have been avoided any time before the decision to get airborne was made. But a refusal to abort as soon as the directional control problem became evident cost two lives.

· *Advance power slowly and smoothly on takeoff.* Give yourself a chance to feel what the airplane is going to do and time to react to directional changes. There are short-field situations in which brakes must be released only after full power is developed. But remember, this is a special-circumstance procedure, and you'll have to be especially alert to prevent directional control problems.

Incidentally, on turboprops, hold the brakes until the power levers are halfway forward and the engines and propellers have had a chance to stabilize at the same approximate speed and pitch. Then release the brakes and move the power levers to the limiting parameter.

· *Rotate at the proper speed.* In high-performance singles and light twins, a late takeoff can be as bad as an early takeoff. Most manufacturers recommend that in crosswind conditions the aircraft be held on the ground until a slightly higher-than-normal takeoff speed is reached, then rapidly rotated to avoid sideloads. Follow this advice, but *don't overdo it.* Most light twins, and many high-performance singles, will wheelbarrow if accelerated much more than five knots above normal takeoff speed. As you can imagine, this can be disastrous in a strong crosswind.

Inattention is the only reason anybody ever stalls an airplane accidentally. If you're paying attention to what's going on—IFR or VFR—you won't spin in. It's easy to get sloppy with airspeed control, though, especially in an airplane you've flown for hundreds of hours. A pilot of our acquaintance took off a while back in a high-performance single and was off the ground before he realized that something had choked the pitot system. The lack of airspeed indications obviously caused no operational problems, but surely a glance at the airspeed once in a while wouldn't hurt either.

When we installed an angle-of-attack system in our 310, the device made better pilots of us all. On approach and departure, we check angle of attack continuously. The instrument itself has increased our awareness of the peculiar problems associated with low-speed, high-angle-of-attack flight.

At B/CA we firmly believe that approach and departure stalls would practically disappear if all aircraft were equipped with relatively inexpensive angle-of-attack systems and, of course, if pilots learned how to use these systems. Next time you've got a couple hundred bucks burning a hole in your pocket, give serious thought to an angle-of-attack indicator. It could be the most valuable instrument in your airplane.

We rarely break airplanes through ignorance; we have accidents because of slight inattentions and sloppiness.

Airport Performance for Business Jets

9

by James W. Powell

Perhaps no single subject commands attention from the aviation industry as does aircraft performance. Engineers, accountants, pilots, passengers and management are concerned with what an aircraft can do—whether or not it can fulfill the needs of the operating individual or company. Transport category jet performance, which covers all but one of the business jets, seems to be confusing to almost everyone except the pilots themselves.

In light of this interest by so many people in the companies that own and operate jets, a synopsis of performance standards as contained in the Federal Aviation Regulations, Part 25, "Airworthiness Standards: Transport Category Aircraft" seems fitting. Particular attention will be directed toward sections 25.101 through 25.125, termed "Performance: Turbine Engine Powered Airplanes."

On February 1, 1965 FAR 25 became the successor to the old CAR 4b. Several "Special Air Regulations" were also adopted in establishing airworthiness standards for transport aircraft certification. Additionally, SR-422, SR-422A and SR-422B containing operating rules applicable to transport category aircraft used in scheduled air carrier service were placed in FAR 121 after April 1, 1965. Provisions for an airplane flight manual, carried over from these "Special Air Regulations," are also included in FAR 25.

No performance computation can be safely applied without an awareness of assumptions and parameters that went into the specific calculations. Many operational and aerodynamic factors are considered by test engineers responsible for collecting and plotting performance data. Included are evaluations of the effect of still air versus ground effect, temperature and humidity, average crew abilities, time delay segments (recognition, decision, operation), effective runway gradients, headwinds and tailwinds and runway coefficient-of-friction.

It's also necessary to understand the pertinent parts of the general conditions specified in FAR 25.101:

"Unless otherwise prescribed, turbine powered airplanes must meet the applicable performance requirements of this subpart for ambient atmospheric conditions and still air.

"The performance, as affected by engine power or thrust, must be based on a relative humidity of 80 percent, at and below standard temperatures; and 34 percent, at and above standard temperatures plus 50° F. Between these two temperatures, the relative humidity must vary linearly.

"The performance must correspond to the propulsive thrust available under the particular ambient atmospheric conditions, the particular flight condition and the relative humidity specified. . . . The available propulsive thrust must correspond to engine power or thrust, not exceeding the approved power or thrust, less installation losses; and the power or equivalent thrust absorbed by the accessories and services appropriate to the particular ambient atmospheric conditions and the particular flight condition.

"Unless otherwise prescribed, the applicant must select the takeoff, en route, approach and landing configurations for the airplane.

"The airplane configurations may vary with weight, altitude and temperature, to the extent they are compatible with the operating procedures required by the following paragraph. . . .

"Unless otherwise prescribed, in determining the accelerate-stop distances, takeoff flight paths, takeoff distances and landing distances, changes in the airplane's configuration, speeds, power and thrust, must be made in accordance with procedures established by the applicant for operation in service.

"The procedures established under [the above] must be able to be consistently executed in service by crews of average skill; use methods or devices that are safe and reliable; and include allowance for any time delays, in the execution of the procedures, that may reasonably be expected in service."

Four principal limitations are applicable to business jets vis-a-vis the takeoff phase of flight. Let's look at them individually:

· *Structural*—Every jet has a maximum takeoff weight. The limit may be determined by any one of a half dozen or so considerations: brake effectiveness, engine thrust, climb capability or simply the capacity of the aircraft for fuel and people. The usual limitation, however, is structural. The strength of the landing gear, and the structure to which the landing gear is attached, is often the primary consideration here. Landing gear strengths are meticulously spelled out in FAR 25.471 through 25.511.

· *Takeoff field lengths*—Takeoff field lengths are broken into three parts, but before getting into them we must first come to grips with the pertinent parts of FAR 25.111, "Takeoff Path." That regulation specifies, "The takeoff path extends from a standing start to a point in the takeoff at which the airplane is 1500 feet above the takeoff surface, or at which the transition from the takeoff to the en route configuration is completed [see the "Final Segment" column in Figure 1] . . . whichever point is higher. In addition, the takeoff path must be based on the procedures prescribed in Part 25.101(c):

"The airplane must be accelerated on the ground to V_1, at which point the critical engine must be made inoperative and remain inoperative for the rest of the takeoff; and after reaching V_1, the airplane must be accelerated to V_2.

"During the acceleration to speed V_2, the nose gear may be raised off the ground at a speed not less than V_R. However, landing gear retraction may not be begun until the airplane is airborne.

"During the takeoff path determination in accordance with the first two paragraphs in this section; the slope of the airborne part of the takeoff path must be positive at each point; the airplane must reach V_2, before it is 35 feet above the takeoff surface. . . ."

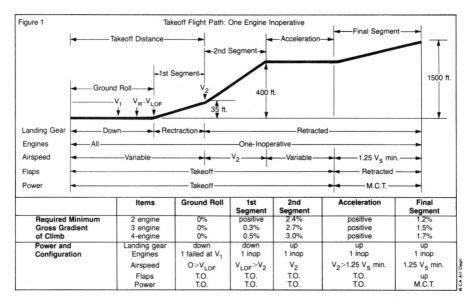

Figure 1

	Items	Ground Roll	1st Segment	2nd Segment	Acceleration	Final Segment
Required Minimum Gross Gradient of Climb	2 engine 3 engine 4-engine	0% 0% 0%	positive 0.3% 0.5%	2.4% 2.7% 3.0%	positive positive positive	1.2% 1.5% 1.7%
Power and Configuration	Landing gear Engines Airspeed Flaps Power	down 1 failed at V_1 $0 > V_{LOF}$ T.O. T.O.	down 1 inop $V_{LOF} > V_2$ T.O. T.O.	up 1 inop V_2 T.O. T.O.	up 1 inop $V_2 > 1.25 V_S$ min. T.O. T.O.	up 1 inop $1.25 V_S$ min. up M.C.T.

Now, returning to those three parts in reference to takeoff field lengths, let's examine each:

(1) Takeoff distance is defined by FAR 25.113 as "The horizontal distance along the takeoff path from the start of the takeoff to the point at which the airplane is 35 feet above the takeoff surface (following an engine failure at some arbitrary speed, V_1) . . . or 115 percent of the horizontal distance along the takeoff path, with all engines operating, from the start of the

takeoff to the point at which the airplane is 35 feet above the takeoff surface. . . ."

All that is illustrated in Figure 2, with V_1 in 2A referring to the point at which an engine fails and V_{LOF} referring to the points on the runway (in both 2A and 2B) at which the aircraft becomes airborne, or lifts off.

In most cases, takeoff distance charts do not define which of the two methods used for determining takeoff distance is most limiting, but only display the longest distance. Takeoff distance may only include runway length plus the legal clearway.

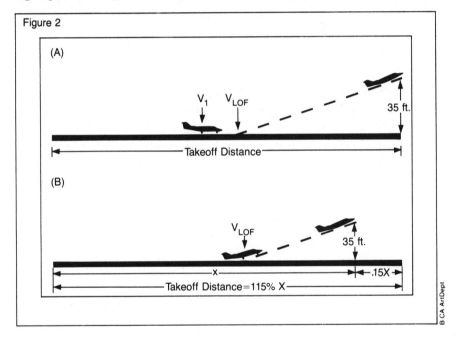

Figure 2

(2) Takeoff run is a term applied when the takeoff distance includes a clearway and is the greater of the two distances established in Figure 3. Those two distances are: (3A) the distance from the start of the takeoff roll to the horizontal mid-point between liftoff (V_{LOF}), and the point where the aircraft attains a height of 35 feet above the takeoff surface, following a critical engine failure at V_1; or (3B) 115 percent of the distance from the start of the takeoff roll to the mid-point between liftoff and the point where the aircraft attains a height of 35 feet above the takeoff surface, with all engines operating.

Of course, the takeoff run must be completed by the runway end.

(3) Accelerate-stop is the sum of the distances required to accelerate to V_1 and bring the aircraft to a complete stop, assuming critical engine

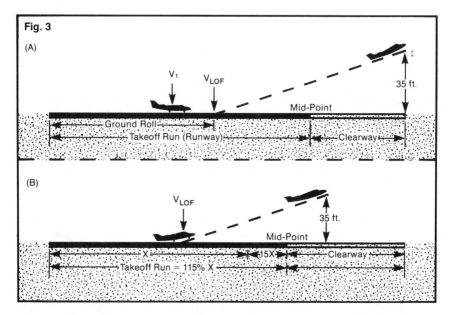

failure at V_1, as shown in Figure 4. Only the runway, plus the charted stopway, may be utilized for this computation. The aircraft need not have taxi capability following a rejected takeoff. Even brake fires of a limited nature are allowed.

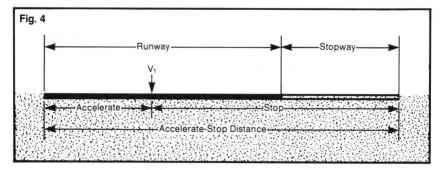

Interestingly, FAR 25.109 specifies that, "Means other than wheel brakes may be used to determine the accelerate-stop distance if that means is safe and reliable; is used so that consistent results can be expected under normal operating conditions; and is such that exceptional skill is not required to control the airplane."

In spite of that, thrust reversers are not allowed, nor is a drag chute, in computing the accelerate-stop distance for a jet. The FAA evidently feels they aren't safe, reliable or consistent in the context of FAR 25.109.

There's another condition that enters the equation when a stopway or overrun is available, as follows: "If the accelerate-stop distance includes a stopway with surface characteristics substantially different from those of a smooth hard-surfaced runway, the takeoff data must include operational correction factors for the acceleration-stop distance. The correction factors must account for the particular surface characteristics of the stopway and the variations in these characteristics with seasonal weather conditions (such as temperature, rain, snow and ice) within the established operational limits."

Incidentally, the FAA specifies that "the landing gear must remain extended throughout the accelerate-stop distance." No fair retracting the gear to slide to a stop quicker.

With respect to the three parts of the takeoff distance, the specified field length limitation will be the most restrictive of the takeoff distance, takeoff run and accelerate-stop distances.

Takeoff flight path: one engine inoperative—Yet another limitation that may determine the maximum takeoff weight is the takeoff flight path following a critical engine failure at V_1. The takeoff flight path begins at the end of the takeoff distance (that is, when the aircraft has achieved an altitude of 35 feet, as described above) and ends at 1500 feet above the takeoff surface or en route altitude, whichever is higher.

Gross gradient—the climb expressed as a percentage of the horizontal distance covered—actually achievable by an "average" aircraft of the type in consideration must be met. "WAT" charts display this information predicated on the maximum aircraft Weight for the airport pressure Altitude and Temperature. Figure 1 presents the minimum takeoff flight path requirements when computed by the conventional segment method. Manufacturers may seek certification of more stringent standards, such as direct second segment climb to 1500 feet.

Takeoff flight path: obstacle clearance—A final limitation to weight carrying ability on takeoff concerns obstacles within the departure path. FAR 25 dictates that a reduced takeoff flight path be assumed where obstacles are concerned. FAR 25.115 spells this requirement out: "The net takeoff flight path data must be determined so that they represent the actual takeoff flight paths . . . reduced at each point by a gradient of climb equal to 0.8% for 2-engine airplanes; 0.9% for 3-engine airplanes; and 1.0% for 4-engine airplanes."

Operating rules in "Special Air Regulations" required that the obstacle be cleared by specified limits. These rules are now incorporated in FAR 121, the rules applicable to the air carrier operations, but not in the FAR 91 rules that apply to corporate jet operators. (FAR 121 does apply, however, to business jets operated in air taxi service.) Corporate operators should adhere to the 121 regulations regarding obstacle clearances although that isn't mandatory.

Provisions are made in FAR 25 for inclusion in the airplane flight manual data on en-route flight paths with an engine, or engines, inoperative. Again, as with obstacle clearance on takeoff, a reduction is made of the gross performance as measured during certification testing. That reduction is charted in Figure 5.

Figure 5		
Number of Engines	Reduction from Actual % (1 Engine Inoperative)	Reduction from Actual % (2 Engines Inoperative)
2 engines	1.1 %	No provision
3 engines	1.4 %	0.3 %
4 engines	1.6 %	0.5 %

Specific operational considerations such as vertical separation from obstacles and drift down altitudes (the altitude to which the airplane sinks following an engine loss) are left to operator judgment. Hopefully, this factor is considered in every flight over high terrain or large bodies of water.

As is true for the departure, several factors limit the permissible weight of an aircraft at landing. Let's take a look at those.

Structural—Again, the strength of the gear and the structure to which it is attached is the first limiting factor on landing weight. However, there can be other structural factors that have a side effect on the landing weight. For example, aircraft with various forms of external tanks are often restricted from landing with more than some specified maximum amount of fuel in those tanks. Therefore, in certain situations it may be that the aircraft is below its maximum landing weight, but still cannot be landed (except in an emergency) because of fuel on-board in excess of a limit.

Should it be necessary to land an aircraft at a weight above the maximum landing weight, or with excess fuel in a tank, an over-weight landing inspection is required to insure that no structural damage or deformity resulted. In extreme instances, replacement of certain parts may be mandatory.

Landing climb: one engine inoperative—In event of a rejected landing while in the landing configuration (landing gear extended and flaps full down) the regulations specify a minimum flight path gradient in *each* configuration labeled "approach" by the manufacturer. The maximum weight allowed in a landing WAT chart is a function of the airworthiness climb requirements in landing configurations. The minimum climb gradients, one engine inoperative, are: for a 2-engine jet, 2.1%; 3-engine, 2.4%; 4-engine, 2.7%.

Landing climb: all engines operating—In the landing configuration (landing flaps and gear down) the gradient of climb may not be less than 3.2% with all engines operating at thrust levels available eight seconds after the throttles were moved from idle to full open. The airspeed must be 130% of the stall speed for the aircraft.

Landing field lengths—Landing field lengths consist of the horizontal runway surface necessary to cross the threshold from 50 feet at 130% of the stall speed, then maintain a steady glide to the landing surface and come to a complete stop using brakes only. (Again, reversers aren't allowed in determining minimum landing distances.) Accountability for altitude and temperature above or below the average for that altitude, is individual to each airplane flight manual.

No provision is made in FAR 25 for utilization of only a percentage of the total landing runway length. That is, in corporate operations, the available runway need not be any longer than the actual distance required as shown in Figure 6. FAR 121, applicable to for-hire and air carrier operations, does require additional runway to insure a safe stop in event of a miscalculation or a brake failure. The 121 requirement is obtained by multiplying the actual runway needed times 1.67. In the opinion of most aviation safety experts, and of most pilots as well, the 1.67 factor should be applied as a hard and fast rule for every operator of a Part 25 jet.

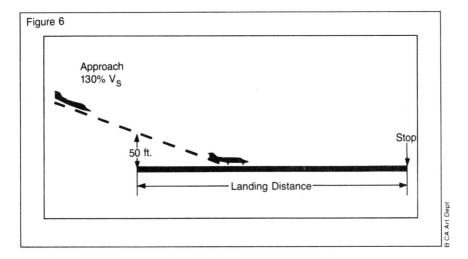

Figure 6

Approach
130% V_S

50 ft.

Stop

Landing Distance

B CA Art Dept

Your performance manual may, in fact, give landing distances in terms of 121 rules, as this enables the manufacturer to have an FAR 121 acceptable airplane flight manual and thereby a more attractive product offering.

Obstacle clearance on landing—Generally, and obviously, obstruction clearance on landing involves missing the obstacles in the approach path. In addition, consideration must also be given to the capability to achieve and maintain adequate clearance above obstacles in the airport vicinity should a go-around be necessary. Provisions for this determination will be individual to each airplane flight manual, and not all of them contain it. In that event, the chief pilot should create safe standards for the aircraft involved and each airport it visits.

While discussion of FAR 25 performance standards may seem abundantly detailed at times, each individual limitation can be considered in concise and quick fashion by a pilot who is master of the performance manual for the aircraft he flies. For that reason, reviews of the manual should be a major part of each pilot's recurrency training program, as well as a review of the pertinent Federal Air Regulations.

It is equally important that those who manage the aircraft, and those authorized to schedule it for trips, have some knowledge of its performance as set forth in the performance manual and the pertinent Federal Aviation Regulations briefly discussed here.

The reason for that should be obvious. If company management does not fully understand the limitations of the aircraft and the rationale for them, those officials may from time to time ask an aircraft captain to attempt a departure from an airport, or a landing at one, that is unsafe in event of an emergency. Depending on how secure that captain feels in his job, he may attempt the operation in spite of his better judgment and thereby place the involved company management in jeopardy.

For the reasons immediately above, the editors of B/CA recommend that management request from their chief pilots a performance limitations summary for each aircraft operated by the company. The limitations summary should include data on maximum safe ranges, maximum loading capacities and minimum runway lengths.

Such a summary should be used as an inviolate guide to what company management may and may not ask the captain of a flight segment to do.

Noise-Abatement Procedures

10

by Bill Cotton

Only a handful of airports around the world have been given a black star rating by the International Federation of Air Line Pilots' Associations for being "seriously deficient". Most of them have received this dubious distinction for substandard runways, lighting or approach aids. But Los Angeles International Airport has been given a black star rating for a different reason—dangerous noise-abatement procedures. Due to the threat of multibillion-dollar noise lawsuits, the Los Angeles Board of Airport Commissioners forced the FAA to institute special operational procedures between the hours of 2400 and 0600. These procedures require landings from the ocean and takeoffs over the ocean. Result: opposite direction takeoffs and landings. The landings are frequently downwind in poorer weather than that on the normal approach from the east due to the sea fog. A pilot's only recourse to those procedures is to divert to his alternate.

The Los Angeles story is only one illustration of how a growing number of new procedures and policies are being implemented in an effort to ease the aircraft noise problem at airports. Airports in every section of the country are coming under pressure to regulate aircraft noise; night curfews have already been imposed at San Diego, Washington National and Boston. Business jets are not immune to these threats to free airport access, which until recently have primarily been the airlines' problems. Frequently, corporate aircraft are the only jets using a particular airport, leaving no question about who will receive local airport noise complaints.

But how far does the responsibility of a corporate pilot go? How much noise relief can be provided to airport neighbors by a pilot without seriously jeopardizing the safety of his passengers or the economical operation of his aircraft? This is one of the most difficult questions facing corporate pilots today and the stakes are high—the safety of a flight and the right of access to an airport, or even the existence of the airport itself.

Caught in the middle of the noise controversy are the air traffic controllers who, through the clearances they must issue, implement the noise-reduction programs. The controllers are criticized from both sides—from the irritated local resident who has learned the phone number of the control tower and from the pilot who is irate at having to compromise safety for the purpose of noise abatement.

The conflict between pilots and ATC resulting from noise-abatement procedures is illustrated by an incident that took place in Boston. A tower controller on the midnight shift cleared an Aztec to land on a runway that was directly crosswind. "How about 15R for landing?" asked the pilot, wanting to land into the wind. "Well, I can give you that if you insist, but I think you should know the sheriff will be meeting you at the ramp if you land on it."

On the other hand, controllers in San Diego feel it is unfair to expect them to enforce a local airport curfew ordinance that may prove to be unsafe or even illegal. "If an airplane arrives during the curfew, I'll provide him traffic separation and clear him to land. That's as far as my duty extends," claimed one San Diego controller.

Keeping in mind the conflicting desires of pilots, traffic controllers and local residents, three solutions to the noise problem seem possible:

(1) Remove those who complain about the noise.

(2) Reduce the noise at the source.

(3) Procedurally or operationally move the noise away from sensitive areas, or at least spread it around.

Removing those who complain about the noise is the most effective solution, but it's also the costliest and politically most difficult. Los Angeles Airport did buy up and raze whole neighborhoods that lay under the final approach paths to the airport. Cleveland Airport authorities did the same thing. Some airport planners were farsighted enough to prevent, through zoning, the residential development of land surrounding their airports. However, this approach does not always work since zoning variations or changes to the law itself can negate the good intentions. Homes just seem to spring up around airports like mushrooms after a spring rain. The fact that the airport was there before they were does little to quiet the complaints.

While buying up the land around an airport may be the ultimate solution at a few major terminals, it is impractical at many of the places where corporate jets fly. The most that can be hoped for is that protective zoning was put in place when the airport was constructed.

Noise *complaints* are one thing; lawsuits, curfews and threatened airport closures are something else. When legal action is threatened, airport operators have to show they are doing something to alleviate the problem or they may lose the whole thing. One legal defense for an airport threatened with lawsuits based on noise complaints is for officials to fall back on

FAR Part 36. Los Angeles Airport, for example, will permit aircraft meeting this noise specification to land to the west during the early morning hours if the weather is below minimums for an east approach; all other aircraft have to go somewhere else.

Reduction of noise at the source, through improved engine or nacelle design, is receiving a great deal of attention from government and industry right now. In the business aircraft fleet, all new jets coming off the production line since January 1, 1975, meet Part 36 requirements; many older business jets and BAC 1-11s and DC-9s being used for business purposes do not. Retrofit is a possibility on the noncomplying aircraft, but the cost is up to $500,000 per engine for both airliners and business aircraft. There is a proposal to use Aviation Trust Fund money to help pay for aircarrier engine retrofit costs, but so far this has not been proposed for the business jets.

Since reaction to perceived noise levels is subjective on the part of airport neighbors, many people question the wisdom of spending billions for a very small reduction in the decibels reaching the ground. An alternative plan favored by the airlines, and also being given consideration by the government, is the establishment of an escrow fund to finance the purchase of new, more fuel efficient aircraft which meet both Part 36 noise criteria and EPA emissions standards. This fund, generated by a passenger ticket and freight waybill tax of about $1, would be used to stimulate private investment in new airframes and engines, as well as speed the replacement of old equipment. A variation of this plan would also use Trust Fund money. But of course, while a fleet replacement fund may eventually ease credit and noise problems for the airlines, it doesn't help the corporate operator whose aircraft already meets FAR 36, but whose neighbors don't think that's good enough. Besides, the corporate operator can't start collecting a dollar from the boss every time he flies.

Progressively stricter environmental legislation compounds the problems of the aircraft operator. When noise and emissions standards are tightened, it is possible for an aircraft to become illegal overnight though it's still mechanically healthy. Moreover, removing the noise at the source is a good long-term solution, but the promise of quieter days to come does nothing to quench the flaring tempers now threatening airports. Citizens' groups can amass tremendous political pressures to close or restrict airports. The owners of private airports open to public use, already burdened by overtaxation and small yield on investment, often find the noise issue to be the final push required and give in to attractive offers from land developers. At publicly owned airports, while closure is not as likely, the political pressures are even greater, and there is an alarming trend toward imposing a nighttime curfew.

At Heathrow in London and Orly in Paris, as well as at other European airports, a ban on night operations has been in effect for years. The curfews at San Diego, Washington National and Boston are feared by many to be just the beginning of more local regulatory actions at U.S. airports. For this reason, most of the aviation community is pushing hard for federal preemption of the airport access law and for firmer federal guidelines on noise and pollution standards as well as flight procedures which, when complied with, would constitute a complete legal defense against public noise suits.

Faced with the fact that quiet airplanes and legal and political relief are way down the road, operators of jet aircraft today have turned to the third avenue of relief, namely, to procedurally or operationally move the noise away from the sensitive areas. Some of these procedures require just common sense on the part of the pilot; others are formal FAA/ATC programs. Some require additional airborne hardware; others do not. In every case the operational considerations have an impact on safety and must be applied carefully to avoid quietly descending through an airport neighbor's roof.

The most obvious procedural remedy for noise relief is the preferential runway system. When one runway is poorly located with respect to noise-sensitive areas and another is not, it makes sense to use the less sensitive one whenever it is operationally sound.

Most airports with towers already have such programs in operation and it is ATC that provides the clearance for the appropriate noise-abatement runway. Unfortunately, this also requires the air traffic controller to make an operational judgment he is not properly equipped to make. The amount of crosswind or tailwind that an airplane is certified to land or take off with is by no means a fixed value. Gross weight and temperature must also be considered in runway selection. Add to these the condition of the runway surface, the weather and approach aids available and the degree of pilot fatigue, and it is easy to see that the air traffic controller has no hope of selecting the appropriate runway for a particular aircraft operation. He can only issue the runway shown in the noise-abatement procedures for the airport according to the hour of day, the existing wind and the basic weather conditions.

Pilots should be aware that they must carefully consider all factors before accepting the runway as given and they need not hesitate to opt for another when in their judgment the one specified is inadequate. At the same time, if safety will not be compromised, the pilot should himself suggest a less noise-sensitive runway when appropriate. Also, where no tower exists, he should select one that causes the least distress to airport neighbors. This will go a long way toward improving relationships with the community and toward assuring the continuation of that airport's existence.

At most airports, preferential runways are just that—preferred. Any time a pilot requests the use of another one for operational reasons, his request is granted. The dangerous precedent set by Los Angeles is that the preferred runway usage has become mandatory. Thus, pilots are forced into choosing between what may be a marginally safe landing at the destination, or diverting to an alternate airport when another runway at LAX would have been more acceptable.

Los Angeles has quite a number of nearby alternates to choose from. But if this type of procedure should spread to other, more remote locations, the choice of an alternate could become much more critical and complex. During his pre-flight planning, a pilot would have to look not only at the forecast weather for approach minima, but also the wind direction and velocity, even on CAVU nights. He may find that the weather is fine but the wind is wrong, or that the weather requires an instrument approach, but there is no approach to the mandatory runway. What started out as just an idea to provide noise relief could force a number of emergency situations to develop because of the mandatory nature of anti-noise procedures.

It has been said that the noise of a 747 flying low over a house, even if it were a sailplane, would be objectionable. Whether that is true or not, many hours have been spent trying to devise ways of getting to the runway end while flying either higher above or further to the side of those houses and schools under the approach zone. ALPA, FAA, NASA, NBAA and the airlines have been working on a number of techniques designed to do just this. While each of these offers a degree of relief for the noise problem, they all fly in the face of what has become the watchword for safety in jet landings—the stabilized approach.

Being stabilized means that the speed is constant, the airplane's drag devices are fully deployed, the rate and angle of descent are slow and shallow and the power is set high enough so that engine spool-up time to a missed approach power setting is minimal. Before noise opposition became a powerful force, every government and industry admonition was for just this approach, but now one hears there must be an exception to this rule.

The steep approach was the first proposal for procedurally reducing the noise perceived on the ground. Not only does this place the aircraft higher over the houses at any point along the approach, it requires a lower power setting to keep the airspeed from building up. But if this procedure were implemented, all the VASIs and ILS glideslopes in the country would have to be adjusted upward to provide proper vertical guidance.

It is possible in visual conditions for a pilot to eyeball a steeper approach to any runway, but not without introducing several hazards. Engine power will be down, making a possible go-around more critical. Some engines spool up very quickly and this is not a serious limitation. But the sink rate will be higher—probably close to 2000 fpm. This requires about 10 extra knots of airspeed to provide for the higher load factor during the flare, or alternately, to provide for a speed bleed during the additional time it takes for a normal flare rotation begun at higher altitude.

Since a higher speed is required on the steep approach, an aiming point nearer the landing threshold must be used in order to touch down in the normal zone on speed. Otherwise longer runways must be available.

One pilot who tried to accommodate his neighbors in this manner, after making a very quiet approach, was requested by the tower to make a short turnoff. He attempted to comply and blew four tires.

Safety considerations must always be first in the pilot's mind. As noise procedures proliferate, safety is covered less and less by the procedures themselves and becomes more a matter of the captain's judgment. When, in his judgment, all aspects of safety are covered, a steeper than normal approach should be flown as a gesture of good will.

More recent NASA tests have been conducted on a decelerating approach along a standard glideslope. Energy management is the term used to describe the gradual transition from a fast, clean idle power configuration to a full flaps, on reference speed, spooled up condition just before landing. A Convair 990 is being used in the tests with an onboard computer, programmed by the pilot, which calculates the deceleration, calls for the deployment of flaps and gear, gives the pilot a continuous "how goes it" energy readout and even reminds him when he reaches the point where stabilized flight commences. Figure 1 shows the profile for this approach.

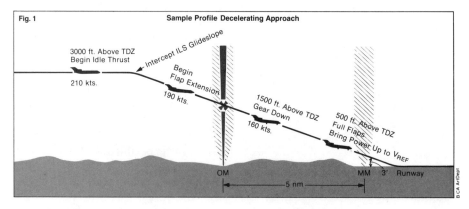

Fig. 1 — Sample Profile Decelerating Approach

Many pilots are, in fact, doing a form of this procedure today in visual conditions simply as a result of ATC requests to maintain a high speed to the outer marker for separation purposes. The same limitations apply with respect to tailwind, wind shear and engine bleed requirements as with the two-segment approach because of the possibility of being caught with the engines at idle thrust. When conditions permit, a pilot can do this procedure at any airport having an ILS by beginning fast and clean and using the computer in his head to get the aircraft slowed, configured for final approach and the engines spooled up before reaching 500 feet agl while following the glideslope.

Both the two-segment and decelerating approaches are designed to reduce the noise heard below the conventional approach path, which is the extended centerline of the runway. Another way to avoid noise-sensitive areas, if they happen to lie on this line, is to fly a curved approach path to the side of the sensitive area. The ability to do this in all weather conditions is a highly advertised feature of the new Microwave Landing System (MLS).

What is not advertised by MLS proponents is that in order to fly a curved approach, an aircraft must be equipped with either a flight director or an electronic map display in addition to the MLS receiver-computer. The reason is that a flight path with constantly changing magnetic bearing cannot be maintained by comparing a left/right needle to a magnetic heading, as is done in all VOR and ILS localizer flying. The bearing of a curved approach is constantly changing.

Also, little consideration has been given to the ATC problem of merging traffic on a curved approach with other traffic flying a straight-in approach. With MLS, the merge point is much closer to the runway than with today's ILS operation. Normally, final spacing adjustments are made prior to the outer marker and pilots are left alone after that point. These final adjustments will be more difficult for the controller to make when the aircraft involved are flying different paths at the time they must be released.

An airborne electronic navigation display, showing pertinent traffic, could solve both the problem of navigating the curved approach and arriving at the runway threshold with proper spacing behind the preceding aircraft.

Further back in the arrival stream, other measures have already been taken by FAA to reduce noise. The "keep-'em-high" order, which was originally designed to minimize the low-altitude collision exposure of high-performance jets, has become a noise-abatement procedure. This is an ATC technique designed to keep jets at 10,000 feet agl until 30 to 40 flight path miles from touchdown, and above 5000 feet agl until entering a "descent corridor" whose dimensions are shown in Figure 2.

These descent corridors are not depicted on any pilot's chart, but pilots become painfully aware of them when approaching an airport from a direction opposite to the landing direction. Nearing the airport, the pilot accepts a visual approach, expecting to continue his descent on the downwind leg. He is then told to maintain 5000 feet until passing the airport. At this point he is often faced with a choice of doing a split-S to the runway or extending so far downwind before turning that he loses sight of the airport.

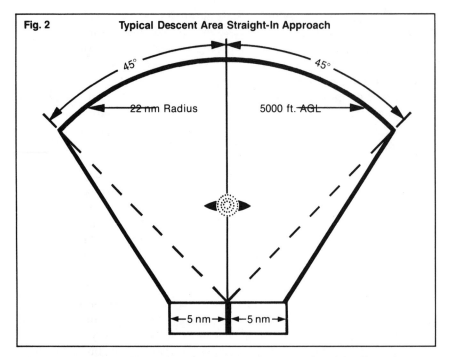

Fig. 2   Typical Descent Area Straight-In Approach

45°   45°

22 nm Radius   5000 ft. AGL

←5 nm→ ←5 nm→

Another problem with this procedure is that most local facilities have not applied the "flight path miles" portion for the beginning of descent from 10,000 feet. This results in either a dive to the runway if landing straight-in, or unnecessary dragging around at low speed to the far side of the airport if that is the landing direction. This is not a problem with the "keep-'em-high" order, but local implementation of it. The order also includes a section calling for uninterrupted climbs to cruise altitude which a number of terminal facilities on the East Coast have chosen to ignore.

An extension of the "keep-em-high" procedures in the arrival phase has been instituted at a number of terminals. In short, this procedure permits pilots to make uninterrupted descents from cruise altitude to touchdown, most of the way at idle thrust, other conditions permitting. Because of sequencing and spacing requirements, this technique is normally used only during periods of very light traffic. This procedure is known as the "profile descent"; it was designed to minimize fuel burnout during descent and approach, but it also carries a low noise side benefit.

The takeoff also generates a great deal of noise, and attention should be paid to the profiles developed for this phase of flight. The airlines, ALPA, NBAA and several local airport authorities and pilot groups have each developed noise-abatement takeoff profiles to minimize noise impact on the departure area just off the airport. They are all similar in certain respects.

NOISE-ABATEMENT PROCEDURES

In a typical procedure for jets, the aircraft lifts off and climbs at V_2 plus 10 knots until 1500 feet agl, then power is reduced and the takeoff flaps partially raised while climb is continued to 3000 feet. Then the balance of the flap retraction is accomplished and normal climb thrust and climb speed are used to cruise altitude.

One of the most important variations within this procedure is a limit of 15° nose-up body angle applied by most airlines. This limit is applied to permit better forward visibility for traffic watch as well as a more reasonable attitude from which to recover should a wind shear or wake vortex encounter occur.

Another variation in technique is the speed used during the second segment while the reduced thrust setting is used with partial flaps. Some carriers continue to use V_2 plus 10 knots in this configuration and limit the bank angle to 15° to account for being at less than maneuvering speed. Others recommend using the maneuvering speed for the flap setting selected. While the latter does result in a slightly lower rate of climb, the crew is in a better position to maneuver out of harm's way.

In summary, there seems to be no end to the techniques being devised to solve the noise problem—legal, financial, technical and procedural. The procedural solutions almost always require a compromise of standardization, or a relaxation of basic safety rules for jet flying. Many things can be done by a pilot to reduce the noise he sends to the surface, but he must use great care and judgment in applying noise-abatement procedures since no one else will take all factors into account. Nevertheless, it is worth the effort to be as thoughtful about noise as is safely possible. Today the alternatives are denied use of the airport during curfew hours or outright closure of the facility.

Wake Turbulence: The Invisible Enemy

11

by Marcus R. Bryan

In 1972 the crash of an air carrier DC-9, which the NTSB found was caused by wake turbulence generated from a DC-10 that had preceded it to the runway by one minute, tragically crushed any complacence that pilots of transport category aircraft might have had concerning the danger of turbulence generated by wide-body aircraft. NASA and FAA research subsequent to that crash now suggests that even pilots of wide-body aircraft should exercise concern for wake turbulence under certain conditions. This research also provides some useful information that allows pilots to establish guidelines of their own for distance and time separation to minimize wake turbulence encounters.

To put results of this research in context, it will help to review a few of the more important aspects of a wing trailing vortex. As Figure 1 shows, a wingtip vortex is formed because pressure on the underside of a wing, producing lift, is greater than on the top so there is flow around the wingtip. When this flow combines with the forward motion of the aircraft, it curves into a whirlpool shape. Because the vortex is a basic part of lift generation by a wing, it increases in strength with increasing lift or angle of attack. For a wing with no flaps extended, the trailing vortex from each wingtip

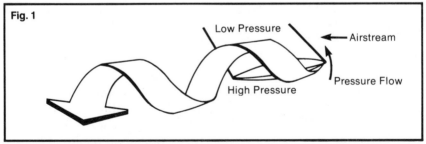

Fig. 1

Low Pressure

Airstream

Pressure Flow

High Pressure

A vortex is formed when the spanwise flow of high pressure air on the bottom of a wing curls around the tip seeking the lower pressure area above. Thus it is a necessary by-product of lift.

is strong and well defined. However, when high lift devices are used, each individual section acts like a wing and generates its own set of tip vortices. As a result, they all tend to interfere with one another. Therefore, the total vortex system behind an aircraft with flaps extended is more diffuse and dissipates more rapidly than it does behind the same aircraft in a clean configuration.

If air were a perfectly frictionless fluid, the vortex system behind a wing would last forever; but since air has a slight amount of friction, a vortex will eventually lose its form and decay into random turbulence. The amount of time a vortex takes to decay is highly dependent on the state of the atmosphere in which it was formed. Generally, the factors which seem to contribute most to vortex persistence are a stable atmosphere, as when there is an inversion; when surface wind is less than five knots with no thermal activity; when there is flat terrain with no protrusions to induce vortex breakup.

Since tip vortex generation is a basic component of the lift generated by a wing, its intensity depends on the amount of lift produced, or the wing loading of the aircraft. Consequently, large aircraft, particularly the wide-body jets such as the DC-10, L-1011 and C5A, which have high-wing loadings, also generate severe vortices. Also, for reasons not entirely understood, aircraft with T-tails and fuselage mounted engines, such as the Boeing 727, DC-9 and G-11, generate more severe vortices than their mere size and weight would imply. Flight tests indicate that the vortex behind a wide-body jet can have peak velocities exceeding 220 fps with a diameter of eight to 10 feet. This diameter refers only to the core containing the peak velocities, but dangerously high velocities exist over a much larger area. Measurements and visual observations indicate there is no significant decay of the vortex strength for one minute after generation, and that significant vortex cones frequently still exist two minutes after generation.

Of course, what is important to a pilot is not the exact size and strength of a theoretical vortex, but how his aircraft is likely to react if it encounters one. An aircraft can penetrate a vortex in two distinct ways: transversely across the wake (Figure 2, aircraft A), or longitudinally along it (Figure 2, aircraft B). A glance at Figure 2 immediately shows what is likely in each situation.

An aircraft's flight path across the wake will encounter an upward angled gust. Since the aircraft would not instantly be subjected to the full strength of the vortex, a factor of around 50 percent would apply to the actual velocity to get an equivalent sharp-edged gust affect. The maximum gust used for aircraft structural strength determination is usually 50 fps with a safety factor of 1.5. Therefore, hitting a vortex with a peak velocity of 220 fps would exceed the ultimate structural strength of most aircraft by around 50 percent. After two minutes, vortex velocities generated by a

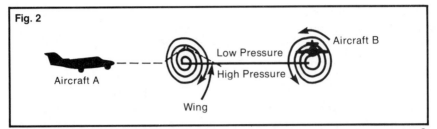

Expected results upon intercepting a vortex. An aircraft crossing it can expect a moderate to severe G loading, which can cause structural damage. An aircraft encountering a vortex parallel to its longitudinal axis will be subjected to strong rolling moments.

DC-10 or L-1011 are around 50 fps in the landing configuration (flaps and gear down) and between 90 and 150 fps in takeoff or clean configurations (zero or takeoff flaps, gear up). Vortex velocities one minute after generation are around 80 fps in landing configuration and exceed 200 fps in takeoff or cruise configurations. Crews must be aware of these potentially destructive forces and slow down when transverse penetration of wake is a possibility.

Because the likelihood of a longitudinal vortex encounter is significantly increased during takeoff or landing, this possibility has received, by far, the most attention. Figure 2 (aircraft B) points out that the probable events in this case would be loss of roll control or being slammed into the ground because of the downwash between the two vortices.

One of the more important results of the current research has been the realization that relative wingspan of the aircraft involved is probably the most important factor in establishing safe separation distances. For example, if the relative wingspan of a trailing aircraft were small enough for it to be completely immersed in the left vortex of a large aircraft (Figure 2), an uncontrollable roll to the right would occur, although an aircraft with a large wingspan might have enough wing area outside the wake to successfully maintain control.

However, even if the wingspans are comparable, considerable control difficulties can be present. For example, in one series of tests, a C-141 (a four-engine heavy military jet transport) was flown two miles behind another C-141. To remain in a particular vortex required maximum continuous thrust, one half to full aileron displacement and considerable rudder input. Obviously, this would be a pretty exciting experience at 200 feet during an ILS approach.

Another aspect of a vortex encounter, not usually stressed, is the possibility of a jet-engine flameout or compressor stall due to the disturbed airflow at the intake because of the vortex. Engine problems, combined with even minimal control difficulties at a low altitude, would concern pilots of any size aircraft.

But more important to the pilot than exactly what severe vortices can do to his aircraft, is what he can do to avoid them. The FAA has an Advisory Circular (AC No. 90-23D) on this subject that is probably familiar to most pilots and AIM Part I has information on vortex hazards, but most of this information is of only marginal use to the pilot operating jet or heavy-prop equipment. Since the present ATC system at even moderately busy airports precludes much pilot option as to his choice of routing, wake turbulence avoidance generally depends on how much separation is necessary to sufficiently reduce the hazard. It was this particular problem that NASA and FAA explored in their experiments. Probe aircraft were positioned in a vortex behind a generating aircraft at varying distances and available aileron control was compared with the vortex induced roll. In addition to specific measurement, test pilots assessed the possible hazard during flight, considering such factors as structural strength of the probe aircraft, passenger comfort, possible loss of control during IFR conditions and maneuvering hazards close to the ground. The aircraft used were a C5A, Convair 990, DC-9, Learjet 23 and a Cessna 210. Figure 3 summarizes the most severely induced roll with each combination of aircraft tested, as well as the maximum distance at which vortex-induced roll overcame the available roll control. Figure 4 shows what might be considered final results of the tests: safe separation distances are a function of the relative wingspan of the aircraft involved.

Generating Aircraft	Probe Aircraft	Ratio of Vortex Roll to Aircraft Roll Capability	@ Distance (nm)	Maximum Distance at Which Vortex Roll Exceeded Aircraft Roll Roll Capability (nm)
C5A	Convair 990	1.25	3.00	7.00
C5A	DC-9	1.50	4.00	8.00
C5A	Learjet 23	3.00	7.00	8.00
Convair 990	DC-9	0.60	2.25	_____
Convair 990	Learjet 23	2.00	3.00	5.00
Convair 990	Cessna 210	1.50	5.50	5.50

Figure 3: Results of FAA and NASA research. When the ratio exceeds one, an upset is likely to result.

So what does all this provide in terms of useful information to the pilot looking to minimize his chances of a wake turbulence induced upset? First of all, every probe aircraft had insufficient roll control to remain upright in the wake turbulence generated by a C5A in clean configuration at the normal IFR radar separation of five miles from heavy aircraft. It is worthy to mention that vortex velocities in a C5A wake average 75 to 100 fps, *lower*

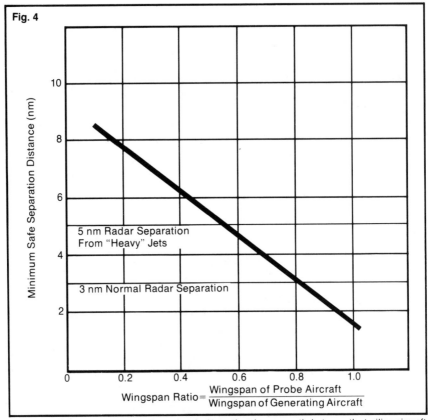

Fig. 4

Minimum Safe Separation Distance (nm)

5 nm Radar Separation
From "Heavy" Jets

3 nm Normal Radar Separation

$$\text{Wingspan Ratio} = \frac{\text{Wingspan of Probe Aircraft}}{\text{Wingspan of Generating Aircraft}}$$

FAA and NASA research results indicate that the lower the wingspan ratio between the trailing aircraft and the generating aircraft, the greater the separation distance must be.

than are common behind a DC-10 or L-1011. It is also important to remember that the pilots involved in this experiment were looking for the most severe part of the trailing vortex system, so the results really represent the worst possible situation rather than the average.

Pilots flying aircraft having a relatively short wingspan should be especially careful following larger aircraft since the safe separation distance can be nearly 10 miles for wingspan ratios less than 0.2. This is even more important following aircraft such as the Boeing 727, which generate unusually severe vortices because of their designs.

One should be very wary of canceling an IFR clearance in a busy area, or accepting a visual approach behind a much larger aircraft because then the pilot is solely responsible for safe separation. Tests have shown that even experienced pilots can make errors of over 50 percent in judging distances from other aircraft in flight. In addition, it is much harder to

The Nine Commandments of Wake Avoidance

Even though avoidance of wake turbulence has been the subject of numerous safety articles, there are still professional pilots who haven't gotten the word. Therefore, to emphasize once again how to avoid wake encounters, B/CA makes the following suggestions:

(1) The basic rule of thumb in all cases (whether en route, taking off or landing) is simple: STAY *ABOVE* THE FLIGHT PATH OF THE WAKE MAKER.

(2) Do *not* accept intersection takeoffs. Controllers are required to separate smaller aircraft from heavies taking off from intersection on the same runway by a three-minute interval. This interval can be waived by the pilot—except when departing behind a heavy jet—but don't you do it.

(3) When taking off on the same runway behind a *departing* heavy, lift off shorter than the heavy and climb out above his takeoff flight path.

(4) When taking off on the same runway behind a *landing* heavy, note where his nose gear touched down and lift off after that point.

(5) When landing behind a *departing* heavy on the same runway, note his rotation or liftoff point and land well beyond it.

(6) When landing behind an *arriving* heavy on the same runway, stay *above* his approach flight path, note his touchdown point and land well beyond it.

(7) Be super cautious when using a parallel runway. When operations are conducted beside heavy aircraft on a parallel runway, note the wind component for possible vortex drift and if feasible, request the upwind runway. Stay *above* the wake maker's approach flight path as though he were on the same runway. Note his liftoff or land as appropriate at a point abeam it.

(8) When landing behind a *departing* heavy on a crossing runway, note his rotation point. If he rotated *past* the intersection, there is no problem for you—*unless* a vortex drifts into your touchdown zone. Watch the wind. If he rotated *before* the intersection, abandon the approach unless your landing is assured *before* reaching the intersection.

(9) Remember this simple rule of thumb: STAY *ABOVE* THE FLIGHT PATH OF THE WAVE MAKER.

judge the descent path of an aircraft three or more miles away so as to remain above it, and equally difficult to judge the touchdown point because it is hard to distinguish whether an aircraft is airborne or rolling on a runway when seen from above.

Finally, it is useful to note that when encountering a vortex at a shallow angle from outside the path of the generator, the initial rolling tendency is away from the vortex, as can be seen from Figure 2. An encounter from the other side will roll you into the vortex. So if there is a chance of hitting a vortex and your aircraft starts to roll, it is a good idea to make a turn in the appropriate direction rather than try to maintain wings level. In the NTSB report on the DC-9 crash mentioned at the beginning of this article, the pilots commented on "a little turbulence here" seven seconds before they lost control. The Board theorized that the pilot action in maintaining wings level at the onset of the initial roll drew the aircraft into the heart of the vortex. Although there is no accepted procedure for escaping from a vortex, as good a method as any might be to let the airplane have its own way initially, so you either turn away from the danger or pass through it as quickly as possible.

Unfortunately, wake turbulence is one of those things that breeds the attitude that it will always happen to somebody else. But it is very real even though it is usually invisible. Undoubtedly there are NASA and FAA pilots with a lot of first-hand knowledge who are going to be careful.

DEPARTURES

Just as a journey of a thousand miles begins with only a few steps, in aviation, each journey begins with taxi, takeoff and area departure. The time these first steps consume is relatively short considering the length of most non-local flights, but that time is filled with unique safety challenges. Far too many accidents occur on takeoff and departure for far too many reasons. This section is dedicated to dealing with those reasons.

In jest, turbine pilots like to say that they just kick the tires, light the fires and go. But the real professionals know that a safe departure requires careful preplanning and precise execution. Each departure is an amalgam of runway limitations, aircraft performance, ATC procedures, pilot-controller communications, masses of technical data and that ever-present intangible, human capabilities. Safe departures demand teamwork from pilots and controllers. Every takeoff therefore demands the ultimate from man and machine to avoid the inevitable errors and complications that accompany demandingly intricate work from being amplified into serious hazards. That is why planning is so important and why correct information is so essential.

Your thousand-mile journey begins with a single departure. This chapter of Staying Current *can help you to make that first step a safe one.*

Anatomy of a Departure

by Arnold Lewis

Well-executed departures don't just happen. Operators of smaller business aircraft can eyeball their loads, runway and temperature conditions and pretty much figure out in their heads the parameters of a departure.

But those flying FAR Part 25 turbine equipment face the same requirements encountered by the airlines, except they usually don't have dispatchers to do all the work for them. Planning a departure that meets all of the takeoff and climb gradient requirements out of an airport that is marginal to begin with demands skill, coordination and resources that aren't always readily available.

To gain an insight into what's involved, let's look at a departure from Aspen, Colorado's Pitkin County Airport. Aspen is really a resort city; we use its airport in our example only because it presents altitude and terrain problems that crisply point up all the considerations of a departure. The aircraft we will use is a Gulfstream II, up to its full 37,000-pound basic operating weight—including crew, cabin stores and other paraphernalia—plus a residual 5000 pounds of fuel from the incoming flight.

Under normal circumstances at a normal airport you'd simply top it off to the maximum 23,300 pounds of Jet A, make a few quick calculations, pour the coal to it and fly to Chicago—home in time for a martini before supper.

But this is not the normal airport and the circumstances are anything but. It's a hot day at Aspen—30 degrees centigrade and, coincidentally, ISA plus 30, field elevation is 7793 feet (we'll call it 7800 for simplicity) and the airport is surrounded by the Rocky Mountains.

We know that according to FAR Part 91.37, we may not operate this Part 25 transport category airplane contrary to the provisions of the "Airplane Flight Manual" (AFM), and that the takeoff weight must not exceed that specified in the AFM when considering such conditions as airport elevation, temperature, wind, effective runway gradient and runway length. We also know that we must assume an engine failure at V_1 and that the aircraft must still be able to meet minimum FAA first-, second- and final-segment climb gradients on the remaining engine in order to return us to the field without any further incident.

These basic considerations—takeoff and climb limitations—make the anatomy of a departure. They are as important to the safety of flight as any other phase.

As a rule of thumb, we know that takeoff weight is usually a limiting factor at the lower elevations because of runway lengths, while second-segment climb limitations generally come into play at the higher elevations.

Second-segment climb is that takeoff phase from the point that the gear is fully retracted (assuming one engine on the plane has failed) at V_2, and approximately 35 feet above the takeoff surface, to a point at which the aircraft has reached 400 feet and is able to level off during the third segment for acceleration.

It is a characteristic of the G-II that second-segment climb performance is improved by the use of only 10 degrees of takeoff flaps rather than the normal 20 degrees—at the expense of takeoff distance, however. (It is generally true of any aircraft that flaps reduce both takeoff roll *and* second-segment climb from a high elevation airport.) Thus, in our initial calculations, we will want to consider both 10- and 20-degree flap settings for takeoff.

We must also consider that by using only 10 degrees of flaps, we are faced with two additional penalties not encountered if we go 20 degrees—maximum brake (heat) energy limitation and a 173-knot-per-hour tire limitation because of the higher speeds on the takeoff roll. Thus the only inputs for these initial calculations are the ambient temperature (30 degrees centigrade) and the airport elevation (7800 feet). Here are the results from the G-II AFM charts (anti-ice off):

	Maximum Takeoff Weight	
	Flaps 10	Flaps 20
Brake energy	54,700	——
173-knot tire	59,500	——
Second-segment climb	57,200	51,700

Thus it appears that 54,700 pounds with 10 degrees of flap is our weight limitation; not because of performance, but because of brake energy limits. But let's not stop there.

Now that these preliminary takeoff weights have been established, we can take a look at additional airport conditions, including wind, runway length and gradient. Although we are looking at a runway length of only 6001 feet, there are a couple of other factors that may help us further—stopway (overrun) and clearway. Stopway information will be found on the airport diagram, but for clearway and runway gradient you need FAA publication 5010-1. Since you probably don't have such an animal, the best thing to do is check with the local commercial carrier or the airport manager.

Aspen is a peculiar airport in that arriving traffic generally uses Runway 15—even with a following wind—because of a 1.98 percent uphill runway gradient. Departing traffic uses Runway 33 because of the downhill gradient and the fact that winds are generally out of the north at six to seven knots. In our case, we'll use 33 and assume a wind out of the north at six knots. Now let's take a look at the runway surface.

Runway 33 is 6001 feet long, but it has a 520-foot overrun at the end, giving us an effective "takeoff distance" of 6521 feet. Takeoff distance is defined as the horizontal distance from brake release to a point—assuming engine failure at V_1—that the aircraft reaches a height of 35 feet above the takeoff surface, or 115 percent of the distance from brake release to 35 feet in an all-engine takeoff, whichever is greater. In this case, we are assuming an engine-failure recognition by the pilot at V_1.

In addition, we are working with a "balanced field length" situation in which the accelerate/stop distance is equal to the takeoff distance. In an unbalanced situation, the two would not be equal because we would be dealing with a "clearway." A clearway is a 500-foot-wide area beyond the runway surface defined as an upward slope not exceeding 1.25 per cent, above which there are no obstacles. Its length cannot exceed one-half of the runway length. Clearways provide turbine aircraft with the additional takeoff distance necessary because of slow acceleration below V_2—thus extra distance after liftoff in which to conform with climb gradient limitations. But since Aspen has no clearway, we are dealing only with the 6001-foot runway plus an overrun of 520 feet, or a total takeoff distance of 6521 feet.

So now we go to our takeoff performance charts in the AFM. Cranking in six knots of wind out of the north and a downhill gradient of 1.98 percent, here are our takeoff weight limitations for both 10 and 20 degrees of flaps, including all parameters to date:

Maximum Takeoff Weight

	Flaps 10	Flaps 20
Brake energy	54,700	——
173-knot tire	59,500	——
Second-segment climb	57,200	51,700
FAAT/O performance	48,500	53,000

Here we can see that if we select 10 degrees of flaps our weight will have to be 48,500 rather than the 54,700 we'd previously supposed because of takeoff performance limits. With 10 degrees of flaps we will be *relatively* fat on second-segment climb because our weight is 8700 pounds less than the max weight (57,200 pounds) we can use and still meet second-segment climb requirements. With a 37,000-pound basic operating weight, plus four passengers totaling 800 pounds, this would leave us with only 10,700 pounds of fuel.

But notice, if we go with 20 degrees of flaps, we find we are second-segment climb limited to 51,700 pounds, compared with 53,000 for the takeoff limitation. Obviously, 51,700 beats 48,500.

But don't go yet; there is more.

Before we go ahead and check our climb gradients and our eventual net takeoff flight path, we might as well get our various takeoff speeds computed and out of the way.

The first and perhaps the most critical is V_1—defined as the "critical engine failure recognition speed," or better explained as the "decision speed." It's the point of no return during the takeoff roll. If we lose an engine prior to V_1, we are fairly safe in the assumption that we can pull back the remaining engine and come to a stop within the limits of the overrun using ground spoilers and brakes only. (We are assuming ground spoiler availability although they're temporarily decommissioned on the G-II.) At V_2 or above, we are committed to continue the takeoff on one engine. In our case, V_1 comes out to 124 knots calibrated airspeed (KCAS) with 20 degrees of flaps and at 51,700 pounds.

Rotation speed, or V_R, is the speed at which the nose is raised off the ground. Of course, V_R is never less than V_2, but it can be the same, depending upon the aircraft and existing conditions. In our case, V_R turns out to be very close to V_1—124.8 KCAS.

Hitting the rotation speed right on the button is important. For instance, early rotation could extend the takeoff roll or cause an early liftoff, resulting in climb below the minimum flight path. Late rotation also extends the takeoff roll and in addition may send the speed up over V_2, resulting in a climb below minimum flight path. These penalties are especially applicable when the takeoff is either field-length or climb limited.

Assuming a proper rotation, we must next look for V_{LOF}—liftoff speed. It is here the aircraft actually becomes airborne—in the case of our G-II at Aspen, it is 128 KCAS. According to the G-II manual, "The ability of the aircraft to meet the climb gradient requirements in the first segment is based on the use of V_{LOF} as the climb speed. However, the procedure for engine failure during takeoff requires the speed after liftoff to be increased to V_2 prior to reaching the 35-foot height."

Remembering that one engine has been inoperative since V_1, it is at V_{LOF} that the first-segment climb begins. The first segment continues until the gear is up, V_2 has been reached and 35 feet has been gained. The only change in configuration during the first segment is retraction of the landing

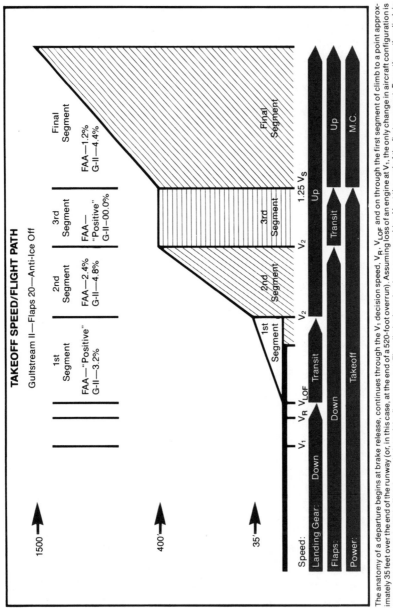

TAKEOFF SPEED/FLIGHT PATH

Gulfstream II—Flaps 20—Anti-Ice Off

The anatomy of a departure begins at brake release, continues through the V₁ decision speed, V_R, V_LOF and on through the first segment of climb to a point approximately 35 feet over the end of the runway (or, in this case, at the end of a 520-foot overrun). Assuming loss of an engine at V₁, the only change in aircraft configuration is gear retraction between liftoff and completion of the first segment. The climb phase begins upon reaching V₂ at the end of the first segment. From there the climb is continued with takeoff flaps to 400 feet while maintaining V₂. Upon reaching 400 feet, the aircraft is pitched over into level flight and the flaps retracted for acceleration during the third segment at zero gradient to the final segment climb. Climb speed is approximately 1.25 V_S. The final climb segment takes the aircraft to approximately 1500 feet agl, from which point the enroute climb phase is initiated.

gear. If all goes well, we will arrive at the 35-foot height with gear fully retracted and at V_2.

V_2 is defined as the takeoff safety speed that will enable you to meet the all-important, second-segment climb gradient with one engine inoperative. Reaching V_2 at the proper time requires proper rotation and liftoff procedures. V_2—in our case 134 KCAS—is maintained throughout the second-segment climb with no change in configuration (flaps still at 20 degrees and gear up). The second segment ends when the aircraft reaches a height of approximately 400 feet above the takeoff surface or higher, if necessary for obstacle clearance. At that point flaps are retracted and the aircraft permitted to accelerate through the third segment to the final takeoff segment climb speed (enroute climb configuration V_{FEC})—148.2 for our G-II. The final takeoff climb segment continues to 1500 feet or at the point where transition to the enroute configuration is completed, whichever is higher. According to the regs, this final takeoff climb speed should be 1.25 V_s—or 1.25 percent of stall speed. A check of the G-II stall-speed chart shows 1.25 V_s at 51,700 pounds to be 148.2.

You may have thought we were off and running and our takeoff profile complete. Not yet. There is the little matter of meeting minimum climb gradients and plotting our net takeoff flight path. So we are right back to that V_{LOF} point with flaps 20 and the gear still hanging down. FAR Part 25.121 requires that a twin-engine turbojet be able to maintain a "positive" climb gradient until gear retraction is complete and the speed has accelerated to V_2, at or below 35 feet. The G-II AFM says we'll be okay during the first segment with a 1.3 per cent climb gradient.

The climb requirement during the second segment jumps to 2.4 per cent for a twin-engine jet. We'll have to call it a squeaker, because that's exactly what we're going to get—2.4 percent. Remember, however, that we based our takeoff weight on second-segment climb limitations with 20 degrees of flaps rather than on takeoff performance with 10 degrees. As a comparison, opting for the 48,500-pound takeoff performance limitation with 10 degrees of flaps would have given us a second-segment climb gradient of 4.8 per cent. But G-II operators tell us they would go as long as they met the minimum requirements, in other words, 20 degrees of flap and 51,700 pounds. During the final takeoff climb segment, we will have a 3.7 percent climb gradient, well above the FAA minimum of 1.2 percent.

Under normal conditions, you very well might conclude your calculations at this point and go with a clear conscience. But this is Aspen on a hot day with mountains all around. So let's make sure our computed net takeoff flight path will get us up over the mountains on only on engine.

Oh, oh! There must be some mistake. Seems that the G-II AFM chart for the first segment flight path has a big void in the curves above 5000 feet with temperatures above ISA plus 20.

When we discovered this, we called our friends at Grumman and asked, "What gives?" They did not have an immediate answer. But they did suggest we apply a "ship's [French] curve" to the chart and see what we came up with. (Ship's curves are those clever little plastic curlicues of many varied shapes and configurations that we remember from grade school.) Oops, the correct curve applied to the 8000-foot line doesn't even come close to the 30-degree Centigrade line. Back to Grumman and one of the performance engineers. "Looks like you'll have to stick with 10 degrees of flaps," he said. And the reason for the voids in performance charts, he added, is simply that the aircraft was not specifically flown under those conditions during certification flight testing. Thus, those parameters could not be charted.

Well and good. Think what would happen to the price of the airplane if FAA forced manufacturers to flight test their airplanes under every conceivable temperature and elevation.

Takeoff Weight Limitations (lbs.)

Brake energy	54,700
173-knot tire	59,500
Second-segment climb	57,200
FAA T/O performance	48,500

Takeoff Speeds (KCAS)
(10 Degrees Flaps)

V_1	126.2
V_R	132.5
V_{LOF}	137.6
V_2	138.7
V_{FEC}	143.5
1.25 V_s	143.4

Climb Gradients

	From AFM	FAA Required
First segment	3.2%	Positive
Second segment	4.8%	2.4%
Final segment	4.4%	1.2%

Net Takeoff Flight Path (ft.)

	Horizontal	Accumulative	Vertical
Takeoff roll	5581	5581	0
Liftoff-35 feet	940	6521	35
35 feet-S_1	2410	8931	90
35 feet-S_2	7880	14,401	334
35 feet-S_3	11,480	18,001	334
End of final segment	46,680	53,201	1500

94

So it was back to the AFM to chart all of the takeoff parameters using only 10 degrees of flaps, which limits us to only 48,500 pounds. We still had to apply the ship's curves when plotting net takeoff flight path, but under these conditions, the extended curves produced logical results. The accompanying chart shows the results of those calculations using 10 degrees of flaps and anti-ice off.

The only remaining obstacle to loading up and taking off is Triangle Mountain—just over six nm out on the runway heading of 330 degrees. In a two-engine departure, we'd zip right over that 9500 feet msl (1707 feet agl) peak with no sweat. But on only one engine at our weight we'll fall somewhat short since our flight path calculations show us needing 9.3 nm to reach 1500 feet above liftoff. This should pose no problem, however, because we are restricted to VFR conditions anyway and the valley makes a left turn about four miles from the end of the runway without another obstruction until reaching Utah.

We started off by using 20 degrees of flaps—which is normal for the G-II —and found we could, if only marginally, meet our second-segment climb requirement without the runway being a limitation. Fat, dumb and happy, we proceeded on that basis, only to find out later that the G-II AFM actually could not guarantee those earlier calculations on the basis of net takeoff flight path. Indeed, a G-II operator told us later that just eyeballing the existing conditions told him it was a 10-degree-flap takeoff situation.

So we went back to 10 degrees of flaps and learned that rather than being second-climb limited, we were now takeoff-performance limited to 48,500 pounds. This represented quite a penalty in terms of fuel—leaving us with 10,700 pounds to play with, or only 46 percent of our total capacity. Whether we could make it all the way to Chicago with that amount or would have to drop into Grand Island is a question we won't address here.

Giving up that 3200 pounds of fuel—the difference between 51,700 pounds takeoff weight with 20 degrees of flaps and 48,500 pounds with 10 degrees of flaps—is a small price to pay, however, for knowing that if you lose an engine at V_1, you've got enough oomph left to get out of there safely.

V₁, the Mythical Decision Speed

by Dan Manningham

Few elements of aviation have been as controversial as the takeoff decision speed, V_1. Manufacturers, regulators, pilots and operators have debated, harangued and argued about it since the inception of jet operations over 20 years ago. Today, V_1 remains a major area of concern to knowledgeable pilots, and with some justification. Unfortunately, that critical go/no-go decision point is conceived and calculated with several basic flaws. What is worse, the FAA has waffled on solutions to even the most obvious problems with the V_1 concept for more than 10 years.

V_1 is defined as the critical engine-failure speed. Pilots think of it as a decision speed, a single calculated point in the takeoff regimen that separates the stop and go alternatives. Specifically, V_1 is the speed at which, if an engine fails, the remaining runway will allow either:

· Deceleration to a full stop, or

· Takeoff to a height of 35 feet in the case of Part 25 airplanes or 50 feet for those certificated to Part 23.

Theoretically, the stop is always possible below V_1 with the go always possible above V_1, with those two possibilities being equal options at V_1. In the past two decades a lot of reputations and lives have pivoted on that very tenuous theory.

V_1 speeds are derived in a building-block fashion using empirical data. The first step is to establish two very fundamental performance criteria called accelerate/stop distance and takeoff distance (Figure 1).

Accelerate/stop distance is the total distance required to:

· Accelerate with all engines at takeoff thrust from a standing start to V_1, or engine failure speed;

· Transition from takeoff thrust acceleration to idle thrust with the speed brakes and spoilers extended and maximum braking applied;

· Decelerate to a full stop.

Takeoff distance is the longer of either engine-out or all-engine takeoff distance where—

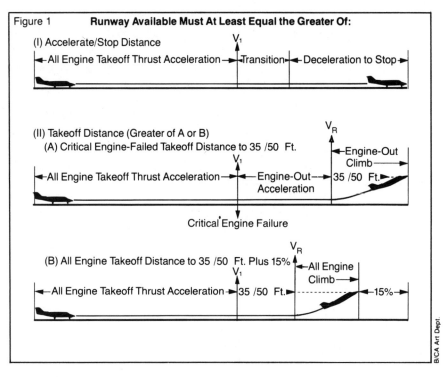

Figure 1 — Runway Available Must At Least Equal the Greater Of:

Engine-out takeoff distance is the total distance required to:

· Accelerate with all engines at takeoff thrust from a standing start to V_1, or engine failure speed;

· Continue acceleration after sudden and complete failure of the most critical engine to V_R, rotation speed;

· Climb with the engine inoperative through 35 or 50 feet as applicable.

All-engine takeoff distance is the total distance required to:

· Accelerate with all engines at takeoff thrust from a standing start to V_R, rotation speed;

· Climb on all engines through 35 or 50 feet;

· Plus a 15 percent margin.

We should make clear that the above description of takeoff distance and the illustrations in Figure 1 are based on FAR Part 25 criteria. Actually, Part 23, the regulation pertaining to small aircraft design, does not define an engine-out takeoff requirement. The only takeoff distance defined in Part 23 is the *two*-engine distance to an altitude of 50 feet. The 15 percent additional distance specified for Part 25 aircraft is *not* required in the stated takeoff distance for Part 23 aircraft.

In summary, Part 23 airplanes are not required to have a one-engine takeoff capability and many do not. Accelerate/go charts are provided by the manufacturers of some light twins having that capability; others do not. Therefore, in the case of aircraft certificated to FAR 23, what follows is applicable only to those for which accelerate/go charts are provided. In no instance does the manufacturer of a FAR Part 23 twin provide balanced field length data; accelerate/stop and accelerate/go are always two distinct distances.

For FAR Part 25 aircraft, the requirements for accelerate/stop and accelerate/go are clearly defined. Since it is impossible to compute these critical distances on a theoretical basis, as one might compute stall speed or critical Mach number, they are established by actual flight and ground test. This test data is obtained under optimum conditions on smooth, dry, hard-surface runways, using highly qualified test crews responding to prearranged failures in perfectly maintained aircraft. Stopping distance is based on the drag from the takeoff flap setting, fully extended speed brakes and/or spoilers and maximum wheel braking with new tires and brakes. Tests are repeated over and over again until the absolute minimum distances are established.

When those tests are completed, the V_1 speed emerges as a natural by-product to be modified by several legal limits:

· V_1 may never be less than V_{MCG} (minimum control speed, ground) because it would not be possible to control the airplane on the runway in the event of engine failure below that speed. As a point of interest, it is not possible to keep the airplane straight *at* V_{MCG} because FAR 25 certification rules allow for specified drift from centerline during the test runs that determine V_{MCG}. Actually, V_{MCG} is the lowest demonstrated engine-out speed at which the manufacturer's best test pilots can keep the airplane within 25 feet of centerline, using primary aerodynamic controls alone. The airplane can do it; the test pilots did it. Maybe *you* can do it on a good day, maybe not.

· V_1 may never be more than V_R, the takeoff rotation speed, because accelerate/stop distance determination becomes an open equation once the airplane begins to fly.

· V_1 may never be more than V_{MBE}, the maximum brake energy speed. V_{MBE} is the maximum speed on the ground from which a stop can be accomplished within the energy capabilities of the brakes.

Now you can see the whole picture. Test pilots establish the optimum accelerate/stop and takeoff distances. Test pilots further establish the minimum control speed on the ground (V_{MCG}), and best V_R. Engineers calculate V_{MBE} based on the total wheel braking capability and then the V_1 charts are compiled. You, as the pilot, have the comforting assurance that at the maximum weight for a given runway, the test crew was able to stop their test airplane on the last inch of runway, or continued the takeoff to a height of 35 or 50 feet within the confines of the runway with an engine failure at V$_1$.

You have often seen references to the "FAR 25 Balanced Field Length" in flight manuals and it has become an accepted term. But, in fact, balanced field length is not defined in FAR 25. Accelerate/stop is defined by FAR 25.109 and the takeoff path is described in FAR 25.111, but one must turn to FAR Part 121—the regulations for scheduled air carrier operations—to find a definition of what has come to be called balanced field length. Actually, there are two definitions: one in FAR 121.177 for piston-powered transport category aircraft that calls for a climb to 50 feet in the accelerate/go case, and the other FAR 121.189 for turbine-powered transport category aircraft that calls for a climb to 35 feet in the accelerate/go case.

In brief, a balanced field length results when V$_1$ is such that accelerate/stop and accelerate/go are equal when a decision is made to stop or go at that speed. To balance the field, V$_1$ is selected as the one, single speed from which the options are equalized. In this case, V$_1$ is a function of regulation and arithmetic, not aerodynamic limit.

If the FARs were written for a 20-foot engine-out altitude, V$_1$ would be slower and the balanced field length shorter. If regulations required a 60-foot engine-out altitude, V$_1$ would be faster and field length longer. V$_1$, then, is simply the speed that balances two otherwise unrelated values, namely the accelerate/stop and accelerate/go distances, to create a decision point.

Typically, balanced field length charts are predicated on the takeoff weight. The pilot or dispatcher goes into the chart for the aircraft in question and determines a minimum runway length requirement and a V$_1$ based on the takeoff weight, temperature, airport elevation, wind and—for turbine-powered aircraft—bleed air settings. If that minimum runway requirement is less than the actual length of the runway to be used, the takeoff can be made, probably safely. If not, the chart is entered at the actual runway length available and worked backwards to a maximum takeoff weight and a new V$_1$. The aircraft is then loaded to that maximum weight and the takeoff is conducted, hopefully safely.

The fallacy of balanced field length and a V$_1$ based on a balance between accelerate/stop and accelerate/go becomes obvious when the runway is longer than the minimum called for in the chart or when there is a stopway and/or clearway for the runway being used. Figure 2 illustrates. At a certain weight, temperature and elevation, all of a 7000-foot runway may be needed to safely takeoff. But if the weight, temperature and/or elevation are reduced, adherence to the balanced concept will result in some portion of that 7000-foot runway being "wasted."

Look at it this way. Whenever the combination of aircraft takeoff weight and/or runway length is such that not all of the available runway length

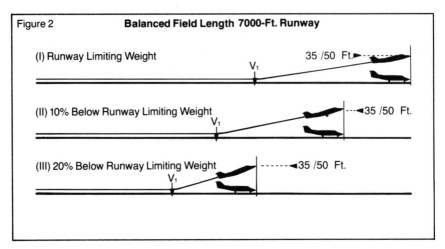

is needed for either accelerate/stop or continued takeoff with an engine failure, a performance margin exists that may be used to slide the V_1 speed. Specifically, that performance margin can be used to reduce V_1 to the point where the aircraft will just reach 35 or 50 feet in altitude by the end of the runway or to increase V_1 until it is just possible to stop on the runway in an abort. The farther below limiting weight for the runway, the greater the range of V_1 within the confines of V_{MCG}, V_R and V_{MBE} as discussed earlier.

Why might a pilot wish to "slide" his V_1? There may be any number of reasons, but let's look at just two (Figure 3). Suppose the balanced field length chart has been consulted and at a certain weight and V_1 the field will be balanced, but you're concerned about stopping capability on a wet runway and want to create a margin. By off-loading fuel and then consulting

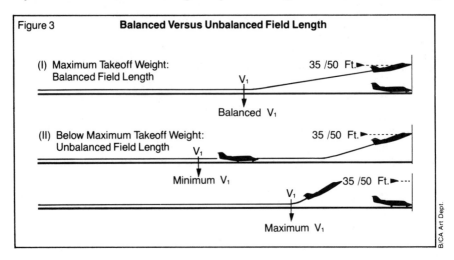

the balanced charts, you'll create a situation like that in Figure 2, part II and have a 10 percent stopping margin. But if at that slightly reduced weight you could also slide V_1, you could create a situation like that in Figure 3, part II for minimum V_1. In this instance, V_1 has been reduced to allow even more than a 10 percent margin in stopping room, but it is still great enough to allow acceleration and go in event of an engine failure after V_1. Note in the illustration that the airplane in the accelerate/go case has just cleared the obstruction. But in the accelerate/stop case it has stopped well before the end of the runway. This illustration assumes a dry runway for stopping; the excess is allowance for the wetness and poor braking.

It has become common practice in jet operations to use a balanced field length concept for computing all takeoff performance, regardless of weight, with a single value for V_1. This practice arbitrarily disregards any excess runway length for the convenience of simplified handbook charts. Although not required by FARs, the balanced approach is easier for you and easier for the manufacturer. Unfortunately, it produces only one V_1 speed that is not related to runway length and not adequate for an intelligent go/no-go decision when some consideration other than an engine failure exists.

One other fallout from the balanced field length concept is that it excludes clearways and stopways from takeoff planning because those legal and practical runway extensions require an unbalanced interpretation.

Balanced field length is necessary for runway limiting weight takeoffs where all of the available performance is being used to meet FAR performance standards. At any weight below that maximum weight for the runway in use, unbalanced takeoff information, with a range of V_1 speeds, would provide the pilot with a more precise measure of aircraft capabilities.

As a broad measure of the airplane's maximum takeoff performance, balanced field length is an interesting comparative figure—like range-to-fuel exhaustion or maximum rate of climb. As an operational planning guide, however, balanced field length is offensive to the professional pilot because it does not reflect actual runway length—it does not allow him to do his own thinking and optimize V_1 for dangers other than a potential engine failure.

Now that you know what V_1 is, balanced or unbalanced, let's see what it isn't. In fact, there is an entire catalogue of serious shortcomings to the very concept of V_1 as a viable decision speed. As you will see, some are more telling than others, but each is capable of extending the required runway beyond those handbook promises. None of the shortcomings are covered by FARs despite years of question and protest by ALPA, FSF, NBAA, NTSB and others.

Recognition time, the allowable delay between noticing an engine failure and reacting to it, is woefully insufficient.

During the certification runs that are made to establish V_1, test crews respond to prearranged engine failures in a clinical, flight-test environment. When the final—and best—data is prepared in chart form for the approved handbook, one second is added to the test crew's reaction time as a margin.

Some margin. Taking into account possible crew inexperience, fatigue, adverse weather, cockpit communications difficulties or any number of day-to-day distractions, makes it more reasonable to assume that reaction time in the real-world situation will be five seconds rather than one. Also, simulator tests and accident findings both supply ample support for an average delay time of five seconds. At a V_1 of 120 knots that extra four seconds amounts to 810 feet of distance traveled beyond the distance promised in the flight manual charts. If the rollout end terminates in water or steep terrain, a disaster is simply unavoidable.

Ironically, in 1975 the FAA proposed an additional 600 feet of runway to compensate for this recognition time. The proposal was withdrawn because of protests from people few of whom had ever crewed a heavy aircraft on a wet runway.

The control action sequence used in certification tests and recommended for takeoff aborts is contrary to well-reenforced pilot habit patterns. The recommended sequence for a rejected takeoff is brakes, throttles, spoilers, in that order—a procedure that markedly reduces the deceleration distance on dry runways by utilizing brakes at the earliest possible moment. But pilot habit, from countless landing decelerations, is more likely to be throttles, spoilers, brakes—with reverse or drag chute further diluting the sequence when available.

One other problem with that brakes-first sequence is that it contradicts preferred deceleration techniques on wet and slippery surfaces. Early, heavy braking induces hydroplaning, but the prescribed abort technique involves use of the brakes at speeds up to 50 knots above hydroplaning speed.

Runway gradient or slope is not properly considered. *Net* gradient, the elevation difference between the runway ends, is used for takeoff calculations except for cases where some intervening point on the runway is more than five feet above or below a straight line joining the ends. Net gradient ignores those middle humps as long as they are five feet or less. But when a hump of any height is present, the aircraft will accelerate uphill and abort downhill with some substantial, but undefined, additional runway requirement. Net gradient is much easier to calculate, but it leaves you with one more possible drain on takeoff performance.

There is another insidious problem with runway gradient. FAR 91.5(b)(2) requires that the pilot-in-command familiarize himself with all information relating to takeoff performance, including runway slope. But when you look for that data to plan your next takeoff, you will not find it in your Jepps or in the AIM, or probably not anywhere else with the single exception of some few NOS charts. The fact is that the FAA's National Flight Data Center has such information for only 38 percent of the public-use airports and it is not readily available anywhere else. A B/CA telephone check of two local airports, frequently used for jet operations, brought gales of laughter from the airport operations people, and several condescending remarks, but little useful information.

The FAA is aware that pilots are facing a conflict between Part 91.5 demands and a lack of runway slope information and it is considering a clever solution. Its answer would be to bury the problem with a change to 91.5, eliminating the slope-planning requirement. It's not safe, mind you, but at least it would make everyone legal.

Runway slickness is never accounted for in the deceleration distance. Water, ice, snow and slush are presumed to have no effect on such matters. Certification data obtained on smooth, dry runways is applicable in even the worst cases of wet and freezing weather.

The matter of runway slickness has been an open subject for years. The British and others have recognized the seriousness of this problem and have written appropriate regulations to reduce V_1 speed (and/or takeoff weight when necessary) on wet and icy runways. The FAA, however, has consistently bowed to pressures from the airlines and aircraft manufacturers to allow operations at normal gross weights in slippery conditions. It is dangerous, unreasonable and naive, but V_1 remains unaffected by runway slickness under U.S. regulations.

Runway alignment distance, the distance necessary to maneuver the airplane into takeoff position, is not taken into account in the FARs. The British do consider alignment distance. The Air Force does. The FAA does not. If you use up 100 feet rolling into position, you will have compromised takeoff and accelerate/stop distances by that amount. If you do not lock the brakes and run the power up to takeoff thrust before releasing them, as specified in the flight manual, you compromise the distances still more. In 1965 the FAA proposed a 200-foot addition to runway requirements to account for these factors, but the proposal was withdrawn.

A complete lack of acceleration information makes the pilot totally dependent on the tenuous principle of speed as a measure of distance. In late 1970, a DC-8 departed Anchorage, Alaska with the brakes locked on an icy runway. By the time the crew recognized, through experience and seat-of-the-pants, that the acceleration was subnormal, it was too late. The airplane crashed and 47 people died.

In response to another takeoff accident, the NTSB recommended:

"... the use of takeoff procedures which will provide flight crews with time and distance reference to associate with the acceleration to V_1 speed." In March 1973, the Flight Safety Foundation addressed the same problem with recommendations for a line-speed check to verify normal acceleration. In 1975, the FAA, in an Advanced Notice of Proposed Rulemaking, called for comments on the installation of distance-to-go runway markers on all runways used by turbine aircraft. The proposal was withdrawn in 1976. As things stand in 1977 you still have no way of evaluating your aircraft's acceleration. V_1 speeds *presume* a normal acceleration. If anything interferes with that norm, actual runway requirements will grow proportionately.

Runway environment temperature is the basis for takeoff performance, but most airport thermometers are specifically located to measure free air over grassy or sodded areas. In bright sunlight, especially with blacktopped runways, temperatures in the pertinent runway environment can be as much as 40° higher than the reported ambient. Every degree higher unaccounted for detracts from actual takeoff performance through degraded aerodynamic and engine efficiencies.

Tire and brake condition is an unknown in most day-to-day operations. Certification tests are conducted using new tires and brakes for optimum stopping performance. Actual on-line equipment is invariably less efficient than that perfect situation, extending the stop distance some undefinable amount. There have been proposals to require certification in the worse-case brake and tire conditions, but those proposals have never become part of the regulations.

The non-engine failed abort is nowhere evaluated in the certification process. Only engine failure is considered. One 13-year compilation of 30 air carrier aborted takeoffs revealed that only seven were the result of engine problems. In fact, seven others were caused by brake and tire failures, seven more by various control problems and at least two by loading problems.

The point is that the engine failure case is one of the easiest to evaluate and quantify. Prescribed test runs provide neat, precise data that results in simple, sterile charts. *Other* serious failures do not lend themselves to such easy analysis and V_1 speeds often are not adequate to handle those more common emergencies.

Aerodynamic drag caused by control surface deflection in a crosswind takeoff is not taken into account. Your airplane flight manual lists some maximum demonstrated crosswind component, but unfortunately, the reduced acceleration that results from control deflection is not factored into field length or V_1 speeds.

Other than optimum CG conditions are not allowed for in the charts. Most takeoff tests are conducted with the aircraft loaded to the aft limit.

The performance may be measurably less at forward CG and in that case an engine failure at V_1 may be critical in some aircraft with marginal performance at best.

You might take comfort from the minimal safeguards that are provided, but it should be small comfort indeed.

· All engine-failure tests are conducted by failing the most critical engine. In a live situation, that may not be the one that fails, which will result in your having a slightly greater margin. The difference, however, is infinitesimal in jet-powered aircraft.

· Your aircraft may be equipped with reverse thrust or a drag chute that is not taken into account in the certification numbers. When used correctly, these stoppers can be of substantial help in the abort case. If you don't have one or the other, now is the time to place your order. They are the only margin you can buy.

· Engine-failure takeoff performance must allow for either a 35- or 50-foot clearance over the runway end. In an obstacle-free situation that altitude may not be necessary for a safe takeoff.

It may seem picayune to highlight each individual deficiency in the V_1 equation as we have above, but that would not be necessary if reasonable safety margins were included by the regulators or manufacturers. Barring such desirable, even reasonable, margins every possible shortcoming is meaningful. Single, seemingly minor exceptions to the idealized test data —such as worn brakes or strong crosswinds—are sufficient to seriously compromise the takeoff. When those exceptions to the ideal are compounded—as when the runway is wet, the tires worn and crewmembers are fatigued—it can make a mockery of even the most careful takeoff planning.

V_1 speeds are patently inadequate. Even worse, they have acquired an undeserved status, by association, with other official V speeds. V_s, the stall speed, for instance, is a reliable, measurable, demonstrable point at which the airplane will invariably experience a specific aerodynamic phenomenon. V_{LE}, the maximum landing gear extended speed, is a single, constant velocity based on engineering analysis of maximum desirable aerodynamic loads on landing gear and associated doors. V_1, on the other hand, has no fixed definition or meaning apart from the legal jargon that supports it. It is useful and necessary, but pilots should understand that this critical speed does not deserve the blind respect normally reserved for other V speeds.

Despite all of that, we need V_1. We must have some specific point or area in the takeoff that separates the go/no-go options. V_1 may be a problem child, but we simply cannot live without it in some form. It is the form that is in question.

Common sense would dictate that the entire V_1 concept be revised to provide at least the following improvements:

· A runway slickness correction.

· Reasonable crew recognition and reaction times.
· Coherent control action sequences.
· Proper education of flight crews as to the meanings and ramifications of any decision speed.
· Unbalanced field length information in all applicable pilot handbooks and flight manuals.
· A thoughtful approach to runway slope and gradient problems.
· Some consideration of the abort for reasons other than engine failure.

It is unfortunate that flight crews must consistently make this critical go/no-go decision with incomplete and sometimes erroneous information. Appropriate corrections to the takeoff performance equation could be made in a single month, with straightforward regulatory changes. They could, that is, if someone would finally sit up, listen and take action.

Meanwhile, pilots must learn to view V_1 with a somewhat jaundiced eye. In the absence of meaningful regulation and criteria, the formula can be loaded to provide a safety margin. When computing takeoff distances you can assume the runway is somewhat shorter than it actually is. Just two or three hundred feet will allow for such things as alignment distance, a runway with a small hump in it, a rough stopping surface or an obstacle that appears a bit taller than the specified 35 or 50 feet.

To give yourself one final bit of edge, keep your tires well inflated to enhance the acceleration factor; stay off the brakes on taxi out to prevent heating them up and thus reducing their stopping power; on a short field, do taxi to the very end, set the brakes and run the power up before releasing.

V_1 is such a mythical number you need all the edge you can get.

Safe Runway Lengths for Propeller Twins

14

by *Archie Trammell*

Recently a reader wrote asking why we use V_{XSE} for a decision speed in our estimates of runway requirements for FAR 23 aircraft in B/CA Aircraft Analysis, Comparison Profiles and in the April directory issue.

The simple answer is because we believe stated runway requirements should be safe for any pilot forced to test the accuracy of them. When you ask *why* we believe required runway lengths based on V_{XSE} are safe and distances based on some lesser speed are not, the answer becomes far more complex.

It must begin with FAR 23. (Aircraft certificated to FAR 25 are less affected by the question, since charts giving more realistic runway requirements are mandatory. But even they are suspect when the operator demands *absolute* safety in the departure.) Read through FAR 23 carefully and you will find only one reference to takeoff distances, 23.51, and it is for normal takeoffs with all engines operating.

There is, however, one paragraph in 23.51 that is critical to any discussion of safe takeoff distances. That is 23.54(4): "No takeoff made to determine the data required by this section may require exceptional piloting skill or exceptionally favorable conditions."

In short, takeoff distance charts assume average piloting skills and average conditions and that philosophy is carried through into even FAR 25.

It's comforting to know that the regulations insure the safety of pilots who have average or better skills, but the FAA certificates pilots to a *minimum* level of skills. So at best, the stated runway requirements in flight manuals protect half the pilot population and the rest end up in the trees at the end of a too-short runway.

We can't buy off on that.

How can twin pilots with less than average skills be protected? After studying and discussing this problem at great length, we settled on V_{XSE} as a decision speed. It's interesting to study some flight manuals and see what that means in real-world terms.

Let's look at the accelerate-stop distances, standard day at gross, for four light twins as shown in 1977 flight manuals. For the Aerostar 601, it is 3450 feet; for the Beech B55, 2700 feet; for the Cessna 310, 3645 feet and for the Piper Aztec, 1970 feet.

Since each of those figures was taken from a flight manual chart titled —and we quote—"Accelerate Stop Distance," they should all mean the same thing, true?

Not true. Those four runway numbers are as comparable as an apple, orange, persimmon and kumquat. That immediately becomes apparent when you look at the decision speeds used to determine those accelerate-stop distances as a percentage above V_{MC}: Aerostar, 14.4%; Beech, 4.4%; Cessna 310, 15%; Aztec, 0%.

Now which of the distances are the most realistic, the most likely to keep a below-average pilot out of trouble should an engine fail at a critical time during the takeoff?

Of course, V_{MC} has little to do with engine-out performance, so let's look at those recommended decision speeds as a percentage of the recommended initial engine-out climb speed stated in the emergency procedures section of the flight manual for each aircraft: Aerostar, 96.5%; Beech 96.9%; Cessna, 100%; Aztec, 80%.

Now, assuming you're an average pilot, which of those twins would you rather be in when an engine fails just at the recommended decision speed? Or one knot above decision speed?

More to the point, since those speeds assume an average pilot, what decision speed is safe for the worst pilot who can legally fly each aircraft in the worst conditions?

We've elected V_{XSE}, which by definition is the speed at which the airplane will climb over an obstacle in the shortest distance. Using V_{XSE}, how much of a fudge factor is added for ineptness, worn tires, fading brakes and tricky winds for each of the four aircraft? For the Aerostar it's 390 feet; for the Beech, 680; for the Cessna, 220; for the Aztec, 830.

Those are short distances to add, considering how long the alternative could be.

The problem with using V_{XSE} to determine the minimum safe runway length is that manufacturers seldom give us a curve for computing accelerate-stop distance versus a sliding decision speed. (An exception is Beech for the B55.) Such a chart should be mandatory. In its absence, as a rule of thumb, add 2 percent to the flight manual distance for each knot of difference between the decision speed used by the manufacturer and V_{XSE}.

In recent years, Beech and Cessna have improved their manuals with the addition of accelerate-go charts. We applaud them for that. But accelerate-go data introduces another problem. Unless the pilot has at least an average knowledge of accelerate-stop versus accelerate-go distances, he will likely get trapped by one or the other.

Examples of this potential can be found in any multi-engine flight manual, piston or turboprop, that has in it both accelerate-stop and accelerate-go charts. The preliminary charts for the new Cessna Conquest provide a classic.

Suppose one day you find yourself sitting on the end of a 2600-foot runway, standard day, at a takeoff weight of 8800 pounds, 1050 pounds under max gross. At the far end of the 2600 feet of asphalt is a 50-foot high stone wall, so you want to make certain you can clear it safely. You look at the accelerate-go chart and find you only need 2585 feet to accelerate, lose an engine at 98 knots, continue the takeoff and clear 50 feet.

Great. You set the brakes, run up to full power, release and rumble down the runway. At 88 knots, a full 10 knots below decision speed, the left engine dies dead and you elect to stop.

You're in for a big surprise. To accelerate the Conquest up to 88 knots then stop requires 3278 feet, 678 feet less than you have to get stopped in before displacing a bunch of stone wall.

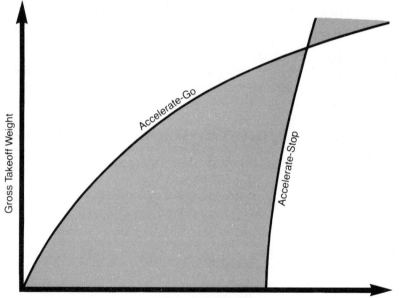

Manufacturers of FAR 23 twins aren't required to furnish balanced field length charts, so we end up with this situation. If you've settled for a runway length anywhere in the shaded area, you'll be in deep trouble should an engine fail at decision speed.

After the repairs, you again find yourself in that situation. But this time you're at gross, 9850 pounds, and the runway is 3700 feet long. You're determined not to make the same mistake twice, so you turn to the accelerate-stop chart this time and find you need only 3665 feet at a decision speed of 98 knots.

Great. You set the brakes, run up to full power and rumble down the runway. At 98 knots everything is lovely and you rotate. At 99 knots, the left one packs in. But no worry, you're a knot above the accelerate-go decision speed.

Guess what. To accelerate-go at gross you need 3965 feet, which is 265 feet more than you have. This time stones will be displaced about 30 feet up on that wall.

The curves in the accompanying graph illustrate the situation. At light weights most aircraft will accelerate-go in much shorter distances than necessary for accelerate-stop at the decision speeds given in flight manuals. The shaded areas represent a graveyard of busted airplanes. To be safe you must *always* have a runway length to the right of *either* curve, accelerate-stop or accelerate-go.

And note that they cross over. Up to the crossover point the accelerate-go chart has absolutely no value or meaning to safety. Above the crossover, the accelerate-stop chart has no value.

If you aren't familiar with this situation for the propeller twin you fly —and you may not be because manufacturers of FAR 23 airplanes don't give us curves like the ones illustrated here—you'd best get out your flight manual and become familiar.

For some few aircraft you will find that you can simply throw away the accelerate-go charts, because at no weight, altitude or temperature will they accelerate-stop in the distances given in the accelerate-go chart. The Rockwell Commander 690B is one of those.

But for most aircraft there is a crossover at some point in weight, altitude and/or temperature. For those aircraft you must consult both the accelerate-stop and the accelerate-go charts and pick the greater of the two for a required runway length.

Then, to allow a margin for skill or other sub-average factors, add two percent for each knot of difference between the flight manual decision speed and V_{xse}.

Stopways and Clearways

15

by James W. Powell

Balanced and unbalanced field lengths for takeoff in any multi-engine aircraft, piston or turbine, refers to only one thing—a comparison of the horizontal distance necessary to accelerate up to a decision speed, commonly called V_1, recognize a critical engine failure at that V_1 speed, then brake to a complete stop (Figure 1), versus suffer a critical engine failure at V_1 and complete the takeoff, attaining V_2 at 50 feet, for piston aircraft, 35 feet for the turbines, above the takeoff surface (Figure 2).

Figure 1 is the accelerate-stop case; Figure 2 is the accelerate-go case.

When V_1 is equal in both Figures 1 and 2, and the distance A to C in Figure 1 and the distance A to C in Figure 2 are equal, the field is said to be balanced.

But what happens when V_1 in the two figures is *not* equal? Let's look at Figure 1 first and assume that V_1 in that illustration is *decreased*, but nothing else changes. Obviously, the distance A to B, the accelerate distance, will decrease because less distance is needed to accelerate up to the lower V_1, or decision speed. Also obviously, distance B to C will decrease as well because less distance is required to brake to a stop from the lower V_1 speed.

So, the accelerate-stop distance can be shortened by simply reducing V_1. But that is not the solution to taking off from a shorter runway safely. The reason? When V_1 is changed in the accelerate-stop case (Figure 1), it significantly affects the distance B to C in Figure 2, the accelerate-go case. In Figure 2, distance A to B will be shortened by a lower V_1, as before, but distance B to C will *increase* so that the total distance A to C is greater than in the balanced field instance described above.

Why does B to C increase? Because it's now necessary to accelerate—with one engine failed—from a lower V_1 up to the V_2 speed and altitude, which remains the same in any case.

So, the effect of a reduced V_1—other things remaining equal—is a

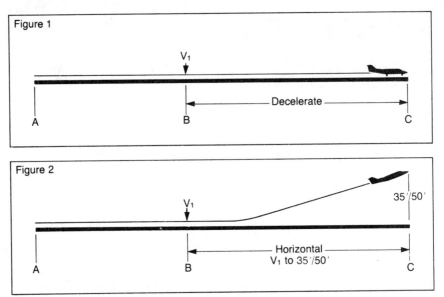

shorter accelerate-stop distance, A to C in Figure 1, but a longer accelerate-go distance, A to C in Figure 2.

Now, what if V_1 is *increased*. In the accelerate-stop case, Figure 1, the distance A to C will obviously *increase* because it's necessary to accelerate to that higher V_1 speed. As a general statement (but not invariably true for all aircraft), the accelerate-go distance, Figure 2, will decrease by some small amount. Why? Because two engines were available for acceleration to a higher speed; therefore, it's necessary to accelerate less on one engine from V_1 to the V_2 gate at 35 feet for jets or 50 feet for piston.

Before proceeding we must understand that for most aircraft there is a value for V_1 in the accelerate-go case of Figure 2 below which it cannot be set. That minimum is V_{MCG}, the minimum speed at which the aircraft can be directionally controlled while on the ground. Except for certain center-line thrust aircraft, if an engine fails below that speed, it will be impossible to steer straight down the runway with the other engine at takeoff power. Therefore, it will be impossible to accelerate and go if an engine fails below that speed. Thus, V_{MCG} determines the minimum balanced field length since V_1 cannot be less than V_{MCG}. Many aircraft would be capable of continuing to V_2 after an engine failure at a speed less than V_{MCG} if they could be steered while accelerating from V_1 up through V_{MCG} to V_R, the rotation speed.

Now, of what use is this fundamental knowledge? Well, it's sometimes advantageous to purposely unbalance the field length by "sliding" the V_1 speed up or down. For example, when there is a stopway for the runway, it may be possible to safely depart at a greater weight. Special Air Regula-

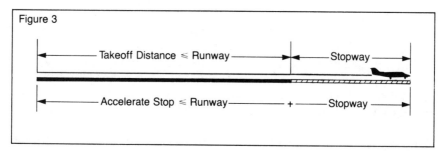

Figure 3

Takeoff Distance ≤ Runway ————→|←———— Stopway ————→

←———— Accelerate Stop ≤ Runway ———— + ———— Stopway ————→

tion 422B introduced the concept of stopway to civil operators of aircraft within the United States. Figure 3 illustrates stopway as an area beyond the runway end, located on the extended runway centerline and not less than the width of the runway. The purpose of a stopway is to provide extra pavement for use in decelerating during a rejected takeoff.

The stopway distance available may be computed as a part of accelerate-stop only, not the takeoff distance or takeoff run. Some pilots add the stopway distance to the runway length and use the sum for determining the maximum aircraft weight for that departure. They consult the *balanced* field length charts in finding that weight.

In most cases that will be safe, but in other instances it may be very hazardous for two reasons. First, there could be a 60-foot solid rock cliff at the very end of the stopway. That would be a stunning discovery if an engine were to fail just past V_1, an accelerate-go situation, because the balanced field length charts guarantee only 35 feet of altitude at the end of the total distance used in calculating the maximum safe takeoff weight for a jet, and 50 feet for a piston aircraft. Second, it's possible that with adequate runway plus stopway for a takeoff, the runway itself may be too short for acceleration to V_1 plus acceleration after V_1 to liftoff with an engine failed.

Simply adding the stopway distance to the runway length and consulting balanced field length charts also may not be legal, so it's not an advisable practice due to the potential for lawsuit in the event of an accident.

The reason it may not be legal is because FAR 91.37 specifies that no person may take off a turbine aircraft weighing more than 12,500 pounds if the *takeoff run* will be greater than the runway length—exclusive of the stopway. What is the takeoff run? It's the distance required to accelerate to V_1 then continue to accelerate to liftoff with an engine out, plus one half the distance from liftoff to the point at which V_2 and 35 feet (50 feet for piston aircraft) are attained. In the case of a short runway and a long stopway, that requirement can easily be breached.

The stopway can be used for accelerate-stop computations, but takeoff run and takeoff distance data for the aircraft must also be consulted. Unfortunately, the manufacturers of most business jets, and of all piston twins, do not give us the charts necessary for computing takeoff run.

Even takeoff distance charts are missing for most piston twins and even many of the turboprops. In some instances you can discover what they are by juggling takeoff roll and balanced field length numbers, but that's not satisfactory. We should all badger the manufacturers for more complete takeoff data. Without it, a truly safe operation is impossible and operators are thus left naked to the potential of law suits.

Design of stopways necessitates consideration of anticipated aircraft weight, for they must not induce structural damage on the aircraft through failure. Caution should be exercised should the coefficient of friction for a stopway be less than that of a good runway. Rough, bumpy stopways have no more usefulness in providing good braking surfaces than do similar runways.

Another instance in which an unbalanced field length may be advantageous is when a clearway is available. Clearway is an area beyond the end of a runway not suitable for stopping an aircraft, but adequate to provide additional takeoff distance for climb to 35 or 50 feet as appropriate. To safeguard operations utilizing a clearway, takeoff run data for the aircraft is again important information. Computation of the takeoff run will insure that the aircraft will be safely airborne by the end of the runway.

The advantage of the clearway is that V_1 for the accelerate-stop case can be low to accommodate a short runway, but the distance available to accelerate to 35 feet and V_2 is extended to allow for the additional time—and distance—necessary to accelerate from the lower V_1 to the V_2 constant.

But we emphasize that takeoff data *must* be available to make use of the clearway. Otherwise you may find the runway so short that you run off the cliff at the end before getting airborne.

Minimum criteria for civil use of a clearway were initially introduced in Special Air Regulation 422A and later made less restrictive in SR-422B. Where a clearway exists, it is considered to start at the end of the runway, regardless of whether a stopway is present.

Airport authorities must have control of clearways to be certain that movable obstacles penetrating a clearway plane will not be present at the time a flight is initiated.

Permanent protrusions into the clearway as defined in the regulations may not penetrate a plane of 01.25% (80 to 1). Runway threshold lights are permitted within a clearway only if they are less than 26 inches in height and are beside the runway.

For calculation purposes the allowable clearway may be no longer than one-half the runway length. Note in Figure 4 that when the clearway plane is positive, the takeoff distance must place the aircraft at the 35-foot, or 50-foot, point above the clearway plane, not above the runway elevation.

A summary of the stopway/clearway concept is illustrated in Figure 5. A clear understanding of the concept, plus the proper aircraft charts for

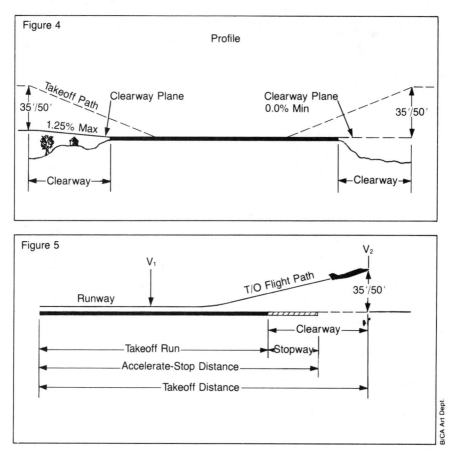

Figure 4

Profile

Figure 5

taking advantage of it, can result in higher takeoff weights from certain airports.

But in conclusion we should leave you with some thoughts relative to V_1, accelerate-stop and accelerate-go.

What happens to accelerate-stop when the runway gradient is zero, but the center, near point B, is higher than the ends?

What happens to the distance A to B if a tire blows out unknown to the crew at the beginning of the takeoff run?

What happens to the accelerate-go distance A to C with heavy slush on the runway?

When the runway is longer than needed for the weight, but it's a hot day at a high-altitude airport, what adjustment should be made to V_1?

Believe it or not, several thoroughly professional, 20,000-hour pilots have wrecked airplanes, because their answers to some of those questions were incorrect.

Always Leave Yourself an Out

16

by Richard N. Aarons

Despite heated scoldings from flight instructors and grim warnings from the National Transportation Safety Board, many pilots still seem to believe that implied in the fact that an aircraft has two engines is a promise that it will perform with only one of those engines operative. And the light-twin stall/spin accident rate further indicates that many multi-engine pilots have not come to grips with the facts that (1) significantly more than half the climb performance disappears when one engine signs out, and (2) exploration of the Vmc regime close to the ground is a sure way to kill yourself.

A while back, the NTSB reported that light multi-engine aircraft are involved in fewer engine-failure-related accidents than single-engine aircraft. However the same report observed that an engine-failure-related accident in a twin is four times more likely to cause serious or fatal injuries.

We don't intend here to debate the relative merits of twins versus singles. The twin offers obvious safety advantages over the single, especially in the enroute phase, and if, only if, the pilot fully understands the real options offered by that second engine in the takeoff and approach phases as well.

Takeoff is the most critical time for the light-twin pilot, but if something goes wrong he *may* have the option of continued flight, an option denied his single-engine counterpart. More often than not that second engine will provide only a little more time to pick a soft spot. (This assumes that the engine is lost before the aircraft reaches maneuvering altitude of 300 to 500 feet.) But even those few extra seconds, representing a few hundred extra yards, can give the twin pilot a hell of a safety advantage over his single-engine counterpart. But I must stress again, this safety advantage exists *only* if the multi-engine pilot fully understands his machine.

We are now going to explore some of the design concepts and certification procedures applicable to current-production light twins and then take a look at light-twin performance tables and attempt to find ways of getting more realistic information out of them. Along the way, we'll establish five rules for technique. We use these rules at B/CA, pilots at the FAA Academy use them, and we're sure many readers are aware of them, but we'll throw them in anyway in hopes of picking up a few more converts.

Let's look first at that implied promise that a general-aviation twin will perform with one engine inoperative. Part 23 sets standards for the certification of light aircraft weighing 12,500 pounds or less. Multi-engine aircraft are further divided by Part 23 into two weight classes, split at 6,000 pounds with the group that weighs 6,000 pounds, or less, subdivided into two, depending on V_{so} (stall speed in the landing configuration). The break comes at 61 knots CAS.

Only those twins that weigh more than 6,000 pounds or have a V_{so} higher than 61 knots need to demonstrate any single-engine climb performance at all for certification. And the requirement is pretty meager. Basically, the regulation says that these aircraft must demonstrate a single-engine climb capability at 5,000 feet (ISA) with the inoperative engine feathered and the aircraft in a clean configuration. The amount of climb performance required is determined by the formula $ROC = 0.027\ V_{so}^2$. The Rockwell Commander 500S (Shrike), for example, weighs over 6,000 pounds and therefore must meet this climb requirement. V_{so} for the Shrike is 63 knots; thus its minimum single-engine climb performance at 5,000 feet is 0.027×63^2 or 107.16 fpm. The Shrike's actual single-engine climb at 5,000 feet is 129 fpm, so the manufacturer bettered the Part 23 requirement, but not by much.

The Cessna 310 weighs less than 6,000 pounds, but stalls at 63.9 knots, so it too must meet the enroute single-engine climb standards. Plugging 63.9 knots into the $0.027\ V_{so}^2$ equation produces a requirement of 110.2 fpm. The 310's actual single-engine climb under Part 23 conditions is 119 fpm.

The Aztec, like the 310, weighs less than 6,000 pounds, but it slips under the V_{so} wire with a stall speed of 60.8 knots. The only requirement that an airplane in this group must meet is that its single-engine climb performance at 5,000 feet (positive or negative) be *determined*. The Aztec climbs at 50 fpm on one engine at that altitude, but the regulation doesn't require that it climb at all at that or any other altitude.

We can see then that where an enroute single-engine climb is required, it's minimal. Consider a hypothetical aircraft with an outrageous V_{so} of 100 knots CAS. The FAA requires only that such an aircraft demonstrate a paltry climb of 270 fpm on one engine at 5,000 feet.

There's another point to consider here. The FAA does not require continued single-engine takeoff capability for any light aircraft other than those designed for air taxi work and capable of hauling 10 or more passengers. Stated another way, there is no reason to assume that an aircraft will exhibit positive single-engine climb performance in the takeoff configuration at sea level just because it had to meet a single-engine climb-performance requirement at 5,000 clean.

FAA Academy flight instructors are fully aware of this situation and believe it's important to stress it with the agency's GADO inspectors. An in-house white paper on light twins used at training courses for FAA pilots puts it this way:

"There is nothing in the FAR governing the certification of light multi-engine aircraft which says they must fly (maintain altitude) while in the takeoff configuration and with an engine inoperative. In fact, many of the light twins are not required to do this with one engine inoperative in any configuration, even at sea level . . . With regard to performance (but not controllability) in the takeoff or landing configuration, the light multi-engine aircraft is, in concept, merely *a single-engine aircraft with its power divided into two or more individual packages.*" (Emphasis ours.)

While this concept of not putting all your eggs in one basket leads to certain advantages, it also leads to disadvantages should the eggs in one basket get broken.

You'll remember from your multi-engine transition training that the flight instructor and check pilot repeatedly insisted that when you lose one engine on a twin, performance is not halved, but actually reduced by 80 percent or more.

That 80-percent performance-loss figure is not just a number pulled out of the air for emphasis. It's easy to figure for any aircraft. Consider the Beech Baron B55 which has an all-engine climb rate (sea level, standard conditions, max gross weight) of 1,670 fpm and a single-engine climb rate under the same conditions of 318 fpm. The loss of climb performance in this case is

$$100 - (\quad \frac{318}{1,670} \times 100)$$

or 80.96 percent. The climb performance remaining after the loss of one engine on the B55 is 19.04 percent.

Performance loss for the cabin twins, turboprops and business jets is similar. The Rockwell Commander 685, for example, loses 83.42 percent of its climb performance when one engine quits; the Swearingen Merlin III loses 75.49 and the Learjet 25C 71.07. The Lockheed JetStar loses 43.48 percent of its climb performance with the loss of one engine, but remember, it has four engines. The loss of one quarter of its thrust results in a loss of almost half its climb performance and if it were to lose half its thrust, climb performance would be cut by more than 75 percent.

Some turboprops and all turbojets demonstrate a continued takeoff capability with one engine inoperative. The turbojets do so because of the tougher certification requirements of FAR Part 25. Although loss of power in terms of percentage reduction is similar in all categories of business aircraft, the turbojets and some turboprops have much better single-engine performance because they're starting with higher numbers. While the Learjet 25C, for example, loses more than 71 percent of its climb performance when one engine is shut down, it begins with an all-engine rate of climb of 6,050 fpm. When this is reduced by 71 percent, it still climbs at 1,750, which is much better performance than you get out of many light-piston twins with both engines running.

Why the performance loss is greater than 50 percent with the failure of one engine needs a bit of explanation. Climb performance is a function of thrust horsepower (or simply thrust in turbojets) which is in excess of that required for straight and level flight. You can convince yourself that this is the case by trimming your aircraft for straight and level at its best all-engine rate-of-climb speed and checking the power setting. If you ease the stick back at this point, the airplane will not settle into a sustained climb. After a momentary climb it may, in fact, begin to descend. However, if you go back to straight and level flight at the best-rate-of-climb speed and slowly feed in power as you maintain airspeed, a climb will be indicated, and the rate of climb will depend on the power you add—which is power in excess of that required for straight and level.

Now trim for straight and level (in the clean configuration at about 1,500 feet) at the best single-engine rate-of-climb speed, adjust one engine to its zero-thrust setting (about 10 inches to simulate feather). You'll notice that the "good" engine, now carrying the full burden, is producing 75-percent power or more. If you increase the power on the good engine, your aircraft will begin a climb, but at a very modest rate. This is so because you've got much less "excess" horsepower available. If you are interested in the math behind this, an approximate formula for rate of climb is:

$$R/C = \frac{ehp \times 33,000}{weight}$$

(ehp is thrust horsepower in excess of that required for straight and level.) To determine ehp, rearrange the formula to read:

$$ehp = \frac{R/C \times 33,000}{33,000}$$

Using the Seneca as an example, with its maximum gross weight of 4,200 pounds and all-engine and single-engine climb rates of 1,860 and 190 fpm respectively, we find that this aircraft has about 236 thrust horsepower available for climb with both powerplants operating and only 24 excess thrust horsepower for climb on one engine. If you refer to the climb-performance-loss formula, you'll see that the Seneca loses about 89.78 percent of its climb performance when an engine stops:

$$100- \frac{190}{1,860} \times 100 + 89.78$$

If you examine the two figures above for excess horsepower and state them in terms of percentages, you'll see that an engine loss in the Seneca represents a loss of 89.83 percent of thrust horsepower available for climb.

Part 23 defines Vmc as "the minimum calibrated airspeed at which, when any engine is suddenly made inoperative, it is possible to recover control of the airplane with that engine still inoperative, and maintain straight flight, either with zero yaw, or, at the option of the manufacturer, with an angle of bank of not more than five degrees." Vmc may not be higher than 1.2 times the stall speed with flaps in takeoff position and the gear retracted. In flight-test work, Vmc is determined with takeoff or METO power on each engine, the rearmost allowable center of gravity, flaps in takeoff position, landing gear retracted and the propeller of the inoperative engine (1) windmilling with the propeller set in the takeoff range, or (2) feathered, if the airplane has an automatic feathering device. During recovery, the airplane may not assume any dangerous attitude or require exceptional piloting skill, alertness, or strength to prevent a heading change of more than 20 degrees.

Vmc is not at all mysterious. It's simply that speed at which airflow past the rudder is reduced to such an extent that rudder forces cannot overcome the asymmetrical forces caused by takeoff power on one side and a windmilling prop on the other.

When that speed is reached and the nose starts to swing toward the inoperative engine, the only hope of regaining control is to reduce thrust on the good engine (or increase airspeed). An increase in airspeed requires a change in momentum and thus a certain period of time to become effective. Thus, for practical purposes, the *only* method of regaining control is to reduce power on the operating engine—quickly.

Vmc is not a static number like flap-operating speed or the never-exceed speed. It changes with conditions. The Part 23 test described above cites the worst conditions. Aft cg, for example, reduces the force of the rudder because it shortens the arm and thus the turning moment. Vmc will be lower with forward cg and all other factors being equal. Conversely if the aircraft is loaded slightly out of rear cg, Vmc will be higher. In normally aspirated aircraft Vmc decreases with an increase in density altitude primarily because the output of the operating engine decreases, thus the asymmetrical power situation decreases.

At first glance, this situation seems to be a good one. The hotter and higher the airport, the lower the Vmc. But actually nothing about Vmc is good and there's a hell of a catch in it. As Vmc decreases (with a decrease in good-engine performance) it approaches the stall speed. This is especially bad news for flight instructors who must purposely explore the Vmc regime with their students. If Vmc and stall are reached simultaneously, a spin is almost inevitable and Part 23 twins are often impossible to get out of a spin. (One northeast flight school lost two aircraft in one summer because of this problem.)

Landing-gear extension seems to reduce Vmc for most light twins and this, like the density altitude situation, can be both good and bad.

Suppose a pilot gets himself in the unhappy position of being 50 feet in the air, gear down, with one engine out, full power on the good side and full rudder to keep the nose from swinging. He doesn't like the look of the trees in front of him so he decides to make a go for it. He reaches down and retracts the gear to get rid of its drag, hoping that will enable the aircraft to accelerate to a climb speed. Suddenly he's looking at the trees through the top of the windshield. Why? Because he was on the edge of Vmc and sucked up the gear, which increased Vmc, costing him control of the aircraft.

The prudent light-twin pilot, of course, would never find himself in that situation because he would know beforehand that his hopes of accelerating without altitude loss from Vmc to Vxse or Vyse are practically nil.

If your aircraft is relatively new, Vmc, as determined by the Part 23 certification test, is marked by a red line on the airspeed-indicator face. Indicated Vmc will never be higher than this line, so the slash can be used as a guide to keep you out of trouble. This does not mean that the airplane will spin out as soon as the line is reached. Under the circumstances described above (such as high density altitude) controlled flight with full power on the operative engine is possible when the indicated airspeed falls below the red line, but it certainly isn't advisable. Exploring this part of the flight envelope in an actual emergency can (and probably will) kill you. So let's establish our first rule for multi-engine flying.

Rule # 1—Never allow the airspeed to drop below *published Vmc* except during the last few yards of the landing flare, and then only if the field is extremely short.

Some aircraft have an all-engine best-angle-of-climb speed (Vx) below Vmc. Using that climb speed under any circumstances can be extremely dangerous. The instructors at the FAA Academy have this to say about the use of Vx near the ground: "Trying to gain height too fast after takeoff can be dangerous because of control problems. If the airplane is in the air below Vmc when an engine fails, the pilot *might* avoid a crash by rapidly retard-

121

ing the throttles, although *the odds are not in favor of the pilot."* Thus we have another rule:

Rule # 2—A best all-engine angle-of-climb speed that is lower than Vmc is an *emergency* speed and should be used near the ground *only* if you're willing to bet your life that one engine won't quit during the climb.

Manufacturers differ on the proper takeoff speed for a light twin. Piper, for example, recommends that most of its twins be rotated at Vmc. Cessna, on the other hand, suggests liftoff at a speed much higher than Vmc and very close to best single-engine angle-of-climb speed. In the case of the Cessna 310, Vmc is 75 knots, recommended rotation speed is 91 knots and best single-engine angle-of-climb speed is 94.

It's important to note that manufacturers who recommend liftoff at or near Vmc do not, as a rule, show figures for continued takeoff in event of an engine failure at the liftoff speed. The reason is simple. Most Part 23 twins cannot accelerate in the takeoff configuration from Vmc to best single-engine rate-of-climb speed while maintaining a positive climb rate. Conversely it is possible to accelerate them (under near sea-level conditions) from best single-engine angle-of-climb speed to best single-engine rate-of-climb speed while maintaining a positive, though meager, climb. Manufacturers who recommend liftoff well above Vmc usually show continued single-engine takeoff performance in their owners or flight manuals.

We have to recommend against lifting off at Vmc for the same reason most flight instructors recommend against "stalling" a single-engine aircraft off the ground. In the latter case, the single will fly to the edge of ground effect but could reach that point behind the power curve. An engine failure at that point could result in a stall and pitch over. In the case of the twin, an engine failure at liftoff at Vmc could produce such a rapid turning moment that control would be lost immediately. The FAA says, "Experience has shown that an unexpected engine failure surprises the pilot so that he will act as though he is swimming in glue." If a pilot rotates at Vmc, loses an engine and begins the "swimming in glue" routine, his odds of survival are minimal.

The alternative, of course, is to hold the aircraft on the ground a little longer. Most multi-engine instructors believe that Vmc-plus-five knots is a good compromise for use in those aircraft with a recommended liftoff at Vmc. Why not hold it down until almost reaching best single-engine angle-of-climb speed like the Cessna folks recommend? The reason again is controllability. Cessna light twins and most cabin twins of all manufacturers are designed to stay on the ground well beyond Vmc. But some of the light twins simply are not. For example, we've tried holding the Seneca and Aztec on the runway beyond Vmc-plus-five knots and have discovered that both aircraft begin to wheelbarrow. (Tests were at maximum gross weight, zero flaps.) High-speed wheelbarrowing can be just as dangerous as liftoff too close to Vmc, especially when we're talking about selecting an appropriate speed for every takeoff. Remember too that the takeoff-performance figures in the aircraft-owners or flight manual are invalid as soon as we use techniques different from those specified in the table footnotes. (More on this later.) Anyway, we've got a third rule now for light-twin operation:

Rule #3—Use the manufacturer's recommended liftoff speed or Vmc plus five knots whichever is greater.

Now that we're in the air, the first priority is to accelerate the aircraft to best single-engine angle-of-climb speed (if we're not already there), then best single-engine rate-of-climb speed and finally best all-engine rate-of-climb speed. Each of these speeds is a milestone in the takeoff and the realization of each reduces the decisions to be made in the event of an engine failure.

Many instructors recommend that best single-engine rate-of-climb speed (the blue line if it's marked on your airspeed indicator) be used for the initial climb to a safe maneuvering altitude. B/CA's pilots recommend the best all-engine rate-of-climb speed, when it is faster (it normally is), for two reasons. First, the swimming-in-glue syndrome is going to cost you time in reacting to an engine failure and this time lost is going to translate into speed lost. So if an engine does quit while you're holding best all-engine rate-of-climb speed, the deceleration while you're getting things straightened out will probably put you pretty close to best single-engine rate-of-climb speed which is where you want to be anyway. Second, the best all-engine rate speed will get you to maneuvering altitude and out of immediate danger.

One caution here is important. Avoid climbing to maneuvering altitude at a speed greater than best all-engine rate of climb—to do so is sloppy and inefficient. Here's why:

As we have seen, climb is a function of thrust horsepower in excess of that required for straight and level flight and drag increases as the square of the speed. At the same time, power required to maintain a velocity increases as the cube of the velocity.

The Cessna 421 has a best all-engine rate-of-climb speed of 110 knots, which produces a climb of 1,850 fpm at sea level. If the aircraft is climbed at 122 knots, drag would increase by 1.2 times and the power required to maintain that velocity would increase 1.4 times with a resulting decrease of excess thrust horsepower available for climb. In this example the climb rate decreases to about 1,261 fpm; thus a 10-percent increase in speed over the best-rate speed produces a 32-percent decrease in climb performance.

These exercises produce another rule:

Rule #4—After leaving the ground above Vmc, climb not slower than single-engine best rate-of-climb speed and not faster than best all-engine rate speed. The latter speed is preferable if obstacles are not a consideration.

You may have gotten the impression by now that we're picking on Cessna and Piper in our examples. Piper twins and the Rockwell Commander 500S have shown up in our examples here because the Ziff-Davis Aviation Division operates (or operated in the case of the Shrike) these aircraft and our observations concerning them were gained from extensive first-hand knowledge. The Cessna twins are used as examples because Cessna, in our opinion, produces the best owners manuals in the industry. This is not to say that the Cessna manuals can't be improved—they are merely the best of a very poor lot. But in any event Cessna manuals provide most of the information a pilot needs to plan for emergencies. A special committee of the General Aviation Manufacturer's Association has been working on standardization and improvement of light-aircraft flight manuals. But until such time as the GAMA committee and the FAA perfect the situation, we're stuck with the paperwork that comes with the airplane. Here comes rule five:

Rule #5—Be a skeptic when reading the performance tables in your Part 23 aircraft owners manual and be doubly sure you read the fine print. Add plenty of fudge factors.

You'll notice first when you look at light-twin takeoff-performance tables (in anybody's manual) that the takeoff is initiated after power has been run to maximum with the brakes locked and the mixtures adjusted to optimum settings. We've attempted to measure the difference in the takeoff roll for brakes held versus a normal throttles-up-smooth start and have come up with figures ranging from an extra 200 to 400 feet. Remember that these figures will increase with increases in density altitude.

If the book gives figures for continued single-engine takeoff and accelerate/stop distances, you've really got it made, because now, by adding a few hundred feet here and there to compensate for real-time situations, you can get a good handle on what's going to happen if one quits—and what you're going to do about it.

We'll use a Cessna 421 for this exercise and remind you again that we're not picking on the 421. It's just that Cessna is honest enough to try to tell it like it is in its owners' manuals.

On a standard day at 7,450 pounds, two engines, a 421 needs 2,500 feet to get off and over a 50-foot obstacle. This assumes a rotate speed of 106 knots, well above Vmc. If an engine is lost at rotation and the pilot elects to go anyway, he'll need a total of 5,000 to clear the obstacle. The ground run in both cases is about 2,000 feet. In the case of both engines operating, the climb from rotation to 50 feet requires a horizontal distance of only 500 feet; but in the case of the single-engine takeoff, the climb to 50 feet requires a horizontal distance of 3,000 feet, a six-fold increase. And keep in mind that we're still only 50 feet above the ground and that to get this far we've made split-second decisions all along the way.

Let's get some real-life factors into the single-engine takeoff equation. Suppose, as is usually the case, we begin the takeoff roll about 75 feet from the approach end of the runway and do so without holding the brakes. This could add 475 feet to the handbook figure. Next, suppose we lose the engine at rotation, but it takes us three seconds to recognize the situation and react. (This, by the way, is a very conservative figure.) The reaction time will cost us about 537 feet. Now the total horizontal distance from the beginning of the runway to a point at which the aircraft is 50 above the surface (assuming engine loss at rotation) is 6,012 feet, an increase of 20 percent. The 421's sea-level, single-engine climb rate is about 305 fpm. Assuming that we want to get at least 500 feet under us before trying anything fancy like returning for a landing, we must continue more or less straight ahead for one minute and 28 seconds. This climb will cover a horizontal distance of some 16,485 feet bringing the total distance covered from the rotation point to 19,485 feet, or *3.7 miles*.

If all this happens at a sea-level airport on a hot day (ISA plus 20 degrees C.), we will not reach the 50-foot level until the aircraft has covered a horizontal distance of 7,040 feet from the point of rotation and engine failure. Assuming calm air the aircraft will reach 500 feet some *5.9 miles* from the rotation point or 6.6 miles from the runway beginning. If the hot condition brought convective turbulence with it, the effective climb rate would be reduced by 100 fpm. Under these conditions, the aircraft would reach 500 feet some *9.9 miles* from the rotation point and 10.6 miles from the runway beginning.

I've been stating these horizontal distances in terms of miles to stress a point. If your flight manual gives figures for continued single-engine takeoff, make sure you look at the climb performance beyond the 50-foot altitude to be certain that continued takeoff is a viable alternative if an engine quits. You might be able to live with that 10.6-mile hot-day figure on a departure from JFK where you could head out over the Atlantic, but the same departure from Teterboro would make collision with obstacles almost a certainty. In the case of the Teterboro departure, a rejected takeoff within the boundaries of the airport or stuffing it into the first available parking lot might be your only survivable alternative. You certainly aren't going to survive if you run into something, or fall out of the air trying to get performance from the aircraft that the manufacturer never built into it.

So, on the subject of rejected takeoffs, check the accelerate/stop tables and the landing-distance charts before each takeoff. Remember to add 500 feet or so to the accelerate/stop distance to compensate for the runway left behind you when you moved into position and the rolling (rather than brakes-held) ground run; add another 500 feet or so for your reaction time and then another 200 feet for "technique." Part 23 sets no standards for the determination of accelerate/stop distances in light twins. The stopping distances are often determined by a 10,000-hour test pilot who does everything short of retracting the gear to stop the aircraft. Even in an emergency situation, you're probably not going to get the same stopping performance he does. (Remember to get the flaps up to increase the weight on the wheels.)

If you're lucky enough to have normal takeoff, single-engine takeoff and accelerate/stop tables in your airplane manual, another check you should make before takeoff is the total distance (adding our real-life factors, of course) for takeoff with both engines operating, climb to 50 feet, then to land from that 50-foot altitude and bring the aircraft to a complete stop. This figure for the 421 (adding all our fudge factors) comes to 5,689 feet. This is less than the distance required (6,012 feet) to climb to 50 feet assuming an engine loss at rotation under the same conditions.

Knowing this number gives you another alternative. If you have 5,700 feet of runway and overrun, you might decide to put the aircraft back on the runway even if the engine failure occurs well after takeoff as you're going through 50 feet. Even if you don't have the full 5,700 feet, you may have enough runway to get the wheels back on the hard surface and begin some serious braking before you run off the end of the runway. B/CA's philosophy, which was copied from that of the flight department of a major manufacturer of light twins, is that it's always better to go through the fence at 50 knots than to hit the trees at 120.

To the best of my knowledge, a takeoff to 50 feet followed by an immediate landing is not taught in twins, although a similar maneuver is taught in single-engine aircraft. It should be, but before you go out and try it, take your aircraft to altitude and practice the transition from climbing flight to gliding flight until you can make the transition without significant loss of airspeed. And it might be a good idea to take an instructor along. If you decide to try it on a runway, allow a good 8,000 to 10,000 feet for the first few attempts—and take your time.

If your aircraft-owners manual does not show performance figures for continued single-engine takeoff, chances are that the airplane simply is not capable of accelerating from liftoff speed to a reasonable climb speed in the

126

takeoff configuration. In this case, your decisions are pretty limited. You really don't have a go-situation until the aircraft is cleaned up and has reached at least best single-engine angle-of-climb speed. An engine failure before that time (on the ground or in the air) dictates an immediate *controlled* descent to a landing. The surviving engine, in this case, can be used to help maneuver to a suitable (nearby) landing place if all of the runway is gone.

You can calculate your own accelerate/stop distances by running the aircraft up to takeoff speed and then bringing it to a stop. (Make sure you start these tests on a good long runway). Do this several times at max gross weight counting runway lights (the airport operator can tell you the distance between lights) and you'll get a good ball-park figure for accelerate/stop. Then use that figure in your future takeoff planning.

To sum it up, we've seen that:

The loss of an engine on a Part 23 twin will decrease sea-level climb performance by at least 80 percent and can decrease it by as much as 90 percent.

There is no requirement for continued single-engine takeoff capability for Part 23 twins, nor, in fact, is there a requirement for any positive single-engine climb at all for twins which weigh less than 6,000 pounds and have a stall speed of 61 knots or less in the landing configuration.

It is vital to know all you can about your aircraft's performance in normal and emergency situations *before* the takeoff is attempted. To arrive at reasonable performance predictions you must adjust the information provided by the manufacturer to take into account real-life factors such as reaction time, runway condition and obstacles, including obstacles five or more miles beyond the airport boundary.

A well-executed Part 23-twin takeoff is one in which the aircraft leaves the ground at least at Vmc-plus-five knots and climbs at a speed of at least Vxse and not more than Vy.

One final comment should be made on the single-engine takeoff. Your personal IFR takeoff minimums should include factors for an engine failure. Certainly your go/no-go decision with an engine failure immediately after rotation or in the initial climb segment is strongly affected by weather. Consider the case of the 421 we discussed above which, in the event of engine failure at rotation, requires about 10.6 miles on a hot day from the start of the runway to a point where maneuvering altitude (500 feet) is reached. Poor visibility and low ceilings could make that situation almost hopeless in any but the most sparsely built-up areas.

Single-engine landings, as you'll remember from your check rides, are not difficult at all. Single-engine go-arounds in Part 23 twins are, on the other hand, damn near impossible unless they are begun from an altitude several hundred feet above the terrain and at an airspeed at or slightly above the best single-engine rate-of-climb speed. The situation is doubly bad if you start a go-around and *then* lose an engine. If you want proof, go to altitude and set up a 500 fpm rate of descent at a speed 10 percent below the best single-engine rate-of-climb speed. Continue the descent until you are within 200 feet of a cardinal altitude, then simulate a single-engine go-around. Attempt to clean up the airplane, and accelerate to best single-engine climb speed without sinking through the cardinal altitude. It can't be done with Part 23 twins—we've tried it in just about everything from the Seneca to the King Air A100. At or above single-engine climb speed it can be done if you're sharp. But don't bank on being sharp after a long flight involving an engine shutdown somewhere along the way.

So establish a single-engine I'll-land-come-hell-or-high-water altitude (agl) and minimum-airspeed combination for your aircraft and stick to it. If you find yourself below that speed or altitude and a truck shows up on the runway, pick a soft spot to hit on the airport. Because it's much better to wipe out the gear by landing off the runway than to wipe out the whole airplane by spinning into the middle of it.

Summing it up—stay proficient (an annual check is a good idea), stay constantly aware of your airplane's performance by analyzing the flight manual information under realistic conditions, and have a plan of action before things start to come unglued. The key philosophy of that plan of action is easy to remember and may save your bottom—*always leave yourself an out.*

ARRIVALS

Arrivals contain many of the same ingredients as departures—traffic congestion, specific ATC procedures, the need for swift and clear pilot-controller communications, changes in aircraft configuration and power settings and so on—but with a critical difference. Arrivals mean convergence as aircraft are funneled into a small parcel of airspace all the way down to the ground. This creates special challenges for all concerned. Safe arrivals do not just happen. They depend upon a multitude of variables which the pilot must carefully balance.

Perhaps the most important thing a pilot must do to effect a safe arrival is to familiarize himself carefully with the destination. Yet even when he has done that, he may find that IFR procedures and ATC coordination can complicate his operation and limit his options. Should he accept a circling approach? Is he current in ADF? Does he understand the prescribed missed approach procedure? He cannot relax even after touchdown, because runway limitations and such hazards as that of hydroplaning could ruin an otherwise perfect arrival.

There is no more critical phase of flight than the approach and landing. The accident statistics prove that every year. Skill and a little luck are sufficient for most arrivals, but knowledge provides a wonderful advantage—knowledge that can be augmented by studying the information in this chapter.

Getting to Know Your Destination 17

by Bill Cotton

"According to this dumb sheet, we're supposed to maintain 3400 to Round Hill."

Those were among the last words of a veteran airline captain on a stormy morning three years ago over the Virginia countryside. The "dumb sheet" he referred to was an IFR approach plate, more formally known as a Standard Instrument Approach Procedure, or SIAP. The SIAP for a runway is constructed by the FAA's Flight Standards Service and converted to chart form by cartographers of the National Ocean Survey (NOS), Jeppesen Sanderson and other map makers.

Shortly after the accident there was a chorus of amazed disbelief by self-righteous pilots who steadfastly maintained that they would never have descended to the altitude that captain did after looking at his "dumb sheet."

In daily operations, however, a very different story was emerging. Upon careful reflection, professional pilots all over the country found that they indeed were descending prematurely while on radar vectors to intercept the final approach course. This technique was an everyday practice because, otherwise, intercept of the approach course would usually occur at too high an altitude to continue a normal approach.

This disclosure, and the accident leading to it, prompted the FAA to issue an emergency change to the regulations requiring pilots who had been cleared for approach to maintain the last assigned altitude until intercepting a portion of the published approach procedure.

About the same time, one of the major U.S. airlines gave its pilots a quiz on interpreting approach charts. The questions related to practical application of the charted procedure, and almost no one got them all right.

How can so much misunderstanding of approach charts exist in the pilot community? That little information sheet is as much a part of a professional pilot's life as a checklist or a flight plan.

The problem is that too many of us have lapsed into just picking off the two or three numbers we need and allowing ATC to guide us from there.

How, then, should a prudent pilot prepare himself for an arrival to an airport he has not frequented for some time, or perhaps never before? He must not only be able to smoothly make the transition from enroute navigation to approach and landing, but also be prepared for any eventuality that may arise to complicate his planning. The first possibility is that his weather will force a diversion to the alternate.

The alternate itself must be forecast to have either 600 and two or 800 and two, depending on the availability of a precision approach or a nonprecision approach. It's all there in FAR 91.83. But some airports have nonstandard alternate minimums, so be sure to check the back of the Jepp plate or the "takeoff and alternate" section of the NOS approach pages.

The takeoff requires careful study of the approach plate too. Finding the available accelerate/stop distance on the chart is basic, but what if you have an engine failure after takeoff? Is the weather good enough to make an approach and get back in? If not, can you make all the required climb gradients and MEAs to another airport where you can land? If you can't, a twin becomes twice as dangerous as a single-engine airplane.

Many airports have special takeoff procedures because of high terrain and these, like the alternate minimums, can be found on the back (airport diagram) side of the 11-1 Jepp chart or the takeoff and alternate pages of the NOS charts.

At Reno, for example, a climb of 350 feet per nautical mile to 8500 feet is required for departure from any runway. Three out of four directions require a turn to the north to avoid even worse climb problems because of the terrain in those directions.

All of this preflight planning is not just "nice to know" information. It's required by FAR 91.5 and includes "all available information concerning that flight." This catch-all regulation is almost as good as "careless and reckless" (91.9) in ensuring that your accident or incident was caused by illegal action on your part. The way to avoid an illegal action, of course, is to familiarize yourself sufficiently so that no incident occurs. FAR 91.0 ought to read, "No pilot shall crash while operating under this subpart."

But, enough of regulations. It is possible for a pilot to study all the available information and pick out that which is pertinent, not missing anything that will cause him to come to grief. The redundancy principle is applied throughout aviation just so a failure in one area or component will not result in disaster.

But experience has shown that failures can still occur in many areas for which there is no backup—save for a prudent pilot. Maintaining separation from terrain while on radar vectors off of published routes very definitely

131

requires pilot backup these days. Several cases of aircraft being vectored into terrain are on record.

Because this kind of accident almost always occurs in the terminal area, either arriving or departing, let's take a look at what a pilot can do to protect himself from this ATC error.

Instrument charts, both approach and en-route, are of very little value in protecting against the off-route vector into terrain. Minimum en-route or obstruction clearance altitudes only apply along the published route segment. MSAs (minimum safe altitudes) are only good to 25 miles from the facility.

The FAA has added a software package called Minimum Safe Altitude Warning (MSAW) to its automated terminal radars that is designed to warn a controller when an aircraft is getting too low for the terrain it is over or approaching. The controller is then supposed to warn the pilot. This system is not in place at terminals without ARTS III equipment, nor will it work if your aircraft does not have an altitude reporting transponder.

Communications are also necessary, even if the other conditions are met. Let's say you are on a vector toward higher terrain and have been asked to switch to another frequency. An error occurs in obtaining the new frequency and communications are lost.

But now where's the backup? That good old VFR standby, the sectional chart, can save the day for NOS users. Every latitude/longitude quadrant has a number printed on it that gives the elevation of the highest terrain contained therein. The newest Jeppesen area charts also show terrain and safe altitudes by lat/long quadrant.

There is a difference between the two altitude references given on sectionals and certain Jeppesen charts, however. While the sectional chart grid altitude depicts the elevation of the highest terrain included, the new Jeppesen charts with terrain contours show a grid MORA, or Minimum Off Route Altitude. This altitude provides terrain *and* obstruction clearance by at least 1000 feet. A pilot accustomed to this built-in buffer on the Jepps would be in trouble using a sectional chart.

Even when you know well the safe altitudes in the vicinity of an airport, there is still difficulty in keeping track of your exact position during off-route vectors. You have to know what section of the grid you are in for the altitude printed there to do you any good. This is difficult, but possible while in visual contact with the ground by using the sectional chart.

While on instruments and determining position by radio, however, it is impossible to always know your exact position with reference to a sectional chart and still perform other IFR duties. Area navigation equipment will be a big help if you have it. If not, your best hope lies with the charts and you should study them with that in mind.

Let's conjure up a couple of real situations and use them to play the

"What-If" game. The first will be a pilot flying a light twin in the further-ance of his own business. He uses the government's NOS charts and fre-quently flies single-pilot IFR. His home base is Memphis, Tennessee and today he's flying to Charleston, West Virginia. It is the first time he has flown to CRW.

There is no IFR area chart for Charleston, and the low-altitude en-route chart shows some very high MEAs to the south and east—one over 7000 feet. This is obviously an airport calling for a thorough audit of the ap-proach chart and any other data available to a man planning a trip into those mountains.

The process should begin with a look at the routine information found in the various data blocks on the chart. There's a south wind today, so the ILS to 23 is probable.

Check that missed approach right now so there won't be a mad scramble to find it if it should become necessary. According to the NOS chart, it's straight out to 1600 feet, then a right turn direct to the Charleston VORTAC while climbing to 3000 feet. Judging from the MEAs on the airways in and out of Charleston, over the VOR at 3000 feet looks like the safest place to go if there's engine trouble.

Now, what about obstructions? Judging by those MEAs in the vicinity, there must be some. Since our pilot is using NOS charts, he'll base his judgments on what's evident on the NOS ILS 23 chart reproduced here.

This approach looks like a tame one. It's apparently toward a river, perhaps into a river bottom, and no obstructions are shown along the final approach path except for one almost 400 feet above the airport elevation about three north of the touchdown zone.

But note those obstructions just to the south of the airport. The airport is at 982 feet, but almost in the departure path from 23 is a 1251-foot obstruction. That's 269 feet above airport elevation. Over to the east of that is an obstruction 313 feet above field elevation and across the river to the south is one 465 feet above the airport.

Notice how few tall obstructions there are farther out from the airport. Doesn't that seem strange for an airport that's apparently in a river bottom surrounded by high MEAs? And pay attention to how crooked that river and its tributaries are.

All that should make you suspect the airport does not, in fact, lie down by the riverside, as this NOS chart makes it appear.

You are so right. If your first approach to Charlie West is in IMC with the ceiling at about 400 feet and visibility a mile, you're going to get the thrill of a lifetime. You'll break out about a mile out over a deep river gorge and directly ahead you'll see a tall mountain.

The airport is on the top of that mountain. That river is *way* down in a canyon.

ILS RWY 23

Amdt 23

AL-852 (FAA)

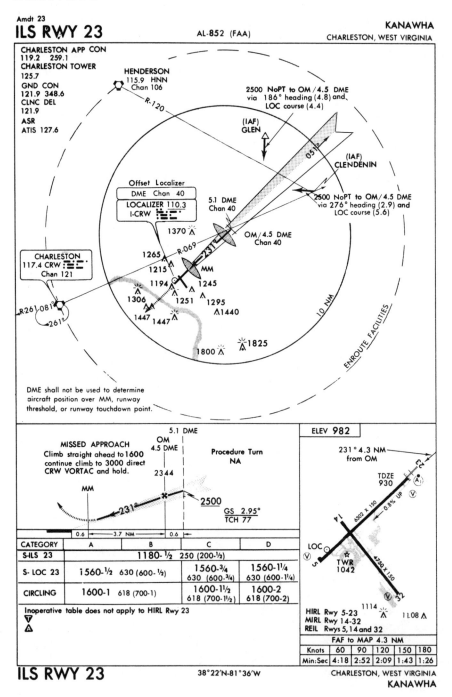

CHARLESTON APP CON
119.2   259.1
CHARLESTON TOWER
125.7
GND CON
121.9 348.6
CLNC DEL
121.9
ASR
ATIS 127.6

HENDERSON
115.9 HNN
Chan 106

R-120

2500 NoPT to OM/4.5 DME
via 186° heading (4.8) and
LOC course (4.4)

(IAF)
GLEN

(IAF)
CLENDENIN

051°

2500 NoPT to OM/4.5 DME
via 276° heading (2.9) and
LOC course (5.6)

Offset Localizer
DME Chan 40
LOCALIZER 110.3
I-CRW

5.1 DME
Chan 40

OM/4.5 DME
Chan 40

1370

R-069

231°

CHARLESTON
117.4 CRW
Chan 121

1265
1215
1194
1306
1447 1447

R-261 081°
261°

1245
MM
1251 1295
A1440

1800   1825

10 NM

ENROUTE FACILITIES

DME shall not be used to determine
aircraft position over MM, runway
threshold, or runway touchdown point.

MISSED APPROACH
Climb straight ahead to 1600
continue climb to 3000 direct
CRW VORTAC and hold.

5.1 DME
OM
4.5 DME

Procedure Turn
NA

2344

MM

231°

2500

GS 2.95°
TCH 77

0.6   3.7 NM   0.6

ELEV 982

231° 4.3 NM
from OM

TDZE
930

6302 X 150   0.8% UP

LOC

TWR
1042

4750 X 150

32

1114

1108

HIRL Rwy 5-23
MIRL Rwy 14-32
REIL Rwys 5,14 and 32

CATEGORY	A	B	C	D
S-ILS 23	1180-½ 250 (200-½)			
S- LOC 23	1560-½ 630 (600-½)		1560-¾ 630 (600-¾)	1560-1¼ 630 (600-1¼)
CIRCLING	1600-1 618 (700-1)		1600-1½ 618 (700-1½)	1600-2 618 (700-2)

Inoperative table does not apply to HIRL Rwy 23

FAF to MAP 4.3 NM					
Knots	60	90	120	150	180
Min:Sec	4:18	2:52	2:09	1:43	1:26

ILS RWY 23

38°22'N-81°36'W

In truth the NOS charts are deficient in cluing you into this. They show all obstructions with the same symbol, so that could be just a nest of antennas south of the airport. The Jepp chart, with much better detail, disabuses you of that thought. Most of those obstructions are granite. Others are tall granite with a short antenna on top. Furthermore, the Jepp chart shows several obstructions—one 370 feet above the touchdown zone —inside the marker and directly under the approach path.

Whichever charts you use, you should be thoroughly familiar with these characteristics and the way terrain features are presented so you can study them and draw a mental picture of the likely terrain around the airport.

With that mental picture in place, play the "What-If" game for each step of the approach. Consider, for example, what your course of action should be in event of an engine failure at any point in the approach or in the go-around procedure.

For this approach, once our light-twin pilot leaves 3000 (the MSA to the northeast which he learned by looking at the VOR chart of this airport) he'll certainly want to stay on the localizer while climbing back up to 3000 feet toward the northwest where the MSA is 3100. (MSAs—Minimum Safe Altitudes—are shown only for approaches based on an omni-directional facility, such as a VOR or NDB. So before beginning any approach always look for it on *all* the approach charts for that airport. If you're not sure what MSA means, now's a good time to refresh your memory.)

Of course, the pilot should have thought about where he must go with an engine out and low ceilings below. From Charleston the only way out in a light unsupercharged twin with an engine feathered is to the west. The MEAs in all other directions are perilously near the engine-out service ceilings of these aircraft.

Of those two broad areas of concern to pilots: terrain and weather, we have learned what we could from the instrument charts about the terrain at Charleston. Now look at the sectional chart for the area. How much more graphic it is in its portrayal of the mountains.

It is now much clearer what to expect. The mountains are more or less continuous in this area with fairly constant top heights and many valleys and ravines. Now it is clear that the airport itself is on top of a mountain that has been sliced off to provide a flat place. In fact, a study of the antenna heights indicates the river is about 300 feet *below* the airport. There is a peak worth keeping in mind just over half a mile from the approach end of Runway 23. Better not be low on that glideslope.

If you need extra ground clearance, and if you have ground contact, it's best to drop down over the river westbound. The city of Charleston is right along the river southwest of the airport, and, as this arrival will be at night, the lights may help in locating the field—weather permitting.

The sectional chart has thus provided more feel for the area than the instrument charts alone. This information will aid in anticipating the landing conditions, and greatly ease the decision making should anything unpleasant arise.

The bare procedures provided by the SIAPs do not provide all the background necessary to obtain that comforting feel of familiarity with an area. The NOS has asked for comment on a combination sectional/instrument chart it designed to provide just this kind of enhanced understanding of the area being flown into IFR.

All this has been part of planning for the flight. We're en route now, about 60 miles away cruising at 7000 feet on V115 coming up from Whitesburg VORTAC. Now's the time to get out all the Kanawha plates so you'll be ready. First check the ATIS frequency, 127.6, and get the weather, approach in use and any pertinent NOTAMs.

The frequency corner of the ILS 23 chart shows there is an approach control, and the ASR, of course, means that they have radar.

The final approach course intercept will most likely be by radar vector. As you discovered earlier from the VOR approach chart, the area northeast of the airport has an MSA of 3000 feet MSL; to the southeast it's 3900. Since the glideslope intercept altitude is 2500 feet, you should confirm with the controller all altitude assignments below those MSAs, as appropriate.

Flying up to the ILS final, the number 1 nav is tuned to the localizer, the glideslope and marker switches are turned on. Note that there's also collocated DME and the localizer is off set.

Checking the airport box in the lower right corner, we see the runway has a U.S. Standard HIRL approach light system.

(The latest Jepp plate shows it also has VASI and that's important on this runway because the 0.8 percent upslope gives an illusion of being high when you're not. A duck under to make it "look right" can be very dangerous indeed. The latest Jepp chart also shows that you're *supposed* to cross the threshold 77 feet in the air, not the normal 50 feet—see the "TCH 77" in the profile view.)

The decision height is 1180 feet on the altimeter, provided all ILS components are working and being received. If you lose the glideslope, three-quarters of a mile visibility is needed to make the approach and the minimum descent altitude will be 1560 feet MSL.

Now let's look at another example, this one an approach into Washington National Airport using the NOS chart for the LDA Runway 18 approach.

LDA stands for Localizer Directional Aid, and in this case it's just like an ILS except that it doesn't lead to a low visibility touchdown straight in to a runway.

A quick check of visual charts shows terrain is not a problem around Washington, but obstructions are. On this approach chart, notice that two antennas over a thousand feet MSL in height are depicted just to the left

Amdt 7

LDA RWY 18

AL-443 (FAA)

WASHINGTON NATIONAL
WASHINGTON, D.C.

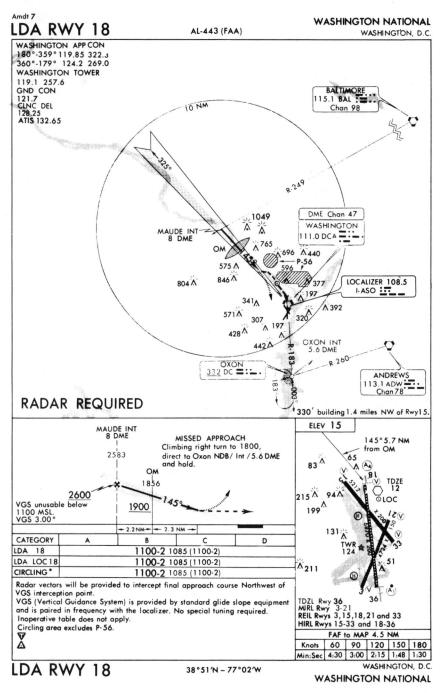

WASHINGTON APP CON
180°-359° 119.85 322.3
360°-179° 124.2 269.0
WASHINGTON TOWER
119.1 257.6
GND CON
121.7
CLNC DEL
128.25
ATIS 132.65

10 NM

325°

R-249

BALTIMORE
115.1 BAL
Chan 98

DME Chan 47
WASHINGTON
111.0 DCA

1049
MAUDE INT
8 DME
OM
765
696 A 440
P-56
575 596
804 846 377
197
LOCALIZER 108.5
I-ASO

341
571 307
320 A 392
428 197
442
OXON INT
5.6 DME
R-183
R-260

OXON
332 DC
183 003°

ANDREWS
113.1 ADW
Chan 78

RADAR REQUIRED

330' building 1.4 miles NW of Rwy15.

MAUDE INT
8 DME

2583

MISSED APPROACH
Climbing right turn to 1800,
direct to Oxon NDB/ Int /5.6 DME
and hold.

OM
1856

2600
VGS unusable below
1100 MSL.
VGS 3.00°

1900 145°

← 2.2NM → ← 2.3 NM →

CATEGORY	A	B	C	D
LDA 18		1100-2 1085 (1100-2)		
LDA LOC 18		1100-2 1085 (1100-2)		
CIRCLING*		1100-2 1085 (1100-2)		

Radar vectors will be provided to intercept final approach course Northwest of
VGS interception point.
VGS (Vertical Guidance System) is provided by standard glide slope equipment
and is paired in frequency with the localizer. No special tuning required.
Inoperative table does not apply.
Circling area excludes P-56.

ELEV 15

145° 5.7 NM
from OM

83
65
A₄
TDZE
12
LOC
215 94
199

131
TWR
124
211 51

TDZL Rwy 36
MIRL Rwy 3-21
REIL Rwys 3,15,18,21 and 33
HIRL Rwys 15-33 and 18-36

FAF to MAP 4.5 NM					
Knots	60	90	120	150	180
Min:Sec	4:30	3:00	2:15	1:48	1:30

LDA RWY 18

38°51'N – 77°02'W

WASHINGTON, D.C.
WASHINGTON NATIONAL

137

of the final approach course. The Capitol prohibited areas are also on the left, so it's wise to favor the right side of the localizer.

No MSAs are shown on this chart, but turn to the VOR and NDB approach charts and you'll find that 2300 is safe in all quadrants. Too bad the DME is on the DCA VORTAC. Anyway, the VGS (Vertical Guidance System, which is simply a glideslope) is to be intercepted at 2600 feet, so MSA is no problem.

But this particular approach shows the lengths officialdom has gone toward public appeasement. Notice that the decision height, MDA and circling altitudes are all the same 1100 feet. This allows a pilot to break off the LDA and follow the river for noise-abatement purposes, as the dashed line indicates. A lead-in light (LDIN) is placed under the Arlington Memorial Bridge to help keep the river in sight (that's the meaning of the circle-and-dot symbol on the dashed line near P-56) and a medium intensity approach light system and VASI light the end of Runway 18 to help in the visual transition to landing while making the 45-degree turn during the last 300 feet of descent to the runway.

Only two miles' visibility is required for this approach, but if that's all you have, watch out. You won't be able to see the approach end of the runway at the missed approach point because a simple trigonometry calculation will disclose that at 1100 feet on the three degree VGS you're still 3.5 nm from the airport. FAR 91.117(b) requires that you remain at 1100 feet (the MDA) until something identifiable with the end of that runway is clearly visible to the pilot.

The Memorial Bridge won't do. If, at two miles out you do see the runway, you have to lose 550 feet per mile to get down to the normal touchdown zone. That's about a 5.25 degree descent all the way down to impact.

That same regulation, 91.117(b), also requires that you remain at 1100 feet on this approach unless you are "in a position from which a normal approach to the runway of intended landing can be made." Is 5.25 degrees a normal approach? When the visibility is at minimums, that's what is required, and two miles is given as "legal" minimums for all approach categories on this approach.

In order to avoid being suckered into this trap, take the visibility (two miles in this instance) and divide it into the MDA height above the airport (1087 feet for DCA). If the answer is more than 300, watch out because you're set up for more than a 3.25 degree descent. This should be checked on any nonprecision approach since virtually all of them suffer this deficiency.

The Visual Descent Point concept is based on this deficiency. Slowly the FAA is to establish a DME or fan marker fix at the point from which a three degree descent from the MDA will contact the normal touchdown zone.

This is identified by a V in the profile view on the chart. Where these exist, do not start down from the MDA until you pass this point, even if the runway is visible. But if you fly past it and still can't see the runway, better get set for a missed approach.

In summary, then, before going into a strange airport always study the approach and sectional charts to get that mental picture of the lay of the land. Always consider the "outs" as you mentally trace the path from each position along the approach to touchdown, and don't be dismayed by the cornucopic information portrayed on the charts.

If you follow your expected path to the airport in this way, checking course and altitude every step, the right questions to ask will suggest themselves, and the answers will begin to pop right out of the page for you.

Arrival Options

18

by Dan Manningham

One pilot had a stock answer for the tower when they cleared him to land. "Oooh" he'd say, keying the mike, "that's the part I hate." He didn't really hate landings at all, but if he were still flying, he might approach them with less enthusiasm in light of the tangled options that now govern the final approach.

Basically, the pilot of an IFR flight will receive one of four possible clearances in the terminal area. He may complete his IFR flight plan. He may cancel IFR and continue VFR. Or he may accept a visual or contact approach. In each case, his authority and responsibility are different.

The IFR Arrival. In most cases, when you fly an IFR trip, it will be terminated by a routine instrument approach and landing. When weather conditions are at or above one statute mile, you may request or be offered an option. When weather conditions are VFR, you can cancel the IFR flight plan and navigate visually. That step often saves a minute or two, but in so doing, you have accepted what would otherwise be ATC's responsibility for traffic separation. Not too bad a trade-off at smaller airports, but a poor compromise at busier terminals.

The Visual Approach. Far more common is the visual approach, which may be issued by ATC to arriving IFR traffic when the ceiling is at least 500 feet above minimum vectoring altitude and the visibility at least three miles. The visual approach is, in effect, a tactic for reducing controller workload and integrating IFR and VFR arrivals. For the pilot, it offers some compromise between safety and efficiency.

ATC defines a visual approach as "an approach wherein an aircraft on an IFR flight plan, operating in VFR conditions and having received an air traffic control authorization, may deviate from the prescribed instrument approach procedure and proceed to the airport of destination by visual reference to the surface." They should add "or by visual reference to a preceding aircraft."

When ceiling and visibility allow, ATC can vector you to the airport area, instead of the final approach course, and then clear you for "the visual" when you have the airport and/or any preceding IFR traffic in sight. When following another IFR flight, you can be cleared for "the visual" if you have only that airplane in sight and the tower is informed of your position by the approach controller. It's easy on the controllers, but it can be a dubious clearance and you are not required to accept it.

When the visibility is three miles at the airport, it may be markedly less at your position five or 10 miles away. In fact, it is not uncommon to be cleared for a visual at some substantial distance from the airport on the strength of having reported the preceding airplane in sight. I'm surely not the only pilot who has been cleared to follow some barely distinguishable traffic through 15 miles of murk to the runway. It's formation flying at its worst, and the problem is best solved by simply saying no.

Then there is the opposite problem of accepting a visual when the field is in sight 40 miles away. In that instance, the navigation is simple, assuming you have the right field in sight. The problem is that in accepting the 40-mile visual, you also inherit responsibility for traffic separation as you slice through a deep altitude structure under conditions conducive to heavy VFR traffic. When you do accept that long visual, ask for radar traffic advisories or actual separation. Then you have the best of both worlds.

Charted visual approaches, such as those found at SFO, DCA and LGA, are even worse. They have no legal standing despite the official appearance of the actual approach page. They are local procedures, designed by gentleman's agreement, and do not conform to FAR Part 97 requirements.

The very concept of a visual approach is a hybrid. It allows IFR traffic to operate by visual flight rules. It allows instrument traffic to follow other aircraft in a tenuous, daisy-chain formation through marginal visibility. And it seriously blurs the lines of authority and responsibility between pilot and controller.

The Contact Approach. Less common is the contact approach, which the FAA defines as "an approach wherein an aircraft on an IFR flight plan, operating clear of clouds with at least one-mile flight visibility and having received an air traffic control authorization, may deviate from the prescribed instrument approach procedure and proceed to the airport of destination by visual reference to the surface."

The contact approach has limited value for several reasons. You must have at least one-mile visibility and be clear of all clouds. You must have ATC separation from all other aircraft, and you, as pilot-in-command, must specifically request a contact approach. The contact approach does have some limited value in the instance of circling approaches, although neither pilot nor controller really benefits from this rare clearance.

One more note on IFR terminations. If you operate under FAR Part 91, you, as pilot-in-command, always have the authority to begin the approach, regardless of the reported weather. If things look bad at DH or MDA, you simply fly the pull-up procedure and make some other plans. If you switch, or alternate, to an FAR Part 135.2 operation, you must satisfy FAR 121.651. That regulation requires that reported weather be above the approach minimums before you begin the approach. Then, if visibility falls below the minimum, you may continue the approach to the prescribed limit if you are inside the OM on an ILS, or have reached MDA on a non-precision approach, or have been switched to the final controller on a PAR.

Terminal arrivals are somewhat more complex today, but the root problem is command authority. Last fall the approach controller at San Jose, California, called the tower to confirm my report of a stratus layer over the field. The tower, surprised to learn the clouds were really there, cancelled the "visual approach" offer and vectored us for a routine ILS.

There are lots of options. Just don't be afraid to insist on your own first choice.

The Approach and Landing   19

by A. Howard Hasbrook

Almost 50 percent of air carrier, business and personal flying accidents occur during approach and landing—*a phase of flight that involves less than two percent of the total flight time.* Obviously then, the approach and landing comprise a hazardous operation that should justify a more thorough human-factors research effort if this disproportionate accident rate is to be modified.

Statistical studies have shown some interesting facts: about 35 percent of air carrier approach accidents have occurred in VFR weather; night approach accidents have been three to four times more prevalent than daytime approach accidents; many nighttime accidents (including 17 percent in one study group of jet air carrier accidents) involved visual approaches over unlighted terrain or over water toward well lighted cities and/or airports.

In many of the VFR approach accidents in which one or more of the crewmembers survived, the pilots involved stated they had the runway in sight and thought their aircraft were on normal, safe approach paths. In some cases, the aircraft struck intervening terrain that was some distance from, but only slightly higher than, the runway. In other cases, the aircraft descended into terrain or water at altitudes well below those of the runways.

From these dreary facts, it appears that pilot perception of the approach path is often seriously in error. Whether such error is due to a lack of needed visual cues (particularly at night), visual illusions, lack of knowledge of available cues, potential error-producing visual concepts or a combination of these, is a question that has been studied many times, but still awaits an answer.

Obviously, there are more visual cues available during a daytime VFR approach than at night, but few pilots seem to be able to describe approach cues in a definitive manner. In fact, many professionals we've talked with have only been able to verbalize their landing approach techniques with such generalities as, "I know the approach is okay when it looks right," or, "It feels right," or, "It looks like I'm in the slot."

However, some scientists and a few pilots have described certain visual phenomena that relate to judging the degree of "correctness" of a visual approach. The perspective (that is, the apparent convergence) of the long sides of the runway trapezoid has been mentioned most often, but the value of this cue is open to question if one considers the thousands of safe landings made on mile-square Army Air Corps turf fields and large circular Navy concrete "decks" during World War II flight training.

"Streamer effect"—the phenomenon of nearby objects and terrain appearing to stream by, as seen in the pilot's peripheral vision—has been suggested as a useful cue in estimating change in altitude (the lower you are, the faster the "streaming" effect). Also, changes in the size of houses, buildings, trees, highline poles, hangars, automobiles, aircraft (on the ground) and other familiar objects may be useful in roughly estimating altitude and vertical descent rates.

Another cue that seems to be important is the outward "expansion" of the terrain and runway surface surrounding the *flight path interception point* (FPIP). (See Figure 1.) Included in this visual phenomenon is the cue the author uses to detect and maintain the desired flight path toward the FPIP; that is, visually acquiring and observing the area (overlying the

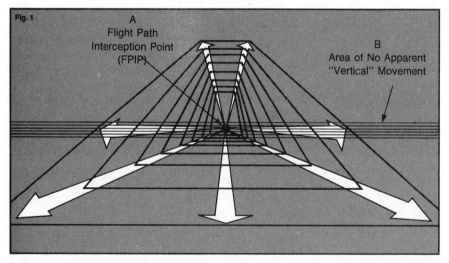

During a straight-line (linear) approach, the trapezoidal runway outlines grow progressively larger in a uniform manner, while the runway surface and nearby terrain move outward (arrows) from the flight path interception point (A). Many pilots use the "no vertical movement" area (B) to identify the flight path interception point (FPIP).

144

FPIP) where no apparent vertical movement occurs in the runway and adjacent terrain.

Other useful cues may include: the diminishing vertical distance between the horizon and the far end of the runway; movement of the intended touchdown point away from the aircraft (indicating an undershoot condition in certain circumstances) or toward and under the aircraft (overshooting); "tilt" of the runway (for lateral alignment of the aircraft's flight path); the vertical angle between the pilot's eyes and the runway surface (Figure 2); and, finally, the expanding shape of the runway.

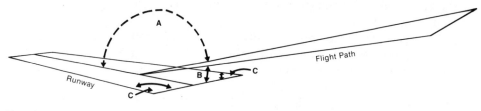

Figure 2

Some pilots say they estimate their flight path angle by evaluating the large angle at "A." Others use the small angle at "B." The latter seems to be the better of the two because restricted visibility would make it difficult, if not impossible, to estimate angle "A" with any degree of accuracy. It is probable that use of angle "B" in combination with the horizontal corner angles at "C" permits the most accurate judgment of the approach angle.

Unfortunately, many of these cues are either subject to illusionary effects during poor visibility conditions or are nonexistent at night. Haze, snow, smoke, mist, patches of fog, rain on the windshield and restricted runway visibility can make the pilot think he is higher than he really is. This, in turn, may induce him to pitch his aircraft down a few degrees and hit short of the runway. Visual loss of the real horizon, or even loss of only the far end of the runway, may also cause the pilot to "depress" the imagined horizon below its actual position and then pitch his aircraft down a like amount.

Estimates of approach path altitude and the point of probable touchdown at any given moment may also be adversely affected at night by the brightness of runway lighting; a runway with bright lights appears closer than one with dim lights. Clear air (still found in some relatively unpolluted areas of the western United States) can make the runway seem closer than it really is. Also, differences in runway dimensions (particularly width) can produce large errors in estimates of altitude and distance to threshold: wide runways may make a pilot think he's lower and closer than he is; conversely, a long, narrow runway can appear to be much farther away than it really is. Also, lack of contrast (as with a snow-covered airport) can produce anxious moments during the final seconds of flare and touchdown.

Worth mentioning are the illusionary effects of upslope and downslope runways. Flying toward an upward-sloping runway (far end higher than the threshold) can cause a pilot to fly a dangerously low approach—particularly at night. On the other hand, a downward sloping runway can result in a steep approach, excessive airspeed and touchdown too far down the runway. Even when an approach is initiated at the proper altitude and distance from the airport by the use of appropriate instruments and navigational equipment, sloping runways can still cause some degree of visual confusion.

Because of the problems associated with accurately assessing and maintaining a proper approach path by the visual cues outlined above, many pilots utilize a technique that works in certain, though limited, circumstances. However, it can, in other circumstances, result in crashes short of the runway. This is called the "gun-sight" approach method, which involves flying the airplane so the pilot's eyes and an appropriate point on the windshield or "aiming index" are kept lined up with the point of intended touchdown on the runway.

Apparently this technique is commonly used, particularly among air carrier pilots. As an article in an airline pilot magazine states, "the PIP (projected impact point) is seen approximately three inches above the bottom of the windshield. Without necessarily being fully aware that he does so, the experienced pilot comes to use this section of the windshield much as a marksman uses the front sight of a rifle. In general, it designates *with remarkable accuracy* the point toward which the aircraft is moving." (Emphasis ours.) Further on, the article also states, "On a dark night, it is more difficult to derive vertical guidance from the natural visual cues ... still, pilots can nearly always maintain an acceptable descent path by keeping the approximate target area in the aiming section of the windshield."

This "gun-sight" method will only work as intended if the air is smooth, there is no wind shear, there are no inadvertent pitch changes nor subconscious vertical movements of the pilot's head (and eyes) relative to the windshield aiming index, the aircraft is flown by the numbers in a steady-state condition, the approach has been initiated from the proper point in space and frequent attention is paid to the altimeter and vertical speed indicator throughout the approach. *It will not, by itself, provide accurate cues as to the angle of the flight path being flown.*

The fact that many pilots use this method has been verified by questioning numerous professional pilots. Several airline pilots have also stated they adjust their seat height so the "aiming index point" is only about ½

146

inch above the bottom edge of the windshield: "If the target area disappears below the windshield, we're overshooting."

Unfortunately, slight, subconscious vertical movement of the head (from stretching or leaning forward) can produce a nonexistent but apparent "movement" of the runway target area. As shown in Figure 3, only a one-inch vertical displacement of the eyeballs relative to the windshield aiming index can seem to move the runway target area several thousand feet. This can produce a pilot-induced (but unnecessary) pitch change to compensate for a supposed flight path error. This unnecessary pitch change may then produce a real—but unnoticed—flight path error of relatively large magnitude. If the pitch change is downward, vertical speed can increase substantially and may go unnoticed due to the pilot's visual concentration on the runway scene. If he continues to "gun-sight" his windshield index point on the runway target area, he can easily descend to a danger-

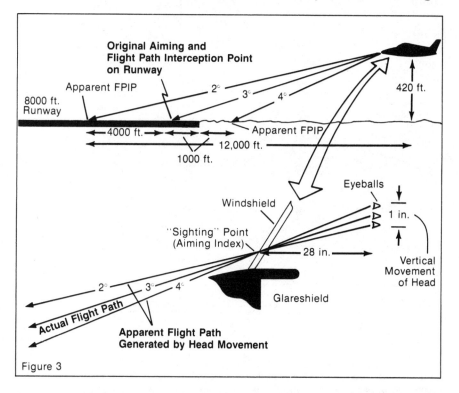

Figure 3

Use of a sighting point (aiming index) on the windshield can cause large errors in the apparent location of the aiming and flight path interception point (FPIP) on the runway if the pilot's eye level is inadvertently changed slightly, or the aircraft is pitched up or down a few degrees. Such errors can result in unneeded, or unwanted, vertical speed and flight path changes, with subsequent under- or overshooting.

ously low altitude and strike terrain short of the runway. (See Figure 4A.)

If altitude and vertical speed are not monitored almost constantly during the approach, a pilot's only means of determining the straightness of his flight path is by "visually remembering" what the runway outline should look like as the approach progresses. The runway outline will expand in a uniform trapezoidal manner if the flight path is straight; if it's non-linear, the runway outline will change in an irregular fashion (B and C, Figure 4). Another easily distinguishable cue is whether the vertical distance between the far end of the runway and the threshold increases or decreases as the aircraft approaches the runway (Arrows, Figure 4).

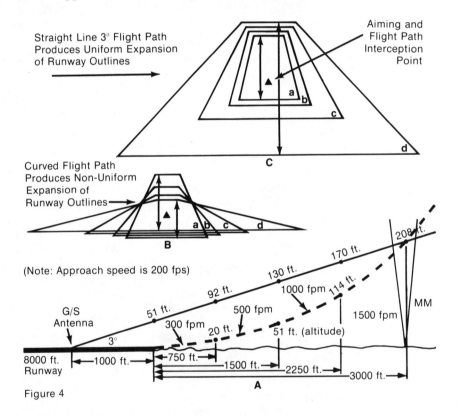

Figure 4

If vertical speed is excessive during descent in the middle marker area, the aircraft may descend to a dangerously low altitude (A) in less than 10 seconds unless cockpit instrument information and the runway pattern cues shown at B and C are used. Irregular expansion of the runway (B), with the threshold appearing to stay at the same distance and at the same altitude, warns of a low, downward-arcing flight path. Conversely, uniform expansion of the runway, with the threshold moving down and toward the aircraft is an indication of a more linear (straight) approach. Another cue to flight path linearity is the apparent expansion or contraction of the vertical distance between the ends of the runway (arrows).

148

THE APPROACH AND LANDING

A preliminary laboratory study of professional pilot estimates of flight path angle (using only computer-generated runway outlines) showed a wide variation in judgment. Most of the pilots judged the flight paths to be much steeper than they actually were. Runway outlines corresponding to five-degree flight path angles resulted in estimates of 10- to 15-degree flight paths. Normal, three-degree paths were judged by most of the pilots to be five to 10 degrees in steepness. Surprisingly, many pilots thought the runway outlines produced by flat (one-half-degree and one-degree) flight paths were indications of flying three- or four-degree approaches. It would seem this tendency for pilots to misjudge their flight paths on the high side could be a major factor in approach accidents at night.

When the runway outline is cut off by poor visibility, one's ability to visualize the runway's vertical dimension and therefore to accurately judge the flight path angle and linearity is further degraded or, in very poor conditions, cut off entirely. Just a slight variation in slant visibility can

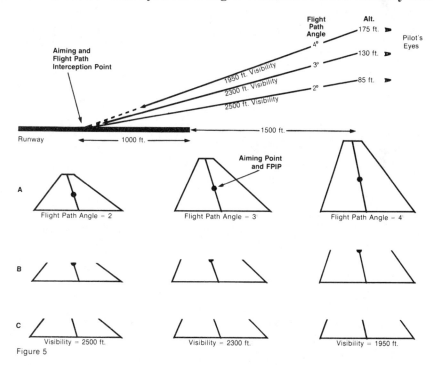

Figure 5

When the entire runway (A) can be seen during the approach, judgment of flight path angle and linearity will be more accurate than when visibility extends only to the flight path interception point (B). Various combinations of visibility and flight path angles. (C) can make it even more difficult for the pilot to determine, in the little time available, if he's on the correct flight path. In these illustrations, the aircraft is slightly left of the centerline, as indicated by the "tilt" of the runway to the left, which further complicates the pilot's judgment.

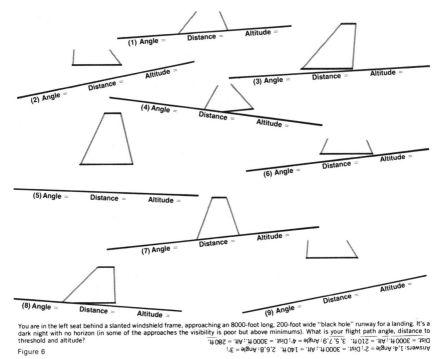

You are in the left seat behind a slanted windshield frame, approaching an 8000-foot long, 200-foot wide "black hole" runway for a landing. It's a dark night with no horizon (in some of the approaches the visibility is poor but above minimums). What is your flight path angle, distance to threshold and altitude?

Answers: 1,4; Angle = 2°; Dist. = 3000 ft.; Alt. = 140 ft. 2,6,8; Angle = 3°; Dist. = 3000 ft.; Alt. = 210 ft. 3, 5, 7,9; Angle = 4°; Dist. = 3000 ft.; Alt. = 280 ft.

Figure 6

make the visible portions of three different runway outlines (generated by three different flight path angles) appear almost identical (Figure 5). Also, too low an eye height in the cockpit can cause the pilot to lose sight of the threshold area too soon.

The runway outlines in Figure 6 show how a runway might appear to a pilot somewhere between the threshold and the middle marker; in some of the examples, restricted but "above minimums" visibility obscures a portion of the runway; variations in aircraft pitch angle and/or in eye height relative to the slanted edge of the windshield are also used in the illustrations to demonstrate the visual affect of restricting the pilot's view of the runway threshold. The reader may test his ability to estimate flight path angles, altitudes and distance to the threshold by looking at these computer-derived runway outlines at a 12-inch (eye-to-page) reading distance. Since the approach speed is 120 knots (200 feet per second), there isn't much time to come up with the answers.

These illustrations serve to emphasize the fact that visual illusions do occur, and they're more apt to happen (and to cause accidents) if the pilot isn't aware of them and doesn't know how to compensate for such illusions.

THE APPROACH AND LANDING

Since only a few degrees of pitchdown during an approach at 200 feet per second can increase the rate of descent dramatically, the nose should not be pushed down unless it's really necessary. If more airspeed is needed, more thrust should be added. (It's always easier and safer to go around than it is to drag the gear through the trees.) Also, it should be kept in mind that the less maneuvering done during the last 20 seconds of the approach, the better the chance of making a good, smooth touchdown on the 1000-foot mark. So the approach should be flown in a stabilized condition during the last mile, and preferably for the last three or four miles, if you're flying a light to medium jet.

Interestingly, many pilots seem to intentionally fly an unstabilized, downward-arcing approach utilizing an initial, excessive vertical speed along with a gradual but constant reduction in airspeed and thrust. The result? The three variables of airspeed, vertical speed and pitch angle interact to confuse the pilot's visual evaluation of his constantly changing flight path and the hoped-for touchdown point.

A stabilized (straight-line) approach, with constant airspeed, vertical speed and pitch angle, gives the pilot an added dividend; it gives him *emotionally unpressured time* to evaluate his progress and make any small flight path corrections that may be necessary. Such an approach also allows the pilot to stay far enough ahead of his airplane to take better care of unforeseen situations, such as wind shear more severe than expected. It also allows him more time to evaluate available visual cues and to monitor the altimeter.

Prior to any approach, VFR or IFR, a wise pilot will double-check the DH or MDA, and just as importantly, he'll compute and memorize the 50-foot threshold altitude. He will never go below the 50-foot minimum, regardless of how good the runway looks, until he's crossed the threshold—unless it's an absolute necessity or an emergency.

Aside from knowing about the visual cues and illusions that relate to landing approaches, an additional requirement for longevity in flying is a fair amount of humility. If things don't look right, "going around" and getting back up where there's time—and altitude—to think things out is a wise move. This is particularly true if visibility conditions are worse than expected or excessively strong wind shears are encountered.

It's also desirable to keep in mind that if there's going to be an accident —and they do happen—it's better to skid off the far end of the runway at 20 knots than to hit short at 120 knots. One is an expensive embarrassment, the other's a catastrophe.

In summary, it's evident that many approach accidents could be prevented if more pilots would:

· Remain visually and intellectually alert to, and prepared for, potential illusionary effects during nighttime and low-visibility approaches.

· Realize the limitations and hazards involved in trying to use the "gunsight" (windshield aiming) method to determine the probable touchdown point and flight path linearity.

· Learn to see and use the "no vertical movement" cue for accurately determining the glidepath interception point on the runway.

· Remain alert to, and compensate for, the tendency to fly nighttime and low-visibility approaches at too flat an angle and too low an altitude.

· Fly a stabilized, straight-line approach, aided by use of terrain and runway "expansion" cues.

· Monitor altitude, vertical speed and airspeed instrument readings as often as possible during the last 60 seconds of the approach.

· Double-check the DH and MDA altitudes *well prior* to the approach.

· Determine and use a 50-foot minimum threshold altitude.

· Resist the desire to pitch down and duck under in response to visual illusions created by visibility conditions.

· Abort the approach and go around if things don't look quite right.

Hopefully, use of these suggestions will cut down on premature terrain contact and make all your landings a piece of cake.

The Low Visibility Approach

by Bill Cotton

Nearing the end of a long day, the crew of the jet airliner discovered the weather at their final destination, Atlanta, was just above Category II minimums. The captain decided on a coupled ILS approach.

During the initial stage of the approach, the captain noticed a slight porpoising in pitch. He was unable to determine whether the culprit was the autopilot itself or the ILS glideslope, but the oscillations didn't seem serious enough to justify a disconnect. The tower reported an RVR of 1,200 feet as the aircraft passed the outer marker inbound, and at 225 feet the first officer announced that the runway lights were in sight. Immediately thereafter, the aircraft began to descend rapidly.

Five seconds later both pilots were horrified to observe the approach lights moving rapidly toward the top of the windshield. The captain initiated an emergency pull-up and the wheels struck a series of frangible approach lights, blowing the tires. Nonetheless, he managed to land on the runway.

The official probable cause of the incident was "an unexpected and undetected divergence of the aircraft from the glideslope centerline induced by a malfunction of the automatic pilot. This divergence occurred at an altitude from which a safe recovery could have been made. However, both the pilot and the first officer were preoccupied at the time with establishing outside visual reference under conditions which precluded adequate altitude assessment from external clues. Consequently the pilot did not recognize the divergence from the glideslope in time to avoid contact with the approach lights."

Short or hard landings after ILS approaches are all too common these days, and business aircraft are not immune. An analysis has been made of 233 general aviation weather accidents that occurred from 1973 through 1975. Of those, 164 were related to low visibility, and a disturbingly large number involved instrument-rated pilots crashing after an approach in IMC conditions. For example:

· "During a night IFR approach the pilot apparently diverted his attention from the operation of the aircraft and became spatially disoriented. The aircraft was landed in water short of the runway."

· "The pilot descended below decision height and was not lined up with the runway. There was a delay in initiating a go-around and the aircraft hit the glideslope antenna, breaking off three feet of wing. The aircraft then hit a warehouse 5,800 feet from the initial point of impact."

The problem is one of inaccurate vertical guidance during the visual (see-to-land) portion of the approach. Civil accidents statistics indicate, and Air Force and NASA studies confirm, that during low-visibility conditions, outside visual cues are inadequate to correctly assess the descent angle and rate. Wind shear or a visual illusion has often led to disaster. By the time an abnormally low altitude or high sink rate is recognized, it is often too late to recover from it.

There have been a few cases in which wind shear was so severe that the aircraft was incapable of climbing out of it. But usually an earlier recognition of the loss of airspeed or deviation from the glideslope by the pilot would have prevented the accident.

FAR 91.117 (b) states, "No person may operate an aircraft below the prescribed minimum descent altitude or continue an approach below the decision height unless:

"(1) The aircraft is in a position from which a normal approach to the runway of intended landing can be made; and

"(2) The approach threshold of that runway, or approach lights or other markings identifiable with the approach end of that runway, are clearly visible to the pilot."

Those criteria are of questionable value because, for instance, at a decision height of 200 feet with a visibility of 1,800 RVR (an approved minimum), the farthest point ahead of the aircraft that can be seen is an approach light 3,000 feet *short* of the touchdown point and 2,000 feet short of the runway threshold!

The NTSB notes in a 1976 safety recommendation on low-visibility landing accidents (A-76-122-128) that "almost every mishap occurred after the flight crew had seen either the ground, the airport or the runway environment . . ." So while it is legal to continue descent without enough visibility to do it safely, any resulting incident is probably the pilot's fault because he must not have been "in a position from which a normal approach to the runway of intended landing could be made."

Often, the visual illusions created by reduced visibility make the problem even worse when that visibility is somewhat above the legal landing minimum; better visibility encourages an earlier transition to visual cues, which can be misleading.

154

Some of the causes of visual illusions are rain on the windshield, scud near the runway threshold, runway appearance, absence of surface lights in the approach zone and a crabbed attitude due to crosswind.

A runway that slopes up in the landing direction creates the illusion of being too high when it is viewed from the proper glideslope. So does one that is especially narrow. In either case, the pilot is tempted to "correct" by increasing the rate of descent. If the runway is extra wide, it appears you are lower than you are.

The "black hole" approach is familiar to many pilots who make night approaches from over the ocean or unpopulated terrain. In the absence of a VASI or electronic glideslope, it's extremely difficult to judge the proper descent angle from the perspective of the runway edge lights alone. A pilot who has made the transition to visual conditions after an ILS approach is in the same boat; few runways in this country are equipped with both ILS and VASI.

The illusion caused by crabbing into crosswinds is treacherous because it varies in degree from one aircraft type to another and appears differently from each of the crew seats. If the windshield panel slopes down from right to left in the pilot's view, the first sighting of the approach lights will give the impression of being too high in a left crosswind and too low in a right crosswind (see Figure 1).

If there are two different flap settings used for landing, use of the lesser one will result in a more nose-up attitude on the approach. The first visual sightings then will appear lower in the windshield and tempt the pilot to push the nose down to achieve a more "normal" picture.

In addition, any crab angle being held for the crosswind will momentarily present a false picture of the ground track of the airplane. Seeing the approach lights angled off to his right, for example, a pilot may correct by turning right only to find he needs an immediate correction back to the left to keep from overshooting the right side of the touchdown zone. Couple any of these visual illusions with the problem of a short or wet runway, and the potential hazards of the low-visibility landing obviously increase.

There have been various attempts over the years to design approach lights that contain height as well as runway alignment information. One such design under consideration by the FAA is called "FAME." FAME, which the FAA is currently testing at NAFEC (Atlantic City), uses a transponder interrogator situated so that it looks up the glideslope to determine whether an aircraft is on, above or below the proper slope. It then turns on colored lights in the approach lighting system—green for "on glideslope," red for too low and yellow for too high. The lights are flashed at an increasing rate for increased deviation from the glideslope.

The single pilot flying an ILS approach in IMC is under particular pressure because he must continue to scan inside the aircraft and out until the

Figure 1   **View Out Captain's Windshield**

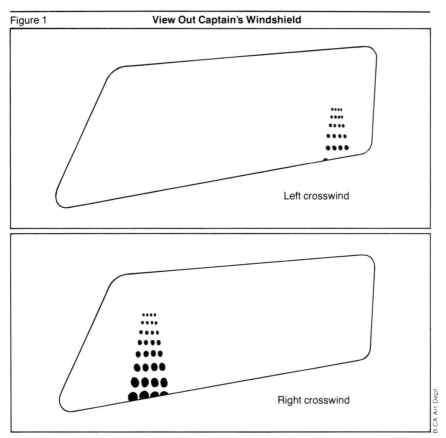

Both views are at the same height above the approach lights, but the left crosswind situation is likely to prompt the pilot to push the nose down.

touchdown zone is clearly in view. After the age of 40, the eye's ability to change its focal distance begins to deteriorate. Even with normal vision focusing can take more than three seconds each time the view is shifted from in to out to back in again. Three seconds can be a long time on a low approach in bad weather. A pilot who has this handicap will sometimes subconsciously decrease shifting his focus because a fuzzy picture during flight below decision height is quite uncomfortable. The safety-minded single pilot who is over 40 will make the go/no-go decision based upon a view of the *touchdown zone* at decision height instead of just the approach lights, as the regulations allow. Having the runway clearly in sight provides a safety margin; the pilot will not have to shift his eyes in and out of the aircraft (and thus refocus) as often.

When two pilots are flying, different techniques can increase both the safety of the approach and the chance that a landing will be made instead of a go-around. Most airlines and corporate operations have adopted a system of altitude callouts to be made by the pilot not doing the flying. Some operators prescribe a call at 1,000 feet above touchdown and another at 500 feet along with the announcement "instruments crosscheck," meaning that no discrepancies exist between the captain's and the copilot's instruments. From there on down, any significant deviations from the localizer, the glideslope or the bug speed are called to the attention of the pilot flying the approach. This is a form of monitoring the approach.

A few operators use a third barometric altimeter adjusted to read zero on the ground (QFE in International Civil Aviation Organization terminology) to discourage altitude errors.

But what the monitored approach does not do is help the pilot flying to make control inputs after he goes to visual flight cues. The monitoring pilot can only call deviations to his attention after they exceed a certain threshold. This is not the same as steering information.

Also, many operators do not require the monitoring pilot to stay head down and make callouts after visual contact is made. The familiar scene is everyone in the cockpit straining for some sight of the approach lights or the runway. A more enlightened procedure is for the monitoring pilot to continue to make altitude calls right to the runway. If a 50-foot call is made and the airplane is not yet over the threshold, it's time for an immediate missed approach.

Using the second pilot to monitor the approach and make callouts to assist the flying pilot will definitely enhance the safety of any ILS approach in low-visibility conditions.

A separate altimeter set to QFE may eliminate some errors of height interpretation (msl to agl), but the two major air carriers who use a third altimeter have very different accident records for low-visibility landings. Clearly, something else is involved. The term "monitor" implies a passive, rather than active role in the approach. While a monitor may call out deviations from the normal flight path, he does not initiate corrective control action. If he did, the captain might well have a few words to say about who was flying the aircraft. But this does present a dilemma to a monitoring pilot whose captain seems to be doing nothing in the face of imminent disaster. There are too many cases on record of an aircraft flying into the ground despite repeated warnings from the pilot who is monitoring.

There are three airlines with extremely good safety records in the low-visibility approach—American Airlines, Aeropostale of France and Ansett Airlines of Australia. Their solution to the problem has been so effective it is worthy of copy by others.

When the visibility is near minimum, the copilot makes the approach—

and he is primed for a missed approach. He will go around automatically unless the captain takes over before the missed approach point. The captain, meanwhile, monitors the instruments and makes appropriate callouts until about 100 feet above decision height. At that time he begins looking outside for visual cues. If the captain finds them adequate to continue visually to a landing, he pushes the copilot's hand from the throttles and says "I've got it." The copilot never takes his eyes from the instruments and continues to monitor and make callouts right up to the landing and into the roll-out.

Aeropostale (now a part of Air Inter Gabon S.A.) once demonstrated an approach to a landing completely under the hood without a flight director for B/CA to prove the effectiveness of its system (and the skill of its pilots). The copilot made the approach, landing and roll-out solely by reference to the ILS and flight instruments. However, completely blind landings are not now legal in Category I and II operations and are not contemplated with standard ILS and flight director instrumentation.

Many corporate flight departments use the monitored approach technique to improve their safety margins. The procedure is standardized, so even if the captain and first officer have never met before, each knows what to expect of the other.

Take a look at United Air Lines's flight profile in Figure 2. Maneuvering flaps are extended, the speed is stabilized prior to the localizer intercept, the landing gear is extended just before the glideslope intercept and the pilot not flying makes the callouts from 1,000 feet on down. At 500 feet above touchdown the pilot not flying begins his outside scan to look for approach light and runway environment cues. If he sees enough to continue below decision height, he says, "I've got it" and takes over the controls. The pilot who had been flying by instrument reference continues to monitor the flight instruments and now makes the callouts to touchdown.

While in the simulator, United Air Lines pilots learning this technique discovered an interesting thing. With the visibility adjusted to the appropriate minimum, about three out of four captains did not see enough to take over before the copilot initiated a go-around at decision height. This discovery suggests that the FAA's current relationship between RVR minima and decision heights is incorrect. If the runway has legal minimum visibility, there should be better than a one in four chance of seeing enough to land at decision height, especially if you've been scanning for outside visual cues for several hundred feet prior to reaching decision height.

Some critics point out that nobody monitors the copilot in his determination of decision height in this procedure. However, when a decision is made to proceed to a landing, the other pilot is monitoring the flight instruments and making callouts on speed, altitude and deviation from glideslope. In

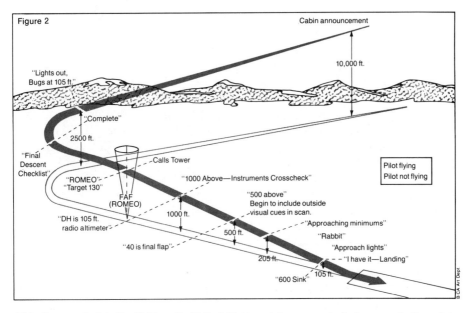

This diagram depicts the flight profile United Air Lines follows on a typical approach. One pilot handles the controls up to decision height and the other takes over from there if the visibility is adequate.

most cases such a procedure will assure a safe, successful approach or go-around.

Three situations can arise in which monitoring the flight instruments and making callouts are not enough to stay out of danger. The first is when a glideslope is unusable below 200 or more feet. Cleveland's Hopkins Runway 28R ILS serves as an example—its glideslope is unusable below 243 feet. If the signal to be monitored is unusable, it cannot back up a pilot using outside references to land.

The second situation occurs when wind shear causes a rapid altitude loss beginning just about decision height. The monitoring pilot will not likely say anything before the airplane is at least one and maybe even two dots below the glideslope. Then it may be too late for the pilot flying visually to take corrective action.

The third situation is when the pilot flying visually does not respond when callouts are made, even when the deviation is slow. Should the pilot monitoring the instruments take over? And if so, at what degree of deviation? The United Air Lines procedure specifies one-third dot maximum deviation from the localizer and one dot maximum deviation from the glideslope at 100 feet, but it does not tell the copilot what to do if the captain exceeds these. There is very little time for discussion at 200 feet agl and lower, so appropriate action must be agreed upon by both pilots in advance. The flare is no time to begin a tug-of-war on the controls. Normally, the pilot making the landing would respond to deviation callouts unless he became incapacitated or was receiving strong contrary visual information himself.

Contrary visual information stems from visual illusions present in the absence of outside steering information. Outside steering information could also help solve the problems of wind shear recognition and unusable glideslopes close to the runway.

This is just what a head-up display (HUD) is designed to do. By superimposing images of the runway and steering information on the windshield, a pilot can accurately control the airplane right through the transition from instrument to visual weather conditions.

More than 30 years after the introduction of ILS, low visibility is still a major cause of civil aviation accidents. But the prudent pilot can, through greater awareness of the problem, strict adherence to a monitored approach technique when two pilots are present and, in the future, better instrumentation, prevent the ground from coming up to smite him.

The Monitored Approach: UA's Better Idea

21

by Richard N. Aarons

From time to time we run across a "better idea" in the management of low-visibility approaches. The cockpit-crew coordination techniques of Executive Jet Aviation and of the Federal Aviation Administration's flight department are examples of some of the best traditional low-visibility-approach workload-sharing plans. However, each of those plans requires that both pilots be heads-up in at least one phase of the approach. Usually, the procedure requires that the copilot obtain visual cues and call "lights in sight" to the captain; whereupon the captain looks up and, if at minimums, makes an instantaneous decision to land or go around.

Back in 1967, United Air Lines supervisory personnel became "concerned over the adequacy" of that procedure, especially since "a major contributor to the accidents and incidents associated with the approach and landing phase of flight has been both pilots looking out." UA undertook a comprehensive investigation into the problems of low-visibility approaches and coordinated its efforts with those of the Air Force, which was involved in similar research with PIFAX (Pilot Factors Program). UA concluded that it is absolutely necessary for one pilot to monitor the flight instruments throughout the approach, landing and rollout or go-around.

Capt. W. L. Thomas, UA's director of flight training, said the decision to keep one pilot head-down at all times was based on three factors:

(1) The industry has had several accidents or incidents directly attributable to the fact that both pilots were looking outside the cockpit and deviating from the proper flight path. (Two Allegheny Airlines accidents at Bradford, Pennsylvania, are examples.)

(2) As we go to lower minimums, the probability of variable fog conditions increases. With the greater possibility of reentering the fog, it is even more prudent that one pilot monitor the flight instruments.

(3) The 100-foot (CAT II) decision height under the old procedures would require an instantaneous decision on visibility and alignment by the captain

after hearing the "lights in sight" call by the copilot. With the copilot monitoring the flight instruments on an autocoupled approach, it is possible for the captain to begin picking up visual cues above decision height and to be better prepared to make a decision at DH.

Thus, United instituted its present procedure, which calls for the captain to make all approaches when the weather is below 4,000 RVR or 300 and ¾. CAT II approaches are made autocoupled and CAT I can be autocoupled or flight-director approaches. The captain flies the approach, picking up his visual cues prior to DH on the coupled approaches, and at DH disconnects the autopilot and lands or executes a missed-approach procedure, announcing "going around." With a DH of 200 feet on a flight-director approach, it would not be necessary to pick up a visual cue prior to DH. Meanwhile, the first officer makes appropriate callouts and monitors the approach by constantly observing the flight instruments to touchdown and through the rollout or go-around.

The following is a detailed explanation of United's procedure:

· Upon extending the gear as the glide slope transits one dot above "on course" index, completion of the final-descent challenge and respond checklist (which occurs near the LOM), and after contact is established with the control tower (a standard requirement), the captain will announce the target approach speed considering all pertinent factors . . . as an example, "Approach speed 140 knots." Both pilots set one bug to that reference speed.

· When the aircraft is 1,000 feet above the airport elevation (baro altitude), the first officer will again cross-check the flight instruments and announce: "One thousand feet above field elevation, flight instruments check (or nature of discrepancy)."

· By use of the barometric altimeter, starting at 500 feet above field elevation and at approximately each 100-foot increment, the first officer will call displacement errors when one-dot displacement exists on the localizer or glide slope. He'll also call deviations of plus 10 knots or minus five knots from the target approach speed and any rate of descent in excess of 1,000 fpm.

Localizer and glide-slope callouts will not refer to displacement error in terms of dots but will be:

"Slightly to the left of localizer."

"To the right of localizer, correcting."

"Low on the glide slope."

"High on the glide slope, holding steady."

Airspeed callouts will be in knots. As long as the airspeed is within established parameters, no airspeed callout will be made. However, if the airspeed is 15 knots above target approach speed, the first officer will announce, "Airspeed 155 knots."

If the rate of descent is in excess of 1,000 fpm, the first officer will announce, "Descent 1,500 feet."

Upon leaving 500 feet above airport elevation, as indicated on the barometric altimeter, and if the airplane is within established parameters, the first officer will announce, "Five hundred feet above field elevation." If outside of established parameters, the appropriate callout will follow the altitude announcement, "Five hundred feet above field elevation, high on glide slope."

Altitudes will be included in the callout only when leaving 1,000 feet and 500 feet above airport elevation. All other calls will state only displacement errors or deviation errors as pertinent. Transitory excursions of instruments, such as caused by an aircraft on the runway, will not be announced.

· The first officer will monitor approach performance by constantly observing cockpit instrumentation to touchdown and through rollout, or through go-around. By use of the barometric altimeter at approximately 100 feet above minimum altitude, he will announce, "Approaching minimums." At minimum altitude (on CAT II-equipped aircraft, the radar altimeter will be used as a reference altitude), he will announce, "Minimum."

· Approaching minimum altitude, the captain will adjust his scan pattern to include outside visual cues and will have his decision formulated at decision height.

· The captain will disengage the autopilot for landing and land, or execute a missed approach should visual cues not be seen or not confirm the alignment of the airplane with the runway. (Maximum deviation at 100 feet is ⅓ of a dot from the localizer and plus or minus one dot on the glide slope.)

· Below decision height, the first officer will call out airspeed changes in five-knot increments and any unusual attitude to touchdown or through the go-around, and also appropriate airspeeds during low-visibility rollouts.

There are various other procedures that will provide the desired flight-instrumentation monitoring, admits United. One British airline has the copilot conduct the approach and the captain looking out. The copilot automatically initiates a missed approach if the captain does not take over at DH to make a landing. (B/CA pilots like this procedure in certain nonprecision approaches, especially in hilly areas where initial visual cues can be misleading.)

United said it chose the copilot head-down approach "to establish one procedure for its 6,000 pilots, considering the possibility of low-time, less-experienced first officers during a period of expansion."

Like all "systems" this one has its problems. Captain Thomas cites three:

(1) It requires a great deal of self-discipline for the first officer to remain heads down at DH and below.

(2) In training and checking in the airplane, the flight instructor or

check-pilot is in the right seat charged with the safety of the flight and cannot really function as a regular first officer.

(3) The flight manager rarely sees his crews in a low-minimum environment, making adherence through supervision difficult.

In defending the system, however, United points out that there "has never been a fatal accident in jets when the full ILS was used and the aircraft flown within accepted parameters. . . . We know of the accidents and incidents due to excursions from the desired approach path while both pilots are looking out; we know the obvious answer to this is that one pilot must be monitoring the flight instruments for out-of-parameter excursions, and we recognize the need for self-discipline, proper training, checking and supervision to assure compliance with such a procedure."

What's an RVR?   *22*

by Dan Manningham

This business of minimums seems to expand a little each year. As you know, the basic concept used by the FAA is that visibility is the sole operating minimum for takeoff and landing, although there are four separate methods of reporting that visibility. RVR, RVV, Sector Visibility and Prevailing Visibility, in that order of priority, could be the controlling report for your departure or arrival, depending on circumstances. Ceiling minimums are no longer used except for alternate airports and a few takeoff minimums under FAR Parts 121, 123, 129 and 135.

Runway Visual Range (RVR) is always the controlling element when reported. In that case, the other three reports are advisory only, and you must predicate your actions solely on the tower-reported RVR.

RVR readings are derived from electronic measurements made with a device called a transmissometer. This unit is actually comprised of two separate elements, a transmitter and a receiver, spaced 250 feet apart, abeam the touchdown zone of an ILS runway. The transmitter is a precisely calibrated light source. The receiver effectively measures how much of that light penetrates the atmosphere in the intervening space. Results are averaged over 60-second segments and transmitted as impulses spaced one minute apart. In National Weather Service offices or Flight Service Stations, the impulses are received and recorded continuously on paper graphs. These recordings, no more than raw data, must then be modified into tables that take into account prevailing daylight, if any, the runway light setting in use and anything else that might alter ambient lighting conditions in the vicinity of the transmissometer. The resultant RVR is reported at the end of NWS sequence reports and to operations offices on the airport.

Airport control towers and approach control rooms receive RVR in digitalized form. The raw impulses from the transmitter/receiver are processed and compensated electronically so controlling facilities receive a direct and simple digital readout. These are updated only once each minute so the tower RVR cannot change more often.

Each airport with RVR equipment has one designated runway for sequence reporting purposes. Chicago O'Hare, for instance, has five RVR runways, but 14R is the designated installation. Therefore, the RVR for 14R will appear on the Aviation Sequence Report whenever the prevailing visibility is one mile or less, or when the highest RVR reading on 14R is 6000 feet or less. That RVR will appear at the end of the sequence as a range of values representing the highest and lowest RVR recorded during the 10 minutes preceding the report.

Actual airport operations are governed by the digitalized readings in the tower and approach control. These instruments normally read from 1000 to 6000 feet in 100-foot increments. Some read down to 600 feet. The raw numbers are modified by use of a "+" or "−" to indicate more subtle differences. Thus, 2700+ indicates something over 2700 RVR but less than 2800 RVR; 2700− shows something less than 2700 but better than 2600 RVR. When minimums are 2400 feet, for example, a reading of 2400− is below minimums. The maximum scale, then, is from 1000− (or 600− in a few cases) to 6000+. RVR cannot measure conditions above or below these limits.

All Category II runways and a few Category I runways are equipped with a second transmissometer at the rollout end. Regulations concerning the use of rollout RVR have changed several times since the inception of Category II, but that situation has now apparently stabilized. When RVR at the approach end is below 1600, rollout RVR is controlling for takeoffs (for some operations) and advisory for landings, in the following manner:

· For takeoff, RVR at both ends is controlling for FAR Part 121, 123, 129 and 135 operations.

· For landing, rollout RVR is always advisory. During Category II operations, rollout RVR is provided when it is less than touchdown RVR. For basic ILS operations, RVR for the rollout end is provided if it is less than 2000 feet *and* less than touchdown RVR. In all cases, rollout RVR is purely informational for landing.

RVR readings for other than the single designated runway at each airport are only available from the local controlling facility.

Naturally, RVR minimums require no ceiling report, but remember one other fact: Runway Visual Range is only an electronic measure of the horizontal visibility for 250 feet of the touchdown zone. It is very local in nature and may not correspond at all to the nearly three-fourths of a mile slant-range visibility you will require for the last 200 vertical feet of your landing approach. Nevertheless, when RVR is reported, it must be used as the controlling information, regardless of any other visibility reports. When there is no RVR, then RVV, Sector Visibility and Prevailing Visibility, in that order, are controlling.

Runway Visibility Value (RVV) is measured by equipment similar to that used for RVR except that measurements are in miles and/or fractions thereof. RVV is the controlling report for that runway for takeoffs and landings. Prevailing Visibility is controlling for all other runways.

Sector Visibility or Quadrant Visibility is sometimes reported when visibility in one direction is markedly different. This Sector Visibility is then controlling in that direction while Prevailing Visibility controls everything else. If, for example, the hourly sequence or tower controller reports VSBY E 1¼ MILES, that visibility is controlling for aircraft departing to the east or arriving from the east.

Prevailing Visibility is controlling for everyone when no other reports are given. At most airports, the Prevailing Visibility as reported in the NWS sequence report is the legal visibility when it is four miles or greater. When visibility is below four miles, controllers have the responsibility to establish Prevailing Visibility.

Watch those visibility reports. Sometimes you need a lawyer to determine the legal minimums.

Flying the ADF

23

by Richard N. Aarons

Few things are nicer after flying a long, hard instrument leg than hearing the words, "cleared for the approach." That is, unless the controller says, "cleared for the *NDB* approach."

For most of us, NDB approaches are bad, bad news, simply because most of us can't fly them worth a damn and have never really tried to master them.

We know ATP certificate holders who have never flown an NDB approach, and if asked to do so, would crumble. There are instrument flight instructors who can diagram incredibly complex NDB approach solutions on lunchroom placemats, only to be foiled by the approach once in the air.

True, the NDB and its associated approach are being replaced by VORs and VORTACs at even the smallest airports around the country. Many airports are, in addition, getting RNAV procedures to replace or support existing NDB approaches. But the fact remains—there are 793 NDBs commissioned in the United States, most of them operated by local governments. At well over 500 U.S. airports, the NDB is the only IFR approach aid.

Practically speaking, pilots for domestic air carriers can forget about NDB approaches, but corporate and businessmen pilots operating into the smallest of the nation's "IFR airports" need a thorough knowledge of NDB-approach theory and a facility with its techniques if they are to take full advantage of small-aircraft flexibility.

Some of the more affluent business pilots equip their aircraft with RMIs (radio magnetic indicators)—devices which take much of the work out of ADF navigation. Much of what we say here is applicable to RMI operators, but our emphasis is intentionally on the plain pointer indicators.

It is not our intent in this article to provide a primer for NDB approaches. You've already been through that. Instead, we'll pass along some cautions, tips and did-you-knows that may make the NDB less fearsome the next time you are so cursed.

We get so used to disturbance-free reception of the VHF nav and com systems we use daily, we tend to forget that low-frequency transmissions are full of error-producing glitches. For example, if you receive a VOR station and you check flags and course width to determine proper station strength, you can fully trust the nav data displayed on the HSI or CDI. Aside from minor course bends and occasional scalloping, you've got no problems. Unfortunately, it's easy for most pilots to forget that low freq is often messy, and therefore, the needle is not always pointing in the right direction. Sometimes, the ADF needle points in the worst possible direction despite your efforts to tune and identify the station properly. The most common source of ADF errors is precipitation static.

Precip static is an interference with the propagation of low-frequency radio waves caused by any kind of precipitation—rain, snow, sleet—you name it. The worst offender is the thunderstorm. You've probably heard oldtimers suggest that the only thing an ADF is good for in frontal areas is to point to the most electrically active cell. At one time this was absolutely true. Modern ADF equipment is not as susceptible to this kind of precip static, but you should always anticipate the possibility that your ADF needle is not being truthful when thunderstorms are around.

By far the most common result of precip static is attenuation of the signal. That is, you'll have to get closer to the beacon to get a good navigable input to the receiver. Station interference presents another possible source of ADF error although this type of anomaly is more common outside the United States. Frequency assignments are made so that an aircraft can't pick up two beacons simultaneously (in theory anyway). But this is a lot more difficult to do than to say, because low-frequency radio-wave propagation varies with time of day, weather conditions, sun activity, and height of and activity within the ionosphere.

Figure 1 shows the power output and service ranges of the classes of NDBs used in the United States. Assuming the station is properly tuned and identified, you can expect reception, free from station interference, within those published ranges in the *daytime*. However, at night, skywaves from distant NDBs operating on or near the same frequency can

Figure 1	Nondirectional Beacon Range	
CLASS DESIGNATORS	POWER OUTPUT (watts)	SERVICE RANGE (nm)
Compass Locator	Less than 25	15
MH	25 to 49	25
H	50 to 1999	50
HH	greater than 1999	75

penetrate the frequency-protected area. (In a moment we'll see how to detect this type of interference when tuning an NDB.)

Night effect is yet another interference type that can mess up ADF navigational information. In this case the ADF receives the NDB ground and skywaves at the same time. Pretty large bearing errors can result. Because this interference type is most prevalent during twilight hours, it is sometimes called "twilight effect."

Mountains and coastlines can bend low-frequency radio waves. There isn't much a pilot can do about these effects other than to remember, when using ADF in mountainous areas or flying over water using inland NDBs, to watch for them.

One of the main reasons the world's airways and facilities planners have gone to VHF navaids is to improve navigational accuracies by getting rid of error-generating, low-frequency interference factors. However, despite these error sources, the NDB/ADF combination is a highly accurate navigational system when used properly and within its limitations.

The flight instructors at the FAA's Oklahoma City facility have put together a list of common ADF errors. This list is applicable to en route or approach ADF operations. If you're having trouble shooting NDB approaches, the reason may be:

· Improper tuning and station misidentification
· Reliance on homing rather than tracking
· Use of the ADF pointer rather than the gyroscopic heading reference to make course corrections
· Poor orientation
· Careless intercept angles due to rushing the initial orientation
· Overshooting and undershooting magnetic bearings due to forgetting course intercept angles
· Failure to monitor selected headings
· Failure to understand ADF limitations
· Overcontrol of track corrections close to the station

The newer ADFs are all digitally tuned. You simply click in (or push in) the frequency and *identify the station.* The importance of identifying the station and *leaving the ident on* cannot be overemphasized. The quality of the ident can tell you a lot about the quality of the nav signal. Crashing bursts of static indicate precip static interference and should put you on guard for associated nav signal errors. A hum or whistle over the ident often indicates station interference, which also can cause gross errors in navigational signals. If you get a good strong ident free of static, a strong needle swing toward the station and you are within service range of the station, you can expect relatively good navigational information.

It's important that, having correctly identified the NDB, you maintain a listening watch on the ident if you are using the NDB for primary navigation. Most nonfederal NDBs (and that means just about all the NDBs you'll be using) are *not* equipped with station-monitoring devices. Sometimes the only indication you'll get that a station has gone off the air is loss of the ident. *So listen to it.*

B/CA asked a half dozen business jet pilots who regularly fly NDB approaches in Canada what their first operational rule is in regard to these procedures. To a man, their advice was to *identify the station and keep listening to the ident.*

On older ADF receivers with continuously variable frequency selectors, tuning requires special attention. Always tune with the system in the receive or antenna mode. Tune to maximum needle deflection if the set is equipped with a tuning meter or to maximum ident volume if it does not. Note the parked position of the needle. Then, after tuning and identification are complete, move the mode selector to ADF.

It's a bit off the point here, but when you're buying a new ADF system, pay particular attention to the park and test modes. Some systems park the needle at a given place on the dial face—usually 45 or 90 degrees—whenever the NDB signal is too weak for navigation.

Of course, if the nav signal is suitable, the needle will be pointing at the station. If test is selected or if the station goes off the air, the needle will move to the parked position. Less desirable ADF equipment does not have a parking place for the needle. If you were settled down on an inbound course and the station failed, the needle would not move. If you were not monitoring the station ident, you could go on boring holes with the needle motionless, probably marveling at your skillful tracking job.

Back to the point, proper tuning and identification are a must. Do not try to stretch signal strength range if you are using NDBs for primary navigation. This is especially important at night when both night effect and twilight effect can raise hell with the accuracy of your ADF.

Type-rating examiners and check-ride inspectors want to see you track (rather than home) whenever you're using ADF as primary. In the real world, tracking means throwing in an initial correction for estimated winds and making sure the errors don't get too big.

It's probably a safe guess that most of us do most of our ADFing when flying direct to a compass locator on an ILS.

These specialized NDBs operate at 25 watts or less and are good for 15 miles at best. An aircraft letting down at 160 knots will cover that stretch in about five and a half minutes. During that five and a half minutes, crew attention must also go to completion of the in-range checklist, monitoring the letdown and setting up and checking the radios for the approach. If "crew" means single pilot, the workload is twice as big. So it stands to reason that the pilot tracking inbound to the NDB doesn't have a heck of a lot of time to mess around with the textbook trial-and-error system of tracking. Here's our suggestion.

Some quiet night, sit down with a CR-type computer—the improved circular version of the old E6B slide type—because it's easier to use for this exercise than an E6B, and work up a rule of thumb for tracking corrections using *your* initial approach speed. For our hypothetical airplane with a 160-knot initial approach speed, we find that a 10-knot crosswind component requires a 3.5-degree correction; a 20-knot crosswind dictates a 7.2-degree correction; and a 30-knot crosswind requires an 11-degree correction. Now you've got a rule of thumb for crosswind correction at 160 knots —the required crosswind correction in degrees is approximately one-third the crosswind component in knots.

(Working this exercise for a speed of 100 knots, you'll find that a 10-knot crosswind component requires a 5.8-degree correction; a 20-knot crosswind requires an 11.6-degree correction; and a 30-knot crosswind requires a 17-degree correction. Thus, for 100 knots, the rule of thumb is that the required crosswind correction is approximately one-half the crosswind component.)

Now, suppose you're within 15 miles of the facility and cleared direct. Estimate the crosswind component, apply the appropriate rule of thumb— the one you worked out for your normal speeds—and add the correction immediately.

Fly heading, go back to your other cockpit chores and cross-check the ADF pointer occasionally. (If the needle moves toward zero, you don't have enough correction. Add an additional correction equal to half the amount of the initial correction and hold that. If the needle is moving away from zero, you've got too much correction. Cut the initial correction in half. Chances are you won't have time for a third correction. But you don't care anyway because you will have reached the station in an acceptable manner.)

Some texts suggest that you use the ADF pointer as primary heading reference when making corrections. *Don't do it.* Most nonservoed ADF pointers suffer from dip errors; besides, using any instrument other than a heading indicator to adjust heading is sloppy flying.

Of the FAA's list of common errors, the *most* common is poor orientation. No doubt about it—ADF is a thinking man's navigational system. If you don't know where you are relative to where you want to go, the ADF can help you out. But you're going to have to do some bookwork first. We're not going to talk about basic ADF orientation here; there are several excellent sources on the subject. But don't fail to do this bookwork simply because you don't expect to have to work an inflight orientation problem. It may happen someday. It has to at least one B/CA pilot.

The rest of the errors in the FAA's list have to do with nothing more complex than heading control. At one time or another, a flight instructor or check pilot probably banged his fist on the panel and explained that you fly *heading* on an ILS and watch what the selected heading does to the localizer needle. The same rule holds for ADF work. In fact, it's probably more important in ADF work. You must remember the course you're trying to make good and the correction you're flying. Failure to do so will lead to immediate disorientation. Use whatever aids you need to remember these figures. Write them down if you have to.

Now let's look at the NDB approach. The rules that follow are the consensus of pilots who regularly fly these approaches in high-performance aircraft.

(1) Determine if minimums exist.

(2) Determine where you're going to break out.

(3) Estimate average groundspeed.

(4) Intercept the inbound leg as far out as possible.

(5) Be at the final letdown fix at least three miles early.

(6) Descend so as to be at MDA no later than half the time to the missed approach point.

(7) Maintain at all times a rapid cross-check. Control of speed, attitude and rate is of prime importance.

Some of these suggestions seem rather obvious at first glance, but they deserve consideration.

For example, the very fact that you have to shoot an NDB approach suggests that the airport's facilities aren't the best. Weather information supplied by any source other than an on-field, qualified observer is likely to be pretty poor—especially if the field is near minimums. There's certainly nothing wrong with shooting the approach to "take a look," but in this case you must *expect* to miss the approach.

Most of the pilots we talked to suggested that you "get out" before reaching the missed approach point. The reason is simple: If you don't have your target before you get to the missed approach, you're not going to be able to complete the approach anyway. The NDB MAP for a straight-in approach is the runway threshold; for a circling approach, it's the center of the runway complex. Why wait until you're directly over the MAP at MDA before missing the approach? Even if you see the ground at the MAP, you won't be able to do anything but go around. So when do you start the missed approach? If your groundspeed is 100 knots, you're going about two statute miles a minute (remember, minimums are statute miles). In this case, it would seem appropriate to break off the approach with 30 seconds to go if you don't have ground contact.

You'll notice in the above list that several items suggest that you do things early—that is, intercept the inbound course as early as possible, be at the final letdown fix at least three miles early and descend so as to be at MDA no later than half the time to the MAP.

Success in an NDB approach is a matter of good planning and careful execution. The earlier you get squared away, the better.

The matter of wind correction angles on the NDB approach can be tackled in the same manner suggested earlier for compass locator tracking. Take advantage of the outbound part of the procedure to get a feel for the wind—if nothing else, at least its direction. If surface winds at the airport are reported and the terrain is relatively smooth, you might apply an old rule of thumb. For winds 1000 to 2000 feet above the surface, add 90 degrees to the direction and double the velocity. Select and fly headings purposefully. Watch the ADF needle. Fast movement means strong crosswind components. Slow movement means relatively weak components.

Sometimes you won't have ground station wind reports. But you should have some idea of what the winds are from the winds aloft forecast (which you checked and recorded before takeoff) or even the observed winds during the latter part of your flight. Make an estimate and use the rule-of-thumb corrections that you worked up for locator tracking.

By the time you reach the final fix inbound (assuming an off-airport NDB), you should have the crosswind correction pretty much nailed. Fly *heading* out of the fix and during let-down to MDA. Don't fly the ADF needle or mess around with new corrections. You will be in too close to the station and your corrections will only beget larger errors. Once established at MDA, check the ADF pointer to make sure its presentation seems logical relative to your inbound course and crosswind correction.

(Of course, during the entire approach, you've been listening to the ident and watching carefully for signs of interference. If the needle shows short-period fluctuations, be alert. The receiver may be experiencing signal fades or station interference.)

A while back, we mentioned that turbojet pilots who fly NDB approaches always listen to the ident during an approach. For them, it's rule number one. Their rule number two is "always tune both ADFs to the same facility." Most of us stuck with NDB approaches don't have dual ADF installations, but if you do, remember rule two.

One of the best ways of coping with the ADF approach is to avoid it altogether. But obviously this isn't always practical. However, one way of doing so (kinda) is to set up the approach on an IFR-approved RNAV system. In this case the approach is flown on the RNAV while the ADF is monitored. If you use this technique—and many pilots do—remember that the ADF is primary and any hokey indications on that instrument dictate an immediate missed approach.

When you're not using the ADF for primary nav reference, keep it going anyway. It can be a great backup. (And constant use, even as a how-goes-it aid, will help you gain proficiency in its use against the time when it's all you have.)

One of the most interesting uses of the ADF pointer is as an emergency attitude-reference instrument. In coordinated flight, the aircraft will turn only if the wings are banked. Or, looking at it from the other side, if the aircraft doesn't turn, the wings must be level. You can maintain an attitude quite easily by keeping the ADF needle pointing straight up using only slight aileron pressures for corrections.

Many veteran instrument flight instructors require their students to shoot at least one practice ADF approach with all gyro flight instruments covered—that includes turn and bank. (Try it the next time you're out practicing.)

Most NDBs are located on or within a couple of miles of an airport. And several cockpit flight guides publish bearing and distance from a beacon to its airport. Many pilots tune their ADFs to NDBs sequentially as they move along airways, especially on dark nights. If everything else goes to hell, they can always find an airport immediately.

Someday the younger pilots among us will be wowing the airport bums with stories of what it was like to fly an NDB approach much in the way some of the veteran pilots now tell hair-raising stories about four-course ranges.

But until the NDB disappears completely—and it's going to take a while —businessmen pilots will need them. Being good at ADF approaches is a rare skill. But it's a fun skill to acquire. Do a little homework, then head out to your nearest beacon and give it a try. You'll be surprised how satisfying being really good at nasty NDBs can be.

Straight Talk on the Circling Approach 24

by Richard N. Aarons

Undoubtedly, we all agree professional pilots should not have accidents, but the unhappy fact is they do. And even unhappier is the fact that the majority of accidents that befall professional pilots, like the majority that involve amateur pilots, are avoidable.

A few months ago, B/CA pilots reached the conclusion that circling approaches are inherently dangerous. This conclusion (at that time) was not the result of scholarly research into the statistics, but rather a couple of sticky, wet-palms approaches involving our company airplanes.

After these incidents we went to the NTSB and asked its statisticians for a computer run on circling approach accidents for the three-year period ended in December 1972. We figured we'd find maybe a dozen incidents which could be further investigated to isolate the dangers of the big circle.

As it turned out, the NTSB's computer found 42 accidents involving circling approaches in the sample period. And the computer also discovered the circling approach accident is strictly a professional pilot's accident.

Consider these facts:

· Sixty-four percent of the pilots involved in these accidents held either an ATP (24 percent) or commercial (40 percent) certificate.

· Average flight time for pilots involved was 5,201 hours with 555 hours in type. Seventy-one percent of these pilots had over 1,000 hours total time; 16 percent had over 5,000 hours, and six percent had over 10,000 hours.

· The 42 airplanes involved comprised six turbojets, one turboprop, 25 piston twins and 10 singles.

· Seventeen (40 percent) of the circling approach accidents involved personal flights. The rest (60 percent) involved some type of business, corporate or general aviation commercial activity. Corporate/executive, 7; business, 8; air taxi, 6; instructional/flight test/ferry, 4.

· Circling approach accidents tend to be fatal more often than other accident types. Fatalities resulted in a full 52 percent of the accidents in the sample period. The fatality average for all accident types tends to be stable at about 14 percent.

· Injuries of one kind or another—fatal, serious or minor—are the result of 76 percent of the circling approach accidents.

· These accidents, like all other accident types, seem to be pilot-induced. The first-listed "probable cause" in 86 percent of the circling approach mishaps was pilot error; mechanical problems led the causal list in another 12 percent, and airport conditions accounted for two percent.

· As you would expect, the largest percentage of circling approach accidents involved VOR approach procedures. In our sample, VOR accidents accounted for 76 percent of the total. Circling maneuvers from ILS approaches accounted for another 17 percent; backcourse circles, 5 percent, and ADF approaches, only two percent.

Now, these numbers in themselves really don't mean a hell of a lot. But when they are considered in light of each other, they enabled us to draw a picture of the "typical" circling approach mishap. And for our purposes, that "typical" accident involves an experienced businessman pilot, flying a piston twin on a VOR circling approach in near minimums weather.

The accident records indicated this typical pilot received a weather briefing from a flight service facility and that the briefing was substantially correct. As he conducted the approach, the typical pilot made one of two mistakes—either he paid so much attention to aircraft control that he misflew the procedure thus suffering a "controlled collision with ground-/water," or he paid so much attention to the procedure or keeping the airport in sight that he lost control of the aircraft thus suffering an "uncontrolled collision with ground/water."

Take a look at these remarks from the circling approach accident briefs:

Learjet 23A—Lack of visual cues caused the pilot to misjudge altitude.

Navajo—Descended below published approach minimums. Lost control during steep, low-altitude turn.

Piper Arrow—Destination below minimums. Pilot elected to land at alternate also below minimums. Didn't recognize station passage. Hit mountainside.

Beech Bonanza—Lost control on turn to final approach. Severe icing conditions encountered. Aircraft not de-icer equipped.

Navajo—Flew into ground during final turn.

Cessna 320D—Pilot spatial disorientation. Missed VOR approach. Observer saw aircraft re-enter low overcast.

Cessna 421A—Stalled during steep left turn to final on a VOR circling approach.

Twin Comanche—Observed in steep bank from low altitude on downwind leg during circling VOR approach. Stalled. Altitude too low for recovery.

Beech Baron—Missed approach at nearby airport. Attempted VOR approach in known below minimums condition. Descended below MDA. Lost control.

Cessna 310—ILS approach to Runway 36 circling to Runway 31. Pilot made a steep right turn, then lost control in steep left turn.

Beech Baron—Flew into ground in low-altitude turn.

HS/BH 125—Missed two straight-in VOR approaches. Attempted VOR circling approach in below minimums condition. Descended below MDA.

Over one-quarter of these circling approach accidents (29 percent) involved loss of aircraft control. Think about that for a minute, remembering that most pilots involved in these accidents are highly experienced in terms of total time and time in type. Certainly there is no excuse for an experienced pilot losing control of an aircraft. And certainly no experienced pilot *would* lose control of an aircraft unless the control loss was the final result of a chain of minor problems or distractions leading to the final catastrophic problem. If that reasoning is valid, it follows there must be something inherent in the circling approach that can trap an experienced pilot into committing an amateur's mistake.

It's our opinion—shared, we think by many professional pilots—that the circling approach is dangerous because it delivers the aircraft into the worst possible set of operational conditions. The classic circling approach involves low-speed maneuvering at low altitudes (bad in itself) in poor visibility conditions during a high cockpit workload period while the pilot is maintaining attitude through both outside and instrument references and attempting to maintain geographic orientation largely without electronic help. And if we consider additional common complications—the pilot often is unfamiliar with the airport; weather may be a bit worse than forecast; the de-icing system may not be quite up to par—the circling approach may, in fact, be the most difficult task normally required of airplane pilots.

Filing one revision package in your Jepps will convince you that VOR circling approaches are the predominate approach type in the ATC system. And despite this fact, official FAA publications devote only two paragraphs to the entire subject—one in the Airman's Information Manual and the other in the FAA Instrument Flying Handbook. (And neither is very informative.) It could be argued that one of the traps in the circling approach is a general ignorance of exactly what the Flight Standards people have in mind when they establish a circling approach procedure. And it is certainly true that lack of published information on circling approach operational techniques leaves it up to the individual to establish his own techniques on a rather hit-or-miss basis. So here we're going to look at both the construction of the approach itself and several operational techniques which seem to offer the best chance of survival in the maneuver.

STRAIGHT TALK ON THE CIRCLING APPROACH

Most of us have been taught that the circling maneuver is simply something that happens at the end of a straight-in approach that for one reason or another cannot be completed straight in. Although this statement is in some cases correct, it can also be quite misleading, because approach procedure designers think of straight-in and circling approaches as wholly different animals. From a procedure planner's viewpoint, a straight-in approach provides lateral guidance to a *runway,* while a circling approach procedure provides lateral guidance to an *airport*—and that's an important distinction. At the termination of a straight-in approach, you land the airplane; at the end of a circling approach you determine the active runway, maneuver to a final approach position and *then* land the airplane.

The final-approach course in the straight-in procedure converges with the centerline of the runway at some angle less than 30 degrees. But the final approach course of the circling procedure need only fall somewhere within the airport boundary. (In a minimum visibility situation, the pilot may not even be able to see the threshold or any other portion of the active runway.)

Approach procedure planners are primarily concerned with providing the pilot with obstacle clearance. For example, there's an imaginary floor below the glideslope of each ILS approach through which no obstacles can penetrate. In an off-airport VOR procedure, no obstacles may be higher than 300 feet below the MDA between the VOR and the airport.

In the case of straight-in approaches, these obstacle clearance zones are normally wedge shaped (laterally) with their narrow ends at the runway threshold. But circling approach procedures, because they deliver the aircraft to an area (airport) rather than a point in space (runway threshold), require roomy obstacle clearance zones centered on the airport as well as those obstacle clearance zones based on the approach centerline.

These airport-centered obstacle-free areas are called *circling approach areas* and they provide at least 300 feet of clearance over any obstacle within their lateral boundaries.

Aircraft categories—The A-B-C-D speed-weight related groupings— shown on approach plates (and in Figure 1)—are used to establish the dimensions of the various circling approach areas for a given approach procedure. The lighter, more maneuverable aircraft of Category A obviously require smaller circling approach areas than the heavy fast aircraft of Category D. The circling approach area for each category is established by drawing an arc of appropriate radius from the center of the threshold of each usable runway and joining the extremities of adjacent arcs with lines tangent to the arcs.

The height of circling approach areas defines the lowest possible MDA for that category aircraft. Sometimes all the circling approach areas at a

Fig. 1: Speed and Weight Classifications			
Aircraft Category	Approach Speed (CAS kts.)	Weight (lbs.)	Radius (nm)
A	less than 91	less than 30,001	1.3
B	91 or more but less than 121	30,001 or more but less than 60,001	1.5
C	121 or more but less than 141	60,001 or more but less than 150,001	1.7
D	141 or more but less than 166	150,001 or more	2.3
E	166 or more	any weight	4.5

Approach category minimums are specified for various aircraft speed and weight combinations. Approach speeds are based on 1.3 times the stall speed in the landing configuration (Vso) at maximum gross landing weight. Weights shown are maximum certificated gross landing weights. An aircraft fits in only one category and that category is the highest category in which it meets any of the specifications. The radii are used in establishing obstacle-free circling approach areas.

given airport exist in a single plane. But more often, circling approach areas are stacked like inverted wedding cakes and thus the circling approach minimums increase for each larger category aircraft. This is so because the probability of encountering a limiting obstacle increases as distance from the airport increases.

Some airports are approved for only Category A type approaches because obstacle clearance simply can not be provided for larger aircraft. Take the case of a single-runway sea-level airport (hypothetical, of course) which sits in a valley bounded by 5,000-foot mountains, 1.3 nm on either side of the runway centerline. In theory this airport could get a circling approach restricted to Category A aircraft. A pilot straying out of the circling area at this airport would be dead.

Chances are you'll never run into an airport (or approach) as clearly dangerous as this hypothetical one. But it's a good idea to *imagine* those mountains are there whenever you shoot a circling approach. Remember, you lose your obstacle clearance guarantee whenever you stray out of the circling approach area established for your category. Maybe there's no mountain out there, but there might be a TV tower.

Visibility minimums for the circling approach are established with the circling approach area in mind. For example, Category A circling approach minimums will never be less than one sm (0.9 nm). So, in theory at least, you've got a buffer zone. (The boundary of the Category A circling approach area is at least 1.3 nm off the centerline in all cases.) But the catch

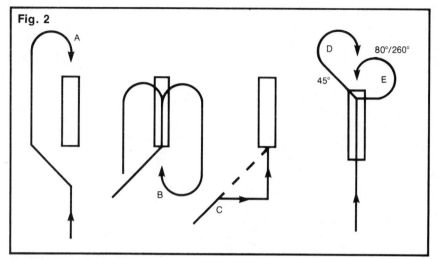

The FAA has diagramed these maneuvers for getting lined up after breaking out on a circling approach. We think maneuvers C, D and E are good ways to bust an airplane.

here is that there are "acceptable" circling maneuvers (procedure D in Figure 2, for example) in which the flight crew loses sight of the runway and sometimes the entire airport. We'll talk about this trap in detail a little later.

Because the aircraft in a circling approach is being guided to an *area* rather than a point in space, the regulations applying to the MAP and MDA are a little hazy. In straight-in approaches the missed approach point is exactly that—a point (though not always an easily identifiable one). In the circling approach, the missed approach point, to quote one FAA official, is "wherever you happen to be when you lose it." *It,* in this case, refers to orientation, visibility, control or any one of a half dozen factors involved in the final portion of the circling approach.

The point here is that the circling maneuver is at best imprecise. So the pilot's task becomes one of making the approach as precise as possible within its rather loose framework. And to do this, the pilot must establish personal minimums, and peak his abilities to fly the airplane while maintaining orientation.

Some of the scheduled carriers have improved their circling approach safety records by forbidding their crews to shoot circling approaches in less than VFR conditions—1,000 and three. This works for the carriers for two reasons: (1) Most of the airports they go into are served by more than one approach so they can usually get lined up for a straight-in during actual IFR conditions; and (2) If they can't get in, they go somewhere else and let

their passengers take the bus. Conversely, business and corporate operators are usually operating into smaller airports which often have only one
approach and only circling minimums. And chief pilots who tell their boss
to take the bus too often may find themselves working full time for Grey-
hound.

Several of the better business jet air taxi operators either demand or
permit their crews to select a higher approach category than they actually
need according to the regulations. For example, an HS/BH 125, which
could be operated as a Category C aircraft for circling approaches, might
be restricted to Category D by the operator. One chief pilot told B/CA he
tells his pilots to use Category D minimums at their option—and all three
of his crews avail themselves of that option regularly.

Many business pilots apply this concept in establishing their own minimums. For example, a Cessna 310 operator who could use Category A
minimums might restrict himself to Category B in circling approaches.
Some guys shoot Category A circling minimums at their familiar home
airport and Category B when away from home. Other pilots elect to use
higher minimums only when they have a bad feeling about the particular
approach.

But suppose for one reason or another you must operate your aircraft
right down to legal minimums. Then what?

B/CA's first recommendation, based on the NTSB computer run, is that
you practice low-altitude, low-speed ground reference maneuvers. Pylon
eights in a Cessna 421? Why not? Chances are the last time you were within
500 feet of the ground in a 45-to-60 degree bank was in a two-place trainer.
And that was probably more years ago than you'd care to admit. But, you
argue, it's dangerous screwing around at low speeds and low altitudes in
a heavy piston twin or a turboprop. You're right—it is dangerous. It's even
more dangerous screwing around at low speeds and altitudes in rotten
visibility during an actual circling approach—especially if you're unprac-
ticed in ground reference maneuvers.

Seat-of-the-pants flying has been out of vogue with instrument flight
instructors and FAA inspectors for years. But I'm afraid the seat-of-the-
pants concept has suffered from overkill. The idea behind the pylon eight
and other ground reference maneuvers required for the commercial certificate is to teach the pilot that his airplane can be controlled while most of
his attention is diverted elsewhere. And there is nothing in day-to-day
aircraft operations which diverts pilot attention from the cockpit quite as
effectively as the minimums circling maneuver to a strange airport. The
ability to recognize instantly deviations from reference speeds and altitudes is essential.

Next go to altitude and practice accelerated stalls—or at least the recognition of them. Almost 30 percent of the circling approach accidents re-

corded in our sample period involved loss of aircraft control, and about half that group involved accelerated stalls out of low, steep turns. And keep in mind that these accidents did not involve light training aircraft and student pilots; they involved highly experienced pilots flying Navajos and 421s and Beech 18s. (It might be a good idea to get a good check pilot to ride along with you the first time you explore accelerated stalls in your piston twin. Some of them can bite you clear to the bone in these maneuvers.)

Figure 2 is based on an illustration from the FAA's Instrument Flying Handbook. It shows five "acceptable" methods for the circling maneuver. Maneuvers A and B are, in fact, acceptable. Procedures C, D and E should be avoided in our opinion.

In the preparation of this study, we talked to several pilots who regularly fly heavy corporate aircraft into strange airports from circling approach maneuvers. The single point they all mentioned first is that the pilot must "normalize" the situation. "I want to establish the aircraft on a downwind or base leg—preferably a downwind—using the center of the airport as an initial reference," explained one corporate pilot. "To hell with that business of breaking out and immediately sliding into a modified base or final. I want to overfly the center of the airport and use that point as an orientation reference. Then I establish a normal downwind leg (it's usually lower than the downwind we use in VFR conditions) and then fly a normal pattern from that point." Specifically what this pilot is attempting to avoid are the maneuvers shown in C, D and E in Figure 2. Procedure C, a quick base followed by a short final, is okay if you're familiar with the airport and you are certain of the traffic conditions. However, if you don't know the airport and its close-in obstructions, this maneuver can get you into a lot of trouble. Suppose, for example, you're on a night approach and there's a clump of barren trees between you and the threshold. You'd be so busy making the turns to base and final that you might not be able to pick out the trees against the runway light pattern. Remember, too, that many of the worst circling approach procedures are at uncontrolled airports. And if the airport is in the boondocks, local VFR minimums may be one mile visibility and clear of clouds (uncontrolled airspace, meaning there could be legal VFR traffic when conditions are at—or even *below*—IFR minimums.) The maneuver in C gives you no opportunity to check for that traffic.

Procedures D and E are both pretty scary because you intentionally lose sight of the landing runway and perhaps the entire airport for a significant length of time.

If you must make the D or E maneuvers, be aware that you've probably got a stiff tailwind or you wouldn't be circling in the first place. And this tailwind will tend to elongate the maneuver depicted in E, making it look more nearly like D. With that in mind, the E procedure seems to be better than the D maneuver, especially considering the relatively small dimensions of the safe maneuvering area.

Procedures A and B are the best. In A you simply set up a downwind and fly it. In B you overfly the runway and again establish a normal downwind. Note that the B procedure solves the problems associated with C.

Timing procedures should be developed for the various stages of the circling approach maneuver. Once you've standardized your procedures based on the approach speed of your aircraft, various key positions in the circling maneuver will be in relatively the same place on each approach. Therefore, you'll always know where to look for the runway during any portion of any maneuver. For approach speeds between 100 and 130 knots, we found the magic number is 15 seconds. For example, if you overfly the landing runway at a 90-degree angle, a 15-second straight ahead segment followed by a 90-degree standard rate turn will put you on a perfect downwind. If you continue the downwind for 15 seconds beyond a point abeam the landing threshold, you'll find that a 180-degree standard rate turn will put you on a perfect short final. The only factors involved in these timing procedures are the airspeed and wind. When a strong wind blows, you'll have to adjust your timed segments accordingly.

Whenever possible you should try to circle to the left. This allows the left-seat pilot a better opportunity to maintain sight of the runway or airport.

Two-man crews have developed various cockpit routines to handle the dynamic circling approach maneuver and some of these coordination drills are quite complex. At night or in poor visibility situations the old "one-man-down, one-man-up" rule is the best bet. Suppose you're using maneuver E depicted in Figure 2. Descent to the circling MDA would be completed on the approach course. Both pilots might take a peek for orientation as the runway was overflown, then the copilot would go head-down and make a standard rate 90-degree right turn followed immediately by a standard rate 260 to the left. The captain would check for traffic and scan his own instruments until the aircraft (in the left turn) was coming up on the downwind heading at which time he'd twist in his seat to pick up the airport over his left shoulder. The copilot would stay head-down maintaining the standard rate turn while holding MDA until the captain was convinced that the threshold was clearly visible and the aircraft was in a proper position to begin the letdown. One jet crew we know uses this technique quite effectively. Often the captain will take over from the head-down copilot when the aircraft is within 60 degrees of the runway heading.

The NTSB's accident briefs indicate that a common cause of circling approach accidents is the premature descent. And it's understandable how a pilot can be lured into a premature letdown. Picture a guy shooting an A-type (Figure 2) maneuver. Suppose he breaks out on the upwind end of the runway in marginal conditions and swings over to the downwind leg only to find that the scud base is another 50 feet lower there. Rather than penetrating the scud at the risk of losing sight of the runway, he drops 50 feet below MDA. Further suppose that he runs into another scud wall further along in the downwind, but he's nearing the point where he'd begin a descent *in VFR conditions* anyway, so he drops down another 50 feet and starts his 180 turn. Suddenly he realizes he's too low, so he stops his descent by pulling up the nose; and if he's got a slight right crosswind, he tightens up the turn. BANG . . . if the turn was coordinated he'd probably crash right side up. If he was sneaking in bottom rudder, he'd probably crash inverted. In either case, he'd be dead.

The rule here is the most important discussed in this article. *Never descend below MDA until the aircraft is in a position to complete the approach to touchdown using minimum descent rates and standard rate turns.* Remember, if you are legal, you've got at least one mile visibility which means your final can be at least one mile long. There is no reason to rush things. Take advantage of that mile and use all of it to establish the aircraft on a normalized final. (Three of the accidents involved in our survey were described as "hard landings." All three involved relatively large airplanes flown by highly experienced pilots. Investigation of these accidents indicated that the pilots were rushed and got into situations involving close-in high-speed descents and either did not or could not flare. Mile-long finals help the pilot avoid these situations.)

The pilots who flew into the ground during steep turns obviously ignored this rule. The pilots who got into accelerated stalls turning onto final ignored this rule too. In fact, when NTSB's list is culled of all violators of this rule and of the mechanical-defect related accidents, all that are left are one poor guy who lost control in a thunderstorm and another guy who was cleared for a night landing on a runway that was covered with 15 inches of snow.

Unfortunately, the definition of the circling missed approach point given earlier is really the only practical definition available—"The missed approach point is wherever you happen to be when you lose it." So, the key to a safe missed approach during a circling maneuver is the "wherever" part. You must know where you are relative to the airport. And to do this you've got to have a plan of action in mind before the approach begins. In a straight-in approach procedure, you've got electronic guidance throughout the approach and into the missed approach. In the circling maneuver you might be droning around in the boondocks out of sight of the airport when things start going to hell. (This is another reason to avoid maneuvers D and E in Figure 2.)

Speed control, standard rate turns and a good mental picture of the situation are absolutely essential if you are going to stay within the protected circling approach area during the maneuvers and then find the missed approach corridor if the circling maneuver flops.

These suggestions might help.

(1) Speed—Turboprop and turbojet flight manuals normally recommend maneuvering speeds and flaps settings. Use them. Manufacturers of smaller aircraft—the piston twins, for instance—normally leave selection of approach and maneuvering speeds up to the pilot. A good way to select the appropriate speed is to check the stall speed charts and pick the speed shown for a 60-degree bank in the approach configuration. In the Cessna 310, for example, this speed is 102 knots, well above the straight and level stall speed of 70 knots. It also approximates the best single-engine climb speed of 101 knots. In actual practice we use 100 knots in our 310 as bug speed for the approach maneuvers. Similar book exercises will work for other piston twins. Once you pick your approach speed, use it all the time.

(2) Standard rate turns—If you overfly the landing runway (from any direction) and then fly standard rate turns and keep track of their direction, you'll always know where the airport is relative to your position.

(3) Mental pictures—Obviously you must study the approach plate before beginning any approach. But this warning is probably more important in the safe execution of a circling approach than in any other procedure. Long before you break out you should have a picture in your mind's eye of the airport's orientation to the final approach course. You should also pay attention to what the wind is doing to you on the final approach course and apply appropriate crab and rollout corrections during your contact maneuvers. Most important, you must have initial stages of the missed approach procedure memorized. There's no time to check the procedure on the plate while trying to stay within the circling approach area and attempting to re-establish your position relative to the airport.

To summarize, the circling approach maneuver needn't be as deadly to professional pilots as it seems to be:

(1) Get back to basics and practice low-altitude, low-speed ground reference maneuvers. Learn how your aircraft approaches an accelerated stall.

(2) Establish your own circling approach minimums. Night circling approaches to unfamiliar airports in hilly terrain are especially deadly. Avoid them if at all possible.

(3) Make and keep a promise to yourself *never* to descend below the MDA until the aircraft is in a position to make a stabilized final approach.

(4) Pick a good maneuvering speed for circling approaches and always stick with it.

(5) Resist the temptation to drop below MDA to retain sight of the airport during ragged conditions.

(6) Make standard rate turns. If your position requires a turn greater

than standard rate to make the runway, abandon the approach and try it again, next time with a little better planning.

(7) Study the approach plate and visualize the position and layout of the airport during the final approach segment. Have a circling plan in mind before you break out. Commit to memory the initial maneuvers of the missed approach.

(8) If you normally fly with a two-man crew, develop a callout procedure and stick with it.

(9) Avoid circling approaches whenever possible.

Remember that a circling approach is a procedure designed to get you relatively close to an airport. Beyond that, it's all up to you.

M Is for Missed Approach

25

by Dan Manningham

I have a confession to make, one I hate to admit. In the last several years I have seldom paid proper attention to missed approach procedures (except when the weather was so bad I fully expected to miss even before beginning the approach.) Fortunately, there have been precious few misses, so my lack of preparation has not bitten me very often.

Maybe success is responsible for the problem. Experience reinforces our expectation of making a successful landing, so we lose incentive to properly prepare for a one-in-a-thousand possibility.

Actually, it's a matter of priorities. A simple review of FAR 91.117, "Limitations On Use of Instrument Approach Procedures," establishes those priorities. Notice the wording of paragraph (b):

"Descent below MDA or DH. No person may operate an aircraft below the prescribed minimum descent altitude or continue an approach below the prescribed minimum descent altitude or continue an approach below the decision height unless—

"(1) The aircraft is in a position from which a normal approach to the runway of intended landing can be made; and

"(2) The approach threshold of that runway, or approach lights or other markings identifiable with the approach end of that runway, are clearly visible to the pilot.

"If, upon arrival at the missed approach point or decision height, or at any time thereafter, any of the above requirements are not met, the pilot shall immediately execute the appropriate missed approach procedure."

Notice the construction of this regulation. It makes the MDA or DH the point at which a missed approach will be made *unless* you happen to see the runway or approach lights well enough to continue. The concept is valid, although it conflicts with pilots' and controllers' experience in a regrettable way. Instrument approaches have such a high incidence of success that we tend to reverse the logic. In real life, the MDA or DH becomes a point from which the *landing* will be made, not the reverse as required by 91.117(b).

I believe that I am not alone in my nonchalance toward missed approaches. There are at least three reasons for this attitude of apparent indifference to the only alternative a pilot has when a safe landing is not possible:

· The IFR environment is so totally controlled we take it for granted that the controller will lead us by the hand in the event of a missed approach. If there were no radio traffic and we really felt isolated in the cockpit, I think we would be much more inclined to plan ahead.

· It is a cop-out to assume that the missed approach procedure will be so simple that a review is unnecessary. We often find, however, that missed approach procedures are more complicated than the approach itself. Look at the ILS Runway 19L approach at San Francisco, for instance.

In order to successfully complete the ILS approach and landing to SFO's Runway 19L, you really need to know only four things: the localizer frequency (108.9), the localizer course (191°), the intercept altitude (1800 feet) and the decision height (285 feet). The missed approach procedure, on the other hand, requires a knowledge of at least nine facts: two altitudes (410 feet and 1900 feet), a programmed left turn, the ISFO localizer frequency (109.5), the inbound course (281°), the Oakland VOR frequency (116.8), the intersection radial (173°), the left-turn hold and the appropriate entry to that holding pattern (tear drop).

· Again, because it so seldom happens, we develop a strong assumption that the missed approach will never be needed; hence the subtle feeling that a review of it is unnecessary. This mental conditioning, which researchers call "expectancy" or "set," is defined as an anticipatory belief or desire. Mixed up in the whole thing is the fact that decisions often are based on how we would like circumstances to be rather than on reality itself.

In its most general form, expectancy works like this:

· We learn a basic skill like flying in an academic, student-teacher environment.

· As we develop that skill, we begin to attach subconscious meanings to the stimuli associated with it. Picture the numeral "3" written twice, one over the other with a line beneath as in an arithmetic problem. If I ask for an answer, you will respond by saying either six, nine or zero, depending on whether you are "set" to add, multiply or subtract. In an airplane we are set to land.

· Once a set or anticipation is developed, we become influenced by it instead of the reality of the situation. The reality of that arithmetic problem is not established until the appropriate sign is added. Likewise, the reality of an instrument approach may not be established until the MDA or DH is reached.

· Finally, our mental set eliminates the viable alternatives by focusing our thoughts on just one possibility such as addition or, in the case of an approach, landing.

The solution to mind set is to recognize its potential and then control the false anticipations. In terms of missed approaches, that solution is a careful review *and* discussion before the approach begins.

Years ago I learned a simple checklist for instrument approaches; I call it WIMTIM:

· Weather checked.
· Instruments and radio set.
· Minimums.
· Time inbound (for nonprecision approaches).
· Instruct other crewmembers about your needs and intentions.
· Missed approach procedure review.
· It's time to put the last M back into WIMTIM.

Keep Off the Grass 26

by Dan Manningham

Before this winter is over, a group of investigators will gather, in the mud, at the far end of some runway and try to piece together another overrun accident. If this case is typical, adverse weather and poor runway conditions will be contributing factors, but whatever the causes, the unfortunate result will be one more airplane off the runway and into trouble. FAA landing-distance criteria are reasonable in most operating circumstances, but a review of those criteria with potential problems reveals that even experienced pilots are sometimes hard pressed to keep off the grass.

Airplane flight manuals are put together from information gathered in actual flight tests and adjusted to conform to FAA requirements for landing distance. For aircraft weighing less than 6,000 pounds there are no landing-distance requirements imposed by the FARs; for aircraft weighing more than 6,000 pounds, whether certified to Part 23 or 25, the FARs are quite specific. Tests must be flown to exact standards by the manufacturer and precise data collected. The ultimate refinement of this data is usually a handy set of graphs showing, for Part 25 aircraft, minimum landing distances or maximum landing weights for specific runway conditions. Unfortunately, this predigested material does not show what, if any, margin there is for error, and as flight-crew members we must often guess at the cumulative effects of runway condition, crosswind, equipment condition and equipment failure. In order to put the matter in perspective, it is necessary to examine landing requirements as they are now computed and used.

For those who operate aircraft weighing 6,000 pounds or more to Part 91 standards the landing-distance requirement is brief: From an approach speed of 1.3 Vso the landing distance is "the horizontal distance necessary to land and come to a complete stop . . . from a point 50 feet above the landing surface . . ." (See Figure 1.)

The distances shown in virtually all general-aviation flight manuals are based on the above description. Although that's what the FARs require, and that's what most manufacturers show in flight manuals, we at B/CA feel that it is at best an imprudent way to tell pilots how much runway an airplane requires for touchdown and stop. It leaves no margin for error. If the flight manual shows 3,500 feet are needed, but you cross the end of a 3,500-foot long runway at a height of 51 feet, instead of the specified 50 feet, you'll run 70 feet off into the grass even with maximum braking. Same thing if you approach at 1.31 Vso instead of 1.3. Therefore, B/CA recommends and uses Part 121 (air carrier) landing-distance requirements in its own operations and that is the standard used throughout this chapter.

Simply stated, the maximum weight for landing on any given runway under Part 121 must be limited so that the *required landing distance* will not exceed 60 percent of the *effective landing length*. By definition:

(1) *Effective landing length* is the distance from the far end of the runway to the point on the approach end where the obstruction-clearance plane (OCP) touches down. (The obstruction-clearance plane is a plane that clears all obstructions and slopes toward the runway at a 1:20 gradient. It may intersect the runway at its very beginning or 1,000 feet or more down the hard surface, depending on the obstructions in the approach path. Regardless of how long the hard surface is, the effective landing length begins where the OCP touches down.)

(2) *Required landing distance* is the distance needed to land and come to a complete stop from a point 50 feet above the effective-landing-length threshold (where the OCP touches down). Test data is gathered from approaches in a steady glide to the 50-foot height at no less than 1.3 landing stall speed. After touchdown, stopping distance is based on the drag from the landing flap setting, fully extended spoilers and maximum wheel braking. Reverse thrust *may not* be used in computing or demonstrating the required landing distance, and stopping distance is based on a dry, smooth, hard-surfaced runway. (See Figure 2.)

Maximum landing weights are based on the ability of your airplane to stop in 60 percent of the effective landing length when flown under the most ideal and carefully controlled conditions. If your airplane is so equipped, reverse thrust will provide an additional, although unspecified, margin. In all cases, excepting alternate airports, 15 percent is added to the required effective landing distance for wet runways. This is an arbitrary figure and may not compensate for the fact that wet-surface braking coefficients are often half those for dry surfaces. In broad terms, then, when you are right up to weight, 40 percent of the available runway is left to cover the difference between your situation and that of the test pilot.

The remaining 40 percent of effective landing length is yours to use as you please; however, under no circumstances may you have 41 percent. With good conditions your margin is sufficient, although the standard winter problems of low ceilings, slick runways and stiff crosswinds can easily consume most or all of that 40 percent in a hurry. As I see it, landing length is composed of two segments, the air distance needed to descend from 50 feet and the ground distance required to come to a full stop. Specifically, then, there are two areas to examine in the case of overruns: approach and roll-out.

Your 40-percent margin assumes precise airspeed, altitude and glide path at the 50-foot window and close attention to those parameters is essential if you wish to preserve maximum stopping distance on the ground. Excess altitude over the threshold will extend the landing distance proportionately and low approaches not only increase the risk of an under-shoot, but may, in some instances, use more runway than a normal approach. Let's look at both cases.

If 50 feet above threshold aims you 1,000 feet down the runway, then 75 feet above will move the aim point to 1,500 feet and so on. When you are high, you have three options:

(1) Continue a stabilized approach and accept the fact that you are going to land long and will have to use heavy braking.

(2) Steepen the approach realizing that you will need added airspeed at the bottom for the flare and accept the fact that you are still going to land somewhat long.

(3) Go around.

Skillful use of power in the flare may allow good recovery from that high and steep approach, however, the final penalty for excess height over the threshold will be some reduction in your 40-percent margin.

Flat approaches may put you onto the hard surface a little early, but you are greatly increasing the risk of an undershoot, which could be far more disastrous than sliding off the far end at reduced airspeed. I have also watched many long, flat approaches that resulted in long landings because, I think, the pilot had mentally fixed on a shallow glide path and failed to compensate for the extra power used in a flat approach and extended aim point after crossing the runway end.

Certification results are based on Vref (1.3 Vso) over the threshold and if the test pilot is off speed he just does it over again. You have the same choice. If you elect to continue with speed above Vref, you again have three options:

(1) Land hot. You will use about two percent added runway for each one percent in excess speed.

(2) Hold the airplane off and reduce speed in the air. This will use roughly 700 to 1,000 feet of runway per each five knots in excess speed and is by far the poorer technique of the first two.

(3) Go around.

When you are fast at the 50-foot window, a larger power reduction may make it possible to lose the excess speed before touchdown, but you will still be ahead of the desired profile and this alone will reduce your 40-percent margin.

193

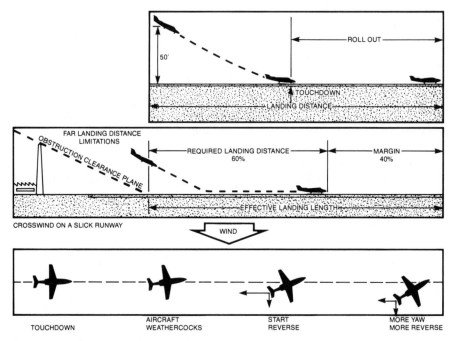

Figure 1 (top): The typical flight-manual landing distance (FAR 91) begins 50 feet over the end of the runway, but there is no margin at the far end.

Figure 2 (middle): Under 121 the landing distance from 50 feet is determined, then 67 percent is added to form a 60/40 safety margin.

Figure 3: (bottom) If the aircraft drifts toward the edge of the runway, turning toward the centerline and applying reverse thrust only aggravates the problem.

There are two final considerations in planning the approach to a tight runway. First, any attempt to flatten out at the bottom for a smooth touchdown extends your landing distance beyond what is assumed in the handbook charts. We all like a "squeaker" and often it is the best technique, but when runway is critical, a firm landing with only minimum time in the flare is necessary to preserve your margin. Second, approaches in high density altitudes are already at a disadvantage since the FAA required landing distance is not temperature corrected and so the higher true airspeeds and flare distances are not factored into your flight-manual landing weights. Those temperatures in your landing-weight charts are only for approach and landing climb gradient specifications.

Some years ago I landed on 10,000 feet of runway from an approach that would have satisfied Steve Canyon. Seconds later, with four engines in reverse, spoilers out and anti-skid braking in full use we skated gracefully off the far end and into an ocean of mud. The moral is—no matter how good the approach to a slick runway, you better get it all together on the roll-out if you are going to stop in time. Deceleration on a slippery runway is a touchy problem so let's isolate one factor at a time.

Spoilers/speed brakes perform two distinct functions:

(1) They increase the total aerodynamic drag of the airframe.

(2) They greatly reduce the coefficient of lift.

In practical terms this means that as soon as you get those spoilers fully deployed, you will have aerodynamic drag and maximum potential wheel braking because the weight of the airplane will be transferred from wings to wheels. Spoilers provide easy and crisp response with little or no risk of directional control problems even on the most slippery runway, so don't waste any time getting them out.

There are marked differences in the operation of reverse thrust between jets and props but the applications are very similar. Any reverse thrust (or ground fine) is most effective at high speed, so use it early, although cautiously, since reverse on a slick runway can cause severe directional control problems. Figure 3 shows a classic example—slippery runway with a crosswind. After touchdown the airplane begins to weathercock and drift toward the downwind side of the runway because the tires have little or no traction and the airframe presents a large sail area to the wind. When reverse is applied in this situation the thrust vectors have a side component which drives the aircraft toward the runway edge. If the pilot reacts instinctively and yaws the airplane back toward centerline he increases the side component and accelerates the sideways drift. Corrective action here is to return to enough forward thrust to regain directional control and, when stabilized, cautiously try reverse again.

Landing-weight and distance charts in your flight manual, recall, do not reflect the use of reverse thrust because the airplane must be certified without it. As a result, engine reverse is a bonus, but remember that it creates the biggest problems when it's most needed. When the runway is tight, get 'em into reverse as soon as possible; but, on slick surfaces especially, get the feel of things at low reverse power settings before using it all.

On dry, smooth runways wheel brake potential is probably much greater than most of us realize. By definition, maximum braking is achieved when the wheels are sustained just above a skid, but even with antiskid, the average pilot may never use more than 70 percent of the braking available to him. Your handbook weights and distances are based on maximum braking and at least one manufacturer figures you will apply this "maximum braking" within two seconds after wheel spinup. So there you are. Anything less than superlative use of the brakes from two seconds after wheel spin-up to a complete stop will reduce the 40-percent margin. And that's on a dry, smooth runway.

In real life things are different. Smooth runways are few and far between and they are often not dry. In fact, no single factor outside your control will affect landing distance as much as the coefficient of friction between your tires and the runway. (See Figure 4.) Normal coefficients on dry concrete run from .45 to .50 although this optimum figure will be reduced by tire wear, runway surface, water, ice, air temperature and ground speed. For example, slush and ice at 32 degrees F. produce braking coefficients of .05 or less, and between the high and low extremes is a whole range of possibilities from dry, smooth and level through damp, wet, standing water (hydroplaning conditions), slush and wet ice. Figure 5 shows some representative stopping distances for various conditions.

In 1961 the FAA conducted carefully controlled and instrumented tests using a Convair 880 on water and slush to determine braking coefficients and stopping distances. Several interesting results were obtained:

(1) Stopping distances on a wet surface were almost double those on a dry surface.

(2) Stopping distances on slush were almost triple.

(3) Braking coefficients are markedly better at lower ground speeds on any surface other than dry.

(4) The tests left a real question as to whether there is any wheel braking at all in standing water or slush at more than 80 to 100 knots because of hydroplaning.

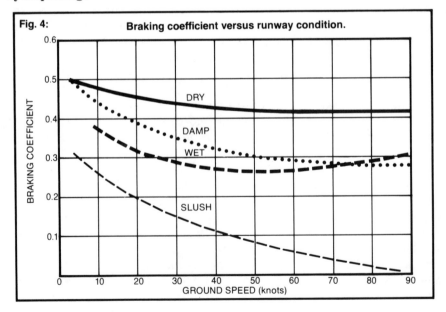

Fig. 4: Braking coefficient versus runway condition.

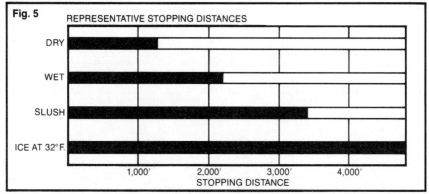

When the runway is wet or iced over, roll-out distances increase startlingly.

Poor braking coefficients are a common fact of life, but there are some ways to optimize that situation:

(1) Carefully preflight tires for proper tread depth and inflation. Worn tires can double the landing roll and under-inflation increases the risk of hydroplaning.

(2) Touch down firm, even hard, to break through the liquid film and place the tires in solid contact with the hard surface.

(3) Touch down at minimum speed, consistent with the above, to reduce total braking requirement, to increase braking coefficient and to avoid the onset of hydroplaning.

Once the wheels are turning, remember that maximum braking will be achieved by sustaining the wheels at a point just above a skid. On a dry surface this may require heavy pedal pressure, but on slick runways you will have to be careful. Your instincts may call for heavy braking in the face of marginal stopping conditions, but best results will accrue by beginning cautiously and then increasing pressure to stay just above a skid as the airplane slows.

Unfortunately, there is still no accurate measure of braking coefficient available to cockpit crews and so we must guess at the cumulative effects of runway conditions based on past experience. With anything less than "smooth and dry" you will use a considerable amount of that 40-percent margin, but there is no way to accurately measure how much or whether you may, in fact, need 41 percent and thus stop on the grass.

Okay, you make a great approach and find out in the early stages of roll-out that braking conditions are nil. Can you take it around from your position on the runway? How long can you delay in making that decision? What are the options?

197

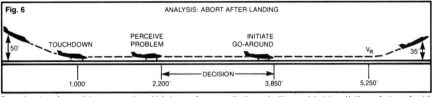

Fig. 6   ANALYSIS: ABORT AFTER LANDING

To touch and scat from a slick runway requires a high degree of crew coordination and split-second decisions. Until manufacturers furnish definitive data, we must recommend against it.

Look at the case of a Learjet 25B or C at 13,000 pounds, ISA, at sea level on a 6,000-foot runway as pictured in Figure 6. Approach speed is 138 knots, required effective landing length 3,690 feet and the pilot aims for the 1,000-foot runway marker. If he is right on the money at touchdown, ground speed will be 230 feet per second. Deceleration will be minimal since braking action is nil in this case. If a go-around is to be made successfully, the airplane will have to be at Vr in takeoff configuration at some limiting point on the runway in order to meet normal obstacle clearances on the climbout.

Touchdown is at the 1,000-foot point and if that limiting point for Vr is, say, 750 feet from the far end, then there are 4,250 feet left in which to attempt a stop, make a decision, transition to takeoff configuration and accelerate to Vr. If I assign some estimated time and distance values as a point of departure, the example looks like this:

Touchdown	1,000 ft.
Spoilers extended	400 ft.
Nosewheel grounded and roll-out stabilized	400 ft.
Wheel brakes tried and problem perceived	400 ft.
Total	2,200 ft.

The airplane is now configured for stopping and the remaining 3,800 feet of hard surface are available for deceleration if you so choose. On the other hand, if you elect to go, you must initiate that action in time to arrive at Vr 750 feet from the runway end. Again, after assigning some estimated values, your distance required to that rotate point looks like this:

Throttles repositioned	300 ft.
Spoilers retracted	300 ft.
Flaps repositioned	300 ft.
Accelerate to Vr	500 ft.
Total	1,400 ft.

Since 1,400 feet of the runway is used from the point where throttles are advanced to the 750-foot rotate point, you will need at least 2,150 feet of remaining runway when you begin the go-around. Subtract that from the 3,800 feet remaining when you first detected a braking problem and you have 1,650 feet, or about seven seconds to delay before making a clear and irreversible decision.

Seven seconds may sound like a comfortable period, but until flight crews have better information there are overriding problems for those who attempt to go-around after touching down.

(1) No one has determined where the decision point is on the runway.

(2) Very few runways have markers which would clearly tell when you are at the decision point.

(3) The maneuver itself requires development of appropriate procedures and thorough crew training and coordination.

(4) The abort decision is irreversible.

Until these problems are resolved and flight manuals changed, flight crews have very little technical or legal basis for attempting to fly out of a poor runway situation. The unhappy truth is that rolling straight off the far end at reduced speed will continue to be the safest solution.

Your 40 percent must handle any and all problems in combination. There is that additional 15 percent for wet runways at regular (not alternate) airports, but none of it is related specifically to engineering test data. There is just the one sweeping assumption that with the worst possible conditions you will never need over 40 percent more runway than was required under ideal circumstances. With this in mind, consider the following, especially when operating close to limits:

(1) Be aware of tire condition and consider starting the winter with new treads.

(2) When approaching an airport with known crosswinds and poor braking conditions, seriously consider diverting to another field.

(3) If you are not close to proper altitude and speed at the threshold, go around. If you are, put the airplane firmly on the ground and save that long grease job for another day.

(4) Raise spoilers and ground the nosewheel as soon as possible.

(5) Modulate brakes to cycle the anti-skid every two to three seconds. Without anti-skid, use enough pressure to keep just above a skid. Remember that the roll-out end of the runway is the slickest part.

(6) When stabilized, use reverse (if available) cautiously at first, and then increase to max allowable.

(7) Reduce speed to a crawl before attempting to turn off a slippery runway.

(8) If you do get into trouble, sliding straight off the end at minimum speed is preferable to any sideways excursion.

ARRIVALS

No meaningful changes in landing weight/distance charts can be made until line pilots have at their disposal an accurate measure of braking coefficient. Until that time, each individual will have to measure his own situation and ability against those of the certification pilot and make some subjective correction to compensate for the differences.

Hydroplaning: Triple Trouble

27

by Dan Manningham

On December 15, 1972, a Boeing 747 landed well below limiting weight on Runway 27L at Miami. Although 250 percent of the dry runway stopping distance was available beyond the actual touchdown point, the airplane hydroplaned off the far end and sustained substantial structural damage. Subsequent tests by NASA on this runway disclosed that wet braking coefficients were at least 70 percent less than assumed by FAR 121. As a result, the NTSB has recommended that the FAA expedite its research in the area of wet runway friction characteristics.

Pilots have long known that landings on wet, smooth runways presented serious potential braking problems and, not surprisingly, much is now being said about hydroplaning and associated incidents on wet surfaces. After all, we may not talk pretty when the runway end is coming up too fast, but the barroom language recorded on the CVR is the only help too many of us have in solving the problem.

Hydroplaning is not new and it is certainly not unique to high performance or turbine-powered aircraft. One B/CA staffer encountered serious hydroplaning in a Cessna 182, proving that any wheeled airplane is susceptible. When you understand the dynamics of this phenomenon, it is easier to see how broad the problem really is.

Experts agree that hydroplaning is really a loose assortment of three different but related phenomena:

· Dynamic hydroplaning, which occurs with standing water on the runway.

· Viscous hydroplaning, which can occur on smooth runways with water depths as shallow as .001 inch.

· Reverted rubber or steam hydroplaning, which requires a locked wheel skid on a damp or wet runway.

Dynamic hydroplaning. Dynamic hydroplaning results from high aircraft speeds on flooded runways. As the airplane accelerates for takeoff,

Aircraft	Main Gear Tire Pressure (psi)	V_p (ground-speed kts)	Aircraft	Main Gear Tire Pressure (psi)	V_p (ground-speed kts)
V_p for Business Aircraft					
Cessna 182 Skylane	42	57	Mitsubishi MU-2K	55	67
Beech Bonanza V35	38	55	Cessna Citation	100	90
Piper PA-23 Aztec	54	66	Dassault Falcon 10	110	95
Beech Duke A60	51	64	Gates Lear-jet 25	140	106
Cessna 421 Golden Eagle	80	80	Rockwell Sabre 60	226	136
Beech King Air E90	55	67	Lockheed JetStar	225	135
Rockwell 690A	60	70	Grumman G-11	155	112

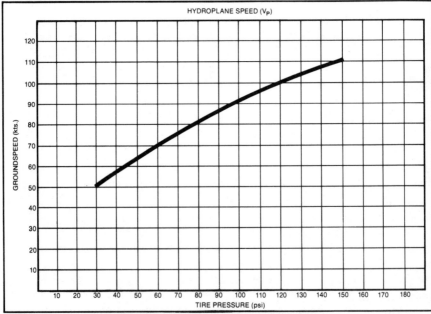

This V_p curve shows why every aircraft down to the heavy singles is subject to dynamic hydroplaning.

a fluid wedge forms that progressively separates the tire footprint area from the runway surface. At tire hydroplaning speed, V_P, the lift developed under the tire is equal to the weight borne by it and the tire is lifted clear of runway to hydroplane on a film of water.

V_P has been determined to be nine times the square root of the main gear tire pressure or $V_P = 9\sqrt{P}$. If your aircraft's main gear tires are inflated to 100 lbs./sq. in., for instance, then $V_P = 9\sqrt{100}$ or 90 knots groundspeed. Smaller aircraft generally have tire pressures proportionate to their reduced groundspeeds, so they too often operate in hydroplaning conditions. If you look at the chart below, you will see that V_P for an airplane with 38 psi tires is 55 knots and V_P for 42 psi tires is still only 57 knots. Virtually all airplanes, regardless of size or type, exceed hydroplaning speed regularly.

During takeoff, speeds up to V_P will produce progressively reduced braking effectiveness and directional capability as more and more of the tire footprint area is lifted out of contact with the runway. Above V_P, full dynamic hydroplaning removes all tire-to-surface friction and, further, the vertical component of the fluid wedge produces a spin-down moment which slows and eventually stops wheel rotation in the extreme situation.

Landing or decelerating on standing water will produce the same general effects, but in reverse order. In fact, experiments have shown that once hydroplaning has begun it may continue to significantly slower speeds. As a result, the problem is more serious for landing or abort situations.

Viscous hydroplaning. Viscous hydroplaning occurs on very smooth runways when they are wet. Water on newly surfaced asphalt runways, or touchdown areas with heavy coatings of rubber from repeated wheel spin-ups, forms a tenacious film that can completely separate tire from pavement at speeds at least 35 per cent below V_P. Unlike dynamic hydroplaning, very little water is required. Total separation can be produced by film thicknesses of .001 inches in this situation with results as potentially hazardous as total dynamic hydroplaning.

Steam hydroplaning. When runways are damp or wet, the heat from a locked-wheel condition produces steam in the tire footprint area that may revert the rubber to its tacky, uncured state. This gummy material creates an excellent seal to enclose the footprint area and entrap steam, which then super heats at temperatures up to 260 degrees C. and lifts the tire clear of the pavement. Steam hydroplaning has been measured to below 20 knots groundspeed in some cases.

Okay, there is the whole bag: dynamic, viscous and steam. If you're unlucky, you may experience all three in one landing. There are several variables that can influence hydroplaning, some of which can be controlled by flight crews. Let's look at a few.

Preflight. Since V_P is directly related to tire pressure, it might seem logical to increase that pressure and thereby raise V_P for your airplane. In fact that would work, although any increase in pressure will also decrease *dry* runway braking coefficients because overinflation lessens the overall contact area of the tire which, in turn, reduces traction. Tire manufacturers' recommended pressures are a compromise between braking coefficients and hydroplane speed (among other things) and you are best off using their numbers. Do, however, check for correct tire inflation.

Tires with deep radial ribs give the best protection against the onset of hydroplaning. Even though the ribs may not be as deep as the pooled water on the runway, they will still function to relieve the buildup of that fluid wedge which acts to separate tire and runway, by providing a low pressure escape route for the water. Deep ribs will inhibit steam hydroplaning and provide maximum cornering effectiveness on slick surfaces, so preflight the tires carefully and don't operate with worn treads or, if you must, use extra caution.

Runways. Runways are constructed from a variety of materials depending on geography, climate, municipal budgets and so on. Each surface seems to have its own personality when it comes to braking coefficients. There are some objective reasons for these differences:

· Runways with a pronounced crown shed water rapidly and prevent the buildup of water depth that is the first prerequisite for dynamic hydroplaning.

· Rough or textured surfaces inhibit viscous hydroplaning by preventing the formation of a smooth and cohesive fluid film. These surfaces also increase the critical fluid depth needed for dynamic hydroplaning by allowing fluid to escape from the tire footprint area.

· Runways with lateral grooves provide the best protection against all three forms of hydroplaning. Heavy rain is more effectively drained away by the channeling action of the grooves, and a pumping action between tires and grooves forces water out of the footprint area to forestall dynamic hydroplaning. Viscous hydroplaning is prevented because the grooves break up what otherwise might be a smooth surface. Steam hydroplaning can't develop because steam pressure in the footprint area escapes sideways through the grooves and because the gummy reverted rubber is scraped from the tire as it slides across the rippled surface.

There is still no objective standard by which braking coefficients on wet runways are measured, so keep your ear to the ground and you will be able to develop your own opinions about specific runways and their relative stopping merits under adverse conditions.

As things now stand, the best information may be the experience of someone who has been there before.

Technique. Pilot technique cannot remove the possibility of hydroplaning, but it can substantially reduce the exposure and the risk if you observe a few simple cautions. You should know what the V_P for your airplane is and be aware that any touchdown above V_P on a wet runway will present a high risk of hydroplaning. When you are in this situation, make the final approach at minimum safe speed (usually 1.3 Vso) to the most favorable runway.

After touchdown, make early use of spoilers, if available, to transfer the aircraft weight to the wheels and aid wheel spinup. Ground the nosewheel for maximum directional control, and once you are stabilized on the runway, decelerate as rapidly as possible with the following precautions:

(1) Sustained heavy braking may induce steam hydroplaning so begin cautiously and be prepared to ease-off pedal pressures as soon as you detect a braked-wheel condition, then reapply brakes judiciously when wheel rotation resumes.

(2) Reverse thrust on a wet runway, particularly with a brisk crosswind, may cause serious directional control problems so use it early, although cautiously, until you have a feel for the situation.

Any amount of water on a runway creates a potential hydroplaning situation and should be treated with respect. Small amounts of anticipation and planning will produce big results when you apply your own good judgment and technique under the prevailing conditions.

WEATHER

Start to discuss the theory of weather, and most pilots will yawn and change the subject. Airmen seem to have a built-in aversion to the study of meteorology even though they spend endless hours coping with the real thing—sometimes on a life-and-death basis. Yet they grouse when forecasts go sour or when they feel that the weather briefer has not been altogether conscientious in providing the whole picture.

Essentially, the serious pilot has two basic problems regarding his confrontations with weather planning and weather flying. First, he must bridge the communications gap between himself and the weather professional so that he can understand the situation as the weather briefer sees and explains it. Second, he must have his own solid grasp of basic weather phenomena and their specific impact on flight. Thunderstorms, turbulence, icing and windshear mean very different things to the pilot in the air from what they mean to the meteorologist on the ground. Being in the weather is very different from consulting charts depicting it. Furthermore, the ultimate weather-founded decisions remain with the pilot in command. Instinct based on experience helps a little in coping with the alternatives, but analysis based on meteorological principles tends to help a lot more.

Forecasting the weather is a complex science that is probably beyond the limits of most pilots' knowledge, but coping with the weather on a practical basis is a necessary skill for the serious airman.

Interrogating the Weatherman

by Richard N. Aarons

Used to be when you called Flight Service for a briefing, all you needed to do was mumble an aircraft N-number and a destination. The FSS specialist would then scrounge around his cluttered table for the appropriate teletype weather reports and forecasts and read you the bad news.

As the briefing progressed, you'd interrupt him from time to time asking for this or that off-route terminal, and he'd comply with a sigh. If you were really sharp, you'd ask for the NOTAMS and NOSUMS.

Then, halfway through your goodbyes you'd suddenly remember that you forgot to ask for the winds. He'd grumble a bit, shuffle some more papers and read off NOA's latest guess.

Times are changing. Like everything else in the aviation business, Flight Service Stations are being computerized to varying degrees of sophistication. In the long run, the use of computers by FSS specialists for weather data acquisition should mean better briefings for the pilot. But the pilot more than ever will have to approach the FSS specialist with a certain degree of professionalism if he is to get a *quality* briefing.

Recently, B/CA editors discussed pilot briefing techniques with several FSS specialists. We are convinced that these men, by and large, *want* to provide quality weather briefings. But we also concluded that many businessmen pilots—more so than the corporate professionals—unintentionally thwart the briefers' attempts to provide good service.

A good weather briefing depends as much on the pilot's interrogation techniques as it does on the briefer's competency. The tips that follow were provided by the briefers themselves. Use these techniques, say the briefers, and you'll get much better service from FSS.

First, remember the briefer is a guy just like you trying to do a job. Like most pilots, he's human. Try to establish rapport with him. If you're a crude grouch, the briefer will want to be done with you as soon as possible. As one FSS specialist put it, "You'd be really surprised at the number of grouches who call us. It's only human nature that you'll keep the briefing as short as possible if you've got 10 other phones ringing and the man you're talking to is busting your chops."

You don't have to fall in love with a FSS specialist to get good service, but a friendly hello will go a long way to get the ball rolling.

If FSS specialists were asked to cite their number-one gripe, it would be pilots who make the briefer guess what they want. Don't waste your time or the briefer's. Tell him right up front who you are, what your qualifications are, where you're going, how you're going to get there and when you're leaving.

Make up your own introductory speech and use it whenever you call for a briefing. For example: "This is November six-two-four-eight Quebec. We're an IFR Cessna 310 leaving White Plains at 1200 going to Pittsburgh. We'll need low-level winds and terminals and forecasts for the route and destination."

Your speech, of course, doesn't have to be exactly like this. But it should contain at least the information items suggested here.

It'll be years before all Flight Service Stations get sophisticated computer terminals. In fact, it's probable that there will be several types of automation in Flight Service Stations. But it's important for the pilot to understand what this computer business is all about.

Basically, the idea is to give the pilot a better briefing by giving the briefer all the data pertinent to the pilot's flight.

Under the old system, the briefer had to shuffle through the stacks of teletype reports to find the information for your route. The amount of information given to the pilot often depended on the amount of time the briefer was willing to spend hunting the information. And the amount of time he was willing to devote to servicing you may have depended on the number of other telephones ringing and your ability to keep him on the line.

Under the modern system, the briefer will take your request to a computer terminal—a thing that looks like a big electric typewriter—and enter your origin, destination, route and off times. Within seconds he'll get a hard copy of the weather information (reports and forecasts) and NOTAMS relative to your flight.

The software systems involved in these automated Flight Service Stations will vary from location to location. In some cases, you'll get sequences and terminal forecasts for all reporting points within 50 miles of the route centerline; in other cases you'll get the data for wider or narrower areas.

The important point is that the briefer (and computer) will assume that you are going approximately straight-line from origin to destination. If you plan a significant dog leg, tell the man up front or he'll have to go back to the computer terminal a second time to extract the rest of the information you need.

For the same reason, you should request any special information immediately. For example, it's not unusual for a pilot to request information to destination A and, when he's gotten a complete briefing, he'll add, "OK. I'll be on to (destination B) for the next leg. What's the weather on that route?"

Remember, it's easier for the briefer to ask the computer about all your legs and destinations on his first trip to the terminal.

While we're on the subject of computers, the Flight Service people we talked to asked us to remind you that IFR flight plans are dropped by the ATC computer two hours after the filed off-time. Therefore, if your departure is going to be delayed more than two hours, give Flight Service a call to update your flight plan. That simple procedure will save everybody a bunch of hassles.

Finally, check AIM regularly for announcements of special briefing services. Some Flight Service Stations now have recorded weather briefings on discrete phone numbers for busy routes out of their areas. Others have automatic flight-plan-filing recording machines. At Washington National, for example, it's possible to call one phone number and get a complete briefing for the Washington-New York City route. Then the pilot calls a second number and reads his IFR flight plan into a recording machine. Obviously, these services save time for everybody.

Summing it up then:

(1) Be pleasant on the phone.

(2) Tell the briefer who you are and what kind of equipment you're flying.

(3) Before he goes to retrieve the weather information for your flight, make sure the briefer knows where and when you're going and how you're going . . . and be sure to ask for any special information in this contact.

(4) Check AIM for any special self-help services available at the flight service facility and use those services whenever possible.

Flying Thunderstorms: 29
The Weather Briefing

Any discussion of how to fly thunderstorms must begin with a disclaimer. Don't.

The authors of this special report, combined with various consultants who added their expertise to ours, have a total of 100 years or more experience in dealing with thunderstorms in every sort of airplane from a J-2 Cub up through DC-8s. Our advice without a single dissenting vote is, *don't* fly in, close to or over thunderstorms. Just don't.

End of special report. Now on to the postscript.

Every pilot who uses an airplane for serious transportational purposes must sooner or later grapple with that most awesome of weather phenomena, the thunderstorm. In summer months every weather forecast has somewhere in it, "Chance of thunderstorms," or "Embedded thunderstorms," or "Lines of severe thunderstorms." If you are to totally and absolutely avoid this monster of nature, then you must hangar your airplane from March through October.

The alternative is to learn everything possible about those weather giants and then work the odds on staying out of the worst of them.

You've all been told what thunderstorms are. For most younger readers, the educational process began on page 105 of the FAA's Advisory Circular 00-6A, Aviation Weather. The rest of us received our thunderstorm educations from some Mil-Spec training manual or the other, which we probably still have. That's all good information and should be reviewed occasionally. But what we really want to know is where are the thunderstorms now, at this instant, and how bad are they?

Unfortunately, there is no book for that. Nor can a forecast tell you, or even a ground observation. Radar, either ground based or airborne, can tell you where they are, but even it cannot reveal the intensity without generous portions of foreknowledge, experience, intuition and skill.

Of those four, the first is by far the most important, whether you have airborne radar or not. Everything else connected with flight in the area of, into, through or out of, a thunderstorm *must* begin with foreknowledge.

You can get it from a Flight Service Station, a National Weather Service office or a private weather company. The trick is to know what to ask for.

It's amazing, but although the thunderstorm is the most feared of all

After obtaining data on the convective outlook for your route, you should look at, or ask about, the Radar Summary. This is what the Summary map looks like. To have any real meaning in predicting storm intensity, it must be studied in conjunction with the map below.

This Weather Depiction map, for the same time as the Summary above, should be viewed along with the Summary so you can see whether storms on your route are likely to be air mass or frontal types. Those associated with a front are normally the more severe.

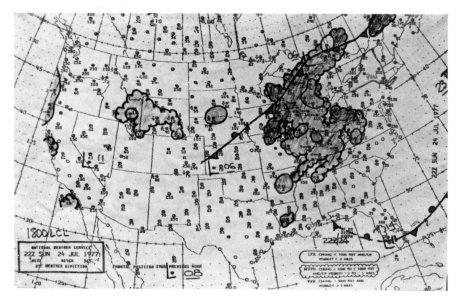

212

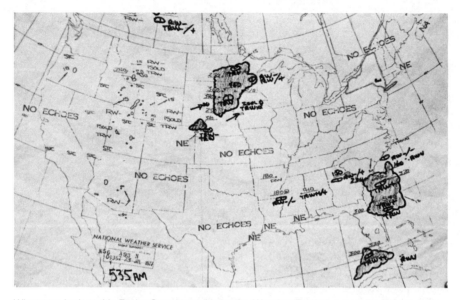

When you look at this Radar Summary without the Weather Depiction map for the same time frame, it has little meaning. You can't tell if those storms in the Dakotas are frontal or not. The areas with no echos may or may not be benign, depending on the AC report.

weather phenomena encountered by airmen here in the United States, one could make a good case for saying there is a conspiracy between the National Weather Service and the FAA to keep vital information out of the pilot's hands. Each day through the summer tens of thousands of bits of information on potential and actual storm activity are collected by the NWS and sent out on teletypes that are never seen by most pilots. FSS specialists rip reams of it off their teletypes and ash-can it without looking to see of what use it might be. There is so much we cannot catalogue it all for you, but we can tell you how we dig some of it out.

For us a weather briefing during the thunderstorm season begins by first just thinking about what time of year it is, where we are and where we're going. Both the frequency and the likely intensity of thunderstorms are known quantities for anyplace in the world and certainly anyplace in the United States. They are rare along the West Coast. They are a daily occurrence all through the middle of the country, but generally less intense the farther north you go. They're less intense in the Northeast, but usually imbedded in smoke and haze or stratus clouds. The farther south you go along the East Coast, the more frequently they're encountered, but they usually top out rather low, tend to be soft and can normally be circumnavigated VFR down low.

213

You don't want to lean too heavily on those generalities, but they help.

After thinking about the potential for storms relative to time of year and locality, the thing we want next is the AC report. When we ask for it, the FSS specialist normally gives us a blank stare or tries to hide his ignorance by fast talk about forecasts or sequences.

Don't let him get away with that. Tell him to use his R and R (Request and Reply) wire to call it up from Kansas City for you. (He got it automatically earlier in the day, but immediately threw it away.) He will get it by requesting RQ MKC AC. While he's at it, ask him to try getting RC FOUS 80 KWBC and RC FXUS 61 KWBC, if east of the Mississippi, or RC FXUS 60 KWBC, if west of the Mississippi. You will also need the Lifted Index and K Index for the day, which he should have somewhere.

We find the AC report to be the most useful indication of what to expect on any flight. It is a convective outlook analysis for the day for the entire United States. It's usually brief. It simply describes areas of the country in which the convective situation will be right for development of severe thunderstorms during the day. The Skywarn areas given on NBC's *Today Show* each morning are based on the AC report.

We've found it to be very accurate. If you add just a bit of common sense to it, it's an excellent guide to when you must be cautious and when you can be optimistic. For example, recently we were westbound in an area not covered by an AC alert, but at Cincinnati ground radar was showing an area of building thunderstorms in heavy lines extending west to Evansville.

With the convective outlook negative, we figured the cells would be shortlived. Experience in using AC reports convinced us of that in spite of it being just at noon when one would normally expect thunderstorms to continue building.

We filed, had a leisurely lunch, then flew through the area without encountering a single raindrop.

Later that afternoon, as we approached Amarillo, Texas, we could see in the distance a nasty line of cells. A nearby FSS told us hail and tornadoes had been reported. But since we were still outside all AC alert areas we continued west cautiously. Sure enough, the cells dissipated in front of us.

By contrast, a few days later over Oklahoma, we encountered an insignificant looking little cell that couldn't have been more than 15 miles across. In another situation—or before we found out about AC—we would have plunged through it. But we were in an AC alert area so we called an FSS just ahead and got an excited reply that the field was zero-zero with heavy rain and half-inch hail.

You shouldn't put all your eggs in the AC report basket, of course, but in the summertime, look at it or have it read to you before you do anything else in preparation for a flight. If the flight will be outside AC alert areas, the odds are that any cells encountered will be moderate and/or short-lived.

If the flight will be through an AC alert area, be super cautious and conservative.

You should also have a look at the Two-to-Six-Hour Probability of Thunderstorms and Severe Weather report. That's such a mouthful, weathermen call it simply the "Charba" report after the man who invented it. The name alone tells you what it is and what use it has. Unfortunately, we find we can't always get it. Supposedly it can be called up by the FSS specialist on his R and R wire with the code RC FOUS 80 KWBC, but often the response is that it's not in the system. Give it a try anyway, because every bit of data helps.

RC FXUS 61 (or 60) KWBC is the MOS Thunderstorm Probability report. It should come off the facsimile receiver and it shows isometric lines of thunderstorm probability. But it too may not always be available.

Finally, look at the Lifted Index and K Index for the geographical areas of interest. The FSS specialist should have them somewhere.

Lifted Index is a broad measure of the atmosphere's equilibrium. This modified Showalter Index uses a scale of $+6$ to -6, with positive numbers representing stability or resistance to thunderstorm formation and negative numbers representing instability. Positive six is stable enough to frustrate all but the most persistent thunderstorms. Minus six is sufficiently unstable to produce tornadoes.

The K Index value shown below Lifted Index on the same chart is a measure of thunderstorm potential based on the vertical temperature lapse rate, the moisture content of the lowest atmosphere and the vertical extent of the moist layer. K values are primarily applicable to the prediction of air-mass thunderstorms. K values less than 20 generally result in no thunderstorms, while values greater than 35 result in numerous thunderstorms.

With the thorough knowledge of the convective outlook you should now have, it's time to look at—or have described to you over the phone—the current Radar Summary and Weather Depiction maps. The two should be looked at together so you can see on the Weather Depiction map what's causing the storms shown on the Radar Summary. You should examine the two with the AC report in hand so you can mentally superimpose the convective situation on each of them.

Now you're ready to make judgments on the likelihood of encountering storms and the severity of those you may encounter. Let's see four scenarios:

1. If your route is through an area not mentioned in the AC report and no storms are present, it's your lucky day.

2. If the AC report and convective indices are low, but there are storms present, they *should* be relatively tame and short-lived. To the naked eye and airborne radar alike, the storms encountered may appear just as wild

and turbulent as any you've ever encountered. By all means, they should be avoided if possible.

But you can lean towards optimism. The bases should be high and the tops not above FL300 to 350. They will almost certainly be air-mass thunderstorms and so rather easily circumnavigated.

3. If the AC and Index reports indicate a potential for severe storms and there are indeed storms shown on the Summary along the route—*but no cold front is involved*—be cautious. If you do not have radar and lines have not formed, you may be able to pick your way through, but don't let yourself become trapped. More on that in the next section. If you do have radar, be suspicious of it. On the trip today you may see on your display a storm just like one you flew through yesterday. Yesterday you experienced just a few bumps. But yesterday you were in an area of low convective outlook. Today that same storm will likely put a permanent set in your wing panels or blast you with hail. Don't take a chance. Go around everything.

4. If the AC and Index reports are positive, *there is a fast moving front* and storms are shown on the Summary, batten down the hatches. The storms encountered will probably be *extremely* severe. Even the most professional and experienced pilots, flying behind the finest radar systems, occasionally get fooled in this situation.

This was the situation when the Southern DC-9 captain flew into a cell west of Atlanta one spring and lost a windshield and both engines in turbulence and hail. It is reasonable to assume that cell didn't look any worse on his radar than scores of others he had flown through in his career. The difference just might have been the subtleties of an AC report plus the front, rather than anything showing on anyone's radar.

To get a feel for the severity of any thunderstorm, find out how fast it's moving. You will occasionally see one setting in one spot churning out nastiness. But as a rule the bad ones are on the move, and the faster they're moving the more nastiness they generate. A cell moving at 20 knots is likely to be four times as severe as one moving at 10 knots even though it looks identical to the eye and on radar.

Here we have been able to give you only hints and ideas. The major point is, you should never takeoff into a potential thunderstorm situation without knowing what *kind* of thunderstorms may be encountered. You *must* be forearmed with that knowledge if past experience, intuition or even the picture on your airborne radar is to be of any use at all to you on the trip.

Now in the next two sections, let's look at the finer points of flying the trip, first without radar and then with it.

Flying Thunderstorms: Without Radar 30

Dealing with the thunderstorm situation has one of those upside-down aspects to it that are so often encountered in life. Flying through them down low in small aircraft with no radar requires far greater skill and experience than flight at FL410 with $20,000 worth of radar equipment.

But guess who gets to do all the down-low flying?

The amazing thing is that the record is so good for the down-low man, considering how many there are. Looking at the record for businessmen pilots, only 10 of them each year, on the average, are involved in thunderstorm accidents.

There is no big mystery about how to cope with thunderstorms in a non-radar-equipped aircraft. You simply have to remain cool and calm although lightning is all around you and rain is flowing up the windshield a half-inch deep.

For that reason, the briefing discussed in the previous section is doubly important for the pilot about to depart sans radar. He has to do all his weather avoidance before departure. But, more important, he has to *know* before takeoff that if his preflight avoidance is unsuccessful, he will be able to fly through any cells he encounters. If he doesn't know that, he cannot stay calm.

For the non-radar-equipped pilot, the most difficult part of the trip will be deciding whether to go at all or not. If he doesn't have an instrument rating and he isn't prepared to fly short periods of heavy instruments, the answer is easy: He must not go.

A study we conducted last fall disclosed that non-instrument-rated pilots flying non-radar-equipped aircraft are 3.4 times more likely to become involved in a thunderstorm accident compared to an instrument-rated pilot in a non-radar-equipped aircraft.

Assuming you are instrument rated, the go/no-go decision hinges on the four scenarios described in the previous section. If the situation is as in scenario one, you of course go without hesitation.

If scenarios two through four prevail, you'll need more information. First, reflect on the part of the country you're in, the terrain you will cross and the time of day. Couple that with cloud base and visibility reports along the route.

The possible combinations of all that are endless, so only generalizations are possible. But as a rule, if the convective outlook is favorable, thunderstorms are easy to deal with anywhere west of the Mississippi. Normally, the bases in the West are high and visibilities are good, so the flight can be conducted VFR clear of all clouds and heavy rain shafts.

If bases are low and visibilities poor, you shouldn't try to go without radar if the route lies west of a line from Eagle Pass, Texas, up through Regina, Saskatchewan. Experienced mountain pilots may be able to handle thunderstorms out there IFR without radar, but it's not for the rest of us.

East of that line, all the way to the Atlantic, if the convective outlook is favorable, but the weather is down, storms are reported and you have no radar, you'll need one more report from the National Weather Service. Somewhere the FSS specialist should be able to locate an MDR plot and paper doll for you.

An MDR—Manually Digitized Radar—plot is a plot of thunderstorm activity based on 44-nm squares. A code is placed in each square denoting the severity of the heaviest thunderstorm within the square. MDR intensity codes run from one, very light, to nine, extremely intense. When you see it, the MDR data will be old, so don't put too much faith in it. But if it shows nothing stronger than a four, your ride probably won't be too bad should you get into a cell. If many codes are five or above, you don't want to go anywhere without radar, favorable convective outlook or not.

Before filing and going, you should also carefully examine top reports along your route of flight. They're a good indication of how intense the cells may be. A study conducted some years ago disclosed that if tops are less than 24,000 feet, there's a 40 percent chance the intensity will be light and a 90 percent chance the storms will be no worse than moderate. If the tops are running between 25,000 and 34,000 feet, the chance they'll be light is 12 percent and there's a 70 percent chance that they'll be moderate or lighter. If tops are above 35,000 feet, the chance that they'll be moderate or lighter drops to 33 percent, meaning that two out of three storms with tops above FL350 are more intense than you should tackle without radar.

If scenarios three or four prevail, you can expect to see top reports running to 45,000 feet and higher. To impress you with the odds against flying through one without getting a severe pounding, there's an 82 percent chance that any storm topping out at 45,000 or above will be intense; there's only a 1 percent chance that it'll be light.

That should give you a clue as to our advice relative to flying actual instruments without a functioning radar through an area with an unfavorable convective outlook. If the convective outlook is poor and you can't see what you're about to get into, the game is called Russian Roulette.

Seventy-eight percent of the thunderstorm accidents occur to pilots *not* on an IFR flight plan. That must be viewed with suspicion, of course, because no one knows what the relative exposure is. Much flying in the vicinity of thunderstorms without airborne radar is out in the West, VFR.

East of the Mississippi, VFR is less frequently possible. Often the haze is so heavy you simply can't see the cells to avoid them. As a general rule, if you go at all without radar when the bases are lower than 2500 feet and the visibility is under seven miles, it should be IFR.

When should you not go at all? Certainly you should never file into a line squall when visibilities are down unless you have radar. If severe air-mass thunderstorms have been forecast and reported, you *may* be able to file and go safely, but only if you have reliable ground radar and pilot reports of localized activity well off your route. Often the FSS specialist can call center directly and a controller can say whether or not he's painting weather along the airways you plan to use.

What happens when all the above fails and you plunge into a cell?

Nothing—*if* you stay calm.

If you've adhered to the precautions above and have not flown into a severe line of cells or a severe air-mass cluster, you will come through the rest okay.

This is not meant to inspire complacency. Finding yourself inside a thunderstorm, even a light one, is no fun. It terrifies passengers, is hard on the equipment, creates an unsafe situation for ATC and puts you—the pilot—just one slip away from disaster. But even a small single-engine airplane will ride through a cell of light to moderate intensity if it is properly flown.

In a small aircraft operated by B/CA, we have been in cells throwing off more lightning than you would believe possible. One day we even heard thunder above the sound of the engine. We've been in rain so heavy the engine had to be switched to alternate air to keep it running.

Through all that we've never experienced more than moderate turbulence and even *that* has always been of short duration. If you stay calm and maintain attitude and heading, you'll come out the other side in good shape.

There are some tricks that help. First, of course, tighten up the lap belt. Often even that isn't enough. Sometimes the bouncing will make it difficult to read the instruments and you will have to reach down between your legs and grasp the seat structure to stop it. That's good because it keeps you from doing two things that could be bad.

One is messing with the throttle or throttles. Don't. Know before you get into weather what power will result in holding a speed just below V_A in level flight, 500 fpm sink, set it and then leave the power alone. (More on why the sink in a moment.) The second good thing about having to hang onto the seat is that it keeps you from flying with two hands on the wheel. The last thing you want to do is over-control. That will add to the G forces.

Fly with one hand and try to coordinate with rudder but don't over-rudder.

Fly attitude and direction and forget everything else. If the power and attitude are right, airspeed will take care of itself. We just ignore altitude after telling (not asking) ATC that we're descending to MEA or the next higher cardinal altitude. We've found that in a thunderstorm lower is better. We've also found that the jolts are lighter when the airplane is allowed to sink down. Certainly the number of times you have to raise the nose are fewer in a descent and that helps avoid positive Gs. Your entire concentration should be on keeping the airplane unloaded and holding a heading.

We repeat: Do all you can to avoid cells of every size. Brief carefully, and file so ATC can help you to the extent possible. If they don't see the weather—even when they're on circular polarization—it's not likely to be severe.

If all that fails, just stay calm and fly out the other side.

Flying Thunderstorms: 31
With Radar

by Dan Manningham

The art and science of interpreting airborne weather radar is predicated on two basic facts:

First, weather radar can see only precipitation. Turbulence, clouds, moisture, lightning and wind shear are invisible to the normal airborne radar eye. Only water in the form of precipitation (or something more solid than water, like the earth) will reflect those 3.2-centimeter, X-band waves back to the antenna.

Second, the returns you see on the cockpit indicator are only an indirect representation of turbulence; indirect because those electronic pictures of precipitation must be interpreted by a pilot with experience, intuition and prior knowledge of the weather situation he is flying into before they can reveal anything to anybody. Radar cannot show turbulence directly. At best it is only a presentiment of what may lie in store.

The theory is simple. It is unlikely that water droplets, hail or snow—precipitation—of any consequence in predicting turbulence will be encountered in the atmosphere unless there is, or has been, some degree of localized vertical motion. The more localized the vertical motion, the more likely it is that the precipitation will also be localized. Note that the concept can also be reversed: The more localized the precipitation, the more likely it is that there are localized areas of vertical motion. Hence, localized areas of rain, hail and snow are signs of localized vertical motions in the air—turbulence.

Since radar pulses bounce back—reflect—from rain, hail or snow in proportion to particle size and the density of those particles, they will "paint" a picture of the phenomenon. Radar paints water droplets, rain, far better than it does hailstones or snowflakes, so for most practical purposes, returns from rain form the painted picture.

Light rain reflects few radar pulses and the portion reflected back is weak. Heavy rain reflects many pulses and the strength of the portion reflected back is high. On the radar display this appears as a faint image for light rain and an intense, bright image for areas of heavy moisture concentrations.

If the radar paints a heavy concentration of rain, there is quite likely to be turbulence associated with it. That's not invariably true. There can be a wide area of rain with no associated turbulence, simply because the upward vertical motions that lifted the moisture aloft have ceased and the rain is just falling. So a refinement, a bit of finesse, must be added in "reading" the rain pattern on the radar. If it smoothly varies in intensity from light to heavy over some distance, it's probably just falling. If it abruptly changes from none to intense, there is probably some vertical motion in the air impeding its fall or actually lifting it.

Therefore, the thing to watch for in a radar picture is an area, or areas, in which the paint changes from none to intense over a short distance. The shorter the distance, the more likely that extreme vertical motions are associated with the rainfall.

The distance between the first hint of rainfall in a radar picture and the onset of the heaviest rainfall being painted is referred to as the "gradient." If the distance is great with many gradations in between, the gradient is flat or shallow and vertical motions are *probably* equally shallow. If the distance is short and gradations are few, the gradient is said to be "steep" and the probability of extreme vertical motion in the air within the rain area is high.

In simplified theory, that is how radar provides a hint of thunderstorm-associated turbulence. (It cannot even hint at clear-air turbulence, for the obvious reason.) But at best, the radar picture is only a hazy indication of turbulence. There are thunderstorms and there are thunderstorms. Research pilots flying especially constructed and instrumented aircraft have demonstrated many times that two cells that appear identical on identical radar systems can be of enormously differing intensity when it comes to turbulence.

It's a little like a blind man feeling an elephant. He must rely entirely on size and shape as the measures of potential danger. Unless that blind man has substantial experience and knowledge, his sensory exploration can be very misleading.

If radar operators are to benefit substantially from that really limited information on the radar scope, they must understand the limitations of the radar system itself—which in essence is their sense of feel—and they must have a very clear understanding of the target—the thunderstorm—as discussed earlier.

Radar technology is advancing at an incredible pace. Phased-array antennas, digital processing, color augmentation and solid-state circuitry have enhanced radar capabilities in really exciting ways. For example, digital radars process the returning signals and cause them to be displayed to the pilot as distinct bands of intensity. With older radars it took a highly experienced user to distinguish a light rain shower from a medium one. The digital radars do that for you. Some even display a hard line between the bands of intensity; others show the bands of intensity in distinct colors.

Still, the basic truths remain. Your radar can see only rain, hail or snow. You must interpret the pictures it paints for turbulence potential.

All airborne weather radars have some common characteristics that affect their performance in specific, predictable ways. Effective radar reading depends largely on your knowledge of these specific characteristics:

Attenuation—When a radar pulse is transmitted into the atmosphere, it is progressively absorbed and scattered. The farther that pulse travels, the more it is weakened so that the radar's ability to "see" diminishes rapidly with distance.

Attenuation is caused by dust, water vapor, rain or ice crystals, but it is never less than exponential. In the best case, doubling the distance will reduce the returning signal by a factor of four. Heavy precipitation will greatly increase attenuation and may preclude returns from even strong targets if they happen to be masked by other strong cells, as illustrated in Figure 1.

Attenuation is important to interpretation because as you approach a storm it may *appear* to be gaining in intensity just because of attenuation. If you first detect the storm at 100 miles, and if that storm doesn't change at all, the returning signal will double at 75 miles. At a range of 50 miles the return will be four times as intense as it was at 100 miles, only 10 to 20 minutes before. The storm itself may be growing or dissipating, but your interpretation should be guided by the predictable distortion of attenuation.

At close range your job is simplified by the Sensitivity Timing Control (STC) circuit, and we'll look at that in a minute. But first, there is more to attenuation than the predictable signal strength reduction encountered in clear air. Precipitation greatly increases attenuation, often preventing the radar signals from penetrating fully into a large storm and, even more often, obscuring the picture behind such a cell, as the illustrations above show.

Figures 1 and 2 are based on an actual photograph of one of the latest digital radars taken by a B/CA staff member during an evaluation flight. In Figure 1, a cluster of cells appears to be penetrable using the indicated path. The pilot might choose that path because of the apparent long gradient at the left end of the storm in the rear.

But in fact, as the evaluation flight slipped between the two nearest cells, which were pumping out heavy rain, that left rear cell appeared to grow to its left at an extremely rapid pace and the flight was boxed in.

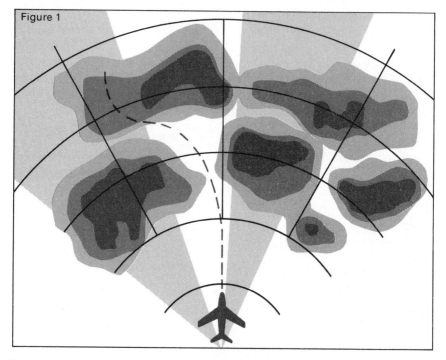

This illustration shows a classic attenuation situation. On the left one cell is being shadowed by another. The same is true of the rear cell bearing about 20° right. This could trick the pilot into attempting to fly the path indicated.

What happened? The front cell was "shadowing" the left end of the rear one, as in Figure 1. As the heavy rain in the front cell was circumnavigated, the attenuation caused by rain in the front cell ceased and the rear cell seemed to grow on the radar picture as the flight progressed.

Without knowledge of this radar characteristic, the pilot may often find himself in uncomfortable situations. He'll blame the radar or ascribe the experience to some explosive weather phenomenon. But the cause is simply a predictable attenuation.

For this reason, the backside of all weather returns should be considered an open question.

Sensitivity Timing Control—At long ranges, attenuation is a problem because it reduces the returning signal to a marginal or even useless level. At short ranges the problem is reversed.

Consider the signal returning from a cell 100 miles away. At 50 miles its strength will have increased four times. At 25 miles the strength of returning signals will be eight times stronger and at 12.5 miles it will be 16 times

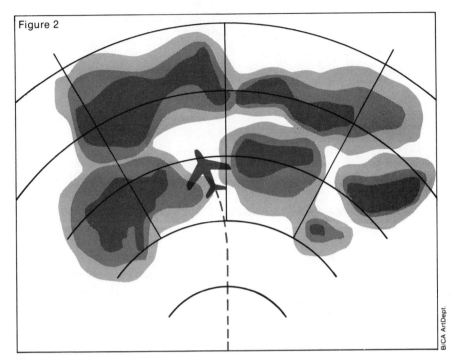

Figure 2

Here's what would happen. As the flight progresses around the nearer cells, the rear ones will appear to grow rapidly in both intensity and size. The cause would not be poor radar performance, but decreasing attenuation as the rain is passed off to the left.

stronger than the initial return from 100 miles. As you approach the storm, the returning radar signal increases so rapidly that the distortion becomes unacceptable. The STC—Sensitivity Timing Control—addresses that problem.

When the radar transmitter fires, it starts a sort of electronic clock that limits radar receiver sensitivity for 700 or 800 microseconds. During that interval the enormous signals returned from close targets are accommodated by that reduced receiver sensitivity commanded by the STC. An echo from 10 miles away, for example, would return to an extremely desensitized receiver. An echo from 15 miles would return to a somewhat more sensitive receiver as the STC circuit progressively returned the receiver to full strength. A return from 30 miles—in this hypothetical example—would encounter a fully sensitive receiver because the STC would have been cut off completely.

The net effect is that, within STC range, targets do not *appear* to grow as the range decreases. As you approach a storm, you can anticipate that

225

the image will grow in intensity due to lessened attenuation right up to the STC boundary. From that point the radar provides a justified image that allows more accurate assessment. Obviously, you should know what the STC range for your radar is so you'll more fully understand what you're seeing at various ranges.

Some digital radars employ computer logic to enhance the image of distant targets. This sort of presentation equalization can be a desirable feature. But, again, you need to know the peculiarities of the radar in order to effectively interpret it.

Gain and intensity—The gain control is your most significant means of regulating radar performance. Technically, gain controls the receiver's sensitivity, and manufacturers invariably suggest that you leave it on automatic or, at least, in one fixed position. Their concern is understandable. If the pilot indiscriminately twists the gain knob to this level and that, he'll never be able to understand what the radar is trying to tell him. A storm that will appear extremely intense to him at one indiscriminate gain setting will turn out to be a small shower; one that appears weak to him at another indiscriminate setting will almost wrench his wings off.

The result will be that he'll show up on the radar manufacturer's door step one day loudly shouting that the products are no good. To preclude that, some manufacturers have simply eliminated the gain control from their radars in the weather mode.

That's unconscionable. It robs the pilot of a very valuable asset, because there is much advantage to varying the gain as long as it is consistently returned to a known setting after each excursion.

The normal gain setting is indicated by the internal noise peculiar to the radar in use. At some upper limit of gain, the receiver becomes so sensitive that it begins to process stray internal signals and display them as "snow" or "noise" on the indicator. A setting just below the noise level will provide maximum searching sensitivity.

Lower or higher settings are often temporarily useful to acquire additional information on the storm or storms in question. Suppose, for example, you're approaching an area of small cells with passengers onboard who don't like turbulence of any intensity. At normal gain, your radar may not paint much of anything. Radars differ, but if you turn the gain up, gradients within even the insignificant little showers may appear allowing you to circumnavigate them. If you use the gain like this with knowledge, *you* will know the resulting radar picture has no real meaning in reference to significant turbulence in another situation, but that day it was helpful.

On the other hand, suppose you're approaching a heavy line of cells that for some reason you must penetrate. Perhaps they block the path to the only airport within fuel range. In that situation, if the gain is turned down, the intensity of the line of storms as displayed to the pilot will be uniformly reduced. This has a benefit other than just making the pilot feel he has a less severe storm to fly through. It will allow him to better pick out the softest spots in the line. The ride through will still be uncomfortable, but this procedure will result in the least discomfort.

The intensity control can be compared to the brightness control on your home TV. It can't enhance the image by causing the radar to paint more of the weather. It merely sets the illumination level for best viewing of the image delivered to it by the receiver's sensitivity.

Contour—Unfortunately, the image on a radar scope is often pathetically uniform, even in the presence of extreme precipitation differences. If the raindrop concentration exceeds some threshold limit, the radar paints it all.

The contour circuit is a crude but effective attempt to distinguish heavier from lighter precip. In the contour mode, incoming signals of an intensity level above some prescribed value are blanked from the display. The result is an image of a storm with a hole in the middle. If the hole is nearer one edge of the storm than the others, the storm is more likely to be turbulent than if the contour hole is dead center. The greatest turbulence is probably near where the contour hole is closest to an edge of the overall storm cell. That's why, in Figure 1, a pilot might elect to try the path indicated around the left end of that rear cell. The gradient appears to be shallower there, so the turbulence should be lightest. (But in fact, as explained, the gradient only *appears* shallow because of attenuation from the nearer cell.)

Many really expert radar operators seldom or never use the contour mode. They prefer to turn the gain down to examine gradients within the contourable area should there be any.

The thing *every* pilot must understand about contour is that it's only another tool. Some believe that if a storm isn't contouring, it will have no significant turbulence. Don't *you* believe it. *If* a storm cell is not contouring, and *if* it's not part of a line, and *if* it's in an area of low convective outlook—then it *may* not be turbulent.

Conversely, just because a storm cell *is* contouring does not guarantee turbulence. Again, you must couple the contour with your knowledge of the convective outlook for the area in which you are flying. In short, contour is only a tool that at best will assist you in judging the gradients within the storm. Remember, gradient is the best indicator of turbulence.

Tilt and ground return—The tilt control allows you to select the pitch angle of the antenna. Aside from the obvious benefits of compensating for the pitch changes of the aircraft, the tilt control is a most important element in radar interpretation. If the blind man mentioned earlier were limited to exploration of the elephant at eye level only, he would never be able to draw a meaningful image. The tilt control allows you to explore at any desired level from toenails to backbone and so develop a comprehensive image of the total target.

Maximum precipitation is likely to occur between 18,000 and 32,000 feet, so that will be the altitude range that usually returns the strongest echo from an active storm. Aircraft flying below that level will want to search with an appropriate amount of up-tilt. Those at higher altitudes will need to search with some degree of down-tilt.

At higher altitudes it is easy to scan over the weather as the radar beam travels straight out tangent to the earth's curving surface. A radar operator using 0° tilt in level cruise at 30,000 feet will be scanning far above any weather at 50 or 100 miles. Best search tilt at high altitude is achieved with the antenna adjusted just low enough to paint some ground return on the outer edge of the scope. At that setting you will be scanning through, rather than over, the weather.

A word on that ground return. It can usually be distinguished from weather returns by its unique arc-shaped appearance. But sometimes mountains or large cities located in areas of level terrain may appear as strong weather returns complete with contoured centers and deceptively changing shapes, especially when the ground is wet. The point here as elsewhere is that radar interpretation demands a constant awareness of radar characteristics and your location relative to cities and mountains.

In a cruise condition, with the tilt set to scan that critical 18,000- to 32,000-foot block, only very heavy rain will return to the radar at ranges of 100 miles or more. Such returns should be considered strong enough to create severe turbulence and you can consider a detour immediately.

As the distance closes, examine the storm critically. If there is no contour, you may be able to force one by momentarily increasing gain. This forced contour can be helpful in determining the most active part of the storm and is well worth trying even beyond the point at which the gain saturates your scope with noise. You already know where the storm is and if you can force a contour in the midst of that noise, you will have found the most lethal part.

If the storm contours at a normal gain setting, you can discern the most active part of that contour by reducing the gain gradually until the contour fades to a speck. In either case, forced or reduced contour, you will have established some initial baseline information from which to build your understanding of the storm's potential.

When the echo comes within your radar's STC range, this analysis takes on some real meaning because the effects of attentuation are eliminated.

After you have analyzed that single slice of storm at the mid-altitude, use the tilt control and gain (if you have that option) to repeat the process at several others. In short order you will have a three-dimensional mental picture of the entire storm. When that analysis is complete, consider the classic indications of severe weather.

· Scalloped edges on a radar echo are often associated with hail, tornadoes or severe turbulence.

· Fingers or hooks, extending out from the edge of a storm return, are prime indicators of severe activity, often in the form of hail or tornadoes.

· Horseshoe-shaped echoes are really a variation of the finger-shaped pattern, twice-repeated, and indicate similar severe activity.

· Any indication of rapid change from no rain to heavy rain is prime evidence of turbulence, probably severe. Always assess the radar picture for every possible indication of such steep gradients.

· Any cell whose radar shape is rapidly changing should be regarded with suspicion. Change itself is a basic characteristic of a turbulent storm.

The frustrating element in all of this is that you can fly through any one of these patterns and encounter no more than a rough ride. Then, when your confidence is up, you may experience wild turbulence caused by the hammer blows of a severe storm. Similarly, hail, tornadoes and severe weather can be found in relatively benign-looking smooth-edged returns. There are no guarantees in radar interpretation, there are only percentages. Circumnavigate all returns by at least 20 nm if possible. If that is not possible, consider the following:

· Absolutely avoid returns with pronounced scalloping, hooks, fingers or any return that is rapidly changing.

· If you must penetrate a cell, do so on the side with the lowest gradient.

· As you approach the storm or line use the gain control to discover the least active area.

· Be aware that you may need some slight additional up-tilt in a turn. The natural articulating motion of the antenna in a turn will tend to position the antenna too high on the outside of the turn and too low on the inside. Since you track toward the inside of a turn, you may need a little extra up-tilt to optimize the picture ahead of your path.

· Never fixate on one single range scale because you may overlook other serious weather. Good technique involves frequent reassessments, including two or more range scales, several tilt angles and probably some gain changes. When there are two pilots aboard, one of them can profitably devote full time to the radar in areas of heavy weather.

Radar interpretation is a very subjective thing. It requires precise knowledge of thunderstorms in general, the synoptic situation in particular and of your own specific radar in precise detail.

Wind Shear Update: The Phenomenon

32

Thunderstorms and local squall line activity plagued the New York metropolitan area June 24, 1975, as the late afternoon airline traffic flowed into JFK International Airport. The spector of wind shear was obvious; several pilots approaching the airport reported significant shear inside the outer marker, and the captain of an Eastern Air Lines Lockheed 1011, Flight 902, abandoned his approach below 200 feet after the indicated airspeed suddenly dropped 30 knots and the rate of descent increased dramatically.

When Eastern Flight 66 made its approach to Runway 22L that day, the crew was aware of the wind shear situation. The L-1011 captain had given a description of his shear encounter to the final-vector controller and the Flight 66 crew acknowledged overhearing that report. The pilot flying Eastern's 66, a 727 loaded with 116 passengers and a crew of eight —stated he was "gonna keep a healthy margin on this one," and another crewmember agreed with his decision; rain was falling, lightning was visible in the area and there was no doubt that conditions on final approach would be rough.

Yet Flight 66 crashed. It struck an approach light tower about 1,200 feet inside the middle marker, hit several more towers and caught fire. One hundred and seven people died.

This accident prompted extensive research into the wind shear phenomenon, a problem that has been with aviation since the first aircraft flew but which has been identified as a universal hazard only within the past five years.

A leading researcher has commented "I spent most of my career up until now telling nonaviation friends that there were no such things as air pockets. Now it appears I was wrong." Obviously, he was being facetious, for there are no airless pockets into which an aircraft could drop as if attempting to fly in a vacuum. But there do develop from time to time, particularly (but not solely) in the vicinity of thunderstorms, air patterns that affect aircraft performance in potentially dangerous ways.

Large changes in wind velocity and/or direction occurring over relatively small distances produce an atmospheric condition known as wind shear. If a tall tower were erected with an anemometer and wind direction indicator located at each 100-foot elevation and each set of wind sensors reported a different velocity and/or direction, we would know that wind shear existed in the vicinity of the tower and that its strength was the equivalent of so many knots of velocity change per 100 feet of elevation. For instance, if the wind velocity is 50 knots at 500 feet and 10 knots at ground elevation, there is a 40-knot loss in velocity and the wind shear is eight knots per 100 feet.

A change in wind direction, however, produces a wind shear even when there is no change in velocity. Assume that the anemometer at 500 feet indicates a wind velocity of 40 knots from the north and the anemometer at ground elevation reads 40 knots from the east. To the aircraft making an approach to Runway 9, there is a 40-knot increase in wind speed relative to its direction of flight. Thus, an eight-knot-per-100-foot wind shear, in the form of an increasing headwind, exists during the last 500 feet of its approach.

It is often said that wind cannot affect an aircraft in flight except for drift and groundspeed. However, changes in wind velocity relative to the flight path of an aircraft also affect airspeed. When airspeed changes, the equilibriums between lift and weight, between thrust and drag and between the various contributors to the aircraft's pitching moment (upon which the aircraft's flight-path performance and trim condition depend) also change momentarily. When that happens, the aircraft assumes a rate of climb or descent and a trim condition different from what it had just prior to the airspeed change, and corrections in power and trim settings are required.

The key to understanding why wind shear affects airspeed lies in a set of fundamental rules of physics known as Newton's Laws of Motion. Newton's First Law states that a body remains in whatever state of motion it last possessed until acted upon by external forces. The quality that causes an object to remain at rest if it is not moving, or continue at its original speed and direction if it is, is known as *inertia*. Inertia is proportional to the mass of an object. Since Newton's laws apply to motion with respect to the earth, we are concerned only with the motion of an aircraft over the ground—its groundspeed—when we consider the effects of inertia.

Changing winds will alter groundspeed, and inertia will resist those changes. For example, consider an aircraft in level flight at 120 knots IAS flying into a 40-knot headwind; you know its groundspeed is 80 knots. Now imagine what would happen if the wind suddenly dropped to 10 knots. The aircraft's inertia would resist any change in groundspeed, and its airspeed would decrease immediately to 90 knots. Since drag is proportional to airspeed squared, and the aircraft initially had sufficient power to maintain stabilized flight at 120 KIAS, the aircraft starts to accelerate. However, the process takes a relatively long time compared with the rapidity with which

231

the headwind ceased, and inertia is resisting any rapid change in ground-speed. Because airspeed has diminished, lift is reduced proportionally to the square of the velocity change. Thus, the aircraft starts to settle as it seeks a new angle of attack where lift and weight are equal. The nose also pitches downward.

Eventually, the forces acting on the aircraft—most significant of which is thrust—return the aircraft to its original airspeed of 120 knots, but that transition takes time. Newton's Second Law provides the clue to how long that transition takes; it states that the acceleration of an object is proportional to its mass and the force acting upon it. Other than gravity, the force attempting to accelerate the aircraft is the difference between thrust and drag. The mass of the aircraft is directly related to its weight. Therefore, the speed with which the aircraft returns to its original speed is related to its excess thrust-to-weight ratio. A lightly loaded Model 24 Learjet, for instance, can accelerate faster than a fully loaded Model 25 under identical conditions of airspeed loss.

If the loss of airspeed is so great that the aircraft cannot maintain level flight at its present weight, even with full power applied to all engines, the aircraft will settle. It will also lose altitude if the pilot does not promptly correct for the changes in lift equilibrium and nose-down pitch trim.

We have been describing the effects of a wind shear that reduces airspeed, such as a decreasing headwind. The effect of groundspeed inertia also causes an *increasing* headwind to increase an aircraft's airspeed, which in turn disrupts the equilibrium of forces acting on the aircraft and results in a requirement to readjust power and trim to maintain a desired flight path. Without those adjustments, the aircraft will experience an increase in climb rate.

There are several reasons why a phenomenon—in this case, wind shear —that has been part of nature for millions of years has only recently been identified as a factor in accidents:

· *Better identification techniques.* Many accidents and incidents that were not thought to involve wind shear have subsequently been related to the wind conditions that existed at the time of the problem. The FAA recently conducted an analysis of NTSB large fixed-wing aircraft accident/incident reports published between 1964 and 1975 and concluded that low-level wind shear could have been a factor in 25 of the situations that were described.

· *Higher approach speeds.* Higher approach speeds typical of the turbojet generation produce faster rates of descent along the glide path. For example, there is 29 percent less time for a 727 approaching at 140 knots to adjust to a wind shear of, say, eight knots per 100 feet, than there is for a Baron approaching at 100 knots. The faster an aircraft descends into a wind shear, the greater the airspeed alteration due to the shear. Because the rate at which an aircraft goes through a shear layer is significant, shear rate (expressed as knots of wind velocity change per second) and the number of seconds the aircraft is exposed to a given shear rate are the key parameters in evaluating a shear encounter.

· *Better records of what occurred.* With the advent of widebody jets, new multi-channel digital flight data recorders were introduced capable of collecting sufficient flight information to enable researchers to determine exactly what winds were encountered. A DC-10 that descended below the glide path on an approach to Logan Airport at Boston in December 1973 and struck the approach lights, causing a crash that destroyed the aircraft due to fire but which resulted in no fatalities, was equipped with such a device. Eastern's Flight 66 had a limited, four-channel foil recorder, which is standard on Boeing 727s, but the probable shear profile was extracted from the digital FDR of the Lockheed 1011 that survived a similar wind problem. Figures 1 and 2 show the winds experienced by the Boston DC-10 and the New York L-1011, respectively.

The crash of Flight 66 also prompted an analysis by the University of Chicago's Theodore T. Fujita of the meteorological situation at New York

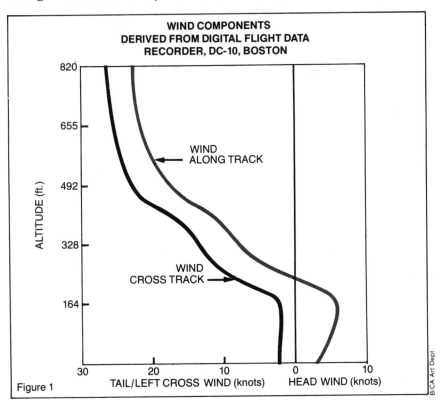

WIND COMPONENTS DERIVED FROM DIGITAL FLIGHT DATA RECORDER, DC-10, BOSTON

Figure 1

233

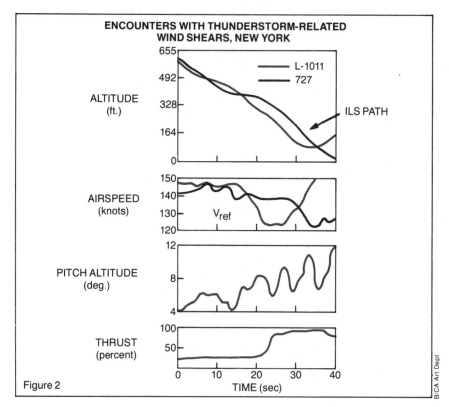

ENCOUNTERS WITH THUNDERSTORM-RELATED
WIND SHEARS, NEW YORK

Figure 2

during the afternoon of June 24, 1975. As the result of that research, which included satellite photographs of the area, a fresh insight into the formation of wind shear and the accompanying phenomenon of excessive downdrafts—called downbursts—around thunderstorms was established. (We'll explore those later.)

Based on the wind profiles generated from the L-1011's digital flight data recorder and substantiated by the Fujita study, NASA simulated the approach experienced by the crew of Eastern's Flight 66, using the Ames Research Center's simulator for advanced aircraft. Six pilots, each qualified on transport category aircraft, flew 20 to 30 combinations of atmospheric disturbance and visibility. Exposure to the wind profile experienced by Flight 66 was included well along in each pilot's approaches with the simulator after he had evaluated disturbances of lesser magnitude. Considerable effort was made to duplicate the levels of warning, readiness and surprise that characterize actual encounters.

The principal conclusion from the simulator studies concerned the promptness with which the pilots perceived the effects of wind shear and downdrafts.

In two of the six simulated exposures to the Flight 66 shear encounter, the aircraft descended to altitudes where obstructions would have been encountered, in almost exact duplication of the 727 accident. A third simulation resulted in a near miss. The remaining three pilots were able to recover with adequate terrain clearance.

In the simulators, the most important factor in the success of the go-around maneuver was the promptness with which corrective action was taken. Successful pilots perceived the sink rate induced by the downdrafts that preceed the wind shear and had added substantial thrust by the time the main body of shear was encountered. They also pitched the aircraft upward to regain near normal sink rates. When the airspeed decayed even further, takeoff thrust was applied immediately.

The rapid application of power and pitch-up maneuvering appear to be fundamental elements in recovery from wind shear. We have seen from our earlier discussion that when an aircraft encounters a decreasing headwind situation, lift is momentarily diminished as airspeed decreases, and if the aircraft is not rotated to a higher angle of attack and power applied, the descent rate will increase. If the pitch attitude is lowered to regain airspeed lost in the initial onset of shear, both the thrust and the gravity force the pilot is attempting to use to restore reference speed are forcing the aircraft further downward, and the aircraft's descent rate becomes exceedingly high.

There is considerable debate concerning which recovery techniques are best when encountering wind shear. Boeing stresses the dangers of pitching the nose downward to recover the reference airspeed once it has been lost due to the presence of shear effects. Boeing engineers also emphasize that Boeing aircraft enjoy reasonable handling qualities and performance at airspeeds approaching the onset of the stick shaker. The Air Line Pilots Association stresses the need to maintain V_{REF} at all times, whereas other experts suggest other techniques.

There is uniformity of opinion, however, in the need for early recognition of the potential wind shear.

As you would expect, the key to early recognition of wind shear is a thorough understanding of the phenomenon and the weather systems that generate it. We saw earlier that the classic wind shear situation involves changes in wind velocity and/or direction with altitude. However, more recent observation has convinced many researchers that vertical air movements are every bit as significant as horizontal movements in the creation of lethal wind shear.

Fernando Caracena of the Environmental Research Laboratories and National Oceanic Survey at Boulder, Colorado, and Theodore Fujita have isolated two important weather systems through analyses of recent wind shear accidents. Those systems are spearhead echoes. Both are associated with thunderstorms.

The term "spearhead echo" describes the general shape and activity of thunderstorm returns seen occasionally on National Weather Service ground weather radars. The significance of the unique shape and movement of these echoes is that several wind shear accidents have occurred when spearhead echoes were located over or near an airport.

Figure 3 shows the formation and advance of a typical spearhead echo. Fujita's analysis of returns from weather radar based at Atlantic City, New

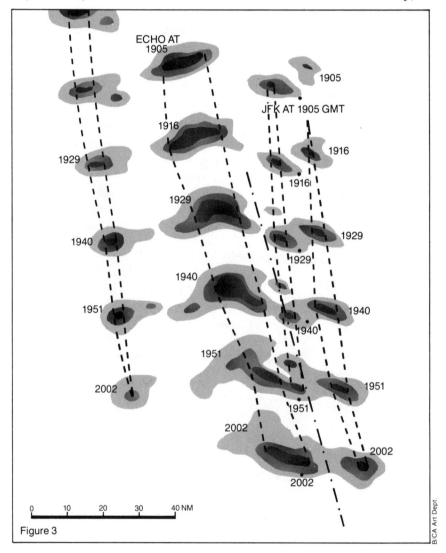

Figure 3

Jersey, and pictures from a weather satellite demonstrated convincingly that the downbursts associated with the spearhead echo were responsible for the loss of Eastern 66.

Fujita describes a spearhead echo as "a radar echo with a pointed appendage extending toward the direction of the echo motion." He has demonstrated that the appendage moves much faster than the parent echo, which is being drawn into the appendage. "During the mature state, the appendage turns into a major echo and the parent echo loses its identity." In Figure 3, the first suggestions of a spearhead echo are seen at 1916Z, when a finger-like projection begins to move out from the main echo. By 1940Z, the appendage is well developed, moving rapidly and drawing the parent echo into itself. Figure 4, from Fujita, suggests a structure for the spearhead echo. Simply stated, the spearhead echo return comprises the main cell with decaying downburst cells moving quickly before it. The downburst cells themselves are formed, says Fujita, when the main cell updraft rises and overshoots the top of the storm, where it encounters fast-moving, low-humidity, stratospheric air. The tremendous energies of both moving air masses combine into a downburst cell, and the top of the storm literally collapses into itself. The energy in a downburst is great enough to smash vegetation directly under it.

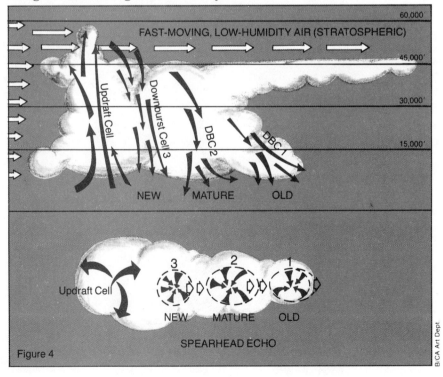

Figure 4

SPEARHEAD ECHO

B/CA Art Dept.

The spearhead echo is formed as the downburst cells move away from the main storm. Fujita describes it this way: "By virtue of large horizontal momentum drawn into a downburst cell, the cell moves faster than other portions of the echo. In effect, downburst cells run away from the parent echo and weaken, resulting in a pointed shape on the advancing end of the echo."

The spearheads are easily recognized on NWS ground-based radar. Unfortunately, airborne radar paints only small circular echoes when range is close and altitude is low. This is especially true when the airborne radar antenna is looking forward from a position below the cloud base.

Figure 5, also adapted from Fujita, shows how three downburst cells paraded across the approach path to JFK's Runway 22L within the space of 25 minutes, creating significant problems for some approaching aircraft (B, C, H, I and, of course, L) while leaving others completely untouched (A, D and E). Still other flights within that 25-minute period experienced varying degrees of shear-associated turbulence, but nothing that threatened control (F, G, J, etc.).

Figure 5 is a time-space analysis of the situation. All aircraft shown were flying nearly identical paths to Runway 22L. However, by spreading out

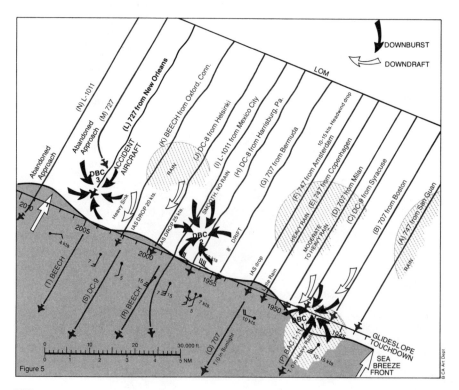

Figure 5

the flights against a time line, the procession of downburst cells can be seen. So, too, can the areas of relative calm, thus explaining why, in a sequence of arrivals, some aircraft have problems with shear while others don't.

Figure 6 is Fujita's analysis of downbursts on the Eastern L-1011 that narrowly averted disaster and on the Eastern 727 that crashed seven minutes later. Between these incidents, two aircraft negotiated the approach with only moderate downdraft problems. Notice that the downburst velocity in DBC 3 is about 1,700 feet per minute. Now imagine your own aircraft's climb capability at the beginning of a rejected approach and you'll have a good idea of just how lethal these things can be.

The discovery of the spearhead and downburst phenomena is important for several reasons. Certainly, recognition of the spearhead and its associated severe downdrafts can lead to early warning of developing downburst situations. Runways and approach paths can be changed and, when necessary, airports can be closed until the danger passes. Recognition that vertical air movements can be as lethal as horizontal movements in "shear" situations is important not only to flight crews but to engineers now working on wind shear detection and avoidance systems. And, finally, it's important that researchers have documented the existence of downdrafts that, if encountered near the ground, are not survivable. This knowledge should encourage us to be on the alert anytime a thunderstorm is anywhere near an airport or its approaches.

Wind shear situations, as we have seen, can be generated by thunderstorms. However, it's important to remember that much less isolated weather phenomena, particularly frontal systems, can also produce shears.

Forecasting the possibility of a wind shear encounter is relatively easy. However, the forecast is that—a prediction that wind shear is *possible* or even *probable* at a given point in space and time. But as the JFK experience shows, an actual encounter with significant wind shear may depend on highly localized systems with the probability of an encounter changing by the minutes elapsed and yards traversed. It's always uncomfortable to play the "what if" game, but sometimes it's helpful to do so. In the case of Eastern 66, "what if" amounted to nine seconds. That is, if the crew had been aware of the shear situation nine seconds earlier, disaster might have been avoided. Therefore, it's easy to understand why most wind shear R&D today is going into *detection* rather than *forecasting*.

As you would expect, researchers are exploring several approaches to detecting the wind shear encounter once it begins. And, also as you would expect, there is some debate on the best solution. We offer here only a sampling of what's going on. We are sure that it will be a long time before industry and government researchers agree on a single "best way."

The FAA's Wind Shear Engineering and Development Program is look-

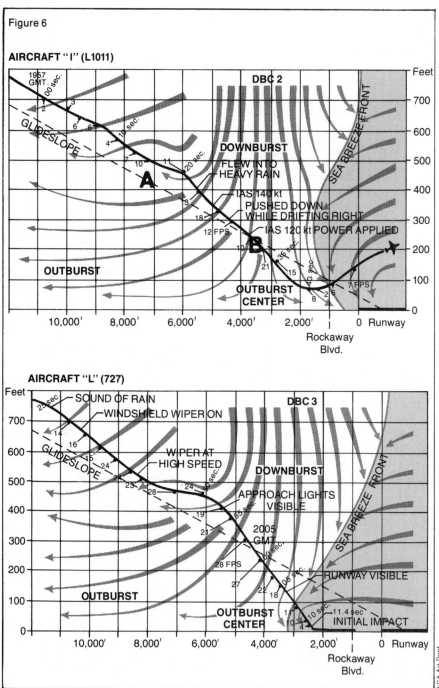

Figure 6

AIRCRAFT "I" (L1011)

AIRCRAFT "L" (727)

240

ing into the problem on three fronts: (1) development of a ground-based system capable of detecting strong wind shear conditions in major airport terminal areas; (2) the provision of a Hazardous Wind Shear Advisory Service for terminal operations (based on NWS-supplied data); and (3) development and evaluation of various schemes for onboard detection of wind shear.

Ground-based detection—This program, called Low-Level Wind Shear Alert System (LLWSAS), is farther advanced than the others with detection equipment now being installed at 13 airports. Ultimately, equipment will be installed at 60 airports.

In a given LLWSAS installation, up to six anemometers are situated near the airport approach and departure corridors from 3,000 feet to 4,000 feet from the runway thresholds. Wind velocity and direction are telemetered to a mini-computer installed in the control tower equipment room, and the computer compares wind velocities reported from the perimeter anemometers with the velocity recorded by a center-field anemometer. Whenever the difference between any one or more remote sensors and the center-field sensor exceeds 15 knots, a display in the tower cab calls the controllers' attention to the situation.

This system should be especially useful in warning of the arrival of sharp-edge weather fronts, localized sea-breeze fronts and thunderstorm-gust fronts, any one of which can cause serious approach or departure wind shear conditions. Pilots will be told by controllers that a wind shear condition exists and will be given readings from the center-field wind-measuring equipment and appropriate peripheral equipment. A typical wind shear alert message would sound like this:

"Baron Three-Four Pop, center-field wind two-seven-zero at one-zero. South boundary wind, one-four-zero at three-zero."

It's up to the pilot to analyze the wind situation relative to his operation.

Forecasting and advisory service—The FAA is currently evaluating results of a five-airport test of wind shear forecasting techniques and the effectiveness of reporting the results of such forecasting over ATIS and other briefing channels. Although reactions to the initial results of the 1976–77 test were mixed, enough positive data were compiled to warrant continued study. The NWS has agreed to look into the implementation of a nationwide wind shear advisory service later this year.

Airborne detection equipment—Perhaps the most promising step in the search for effective wind shear coping tools is research into onboard detection systems. The FAA, mainly through the National Aviation Facilities Experimental Center (NAFEC), is looking into both sensors and display schemes in hopes of coming up with quantitative data for design. H. Guice Tinsley, head of the FAA's wind shear research effort, described the problem:

241

"The basic requirement of an airborne wind shear system is to detect the condition and inform the pilot of the severity. A decision can then be made to continue the approach or make a missed approach. If the approach is continued, the pilot requires guidance in the form of information displayed in the cockpit for controlling the aircraft through the shear condition. Ideally, such a system for aiding the pilot in detecting and coping with wind shear should be predictive in nature."

As it turns out, measuring the dynamics of the system in which the aircraft is operating can be a pretty tricky business. And experts in meteorology and aerodynamics are far from agreement on the technical approach to best meet Tinsley's targets.

Most of the airborne wind shear detection systems tested to date compare airspeed and groundspeed in some manner and present the difference to the pilot. Here's a brief overview:

Airspeed/groundspeed comparison—This concept, according to researchers, has been most successful in manned simulations for a variety of shear conditions. Using this procedure, the pilot computes a minimum desired groundspeed by subtracting the headwind component of the runway wind from the approach true airspeed. He then flies a normal approach. However, at no time will he allow groundspeed to fall below the predetermined value. The concept's proponents point out that the procedure causes the pilot to add airspeed to compensate for any airspeed loss that occurs when a tailwind shear is encountered.

This procedure is "predictive" in nature, say the experts, in that "the pilot is given an indication to perform a missed approach prior to penetrating the shear condition whenever the amount of correction needed to maintain groundspeed exceeds the known performance capability of the aircraft."

Wind difference—A modification of the airspeed/groundspeed comparison technique is one in which the wind component at the aircraft's position is compared with the wind at the landing area. (Groundspeed is used to compute wind aloft.) The pilot sees a presentation of the difference between the inflight and ground wind components. The larger the difference, the greater the shear.

Presentations of the data generated by the sensor and computer systems discussed above are the subject of much continuing research. Some researchers have suggested additional pointers and bugs on airspeed indicators—for instance, one pointer with the traditional function and another that indicates either actual groundspeed or commanded groundspeed. Other researchers believe groundspeeds should be commanded on the Fast-Slow bar on the pitch command bar of a flight director system.

The approaches discussed so far each require an accurate source of groundspeed information. Those flight crews lucky enough to be equipped with INS, VLF or Omega can usually get a pretty good handle on wind direction and speed at maneuvering altitudes, although some INS computers drop out of the wind computing business below 150 knots. DME groundspeed computation has proved too slow to be of much value, but DME manufacturers and NAFEC are looking into that situation.

One problem with various airspeed/groundspeed comparison schemes is that they often fail to predict (or even measure in real time) the effects of vertical air movement such as thunderstorm-generated downdrafts and downbursts. In Figure 5, for example, aircraft A is experiencing a headwind shear that would be detectable using airspeed/groundspeed comparison techniques (assuming the groundspeed calculation was fast enough). The headwind shear in this case is called an "outburst" and is created as the cold air of the downburst hits the ground and spreads outward from the core of the downburst cell.

Aircraft B will suffer a large performance loss similar to that caused by a horizontal shear, yet all the shear is in the vertical plane—that is, all the shear is generated by the downburst.

Engineers at Safe Flight Instrument Corporation, of Armonk, New York, are working on the wind shear problem and believe that onboard shear detection will be meaningful *only* if horizontal *and* vertical components are measured. Under development at Safe Flight is a device designed to do just that. It's called a "Wind Shear Warning Computer" and analyzes various shears and downdrafts in terms of the aircraft's capability of climbing out of them.

The Safe Flight device measures horizontal shear by comparing ground-referenced acceleration. Downdraft drift angle is computed from flight-path angle, vertical acceleration and airspeed. The system monitors the operation continuously and is at all times telling the flight crew what proportion of total available thrust is being used to cope with existing shear and, therefore, what portion of total thrust is still held in reserve. Long before performance degradation can be seen on standard instrumentation the Safe Flight system warns that the situation is getting critical.

Quantification of weather phenomena and development of wind shear detection and forecasting techniques hold great promise for the future. But the unhappy fact is that flight crews must face wind shear *today*.

And, as you have probably guessed by now, there are as many approaches to pilotage in the wind shear encounter as there are schemes to measure it.

As we noted earlier, some of these piloting techniques are subjects of growing debate among the large aircraft manufacturers and the crews that fly their products. Every pilot should be aware of the techniques that have been advanced for coping *today* with wind shear.

Wind Shear Update: Pilot Techniques

33

by Dan Manningham

Preparation is the essential element in successfully combating wind shear. Although the experts have yet to agree on what are precisely the best piloting procedures for handling extreme shear once it is encountered, they concur that recognizing the nature of the weather problem is the first step in coping with it.

Not all wind shears are caused by exotic downbursts, and not all shear encounters result in *catastrophic* accidents like the crash of Eastern's Flight 66 at JFK June 24, 1975. A shear associated with a seemingly benign front can cause an embarrassing, if not damaging, landing incident; local winds or wave effects can influence an aircraft's speed during approach or departure and increase the risk of a mishap. After encountering shear recently, a Continental Airlines aircraft taking off from Tucson flew through wires located near the departure end of the runway, but the incident received little publicity because the pilot was able to remain airborne, make a successful circuit of the airport and then land safely.

No aircraft is *immune* to the problems shear can cause, although heavy jets may be more likely than light twins or singles to experience dramatic shear effects due to their higher vertical speeds when traversing existing shears. The FAA recently completed a study of single-engine and light-twin accidents in which wind shear was involved. The ensuing reports emphasized that shear problems are not unique to large aircraft.

Wind shear is as much a universal characteristic of weather as other meteorological occurrences, such as low ceilings and visibilities. While shear may not be as easy to detect as zero-zero conditions, and in extreme forms may not exist as frequently, all pilots need to be aware of its character.

We have examined thunderstorm-induced shear quite extensively and have reviewed in detail how the concentrated downward flow of cool air (which Professor Theodore Fujita defines as a "downburst") creates both

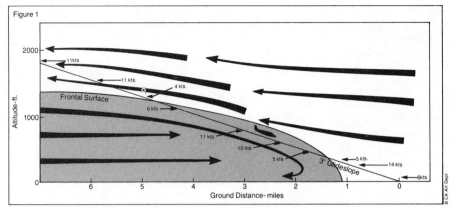

Figure 1

When an ILS course crosses a frontal surface, even something as benign as a sea-breeze front, an aircraft on the approach will encounter large changes in wind direction and velocity. Knowing how your particular aircraft reacts to these changes may prevent significant problems.

downdrafts and wind shears that can compromise the climb performance of a transport-category aircraft. Thunderstorms of light to heavy intensity were present in 13 of the 25 accidents that the FAA isolated as possibly involving wind shear in its analysis of NTSB accident and incident reports for the period of 1964 through 1975. Usually, the cells were within a radius of less than two nautical miles of the runway threshold and were reported or recorded prior to each accident. Consequently, it is wise to hold off from either an approach or takeoff when thunderstorm activity is in the immediate vicinity of the airport.

One airline recommends holding clear of the intended destination for 15 to 30 minutes to allow thunderstorm-related phenomena to pass by whenever airspeed losses or gains of 25 or more knots have been reported due to shear. It suggests that its pilots delay takeoffs by 30 minutes when wind shears capable of producing 15-knot changes in airspeed are suspected in the area and the conditions are building in intensity. When conditions seem to be dissipating, the same airline recommends a 15-minute delay to allow the thunderstorm's influence to subside.

Even with these rules of thumb, however, the pilot must not proceed in the face of obvious indications that wind shear is still present, such as blowing dust associated with thunderstorm-induced gust fronts or sharp differences in wind velocity and direction at different points on the airport. Studies of thunderstorms have shown that gust fronts—actually, "walls" of high-velocity, low-level wind that reveal themselves by the dust they blow along—can precede the storms that feed them by as much as 30 miles, although a range of five to 15 miles is more typical. That Continental

245

Airlines pilot who encountered the performance-compromising shear on takeoff from Tucson had delayed his departure until a thunderstorm moved off the airport, but his wait was not sufficient to avoid a shear created by the storm's outflow.

Shears caused by fronts are not as easy to anticipate since telltale thunderstorms may be absent, but low-level wind gradients can be present near the frontal zones of stationary, cold or warm fronts. (Occluded fronts generally do not produce shear conditions.) Wind shifts as well as velocity changes close to the surface can occur near the edge of most fronts, but considerable shear should be anticipated when there is a temperature change of 5°C across a front or when the front is moving at a speed of 30 knots or faster.

Other indicators of shear-producing weather are:

Mountain waves—These weather phenomena often create low-level wind shear at airports that lie downwind of the wave. Altocumulus standing lenticular (ACSL) clouds usually depict the presence of mountain waves, and they are clues that shear would be anticipated.

Virga—Precipitation that falls from the bases of high-altitude cumulus clouds but evaporates before reaching the ground is a strong indication of low-level wind shear whenever surface temperatures are above 24°C and the dew point spread is 20°C or more.

Strong surface winds—The combination of strong winds and small hills or large buildings that lie upwind of the approach or departure path can produce localized areas of shear. Observing the local terrain and requesting pilot reports of conditions near the runway are the best means for anticipating wind shear from this source.

Sea-breeze fronts—The presence of large bodies of water can create local airflows due to the differences in temperature between the land and water. Changes in wind velocity and direction can occur in relatively short distances in the vicinity of airports situated near large lakes, bays or oceans.

The key to recognizing a shear encounter is to know your aircraft's normal performance and power parameters. When the rate of descent on an ILS approach differs from the nominal values for your aircraft, beware of a potential wind shear situation. Since rate of descent on the glideslope is directly related to groundspeed, a high descent rate would indicate a strong tailwind; conversely, a low descent rate denotes a strong headwind. The power needed to hold the glideslope also will be different from typical, no-shear conditions; less power than normal will be needed to maintain the glideslope when a tailwind is present and more power is needed for a strong headwind.

By observing the aircraft's approach parameters—rate of descent and power—the pilot can obtain a feeling for the wind he is encountering. Being

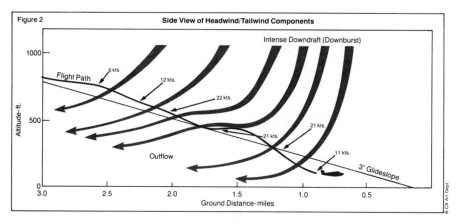

The downdrafts and outflows from a nearby thunderstorm can cause performance compromising wind conditions. Notice that an aircraft on the approach shown here experiences an increasing headwind followed by a decreasing headwind component and a strong downdraft.

aware of the wind-correction angle needed to keep the localizer needle centered provides the pilot with an indication of wind direction. Comparing wind direction and velocity at the initial phases of the approach with the reported surface winds provides an excellent clue to the presence of shear before the phenomenon actually is encountered.

The track of the aircraft on the glideslope and the manipulation of power to keep the glideslope needle centered are also specific clues that a shear is being encountered.

Consider these two cases, one involving a decreasing headwind and the other an increasing headwind:

Decreasing headwind—In this situation the wind at altitude is blowing faster or more in line with the runway than is the wind at the surface. As a result the aircraft starts the approach with a lower groundspeed than it has when it crosses over the runway threshold. But remember Newton's First Law of Motion, which states that a body in motion with respect to the ground tries to keep that motion at a constant speed. The aircraft's "ground inertia" resists the aircraft's attempt to increase its groundspeed as the headwind diminishes with altitude. Thus, the aircraft's airspeed falls off about as fast as the wind velocity drops off with altitude, and the subsequent response of the aircraft is a loss of altitude and a nose-down trim change.

In order to correct for this deviation and to recapture the glideslope, the pilot adds power and pitches the nose upward. The increased angle of attack arrests the descent and the added power gradually accelerates the airframe to recover the lost airspeed. The application of pitch and power

247

may result in the aircraft actually overshooting the glidepath, and a power reduction eventually will be needed to establish the high rate of descent that is required to track the glideslope at the new, higher groundspeed.

This type of wind shear is equivalent to an increasing tailwind; both changes in wind decrease the aircraft's performance. Therefore, a decreasing headwind and an increasing tailwind are often referred to as decreasing performance wind shears.

Increasing headwind—In this situation the wind vector along the localizer at altitude is of lower magnitude than is the wind vector along the localizer at the runway. (The increasing of the wind's magnitude in a direction of the localizer could have resulted from either the wind's velocity being higher at lower altitudes near the runway or from the wind being directed more in line with the runway.)

As a result, the aircraft starts the approach with a higher groundspeed than it has when it crosses over the runway threshold. Since the aircraft must lose groundspeed and its "ground inertia" resists that change, the aircraft's airspeed increases practically as fast as the headwind increases. The aircraft responds to this increase in airspeed with an altitude gain and a nose-up trim change.

The pilot corrects for the subsequent ballooning on the glidepath by reducing power and pitching the nose downward. The decreased angle of attack stops the ballooning and the reduced power gradually decelerates the airframe toward the desired airspeed. But to maintain the glideslope once it has been recaptured, the pilot must add more power than what he was initially carrying because the rate of descent that corresponds with the slower groundspeed will be less than what was required for the initial phase of the approach.

The increasing-headwind situation, which is identical in character to that of a decreasing tailwind, acts to increase the performance of the aircraft. Therefore, this type of wind change is known as an increasing-performance shear.

Certainly, these descriptions of decreasing and increasing headwinds are stylized and simplified, but they do illustrate the normal responses of an aircraft to longitudinal wind shear on the approach.

In real life an aircraft would likely encounter more than one shear level and typically experiences both increasing and decreasing headwinds on the same approach.

By observing the aircraft's airspeed and altitude changes along the glideslope and by being critically aware of the pitch and power manipulations required to track the glideslope, a pilot can detect the existence of shear even when other indicators, such as thunderstorms, are not present.

To illustrate this point (with the advantages offered by five years of analysis by several agencies and wind data extracted from the aircraft's

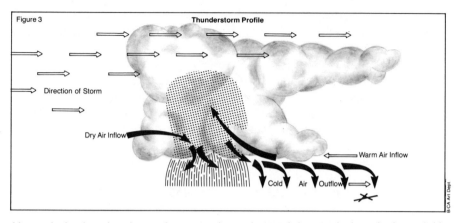

Figure 3 — Thunderstorm Profile

Direction of Storm

Dry Air Inflow

Warm Air Inflow

Cold Air Outflow

B·CA Art Dept

Meteorologists have long known that tremendous volumes of air cascade down the forward side of a mature thunderstorm cell and push out in front of the storm, sometimes as far as 20 miles. Thus, a dangerous shear can exist in this "gust front" over an airport many miles from the associated storm.

digital flight-data recorder), consider the approach parameters of the DC-10 that crashed at Boston's Logan International due to wind shear. The aircraft, approaching with its autothrottles engaged, encountered an increasing headwind (actually, the wind went from a strong tailwind to a light headwind), which caused the aircraft to balloon and increase airspeed. The autothrottles reduced power to flight idle in an attempt to recapture the target airspeed.

Then the aircraft entered a slightly decreasing headwind, which caused the airspeed to decrease and a high, apparently undetected sink rate to develop. By the time corrective action was taken the engines could not spool up fast enough to prevent the aircraft from striking the approach-light standards and crashing, fortunately with no fatalities.

At no time during the flight was the shear strong enough to compromise the performance of the DC-10—in fact, the aircraft struck the obstructions at an airspeed slightly *above* its reference approach speed.

Monitoring airspeed and the time required to reach various reference speeds during the takeoff can provide clues to impending shear situations. The time required to accelerate to V_1 will be less than normal in an increasing headwind and greater than normal in a decreasing headwind. Since wind shears (particularly those associated with localized thunderstorms) frequently include both increasing and decreasing headwind situations, unusual variations in the time to accelerate to V_1 and from V_1 to V_2 plus 10 knots can be clues to potential shear. Certainly, if there were no headwinds when the takeoff was initiated, but the aircraft seemed to accelerate more rapidly than usual in airspeed between, say, 50 knots and V_1, an increasing headwind is present and shear effects should be anticipated after takeoff.

For something as important as establishing the best technique for coping with a strong wind shear encounter, there is a surprising lack of unanimity among knowledgeable parties. Most airlines operators and the manufacturers of airline aircraft agree that when conducting an approach in the presence of known decreasing-headwind shear, the pilot should increase his approach reference speed by as much airspeed as he expects to lose due to the shear, but by not more than 20 knots; then, he should attempt to fly a stabilized approach on the normal glidepath. If there are no pilot reports concerning the airspeed loss to be anticipated, the typical formula used by several airlines is to add one half the steady-wind speed and all of the gust speed, with the total not to exceed 20 knots.

For the increasing-headwind situation, where ballooning and an airspeed increase can be expected, pilots of turbine aircraft are cautioned not to reduce power to flight idle in an attempt to increase the rate of descent and to return rapidly to the glidepath. A rough rule of thumb employed by at least one airline is not to reduce thrust to a setting lower than that used on a normal approach when below 400 feet.

Any technique that encompasses approach speeds in excess of VREF runs the risk of an aircraft crossing the runway threshold with excessive groundspeed and thus running out of runway before it can be stopped. The pilot's option is then to balk the landing and effect a go-around but the decision must be made early and the possibility of encountering a shear situation on the initial phases of the go-around, when the aircraft is transitioning from its high-drag landing configuration, must be considered.

Because of the possible need to go around, either because of an overspeed situation at the threshold or due to a performance-compromising shear encounter during the approach, some experts are suggesting that the minimum flap setting consistent with the manufacturer's approved procedures and the available runway length be used when shear is anticipated. However, there is less than complete agreement in this area. A reduced flap setting results in a higher approach speed and a greater exposure to the effects of shear since the aircraft then descends faster through the shear layer.

There also are some differences of opinion concerning what flap setting and climbout airspeed should be used if a wind shear is anticipated during the takeoff. One airline recommends selecting the longest runway and executing a maximum power/minimum flap setting through the rotation, then maintaining a low enough pitch attitude after liftoff to accelerate to V_2 plus 25 knots.

Other parties suggest that the normal takeoff procedure, in which V_2

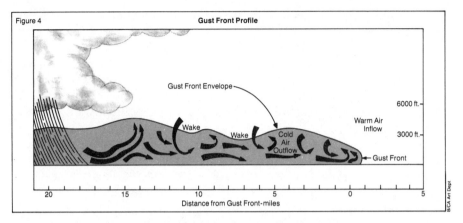

Figure 4 — Gust Front Profile

A closer look at the gust front described earlier shows that significant vertical activity can exist as well as a clearly developed shear line between the outflowing and inflowing air masses. Note that the irregular gust front surface runs from ground level to about 3,000 feet at the base of the storm.

plus 10 knots is used for the initial climb, is better because it provides the advantage of more altitude—which might be needed if a shear caused a loss in climb performance.

The controversy concerning the best speed and configuration for encountering a shear fades into near insignificance when the question of how best to extract an aircraft from an extreme wind shear situation is discussed. The manufacturers and most airline pilots agree that a rapid nose-up pitch correction and an immediate application of power are necessary to arrest a descent that is caused by a severe decreasing-headwind shear and/or a downburst, but there is considerable disagreement concerning how far the airspeed should be allowed to decrease in an attempt to convert speed into altitude.

Manufacturers of airline equipment state that their aircraft possess reasonably good handling qualities and climb performance down to speeds that approach the onset of their stick-shakers, so they are recommending that pilots be aware of stick-shaker speeds and be prepared, in an emergency, to pitch the aircraft's nose upward toward that limit.

Airline pilots, on the other hand, do not want to reduce their speed that far below VREF, preferring instead to leave some airspeed in the bank, so to speak, in case they are forced to flare the aircraft due to impending ground contact.

Other parties, such as the manufacturers of flight-path guidance equipment, feel there are more optimum solutions to tradeoffs between pitch attitude, angle of attack (airspeed) and longitudinal acceleration that will

251

yield better results when a pilot is attempting to get out of an extreme wind shear situation.

Of the general aviation airframe manufacturers and the professional-pilot training organizations B/CA contacted, none had a recommended procedure for coping with extreme wind shear. There are some bright spots in the wind shear situation. Here are some things a pilot can do in the cockpit to reduce his risks of a serious encounter with shears and downbursts:

Be prepared—Use all available forecasts and current weather information to anticipate wind shear. The National Weather Service is conducting an experimental program that will lead to inclusion of shear forecasts in regular aviation weather reports, and the Air Force already has such a program operational. Also, make your own observations of thunderstorms, gust fronts and telltale indicators of wind direction and velocity available to other pilots.

Give and request pilot reports—PIREPs on wind shear are essential. Request them and report anything you encounter. A suggested format that we feel is worthy of repeating here is as follows:

(1) Location of shear encounter.
(2) Altitude of shear encounter.
(3) Airspeed changes experienced, with a clear statement of:
   (a) the number of knots involved;
   (b) whether it was a *gain* or a *loss* of airspeed.
(4) Type of aircraft encountering the shear.

Avoid known areas of extreme shear—When the weather and pilot reports indicate that extreme shear is likely, delay your takeoff or approach.

Know your aircraft—Monitor the aircraft's power and flight parameters to detect the onset of a shear encounter. Know the performance limits of your particular aircraft so that they can be called upon in such an emergency situation.

Act promptly—Do not allow a high sink rate to develop when attempting to recapture a glideslope or to maintain a given airspeed. When it appears that a shear encounter will result in a substantial rate of descent, promptly apply full power and arrest the descent with a nose-up pitch attitude.

Remember that the lift and drag characteristics of an aircraft are such that a change in angle of attack quickly produces more pounds of lift force than it does pounds of drag force over the speed range the pilot will be using during his shear encounter, and those pounds of lift can be used to check the initial impact of a shear or downburst before large descent rates are allowed to build.

Encourage more knowledge—Pilots should seek specific information about the best techniques for extracting themselves from extreme shear encounters. The available information concerning flight below VREF has been generated by the manufacturers of airline equipment for their specific aircraft. Many of their techniques may be type-limited and not applicable to business jets and light aircraft. Considering the simulation and analytical tools available within the business aviation community, it should be possible to develop procedures for the aircraft we fly.

Signs of the CAT

34

by Dan Manningham

Let's start this off right. We have no intention of producing another theoretical paper on the subject of Clear Air Turbulence. Hundreds of brilliant meteorologists have been doing that routinely since 1946 when the problem was first recognized. On the contrary, we would like this to be a meteorology lesson for pilots who hate meteorology.

The basic problem with Clear Air Turbulence is simply that it is easier to forecast than to avoid. By definition CAT is the disturbed air created by wind shear. It is not necessarily associated with clouds. Clouds, when present, indicate the presence of moisture, but do not affect the mechanics of this non-convective turbulence. The accompanying aircraft motions can produce mild annoyance, severe discomfort or very real hazard, and pilots need no further inducement to avoid CAT areas. The key to avoidance is to identify wind shears before and during flight, and therein lies the problem.

There are many different atmospheric scenarios which produce sufficient wind shear to generate CAT. Often this turbulence can be predicted with fair accuracy, but on such an enormous scale that the forecasts have only minimum usefulness. The following National Weather Service CAT forecast for April 5, 1974 is typical:

Area 1—FL 250-FL 390 in area bounded by Dickenson, N.D.; Abilene, Tx.; Memphis, Tn.; Tulsa, Ok., and Aberdeen, S.D.

Area 2—10 Thsd to FL 390 in area bounded by Abilene, Tx.; Memphis, Tn.; Flint, Mi.; Montreal, Qu.; Albany, N.Y.; Atlanta, Ga., and Houston, Tx.

Discouraging, isn't it? Broad areas are routinely forecast with the now familiar qualification "50 percent probability of moderate or greater—." More accurate forecasts may never be practical because turbulent areas, by definition, are in constant motion and change. So, like thunderstorms, the areas can be defined, but specific locations cannot be identified before the fact. Although we dream of some CAT detector in the cockpit for real-time information, the fact is that we will have to rely on skill and daring for at least several more years. There are many ways in which CAT telegraphs its existence to the alert pilot, however, and for the foreseeable future that may be your best defense.

Over the past few years, meteorologists have begun to see atmospheric wave action as the predominant cause of turbulence. In fact, the very term "CAT" is now falling into disfavor and being replaced by the more appropriate name, WIT (Wave Induced Turbulence). The amplitude (and, thereby, potential turbulence) of such waves varies enormously. They may well be present in clear air or associated with clouds.

When air moves and accelerates in the normal process of atmospheric changes, wave action develops on the interface between two layers of different stability. Such waves are produced by fronts, jet streams, terrain, or the damming effect of squall lines. The frequency may be measured in meters or miles. The action can cover a few miles or a few hundred miles. The results, however, bear certain marked similarities.

The wave action begins with an initial smooth motion called undulance. You may detect some fluctuations in airspeed or altitude but little, if any, turbulence (Figure 1).

As the vertical distance from the troughs to the crests (amplitude) increases, the crest may develop a roll or curl from the different windspeed in the higher layer. These cresting waves will produce light to moderate chop or turbulence and may leave a tell-tale "coat-hanger" pattern on stratus layers when they are present (Figure 2).

Sometimes wave trains are formed with each succeeding crest higher than the last until some critical height is reached and the largest wave breaks into a chaotic and turbulent area of disturbed air similar to ocean waves breaking on a beach (Figure 3). Such breaking waves will always produce discernable turbulence, usually in the moderate or severe category.

Okay, that's the basic action, but you need to know what triggers it and how to identify those areas. As you can see, WIT is started by some contrast in the atmosphere. Because of that, it is far more common in winter than in summer. The peak frequency is January and February over the continental United States although there are some large occurrences in spring and fall.

Summer CAT is usually generated by the blocking action of thunderstorms and squall lines in a wind field. Summertime CAT is annoying, but local and predictable.

Several phenomena can create the atmospheric contrasts needed for strong WIT, but none does so on such a large scale as the tropopause. You will recall from basic meteorology that the tropopause is the boundary between the lower atmosphere (troposphere) and the upper atmosphere (stratosphere). Actually, it is the absolute height affected by surface heating and accordingly it is far higher at the equator than at the poles. It's absolute extremes are probably near 18,000 feet and 70,000 feet although

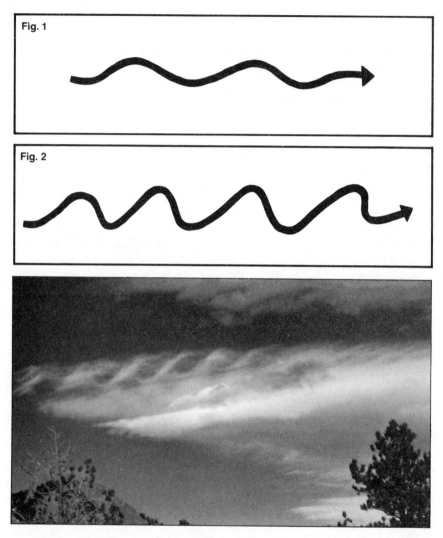

Fig. 1

Fig. 2

trop height over the continental United States will normally be confined between 30,000 and 45,000 feet. Naturally, it is lower in winter, higher in summer.

The tropopause is defined by meteorologists as that level where the rate of cooling with altitude (lapse rate) becomes less than two degrees C, per 3000 feet. This lapse rate provides a clear measure of the resistance to vertical motion and so the trop is that boundary where vertical air motion essentially stops. When that boundary is abrupt, there is a marked energy potential because any vertical motions will spread out horizontally in a turbulent wave action. This occurrence is so common, especially in winter, that one study of almost 15,000 CAT reports indicated that 47 percent were

Clouds are the signs of upper-air turbulence. As the wave builds from undulance (Figs. 1 and 2 and the photograph on the preceding page) to cresting and swirling (lower illustration and photograph, this page) turbulence is increasing.

in the vicinity of the tropopause, although only 34 percent of the total flying occurs at those altitudes.

The solution is simple. Stay away from the tropopause and save yourself a lot of grief. There are several ways to do this. The most obvious is to check National Weather Service charts for trop height along your route. Unfortunately, there is no concise chart of tropopause height since that specific chart has been removed from the NAFAX circuits. For the time being, you will have to make do with the 12-hour upper air progs and the two small tropoause height/wind shear/max wind panels sent as N3 and N54. One other chart, the tropopause height and vertical wind shear (Trop-VWS) is most helpful, but you will find it only at a very few stations where long overwater trips are commonly planned. Lacking these charts, check temperatures aloft and look for the altitude above which temperatures remain constant.

If this information is not available, or if there is a need to determine trop height enroute, look for the following:

(1) An abrupt top to the haze layer which is often present at the trop. Any visible stratus top between FL 300 and 450 should be suspect since the moisture is obviously not penetrating upward and the lapse rate change is apparently sharp enough to create discernable wave action. Often the wave action can be seen on the stratus layer as in Figures 1, 2 and 3.

(2) The level of thunderstorm tops en route may well indicate the trop although strong TRW will penetrate 10,000 feet or more into the stratosphere.

(3) The level on climbout, and above 30,000 feet, above which temperature remains constant.

When you can clearly identify trop height, avoid it by at least 4000 feet, although you may be faced with an annoying choice. Either hang on in light to moderate chop at the best altitude for specific range or descend 4000 to 10,000 feet for comfort and accept the increased fuel flow.

Locating and avoiding turbulence associated with the tropopause can be a frustrating task. There is no question that a very large percentage of all turbulence is near the trop, but the truth is that the pilot has problems:

(1) Desirable altitudes are often not available.

(2) Trop level may fluctuate considerably over long trip lengths, making it difficult to avoid.

(3) Trop depth may be large enough (5000 to 10,000 feet) to contaminate a substantial amount of the available cruising levels. Even with the best information, you may be able to avoid trop-generated WIT only a fraction of the time. When it is unavoidable, you must plan the trip accordingly.

Sometimes a break or step develops in the tropopause in a manner which translates horizontal motion into a narrow band of high velocity wind which we call the jet stream.

The core is typically 100 miles wide and 5000 to 10,000 feet deep. Winds in the jet stream can approach 300 knots and even at substantially lower velocities the shear effect is announced enough to produce turbulence. Once again, the mechanics of this turbulence hold the key to minimizing your exposure.

Fortunately, jet streams have received so much attention from meteorologists and pilots that it is possible to draw a fairly accurate cross-section looking downwind. In Figure 4 notice that the isotachs (lines of equal windspeed) are much closer together on the north side. These lines indicate stronger wind shear and turbulence.

Above the core, temperatures increase to the north and decrease to the south and that relationship is reversed below the core. This relationship can be of very practical value to the jet pilot searching for the most favorable winds at altitude. We have used it several times when operating near the jet stream. It is sometimes possible to add 20 or more knots to groundspeed simply by playing the temperature gradient.

The jet stream engenders a wave motion of its own which can produce

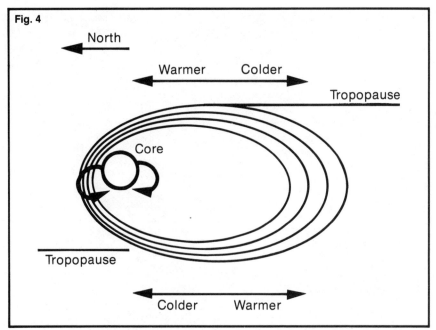

Several features stand out in this jet stream cross-section. If you can picture these relationships en-route you may avoid some lumps and even pick up a little groundspeed.

WIT of a magnitude to interest pilots. Those hooks radiating outward from the core in Figure 4 represent eddy currents generated by the strong shear in that area. These vortices parallel the main stream and are often felt as moderate chop.

If moisture is present they will leave a band of herring-bone clouds where the moisture has condensed at the top of each spiral. When present, this narrow line of ribbed clouds is an important visual clue to the high-shear zones at the edge of the jet stream.

Two other cloud patterns have been identified with known jet stream activities. Cirrus clouds in the presence of jet shear and eddy currents will often display a distorted and fractured appearance characterized by pro-nounced tufts or curls (Figure 5). Sometimes the atmospheric contrasts which are responsible for the jet can be seen. You'll notice clear polar air to the north and warm moist clouds to the south of an extensive east-west cloud break.

Any or all of these cloud patterns are possible apart from jet stream activity, but when you are in the vicinity of a known jet stream try it out. If at least one of these patterns is repeated within five minutes, then you can feel quite confident that the jet is leaving its tracks.

Blowing dust on the lee side of a mountain range tells you where the wave is touching the surface and bouncing aloft.

Wave induced turbulence can be encountered anywhere, but its most severe form, mountain wave, has received the greatest attention, and rightly so. Mountain wave forecasting techniques are now so reliable that few surprises are left, although you certainly need a basic understanding of the mechanics and problems of this phenomenon.

Terrain induced wave has been found at heights up to 75,000 feet over rolling hills only a few hundred feet high, although severe wave is usually associated with major mountain ranges. The Rockies, just west of Denver, and the Sierras near Bishop, California, are prime wave producers and turbulence in these areas occasionally approaches destructive proportions. Let's look at the process.

When there is a strong pressure gradient directly across a mountain range, the air is mechanically lifted by the hills as it flows from high pressure to low. If the lifted air is very stable, it will cascade down the lee side of the range like water over a dam, setting up a large-scale imbalance at all levels. The proportions of this downdraft system will greatly exceed that of any topographical features because of the enormous disturbances that result when the atmosphere seeks equilibrium after having the bottom fall out.

The National Center for Atmospheric Research (NCAR) at Boulder, Colorado, has studied mountain wave for several years with instrumented aircraft and has contributed as much as anyone to the present body of knowledge on this subject. On January 11, 1972, the NCAR was able to accurately document a very large wave over the Rockies. This wave was penetrated at selected altitudes and routes by NCAR's Sabreliner and Queen Air, both of which are equipped with special measurement equipment and INS. All data was subjected to computer reduction and the remarkable cross-section shown in Figure 6 was produced.

The solid lines are potential temperature isolines (in degrees Kelvin) which may be considered mean streamlines of the actual airflow. As you can see, the dominant feature is an enormous downdraft region from the mountain peaks to Jefferson County Airport, followed by intense updrafts and somewhat chaotic wave motions further downstream. Severe turbulence was experienced by the Sabreliner at 20,000, 30,000 and 39,000 feet and by both aircraft at all levels below 15,000. At one point in the wave trough, windspeed fluctuated from 0 to 95 knots over a three-mile track. During this period two DC-8s reported near loss of control when transiting the area and surface wind-speeds exceeded 100 knots causing $2.5 million damage. Ironically, the NCAR hangar at Jefferson County Airport was blown in and nearly demolished.

Clearly, mountain wave must be treated as potentially destructive, and the prudent pilot will simply not route himself through an active area. Forecasting techniques are well refined and reliable. NWS forecasts will normally be adequate, but a brief look at the most important forecasting tools is helpful in understanding the nature of mountain wave. Meteorologists look for:

(1) Reports of pressure falling rapidly (PRESFR) at stations near the lee side of the mountains.

(2) Strong temperature gradients (−6.7 degrees C. or more) across the mountains or between two stations near the mountains.

(3) Winds blowing across the mountain range at 30 knots or better.

(4) Reports of altocumulus standing lenticular clouds (ACSL) over the mountains.

(5) Reports of strong surface gusts and/or blowing dust near the lee side of the mountains.

When these signs are present, there is excellent wave potential as that cool, high pressure air flows east over the mountains. Seventy percent of the significant wave action in the United States occurs in January and February, although strong polar outbreaks can breed mountain wave from September through May. The flight planning process is quite simple.

Frayed and ragged cirrus are a prime indicator of high-level turbulence.

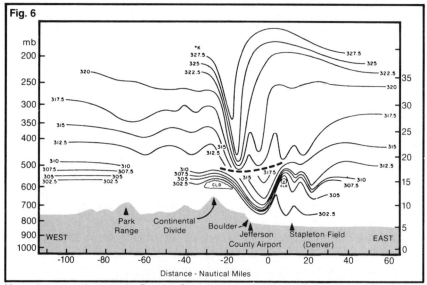

Mountain wave action over the Rockies. Solid lines representing the mean streamlines of airflow leave no doubt about this wave's intensity. Degrees are shown in Kelvins. The wave/mechanical boundary is at the dashed line.

· Be especially alert during the cold months and particularly during strong polar outbreaks, which generate jet stream and trop/WIT weather.
· Check the NWS mountain wave forecasts and believe them. They are very accurate.

· Avoid active areas. J-94 or J-78 will provide minimum exposure over the Rockies.

When sufficient moisture is present, mountain wave telegraphs its existence with three distinctive cloud formations. If you can interpret these in flight, you will have a real advantage in avoiding the worst situations. See Figure 7.

Lenticulars. As the stable air on the windward side of mountains is forced upward by the terrain, condensation will occur above the level where temperature and dew point are equal. This condensation acts to further cool this already stable air so that it will begin to descend again as soon as the terrain allows. Often this condensation occurs just at the peak of the wave action, leaving a smooth, lens-shaped cloud which is called lenticular. In a well developed wave, these lenticulars will form in stacks as several different layers of the troposphere leave their individual marks. That's when the sequence reports for near-by terminals will end with the notam "ACSL" (alto cumulus standing lenticular).

When these lenticulars are smooth in appearance, they indicate a Jaminar flow that will most likely allow a smooth ride with some gentle airspeed and altitude deviations. We've navigated many well developed waves with no indication other than gentle Mach excursions of ± 0.02 to 0.04.

When the wave builds to breaking stage, lenticulars will clearly indicate the turbulent, chaotic flow associated with any breaking wave action. Lenticulars, showing ragged edges or an otherwise frayed appearance, are a positive warning of rough air.

Rotors. When the stable air finally cascades down the lee side of the mountains to seek equilibrium, it may pick up considerable moisture at the lower levels which will condense out when this low-level wave action rises. The clouds formed by this action are called rotors, and they look like cumulus or fracto-cumulus lines parallel to the ridge line. Although they appear to be stationary, they are actually in a constant boiling motion, forming on the windward side and dissipating to the lee. Their bases will be somewhat below ridge height with tops extending up to twice the height of the highest peaks. Sometimes rotors will merge with the lowest lenticulars, which may in turn extend solidly to the tropopause.

Despite their somewhat harmless appearance, rotors are extremely dangerous with up and down drafts often exceeding 5000 fpm. Positively avoid rotor clouds.

Cap clouds. If there is sufficient moisture in the lower levels on the windward side, it will condense and form heavy stratus over the windward slopes and peaks. This cap cloud, or foehnwall, will hang over the peaks like a waterfall and may extend down the lee slopes. The degree of overhang is proportional to the severity of the downdraft and you can read low level turbulence quite accurately by the extent of foehnwall overhang. Any cap

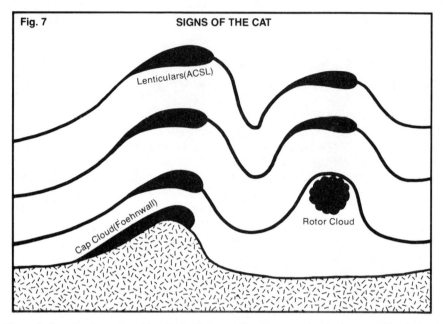

Three distinct cloud types are identified with mountain wave: cap clouds, rotors and lenticulars. Each telegraphs its individual story as thge wave action develops.

cloud with significant leeward extension indicates extreme downdrafts and you should interpret it as a clear warning of active wave action and turbulence.

Strong mountain wave will leave one more track if conditions are right. With clear air and dry ground, you will see blowing sand and dust on the surface where the wave dips to ground level. This is a prime indicator of active wave, especially when associated with other wave evidence.

Bear in mind that all of the action associated with mountain wave can take place in perfectly clear air if there is little moisture to begin with. Wave, breaking wave, rotor action and lee-side downflow are the natural consequences of mountain wave with or without the moisture necessary for cloud formation. When the clouds are present, read them carefully.

When you must pass an area of active mountain wave, you have three options:

· Detour.

· Overfly the area several thousand feet above the tropopause, which acts as a barrier to the upper extension of the wave.

· Reduce to rough airspeed and hang on.

Wave action and especially wave induced turbulence are the natural consequence of contrasts in the atmosphere. With that in mind, look for the following when you flight plan:

(1) Strong temperature gradients at altitude, especially if associated with strong winds. There is a high probability of CAT when the gradient approaches five degrees C. in a distance of 100 nm.

(2) Troughs at altitude with windshift nearing a right angle.

(3) Jet streams, especially with undercutting winds.

(4) Any marked changes in wind speed.

(5) Unusually cold temperatures. Temperatures below standard often permit higher cruising altitudes with resultant better range, but they also indicate a high CAT probability.

(6) Any wind of 150 knots or more.

(7) Avoid flight within 5000 feet of the known tropopause level.

Conversely there is little or no risk of WIT in:

(1) Levels showing little or no temperature change unless they are 10 degrees or more below ISA.

(2) Levels with temperatures well above ISA.

(3) Levels with nearly constant windspeeds and directions (except in mountain wave zones).

(4) Levels with weak winds.

Inflight you can expect WIT in conjunction with any of the appropriate cloud formations and when you encounter any abrupt change in temperature, unusually cold temperatures, especially above 30,000 feet, or wavelike fluctuations in airspeed and altitude or both.

Predicting WIT is a sometimes thing for the line pilot, but even 30 percent success is better than none. Know the mechanics. Read the signs. Keep some records and in short order you'll have your own favorite methods for avoiding those lumps.

Icing Update

35

by Dennis Newton

After all these years of flying in ice, studying it, and designing and building equipment to cope with it, the aviation community is still plagued by icing problems. Except for thunderstorms, icing is the most serious weather hazard for pilots who fly at relatively low altitude. But it can also be lethal to higher flying aircraft; for instance, ice contributed heavily to the fatal crash of a 727 not too long ago when the crew neglected to activate a crucial anti-icing system.

We'll take a look at icing from several points of view. We'll discuss how it forms on an airplane, and where. Next, we'll see what an icing cloud is, where it exists and why. Then we'll look at how to anticipate icing clouds from data available on the ground, and how to recognize and avoid them in flight. Finally, we'll discuss the effects of ice on an airplane, how to cope with them and what the legalities of flight in icing conditions are.

The accretion of ice on the components of an airframe is caused by, and the form of the ice is controlled by, several meteorological and aerodynamic factors. These are cloud liquid water content, cloud droplet size, temperature, size of the ice-collecting object and aircraft speed. The generating factor is cloud liquid water content. The amount of ice that will accumulate on an airframe component is directly proportional to the amount of water contained in the cloud in the form of liquid droplets. However, water contained in the cloud in the form of vapor, snow or ice crystals will generally not stick to the airplane and contributes little or nothing to the overall ice buildup.

The second most important meteorological factor is temperature. It affects both the likelihood of icing and the form the ice will take. The vast majority of icing encounters of any significance occur at outside air temperatures between 0°C. and −10°C. Below −20°C. icing is a very rare event. This is true largely because the likelihood of finding high liquid water content in a cloud decreases rapidly as the temperature decreases. That's a statistical conclusion, however, and should not be taken as gospel. It is possible to get plenty of ice at colder temperatures, and a couple of exceptional cases will be discussed later. It is also possible to get ice at ambient temperatures above 0°C. in aircraft systems where there is a pressure drop, such as engine induction areas. The warmer the temperature at which ice is encountered, the more serious the shape of the ice is likely to be, as we'll shortly see.

The size of the cloud droplets has a significant effect on both how much ice will form and what shape it will take. The effect on total accumulation occurs because of what is called collection efficiency. As the airplane moves through the air, it disturbs the pressure field around it. This results in a pressure wave moving out ahead of the aircraft at the speed of sound. Nearly everyone who flies has seen the effect of this in some sort of wind tunnel picture. The airflow parts and moves smoothly around the disturbing object. The cloud droplets also try to make the turn with the airflow. To oversimplify a bit, the small ones make it and the big ones don't. Therefore, the larger the drops, the more ice you get. The collection efficiency is the ratio of the amount of ice an object *does* collect to the amount it *would* collect if it caught every liquid droplet in its path.

Anyone who spends a minute thinking about all this will quickly conclude that the size of the object collecting the ice, as well as the drop size, have to be factors in how much ice will form—which is absolutely correct. However, the effect of the aircraft size is not what you might expect. The larger the component, and particularly the larger the leading edge radius, the less ice it will collect. This is true because the larger objects give the air ahead more "warning" that they are coming and allow the air to get out of the way with more gentle turns which carry more water, missing the component. The effect of speed is just the opposite. The faster the aircraft is moving through the air, the less warning the air has that it is going to have to scramble out of the way. This results in more of the water failing to make the sharper turn and smacking into the airframe.

By now it will be readily apparent that all of the above factors combine in a complicated way to influence aircraft icing. It should also be apparent why ice collection has to be considered in terms of aircraft components, rather than just in terms of the aircraft as a whole. We can make the following generalizations about the effects of the factors in combination:

Amount of ice—Given suitable liquid water content and temperature conditions, small components moving at high speed in the presence of large drops will collect the most ice. Large components moving through relatively small drops at slow speed will collect the least ice, and possibly none. Typical collection efficiencies for a light twin in an "average" icing cloud are about 45 percent for the wing leading edges, 85 percent for the empennage leading edges and 95 percent or more for small components such as pitot tubes and OAT probes.

Shape of ice—The shape of the ice that forms depends on all of the meteorological parameters we've discussed. The aircraft speed is also a factor, since it influences the temperature of the ice-collecting object. Warm temperatures, large drops and high liquid water content are the worst combination. When the ice accumulation begins, large and relatively warm drops run back and freeze aft of the point on the leading edge where they strike. Further drops then freeze on the ridges formed by this process. The final result is a buildup with a more or less horn-shaped cross section, which is aerodynamically awful. Small drops at cold temperatures tend to freeze where they strike, resulting in a spearhead type of formation. This may affect lift nearly as badly as the horn-shaped ice, but it is much less damaging to drag.

Type of ice—The two shapes of ice just described are commonly thought of as clear ice and rime ice, respectively. However, there is no sharp transition between them. Since higher speed raises the temperature of the leading edges and increases the rate at which water strikes, it is entirely possible to penetrate a cloud at low speed and collect a rime formation, and then to re-penetrate it at higher speed and collect an intermediate or clear ice shape. There is also a point at which aerodynamic heating is sufficient to prevent ice formation altogether, at least on leading edges.

Location of ice—Some of the remarks made about the amount of ice an object will collect lead to the conclusion that icing will be different on different parts of an airframe. Small parts will collect ice first. It is possible to ice a pitot tube without icing leading edges, and to ice the leading edge of the empennage with little or no icing on wing leading edges.

Identifying and avoiding icing conditions requires a basic understanding of how various types of icing clouds are formed. It is then possible to learn to look for areas of probable icing, both on weather charts and through the windshield. The worst conditions can generally be avoided if you know where to look, what to look for and what to do.

If you don't want ice, the first and most important thing to do is stay out of clouds with high *liquid* water content. The primary cause of high liquid water content is the upward motion of moist air, which results in cooling and thus the condensation of large amounts of water vapor into liquid drops. Once liquid water drops exist in the clouds, the primary threat to their continued existence is the creation of ice crystals, a process called glaciation.

Water goes from vapor to ice in a cloud with great difficulty, but it goes from liquid to ice very easily. Once glaciation starts, the cloud engages in a battle between upward air motion, creating more liquid drops, and glaciation, converting the liquid water to nonliquid crystals of ice.

In the absence of energetic lifting of air, a cloud will glaciate in just a few minutes. The colder the temperature, the more likely it is that glaciation will begin and the more quickly the cloud is likely to become dry. Clouds have been penetrated for flight test purposes at temperatures as warm as −3°C., resulting in heavy ice buildups, and then re-penetrated less than an hour later and found to contain nothing but snow. The following can be said about various types of clouds:

· Cumulus clouds with relatively warm temperatures at their bases are likely to be very wet in their building stages. As a ball park number, developing cumulus clouds can produce very heavy ice buildups if the temperature at the cloud base is −12°C. or warmer. The warmer the cloud base, the worse the possibilities.

· Stratus type clouds are far less likely to produce severe icing—there is much less vertical motion going on, or they wouldn't be stratus. The vertical extent of the icing layer will be much less in stratus than in cumulus; icing layers more than 3,000 feet thick are rare. Fast ice buildups are unlikely in any case, and extremely unlikely with a cloud base temperature less than −3°C. The horizontal extent of an icing encounter in stratus is much greater than in cumulus, but still is usually less than 30 miles.

None of this necessarily applies to lake-effect stratus, formed usually in early winter by cold, northwesterly winds blowing across the unfrozen Great Lakes and then over land. There is so much moisture available that these clouds can sometimes stay ahead of glaciation and remain sopping wet well inland as long as the conditions that created them continue to exist.

· Stratocumulus clouds in relatively thick layers may be wetter than stratus, but not so wet as cumulus. This, naturally, is because the lifting in intensity is between the two pure types. Most of the ice is likely to be found in "lumps" in the cloud deck where the lifting is the greatest, and near the top of the deck where the lifting will have squeezed out the most liquid water. Lake-effect clouds may take this form, as well as the pure stratus form, and the same warnings apply. Icing layers are seldom more than 3,000 feet thick.

· A type of cloud that is not known ever to have been studied by itself for icing condition is the wave cloud. Experience has shown that wave clouds are very wet, however. The reason is simply that the lifting in the upward moving parts of the waves is sufficiently energetic to squeeze out a lot of water, and this condition can be very long lasting. The direction of flight through a wave cloud deck will have a great influence on how much icing is encountered. Icing will be intermittent and of short duration if the flight proceeds perpendicular to the waves, but can be disastrous if the airplane flies along the wave in the area of lift.

· Cloud droplet size has an effect on icing for the reasons mentioned previously. Droplets tend to be larger in cumulus than in stratus. In addition, the cloud droplet size is likely to be considerably larger in clouds that form over open water or in clean air than in clouds that form in dusty or polluted air. Consequently, clouds that originate over or draw their moisture directly from bodies of water are usually not only wetter, but also contain larger drops.

The object of the game, then, is to avoid areas, and altitudes, where the clouds are likely to be icing clouds and to spend the least possible amount of time in such clouds when they must be penetrated. This is a chore with two parts. First, it involves study of the weather situation and judicious preflight planning. The second step is to recognize potentially hazardous weather in flight and to know what to do to stay out of it or to get out of it.

When we consider preflight planning, we come to the subject of icing forecasts. The kindest comment about them is that they are not very good. There are a number of reasons for this, which would be interesting to go into if there were space and time. This was done at considerable length at a recent NASA workshop on the subject. Suffice it to say here that the conditions to be forecast are very poorly defined and that the forecasts pretty much amount to the statement that if there are clouds and the temperature in them is 0°C. or lower, there will be icing. Forecasts are virtually useless in avoiding icing. The usual case is that the forecast will be there, whether the icing is or not. The opposite case, icing with no forecast, has also been known to occur.

A weather briefing is a better bet, but it requires going to a flight service station or National Weather Service office and then hoping that the facility has the information you need. A briefing can be obtained over the phone, but that is like trying to learn to fly by reading a book.

Most weather briefings consist of a description of the surface map and forecasts which are read as if infallible, and little more. That is nowhere near enough. To assess an icing situation, you must do four things. First, you must find out where the moisture is. Second, in the areas where there is moisture, you must evaluate the temperatures. Third, if there is an area along your route with suspicious moisture at ice-forming temperatures, find out what is going on that might lift the air. Fourth, get some idea of the stability of the air, i.e., how well it will cooperate with lifting forces.

The place to start is not with the surface map but with the upper air. Look at the 850 and 700 millibar charts, which represent altitudes of about 5,000 and 10,000 feet msl, respectively. There is a little circle at each station with the data plotted around it. If the temperature-dewpoint spread at a given station is 5°C. or less, the circle will be shaded. If there are shaded stations along or near your route, look more closely. Check the temperatures. If they are between +1°C. and about −15°C., and particularly if they are between 0°C. and −10°C., there may be trouble. If the temperatures are in the danger range, check the temperature-dewpoint spreads more carefully. If you find an area where the temperatures are right for icing and the spreads are 2°C. or less, treat that area as extremely suspect. Compare the same stations on both charts and see if they are moist at each level. The temperature or the moisture, or both, may be safe at one level but not at the other. Look at the temperature difference between the two levels. If the 700 millibar level is more than 7°C. colder than the 850 millibar level, the air in that area may be, or become, unstable.

These charts are, unfortunately, history. Sometimes they are ancient history. The data are taken at 0000Z and 1200Z and are a couple hours old when the charts are first accessible. Therefore, you will not only want to know where the moisture was when the chart data were taken, but where it was coming from and where it was going. If it is still available, study the chart made 12 hours previously for the same level. Where was the moist area then? Did the area become larger or smaller between the two data times? Did it become wetter or dryer? Colder or warmer? What you want is the trend, less serious or more serious.

Whether or not the previous charts are available, look at the winds on the current charts. Are the winds that are moving the moisture coming from warmer areas or colder ones? Wetter or dryer? Will the temperature and moisture probably get better or worse? Make a particularly good check of the low level winds. This can be done with the 850 millibar chart and the surface map, if necessary, but the low level winds-aloft charts present the information more clearly if they are available.

What you particularly want to spot is a wind field at low levels coming over land from a large body of water. Considering the worst of the ice areas in the United States, this means easterlies or northeasterlies in the Atlantic Coastal area, northwesterlies over the eastern Great Lakes and westerlies in the Pacific Northwest. These winds bring moisture, and there is terrain to lift the air. Southerly winds from the Gulf of Mexico also carry lots of water and will provide the raw material for plenty of ice when the temperature is cold enough. Even if the current chart does not show moisture, the next one will if one of these wind conditions exists.

By following these steps with the upper air charts, you can find answers to the following questions. Where were the areas of suspicious moisture (temperature-dewpoint spread 2°C. or less) and temperature (0°C. to − 10°C. in particular) recently (at the chart time)? Which way were they traveling? Were they getting larger or smaller and more moist or less? Can they be circumnavigated? Can they be topped or flown under? Is there likely to be a lake-effect trap? Which way out?

With a little practice in reading the data, you can learn what you need to know from the 850 and 700 millibar charts in five minutes or so. Then, having had a look at where there is, or possibly will be, enough moisture to be troublesome at the right temperatures, you should look for mechanisms that will lift the air. These come in two varieties, meteorological and orographic. The latest surface map and prog charts will indicate the primary meteorological lifting mechanisms, which are low pressure systems and fronts. The more energetic the lifting is, the wetter the resultant clouds will be. In this regard, it is especially important to understand and appreciate the three-dimensional nature of weather.

Having checked the upper air in the lower 10,000 feet for moisture and temperature conditions conducive to icing, and having flagged areas of possible instability by looking at the temperature difference between the 850 and 700 millibar levels, you can see where the lifting caused by the features shown on the surface map is likely to produce the wettest clouds. If the areas in the neighborhood of a front are wet, and/or if the winds bringing in the air ahead of a cold front or behind a warm front are coming from a body of water, watch out. In either case, the place to expect the most ice is from some distance ahead of the surface position of the front to some distance behind it. It is impossible to specify a distance in general, because it will depend upon the amount of moisture available, its distribution in both horizontal and vertical space, how fast the front is moving (i.e., how energetic the lifting is), and what the stability and temperature of the air are. This is why, if you want to exercise intelligently the pilot's prerogative of route planning to avoid icing (or bothersome weather in general), you absolutely must have some idea of what the low level portion of the upper air looks like.

Orographic lifting—lifting by airflow over rising terrain—can cause some of the most hazardous icing conditions. If you get a load of icing where no icing was forecast, there is a good chance that it is orographic in nature. A low level wind field blowing over a body of water and then moving uphill is an excellent situation for the formation of orographic icing. Two classic cases are westerly winds from the Pacific Ocean blowing over the Olympics and the Cascades, and northwesterly winds from Lake Erie and Lake Ontario moving over the northeastern mountain ranges. These are probably the two worst ice traps in the United States. However, orographic icing conditions can also exist over many other mountainous areas when the moisture and temperature are conducive to them. One often overlooked source of moisture is lots of water lying on the ground from the passage of some sort of storm system a few hours previously.

The wave cloud is a special case in the development of icing conditions caused by lifting of air by terrain, and probably the worst of the orographic types. The typical wave cloud situation will occur when a wind field located perpendicular to a mountain range develops after the passage of a cold front. The moisture may come from the ground, having been dropped there by the cold frontal system. In the northeastern and western coastal mountain ranges, the low level wind field after a cold frontal passage often comes directly from a large body of water. The low level air behind the front is typically unstable because of the cold air flowing over relatively warm land. This results in the available moisture being rapidly absorbed into the air. The winds running more or less perpendicular to the ridges combine with the temperature structure typical of the situation to create saturated wave clouds over and downwind of the mountains.

The orographic situations are typically at their worst from late morning to late afternoon, because the sun's heating helps lift the moisture. If wave conditions exist, some degree of avoidance is possible by planning trips at other than these times. Depending on where the flight is going, studying the 850 and 700 millibar charts and the wind fields may enable you to simply avoid the area where conditions are particularly favorable for wave lifting. If your airplane is capable of it, an altitude 5,000 feet or more above the ridges will usually top the wet orographic clouds.

But enough theory. Let's assume that you've done the best you can with the preflight planning and have decided to take off. Now the problem becomes a very practical one. Avoiding ice, or getting out of it if you have been unsuccessful in avoiding it, really boils down to just two things. Either get to an area where the temperature is warm enough to melt the ice, or get out of the liquid clouds.

The temperature aspect seems elementary at first, and it is really not very complicated. There are a couple of traps worth mentioning, however. If you are encountering icing, and another aircraft has reported an altitude below you to be ice-free due to warm temperatures, the obvious solution is to go there. Before you do, however, try to find out some details about the PIREP. If it was made by a G-II tooling along at 250 knots, and you are flying an Apache with some ice on it at 125 knots, you may get ice that aerodynamic heating prevented on his aircraft. An indicated airspeed of 250 knots will protect leading edges, at least, down to true outside air temperatures of −6°C. or so, which is to say, a lot of the time. See if you can find out what the real OAT is down there. Otherwise, you'll be taking a calculated risk by descending, and you'll be giving up precious altitude. If you leave an altitude where you are picking up a fairly benign ice shape and go to a warmer one where, instead of getting rid of it, you begin to collect horn-shaped ice, you have done yourself no favor.

You can infer something about temperatures above and below you by the kind of clouds you see. If they are very flat stratus types, and the air is smooth, the temperature will probably change very little if you go up or down in them. If there are energetic cumulus buildups, the temperature will theoretically warm up 2°C. or more per thousand feet if you descend. Do not blindly use the standard lapse rate. The standard lapse rate is science fiction. It is an engineering standard used to calibrate airspeed indicators and altimeters and has nothing to do with weather on any given day.

There is a lot that can be done to identify and stay out of highly liquid clouds. Let's start with the assumption that you are clear of clouds for the moment and are looking at them ahead, around or below. The first rule is, *stay out of building cumulus.* Avoid them at icing temperatures like you would avoid a level-five thunderstorm. If you have to penetrate them, do it under the most favorable conditions, which are at temperatures either warm enough to prevent ice formation or as cold as possible. All cold temperature bets are off in very energetic Cu or Cb's, however; they can be wet down to temperatures of $-40°C.$, and possibly even colder, due to the large amounts of water condensed by the lifting.

The second rule is, *stay out of wave clouds.* They are easily identified from above, and they will distribute copious amounts of ice all over your aerodyne at the right temperatures. If you have to penetrate them, holler and scream at ATC to let you stay over or under them until you can be cleared to go all the way through, then do it. Do not go parallel to the ridges down through one of the areas of rising air, i.e., upward moving wave, or you will wind up icier than a mint julep.

The third rule is related to the first two: If you must go through, *penetrate any suspected or known icing cloud by the shortest possible route,* either horizontally or vertically, or both.

The fourth rule is, *read what the clouds are telling you.* Spend a minute looking at cumulus clouds and see if they are building upward; if so, they are most likely to be wet. See if the edges of the clouds are sharp and well defined, or diffuse and fuzzy. The first characteristic indicates liquid water, the second indicates already frozen ice crystals. If the sun is in the clear above you and you are on top, you may be able to tell if the clouds below are liquid. Look directly down sun, where the airplane shadow would be. If you see colored rings around (or instead of) your shadow, the cloud is liquid. If you don't see rings, look down on the clouds in the other direction, toward the sun. If you see a brilliant spot of noncolored light on the clouds, you are looking at a reflection from ice crystals. At least the top of the cloud is not liquid.

Now, suppose you don't have the option of peering at the clouds from safely outside them. Suppose you are in them. The previous rules still apply, but are more difficult to follow. Two more rules, in this case, are *be ready* and *spot the ice early.* Have your available anti-icing equipment on when you penetrate possible icing conditions, whether you actually expect icing or not. Look at some small object exposed to the airstream for the earliest possible indication of ice formation. An OAT probe is good. So is a thin antenna mast. The empennage leading edge is better than the wing leading edge. Remember, the smaller the exposed object, the higher its collection efficiency, and the sooner ice will collect. If there is no small object at all visible in the airstream, consider installing one if you are going to fly in icing conditions. Don't position it where ice shedding from it will damage something, however.

If you are in the clouds, you obviously can't avoid the wetter types visually. If you have radar and you paint cells at an altitude in the icing temperature range, by all means avoid them. However, even very wet (for icing purposes) cumulus clouds will often not paint because the drops are too small. You will have to detect this type of cloud by the seat of your pants. The bumps will tip you off, and if there are updrafts, be especially watchful for ice. A single icing cumulus cell is generally quite small (a couple of miles or so across), so your immediate best course of action if you start collecting ice is generally to bore through. Without good ice-protection equipment, however, you can't loiter in one very long or go through a bunch of them without picking up more ice than anyone wants. If you can get on top of the general cloud cover and pick your way around the Cu, climb quickly while you can. If you are *sure* that there are ice-melting temperatures at a safe altitude below, go on down there. Remember, though, that sooner or later, voluntarily or otherwise, you are going down there anyway. If you continue encountering cumulus cells that deposit ice on your aircraft, and you know or can find out the directional orientation of the cause of the lifting that is setting them off (e.g., a front or a ridge line), proceed away from it by the most direct route.

Wave clouds are more difficult to identify if you are in them. Strong ones are detectable, however, if you know what to look for. In the first place, if you are flying over or downwind of a ridge line when the wind is more or less perpendicular to the ridges, suspect wave clouds. Sometime when favorable conditions for waves exist without enough moisture to create bothersome clouds, look for them. When you find them, play with them a little. The best way is to fly toward the ridges a couple of thousand feet agl and do what is necessary to hold altitude. If you have an autopilot with an altitude hold feature, turn it on. Fly for 20 miles or so and watch. A moderate case of wave motion will result in slow airspeed variations, sometimes very smooth, of ±15 knots or more as you maintain altitude. Variations of ±10 knots are common even in relatively weak waves. This will also be true in clouds, of course, if there are clouds, and may serve as your tipoff as to what is going on. If you are flying more or less parallel to the ridge line and your airspeed to hold altitude seems slow, you may be in a downward moving area of a wave. If your airspeed seems high and conditions are otherwise favorable, suspect that you are in an upward moving wave. This is the likeliest area to be wet, due to the lifting.

If you proceed along an icing wave in the lifting area, your airspeed won't be high for long; the ice will take care of that. Again, an important part of the solution is to catch the ice buildup and analyze the cause early. The ways out are to get the airplane headed in a direction not parallel to the ridges and go up or down, as appropriate. If you can climb 4,000 feet or so, up will almost certainly do it. That is usually preferable to down unless you know that the temperatures below will melt the ice. Remember, you will be going down anyway, unless you are in orbit.

If you decide that you are just in everyday stratus, an altitude change of 2,000 feet in either direction will probably do the job, and 4,000 feet would add near certainty. Stratus not involved with lake effect or waves is not very wet through any great depth. As far as up versus down goes, the remarks made about other cloud types apply here.

An important characteristic of icing is its extreme variability in both space and time. There are good reasons for this. An airplane going right down the updraft part of a wet wave cloud will pick up a terrific load, while an airplane 10 miles away at the same altitude but in a downdraft area may get nothing. If the air is relatively cold, one airplane may get a load of ice in freshly formed clouds and another airplane on the scene 20 minutes later may find only snow in the clouds due to glaciation. One airplane may go through some nice little wet imbedded cumulus cells, and the next airplane may miss them. Two airplanes 1,000 feet apart in a stratus deck may encounter different icing conditions. Two airplanes going through the same cloud at the same time at considerably different speeds may encounter widely different icing conditions due to differences in collection efficiency and ram temperature rise. Icing forecasting could be much better than it is, but one of the difficulties it faces is this variability. Another is the wide difference in the usefulness of pilot reports to which these and other variables give rise. The idea that lends some unity to all this is for the meteorologist to look for areas in which clouds with high liquid water content are likely to form, and for the pilot to assess these areas from available data, to recognize highly liquid clouds in flight and to avoid them.

If you have a load of ice, various nasty things are possible. We do our best, with techniques and equipment designed to prevent or remove ice. However, since actual icing can never be ruled out, it is important to review what ice does to an airplane. A lot of data have been taken from icing tunnels and flight testing with various airfoils and airplanes. Although the effects will vary from one airplane to another, it is possible to give some ball park numbers to point out the relative magnitude of the various problems and possibly clear up some misconceptions. First of all, on the bright side, the weight of the ice does not, in itself, present a serious problem. Ice, as it collects on airplanes in flight, weighs about 50 pounds per cubic foot. Considering how few boxes of one foot on each side could be filled with ice taken from even a heavily iced airplane, you can see that the weight alone, while not totally insignificant, will not bring you down. Put another way, ice collection of five pounds per hour per foot of span is about all you would expect even under very heavy icing conditions.

Now the bad news. Even small buildups of ice on leading edges can decrease the maximum lift coefficient by about 30 percent. Most of the damage to lift is done by the initial accumulation: further buildup has less impact. The conclusion, unfortunately, is that even a small buildup will significantly reduce the angle of attack at which an airfoil will stall. This translates into increased stall speed and increased likelihood of an inadvertent stall in a turn or pullup maneuver. As an example, stall speed data taken on an airplane with a normal cruise configuration stalling speed of 69 knots showed that one-eighth of an inch of ice on the wing leading edge raised the stall speed to 80 knots, a 16 percent increase. A further 1.25 inches of ice raised the stall speed only another four knots.

Drag coefficient, on the other hand, starts to increase as ice begins to build and keeps right on increasing. An ice buildup more or less conforming to the airfoil shape will eventually double, or in severe cases triple, the drag of the airfoil. A horn-shaped ice formation with protrusions above and below the leading edge will triple the drag at about the same thickness that the more benign shape would double it, and may eventually increase the drag by a factor of five. Other data that have been taken in terms of power, which may be more familiar than the engineering terms, have shown that the drag rise due to the horn-shaped ice buildup may raise the power required to maintain altitude in a given airplane by a factor of about 2.5. This may be more than the engine is capable of, particularly if propeller efficiency is also decreasing due to ice buildup.

Which brings us to the age-old controversy of whether it is better to keep the props clean or to keep the airfoils clean. The prop advocates lose the contest handily, according to the data. The power loss from iced airscrews is usually around nine percent and seldom more than 20 percent. This is quite a bit, but still small by comparison to increases in power required to maintain altitude on the order of 250 percent due to ice on the wings. Prop unbalance due to possible uneven shedding of ice is another matter, but this is a problem more likely to be due to malfunction of a propeller anti-icing system on one blade than to total lack of ice protection.

Handling characteristics of an airplane can also be adversely affected by ice accumulation. Roll control can be degraded by icing on the wings in front of the ailerons. Pitch control can deteriorate because of ice on the empennage leading edges and also because of ice on the wings affecting the downwash over the tail. If the position of the elevators in flight exposes the balances to ice accretion, enough ice may build to cause the elevators to bind against the horizontal stabilizer if sufficient clearance has not been provided.

Other components and systems of airplanes not designed for flight in icing conditions or protected by suitable systems can be affected in various ways. Windshields become opaque. Fuel vents exposed to the airstream can become plugged. Generators and avionics can overheat and fail due to blockage of their cooling air scoops. Antennas can break off. Static systems not protected by heating or by their location can be affected. Other effects are possible, but these are a few of the more common ones.

The best way to deal with ice on the airframe is to avoid getting it, or to prevent or remove it with equipment provided for the purpose. However, once the ice is there, it behooves the pilot to operate with great care. Even a little ice justifies a 20 percent increase in approach speed because of the probable increase in stall speed. Do not go to a flap setting near the ground that you have not tried with a little altitude cushion first. If at all possible, simulate the landing flare at altitude before it is necessary to do it for real. If disturbed airflow from the icy wings impinges on the tail during the flare, an abrupt pitch down might be the result. On landing, handle the airplane gingerly. Flare gently with no abrupt power reductions and fly it on. Consideration should be given to the length and condition of the runway, since normal short field performance will not be possible.

This discussion would not be complete without some mention of the regulatory environment relating to flight into icing conditions. Airplanes come in three basic varieties in this regard. They are either certificated for flight in icing conditions, prohibited from it, or neither. Since about 1972, the FAA has been altogether prohibiting newly manufactured airplanes of all sizes and weights from flight into known icing conditions unless and until they have been tested and shown to meet the ice protection requirements given the transport category airplanes in FAR 25. No amount of ice protection equipment installed on the airplane alters this prohibition until the full certification has been conducted. Once certificated in this manner, however, the airplane receives virtual regulatory carte blanche. The basic Part 91 contains no restrictions, and FAR 135 and Subpart D of FAR 91 permit airplanes with this icing certification to fly into known severe icing conditions. (Whatever that means, by the way. There is a large problem of definition here.) Whether this all-or-nothing philosophy is wise is open to considerable debate, but that's the way it is.

Earlier airplanes were in many cases neither certificated nor restricted. There is a provision in the basic FAR 91 that requires a pilot to comply with the operating limitations of an airplane and which makes it illegal to fly an airplane with an icing prohibition into known icing conditions, but there are no other restrictions. Consequently, if the airplane is not prohibited from flight in icing conditions and is not a large or turbojet-powered multi-engine model covered by Subpart D, FAR 91 contains no rule pertaining to operating in ice. In addition, FAR 135 permits airplanes having certain listed items of ice protection equipment (and no prohibition against flight in icing conditions) to penetrate light to moderate icing conditions (again, whatever that means) without icing certification. So, hire yourself a proverbial Philadelphia lawyer and figure it out. Good luck.

278

FUEL VI

However masterful a pilot may be, there will always be a finite amount of fuel in his airplane's tanks. It is fuel that sustains flight. Using it well instead of just using it is where the pilot's mastery comes in. Fuel has always been vital in the air because of the consequences of running out of it, and it is just as precious now on the ground because of what it costs to obtain it. Just as the supply in the tanks is fixed, so is the supply in the world. Proper management can stretch that finite supply for the next trip and for the next decades.

Fuel management for the pilot is essentially fuel conservation, and that means careful flight planning and then alert monitoring of fuel consumption. Management begins on the ground with a careful assessment of the actual quantity aboard and a verification of the proper fuel type. Adequate fuel is essential, and correct fuel is vital.

Conservation begins during the initial climb, for fuel consumed can never again be conserved. By the same principle, the careful pilot maintains the right power settings in cruise to obtain the utmost in miles for the least in fuel consumption. Here again, pre-planning helps. Conservation should continue all the way to shut down, a principle not always followed, as is indicated by the number of airplanes lost to fuel starvation during the approach.

This chapter is based on the obvious premise that fuel is the life's blood of flight safety and the foundation of operational efficiency.

Fuel Conservation: Operations

by Dan Manningham

Fuel conservation is largely a state of mind. There are no secrets left, just an unwieldy assortment of procedures that are employed by the conscientious professional. The B/CA system gathers those individual techniques into a cohesive method that saves precious fuel one pound at a time. At the bottom line you will find better range, minimized burnouts and the satisfaction of knowing you have done your job professionally.

Real operational fuel conservation begins on the ground with the flight manual and at the weather desk. Each must be understood and evaluated with a discerning, critical attitude that takes nothing for granted. Official weather reports and forecasts are not always the final answer, so trip preparations—including altitude selection, the route and alternate airport plans—should be made with liberal doses of your own experience and judgment, plus any available pilot reports.

Flight manuals are generally good, but they are far from perfect. Even when they do contain all the necessary information, it may be presented in a biased format. Some manufacturers are so interested in trumpeting their speeds that cruise control data gets step-child treatment. In one representative flight manual maximum cruise speed data is presented on a chart three times larger than the comparable chart for maximum range. No flight manual, to our knowledge, outlines a systematic approach for minimizing fuel consumption throughout the flight profile.

Operational fuel conservation, then, begins with an intelligent understanding of available flight manual information. This information becomes the established baseline from which the effectiveness of the intuitive and rule-of-thumb shifts in technique can be measured. In this regard, don't underestimate the value of the measurement and record-keeping process. Without it, the entire fuel conservation effort becomes a grey area of unproven hearsay and seat-of-the-pants guesses.

On the ground, fuel conservation may include the following:

· Careful selection of the minimum safe fuel load, closer alternates, selection of a low-traffic-level airport for the en-route refueling stops (or one that is certain to be VFR as opposed to one in weather) and computer assisted flight planning are all classic methods of saving pounds of fuel.

· Careful loading of passengers and fuel for maximum aft CG within limits will save fuel. That's because the horizontal tail must produce a downforce to counter balance the wing's pitching moment. As the CG moves aft, the required downforce is reduced so that the inflight weight of the aircraft requires less lift from the wings. Airlines know this principle well, and they target for some optimum CG when loading their aircraft. With a minimum of research you too can establish a desirable target CG for your airplane. Bear in mind when you do that, aft CG somewhat degrades stability and nose-down pitch authority.

· Taxi fuel can often be saved by coordinating ground delays with the tower and by taxiing with an engine shut down when appropriate in turbine-powered aircraft. (But engine start for takeoff should be at least three minutes prior to full power application to allow the powerplant to completely heat stabilize.)

· Reduced takeoff power settings produce immediate savings in turbine-powered aircraft through reduced flow rates and longer term savings by retarding the hot section deterioration.

· Reduced flap settings, when runway and noise factors are not limiting, will minimize takeoff and climb burn-out in any aircraft, piston or turbine-powered. Similarly, expeditious flap retraction after takeoff will help.

Once in the air and cleaned up, it is essential to begin thinking in terms of ground miles covered versus fuel burned, or Specific Range as it is otherwise known. There should be no mystery to SR. It is the aeronautical equivalent of the miles-per-gallon statistic.

If, for instance, you cover 200 nm while consuming 800 pounds of fuel, your SR is 25 nm per 100 pounds. SR can be expressed in nm per pound, per 100 pounds or per 1000 pounds.

To compute SR, simply divide fuel flow (or segment burnout) by speed. That answer will be in miles per pound, so you may wish to move the decimal point for nm per 100 pounds or nm per 1000 pounds. Remember that if you use True Airspeed, the answer will be in nautical *air* miles. That figure is useful for comparison purposes with other aircraft or with the flight manual claims. If you use groundspeed, you will have nautical *ground* miles per units of fuel, a more useful value on which to base actual enroute decisions. The formula looks like this:

$$\frac{miles}{fuel\ flow} \times 100(or\ 1000)=SR$$

The nice thing about SR is it precisely relates distance to fuel for each segment. Then, when it is time to climb, or change routing, you can evaluate that option in relation to its effect on SR. Higher altitudes, for instance, will normally reduce fuel flows in turbine-powered aircraft. However, when you compensate for possible reduced TAS and the known or estimated wind and temperature, you may well find that SR would be reduced, despite the lower burnout rate. Miles per pound is quite simply the only measure that allows meaningful range calculations.

When the airplane is cleaned up and established in the climb, start thinking in terms of SR. Begin to evaluate every option in terms of its effect on miles traveled per unit of fuel so that fuel flows, power settings, airspeeds and altitudes become mere factors in an equation that optimizes SR.

Pilots flying aircraft powered by non-supercharged piston engines will need to rely almost entirely on winds aloft data to optimize their SR. Such aircraft realize very little, if any, benefit from modifications to the still-air climb profiles. Altitude selection can be critical, however, and it requires a great deal of intuition and knowledge of the characteristics of the particular non-supercharged piston aircraft being flown. But generalizations can be made.

In a headwind situation, the breakeven point on wind is about one percent of the indicated airspeed per 1000 feet. That is, at an IAS of 100 knots, a 10-knot headwind at ground level is as much a detriment to SR as a 15-knot headwind at 5000 feet. So you're as well off at 5000 facing a 15-knot wind as at ground level looking at 10 knots at a given power setting. That's because the true airspeed tends to increase one percent per 1000 feet up to the maximum altitude at which that power setting can be maintained. Climbing above the turbulence layer is good for about five knots of headwind in itself because the TAS will be about that much greater in smooth air. This is illustrated by the stepped line on the left in Figure 1.

In still air, or in a tailwind, the SR will increase with altitude up to about 7000 feet at a given power setting. Actually, maximum SR is about constant at all altitudes up to 7000 feet, but the higher the aircraft, the higher the TAS at a constant SR. Said another way, you can get the same SR at 1000 feet as you can at 7000, but you must fly at a lower power setting and therefore slower TAS to get it at 1000 feet. When considering cruise altitudes above 7000 feet, be aware that the speed versus altitude curve for a non-supercharged aircraft is normally quite flat between 7000 and 12,000 feet, but SR increases significantly as you climb above 7000. In short, TAS will be about the same at 12,000 as at 7000, but SR will be greater. Couple that knowledge with a higher tailwind at 12,000 feet and it can save many pounds of fuel on long stage lengths.

Finally, when choosing a cruise altitude, if the climb will require more than 15 percent of the total en route time, you'll be better off staying low.

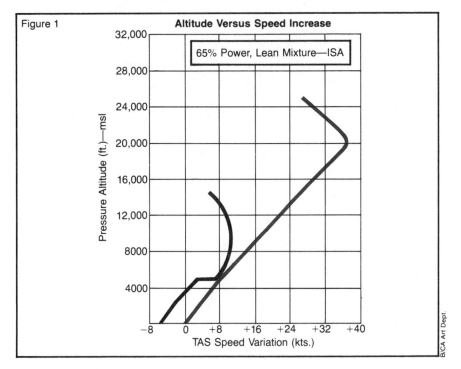

Figure 1

Altitude Versus Speed Increase

65% Power, Lean Mixture—ISA

Pressure Altitude (ft.)—msl

TAS Speed Variation (kts.)

B/CA Art Dept.

That's a loose rule of thumb, but it seems to work for most small piston aircraft.

Aircraft with turbocharged engines will realize an SR improvement at altitudes above 7000 feet as the turbocharger gains efficiency in the reduced atmospheric pressure. But be sure to assess the climb fuel penalty against any potential gains to be certain that trip SR is optimized. In the case of a supercharged piston aircraft, the loose rule of thumb on altitude selection is that the climb should not consume more than 25 percent of the total trip time. Otherwise, so much time is spent going up and down, the supercharging hasn't time to add either speed or fuel economy during the short cruise segment. In a supercharged aircraft it's better to stay high as long as possible to extract maximum benefit from the cruise performance. But the problem of keeping the engine warm while letting down must also be considered.

In many cases, other operational considerations such as choppy air, icing and thunderstorms will frustrate any attempts at fuel conservation.

Turbine-powered airplanes will invariably benefit from cruise in the higher altitudes. (See Figure 2.) Reduced air temperatures provide greater thermal efficiency within the engines so that Specific Fuel Consumption or pounds of fuel per pound of thrust is reduced. Additionally, turbine engines

283

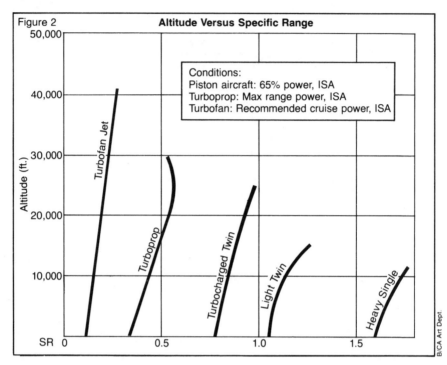

Figure 2 — Altitude Versus Specific Range

Conditions:
Piston aircraft: 65% power, ISA
Turboprop: Max range power, ISA
Turbofan: Recommended cruise power, ISA

achieve best SFC at some design power setting close to maximum cruise thrust. When you consider that these two factors are optimized at altitudes where TAS is close to maximum, it is easy to see why turbine-powered aircraft must go high for best SR.

Turboprops reach a point of diminishing returns, however, usually between 20,000 and 30,000 feet where the propeller efficiency curve turns down. Turbofan engines exhibit a similar efficiency loss at or about 37,000. Turbojet engines normally operate at increased efficiency right on up to certificated altitudes and even higher.

Time to climb versus the total trip time has an impact on the altitude selected for turboprops and jets that is not easily covered with a rule of thumb. Generally, to achieve maximum trip SR a turbine-powered aircraft should be climbed until it is time to start down, with the rate of climb varying as the altitude increases. But that's impractical in the ATC environment.

Altitude versus total trip time, therefore, must be selected based on the characteristics of the particular aircraft. Crews can save fuel on the ground during their layovers by using the time to go into the cruise section of the flight manual and working up charts of optimum altitude and thrust for various stage lengths and weights.

For jet aircraft particularly, the optimum altitude is a function of gross weight. At all but the very lowest weights, airframe considerations will override powerplant considerations so that best SR will be available at some altitude below certificated maximum. Those aerodynamic limitations are complex, but a brief review is essential to understand fuel conservation.

Maximum Specific Range is achieved at one discrete angle of attack, which is essentially independent of weight, altitude, temperature or any other such factors. Careful altitude selection will bear heavily on SR, but the AOA for most efficient operation is the same for any altitude. Indicated speed and Mach number will differ with aircraft gross weight and altitude but that single, most efficient angle of attack is a constant.

Figure 3 shows that for any given AOA there are corresponding values of the lift and drag coefficients. C_D has no specific maximum. C_L reaches maximum just prior to that gross airflow separation pilots know as the stall. The ratio of C_L/C_D is a classic measure of the airfoil's efficiency, and at maximum it provides the best angle for climb and/or maximum endurance. In jet-powered airplanes, the AOA for C_L/C_D max is useful for climb, holding and sometimes for descent.

Quite another ratio, $\sqrt{C_L}/C_D$ Max, yields the AOA for maximum SR. A more direct plot of total fuel flow versus speed for some given value of

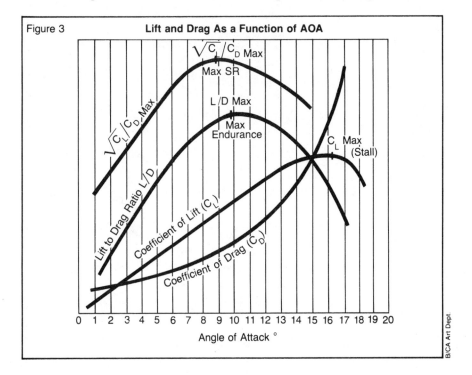

Figure 3   **Lift and Drag As a Function of AOA**

altitude and weight shows the combined engine airframe results for any given TAS in a jet.

The basic curve of Figure 4 is essentially a drag curve, but in this case showing the thrust (fuel flow) required to overcome drag. At a very low TAS, total drag (fuel flow) is high because of the induced drag associated with high AOA. At high TAS the curve rises sharply in response to parasite drag and, finally, at the knee it steepens perceptibly due to rapidly increasing compressibility effects.

The max endurance TAS is right where you might guess, the point of lowest total fuel flow. The more frequently useful figure of MSR ($\sqrt{C_L}/C_D$ Max) is found at the point where a straight line pivoted from the origin runs tangent to the bottom of the drag (fuel flow) curve. That TAS for this particular weight and altitude is the airspeed corresponding to the AOA for maximum efficiency, or MSR as it is called. Cruise at this TAS, or AOA, will produce the absolute maximum miles per unit of fuel.

In Figure 4, you will see that MSR occurs at a rather flat spot on the curve, where very small changes in fuel flow produce disproportionate changes in TAS. Because of this speed instability in jets, and because a one percent sacrifice in SR produces a several knot increase in speed, Long Range Cruise is pegged slightly above MSR speed. LRC speed is, by defini-

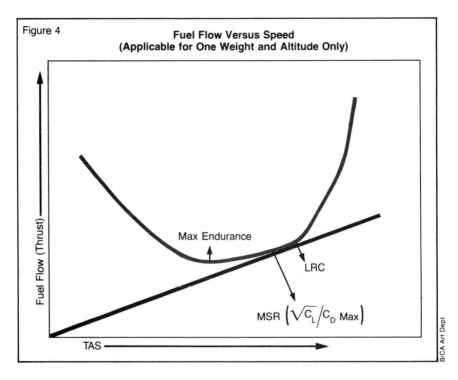

Figure 4

Fuel Flow Versus Speed
(Applicable for One Weight and Altitude Only)

Fuel Flow (Thrust)

Max Endurance

LRC

MSR $\left(\sqrt{C_L}/C_D \text{ Max} \right)$

TAS ⟶

B/CA Art Dept.

tion, the speed at which 99 percent of the MSR will be achieved. LRC is a good, proven tradeoff, and any operation for best fuel economy should be planned at that speed.

If your turbine-powered aircraft is equipped with an accurate, reliable AOA indicator, you can establish LRC at any altitude or weight by reference to one single value of AOA that will always and everywhere provide the optimum cruising compromise. If your aircraft is not so equipped, it is entirely possible to achieve the same results by careful adherence to LRC profiles in the flight manual. If the flight manual is vague or deficient on that subject, tell the manufacturer and insist on this information in a usable format.

We have covered a significant part of the cruise considerations without analyzing the effects of climb. That omission was actually intentional. You can't establish the climb profile until you have some handle on the target cruise altitude. Once that is established trip profile falls into place quickly.

Piston-powered aircraft are not subject to the significant potential fuel burnout variations associated with jets. The best still-air climb profile for piston aircraft, and to a large extent for turboprops, is simply the maximum rate achievable with the power available. However, that must be tempered with considerations of passenger comfort, visibility and engine cooling in the case of piston aircraft. In practice, most pilots of prop aircraft use a cruise climb technique and that is a good compromise if it is shaded toward minimum climb times. As the aircraft climbs away from the ground, the high deck angle becomes less perceptible to passengers so it can be increased toward the optimum. This dovetails with the visibility problem, because as the airport environment is departed the collision potential decreases and ATC surveillance becomes more effective. Just remember that the sooner cruise altitude is reached, the sooner the power can be reduced to optimum and, in a piston aircraft, the cowl flaps can be closed and the mixture adjusted for best economy.

Wind effects in the climb can normally be ignored in a prop aircraft. In the case of extreme headwinds, the cruise altitude is usually low. In a tailwind situation it's still normally best to get altitude quickly because wind velocities normally increase with altitude.

The absolute optimum technique for minimum burnout in a jet is to climb at best rate to the highest altitude at which maximum cruise thrust will just hold the AOA for LRC. Best cruise economy will then result from continued operation at max cruise thrust and LRC angle of attack, allowing the aircraft to drift up as fuel is consumed. This slow steady ascent will result in a constant Mach number and a minimum fuel burn for the trip. Figure 5 displays this optimum profile. Unfortunately, real-world considerations usually preclude any such flight profile although a clear image of the optimum is a necessary first step toward maximizing trip fuel-economy.

287

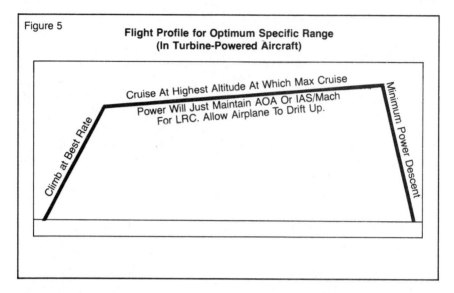

In a no-wind or tailwind condition best economy in a jet is achieved by climbing at best rate so as to reach those higher altitudes of thermal efficiency and higher TAS as quickly as possible. Headwinds at altitude might suggest some slight modification towards a faster airspeed in climb, but that can be worked out with basic navigational arithmetic.

Manufacturer's suggested climb speeds are normally compromise speeds that combine faster airspeeds for shorter trip times with adequate climb rates. The degree of compromise depends on the manufacturer's assumptions. Usually, such recommended climb speeds are slightly faster than the speed for best economy.

Because the optimum climb speed for any given trip is the product of complex variables such as gross weight, temperature and wind, it is impossible to suggest one single speed value for all conditions. There is, however, a simple procedure that will provide near maximum economy, at least in theory.

It is fair to assume that your manufacturer's recommended climb speed is faster than the speed for best rate of climb and best economy. If you cannot extract a definitive max efficiency climb profile from him, make a small, arbitrary reduction to the recommended climb speed of 5 percent. If, for instance, the book recommends 260 knots IAS, try reducing 13 knots for the initial climbout. As altitude increases, reduce IAS to conform to the speeds for LRC. In a Sabre 60, for example, you would target the climb for 240 KIAS at 20,000, 230 KIAS at 30,000 and 220 KIAS at 40,000. In broad terms, higher airspeeds are more economical with headwinds and/or high gross weights; lower speeds are economical with tailwinds and at light weights.

Precisely because climb schedules are complex, you may well find that theoretical profiles do not always work best. One careful Sabreliner operator we talked to believes that *increased* climb speeds actually improve SR in contradiction to the theory.

Your best option is to begin with some speed close to the speed for best rate of climb and keep careful records of climb economy to establish a baseline. Then when you really do know how well some specific climb program does, it is simple to measure other schedules against that baseline to find the one still-air schedule that contribute the most to trip SR. When you have an optimum climb schedule for your aircraft figured out, make appropriate adjustments for wind and temperature at altitude.

You know that best initial cruise altitude for a jet is that flight level where max cruise thrust will just maintain the AOA (or IAS/Mach) for LRC. If you must compromise on altitudes because of ATC restrictions, opt for the higher practical one so that the reducing gross weight will tend to bring the airplane to an ideal weight/altitude balance.

Naturally your speed should *always* conform to LRC values with one exception. Flights into substantial headwinds may benefit from some speed increase above LRC to minimize the time exposure to those adverse conditions. Operations in a tailwind, crosswind, calm wind or moderate headwind will always benefit from LRC or the compromise speed. As headwinds increase above some moderate level, best economy is achieved at a higher speed. The classic thumb rule is that when headwinds approach 25 percent of cruise indicated airspeed, a faster speed will save fuel. This classic principle is seriously tempered in jets by the very substantial increase in compressibility drag at any speed above LRC, but some increased speed may help.

Notice that speed reduction in a tailwind does not provide the same benefits for a turbine aircraft already flying at a LRC speed schedule, but slowing down can definitely add to the SR in piston aircraft, which are normally cruised at some speed well above the maximum SR.

At level-off in any aircraft type, plan to spend two or three minutes trimming. For some reason, the task of fine trim has been underplayed, especially in high-performance aircraft where it is most critical. Really precise trimming involves at least the following steps:

· Turn off the yaw damper, if feasible, to remove any possible interference, especially if it is a parallel type.

· In multi-engine airplanes be particularly careful to balance the power, using the most reliable indicators for your specific airplane.

· Spend whatever time is necessary to balance the fuel load across the airplane centerline. Fuel and thrust imbalances can be trimmed out with the flight controls; however, the net result will be some unnecessary drag.

· Now set the aileron and rudder trim to zero. If the airplane is poorly rigged, you might have to hold considerable wheel and/or pedal forces to maintain level flight, although that degree of misrig should receive maintenance attention ASAP.

· Set the pitch trim to maintain the attitude and/or airspeed desired.

· Roll in enough rudder trim to center the ball or spirit level while holding the wings level with ailerons. When you think the rudder trim is close, mark your heading and check for drift over a period of a minute or two. One degree of drift per minute is equivalent to a 5° skid for 12 minutes.

· When you're entirely satisfied with the rudder trim, and only then, remove any aileron forces with roll trim. Control wheel position doesn't mean a thing, as long as the heading is constant and the wings are level.

· If a large amount of aileron trim is required, check the rudder trim again for possible adverse yaw from the aileron displacement.

· Now check the balls, bubbles, trim indicators and wheel position for later reference. Remember they are indicators, subject to installation error and intended only to be guides, but they can be valuable in the proper context. But the airplane can be trimmed precisely without any indicators.

· During cruise, disengage the autopilot at least once every hour and recheck the total trim blend.

Once established in cruise, there are several possibilities for minimizing burnout in any airplane. The tanks from which fuel is burned should be selected, if possible, to keep the CG aft. In small aircraft, just running the pilot and copilot seats back will add to speed and, therefore, SR. In all aircraft, attention to maintaining the LRC speed will pay off significantly.

The pilot of a piston aircraft should not overlook the possibility of saving fuel with a slight power reduction. Aircraft vary in this respect, but as a rule of thumb each 100 pounds of fuel burn at cruise in a piston aircraft will result in a 0.7 percent increase in SR due to a slight speed increase. But if the power is pulled back to maintain the *same* indicated speed at the lower weight, the SR increase will be 1.4 percent. The indicated speeds involved are so small, the precise speed reduction is difficult if not impossible to read on the indicator. Therefore, another rule of thumb: If the manifold pressure is reduced one-quarter inch per hour, the TAS will remain essentially the same, but the SR will increase substantially.

There are three broad possibilities for saving additional fuel in the cruise segment for jet crews:

· Request an altitude block from ATC so that you can cruise climb at long-range cruise angle of attack or IAS and maximum cruise thrust. This option is too often overlooked.

· Step climb to the next higher altitude, if appropriate, as fuel burns off, remembering to initiate the climb so as to arrive at the higher altitude slightly above optimum weight.

· Maintain level flight when ATC or airplane restrictions prevent a climb, and fly a reducing IAS/Mach schedule as weight decreases. Remember that AOA for LRC is a constant, so at any given altitude the LRC IAS/Mach will reduce with weight.

There is one other rather obvious consideration which can save precious pounds of fuel. A basic theorem of geometry says "the shortest distance between two points is a straight line." We apply that concept to navigation all the time, but not always to the maximum possible degree. When possible, use installed area-nav equipment to the fullest. File direct or request direct routes from the en-route controller.

On departure, minimize speed and expedite turns until reasonably established on course. If you can save just one mile in distance traveled each time you're vectored out of a terminal area, you will reduce an average 600-hour year by one to three flying hours, depending on airplane speed and average trip lengths. The same, of course, is true when being vectored into the airport. With a minimum of effort, one to five miles can be saved on every arrival.

Climb and cruise offer the largest potential for operational fuel conservation because they represent the vast majority of total burnout. Descent from cruise altitude, while not as significant, can contribute measurably to total trip economy.

Unfortunately for piston aircraft operators, and many turboprop operators as well, the manufacturers provide little if any optimum descent schedule data. Operators are left to their own ingenuity.

The general practice is to begin the letdown relatively far out and use the descent for a speed increase. But, in fact, the fuel efficient procedure —and one that costs little in time—is to stay high until closer in, then descend at the cruise segment indicated speed with power reductions as appropriate. The reason for keeping the speed down is simply that a speed increase causes a severe drag increase and a consequent waste of energy.

In turboprop aircraft that profile can be followed very faithfully. In piston aircraft, however, engine temperatures become a major consideration. If the cylinder heads are allowed to cool too much or too quickly, accelerated wear or even costly damage may result. To preclude that, pilots should use a descent schedule of increasing steepness with a stepped power reduction. The first portion of the descent should be shallow with a slight power reduction from cruise. As the descent progresses, the descent rate should be increased as the power is stepped down to progressively cool the engine.

Ideally, the power should be down to 13 to 15 inches at the point in the approach where the gear and flaps must be extended. Those extensions should be as late as safety allows.

In turbine aircraft, descent, like climb, requires some reverse calculations for maximum efficiency. Also like climb, the flight manual descent procedure is very likely designed for speed at the expense of economy.

The absolute best procedure would be to maintain cruising altitude to a point in space from which a power off descent would allow touchdown at the destination airport with only enough power to stabilize the approach at some reasonable altitude on final. Best speed in the descent is somewhat difficult to pinpoint, but LRC airspeeds will provide close to maximum efficiency. In any case be sure to avoid Mach numbers above LRC because you will suffer a significant drag penalty from compressiblity effects. At the same time, avoid any use whatsoever of speed brakes, inflight reverse or flaps because those energy absorbers will definitely add to total trip fuel.

Routine ATC procedures in the United States generally aim for an approximate speed/altitude/distance gate of 250 KIAS at 10,000 feet, at about 30 miles from destination. Add to that 30 nm distance the number of miles required to slow your airplane from descent speed to 250 KIAS. If, for instance, that deceleration distance is five nm, you must target the descent to arrive at 10,000 feet, 35 nm from destination. Now back up from that 35 nm gate and add the distance required to descend at minimum power from cruise altitude to 10,000 feet. Take into account pressurization and any other pneumatic system requirements such as fuel heaters or anti-ice, and compute the descent at absolute minimum power.

Jets will usually descend at a ratio of two to three miles per 1000 feet of altitude in still air. You can find out very easily by comparing distance traveled for each 10,000-foot block on your next trip and taking an average with allowance for wind. When you know the ratio, calculate the descent point like this:

· Add deceleration distance to the 30-mile gate to find the 10,000-foot target point; 5+30=35, in our example.

· Substract 10,000 feet from cruise altitude and multiply the answer by descent ratio. If, for instance, you are cruising at 39,000 feet and your airplane descends at a ratio of 2.5 miles per 1000 feet, the calculation looks like this: 39,000 minus 10,000 equals 29,000. 29,000 times 2.5 nm equals 72.5 nms. In other words it will take about 72.5 nm to descend from a cruise altitude of 39,000 feet to the transition altitude of 10,000 feet.

· Figure the effect of the average headwind/tailwind component during descent. Considering that descent from cruise to 10,000 will require about 10 minutes, make an appropriate distance adjustment.

· Now add the gate distance to the descent distance. In our case 35 nm plus 72.5 nm produces a point 107.5 nm from destination.

· Add five nm for the transition from cruise to descent and the total is your point of descent distance from destination. Our fictitious airplane would begin the transition from cruising flight to descent at a point about 112.5 miles from destination.

FAA is beginning to introduce Profile Descent procedures that will allow the pilot great discretion in planning his descent. If you establish the most efficient descent program now, you will be in position to take full advantage of that discretion when it is offered.

Fuel conservation from this gate point 30 miles out is largely a matter of delaying flaps and landing gear as long as possible while flying the most direct possible track to the runway. Gear and flap programming are a highly individual process, with significant safety aspects, but any delay will save some fuel.

Holding affords its own unique challenges for fuel conservation. Any holding operation should be conducted at the AOA or IAS C_L/C_D Max (Figures 3 and 4) in jets. Maximum endurance in propeller aircraft is achieved at the minimum power setting that will sustain flight. This point of minimum burnout per unit of time is the optimum configuration for maximum endurance. Avoid, at all costs, holding at any other speed or with flaps or gear down. There is usually one option that can minimize holding fuel. When you receive a holding clearance some distance from destination, immediately reduce airspeed to the appropriate maximum endurance figure and tell ATC what you're doing and why (don't *ask* ATC for the reduction, but do inform them.) This type of linear holding can save up to four percent in fuel over a holding pattern.

Once on the ground and clear of the runway, consider shutting down one or more engines. When you set the parking brake, record the fuel remaining so that gauge accuracy can be verified against fuel added for the next trip.

Operational procedures offer a fertile area for very real fuel savings. Begin to adjust your thinking in terms of SR for each segment of the trip so that each pound of fuel contributes the maximum possible range. In the beginning you will have to establish some rigid trip profile and repeat it for several flights of equal mileage so a baseline can be established. When that has been done, you can experiment.

There are four equipment additions B/CA recommends where appropriate for maximizing fuel economy:

· A fuel flow indicator, or indicators, of some kind. The system doesn't have to be precisely accurate as long as it's consistent. With fuel flow knowledge and a DME groundspeed readout, it's possible to instantly calculate the SR being achieved. The formula is groundspeed/fuel flow. Once that's known, power changes can be tried until a maximum SR is found for the altitude and actual winds within the power and speed range available.

· Area navigation equipment. It is impossible to justify area nav purely on the basis of fuel conservation. However, when you consider its significant contribution to operational flexibility, the real promise of *some* fuel savings would seem to tip the balance in favor of this hardware. It is possible that some of the less expensive equipment will pay for itself over several years as inflation and fuel prices steadily escalate.

· Angle of Attack. We have often described the virtues of this instrument and believe that its most significant contribution can be to fuel conservation. AOA offers a host of benefits not available from any other cockpit instrument. It is unsurpassed as an efficiency indicator for cruising flight. In that role alone, AOA could well pay for itself within 12 months.

· An aircraft performance computer.

Accurate record keeping is going to be an essential element in any total fuel conservation program and that is the next and final component of the B/CA Fuel Conservation System.

Fuel Conservation: Record Keeping

37

by Dan Manningham

Fuel conservation is a tedious job. Beginning in the maintenance shop and progressing through the art of weather analysis and flight planning, fuel conservation finally hits its stride in the cockpit environment. At the bottom line you will find increased range, reduced fuel burnout and some added professional pride. You may not always choose to operate for maximum efficiency due to other, more pressing priorities. Nevertheless, when you do finally understand the most efficient flight profile for your airplane, you will be better able to assess the fuel penalty associated with those compromises.

One essential element in developing that optimum conservation profile is to establish a baseline from which to measure and test the individual elements of your total program. If you are not sure how much fuel you are burning now, there is no way to accurately determine the effects of new and altered procedures. The B/CA fuel logs—one for piston aircraft, one for the turbines—are bookkeeping devices designed for careful recording and analysis of trip burnout on a carefully segmented basis. They are supplements to your normal flight plan forms. Using the appropriate fuel log for several trips will allow you to establish, with accuracy, your current fuel utilization. Continued use will show the effects of each modification to engines, airframes and flight planning, as well as to your climb, cruise and descent procedures. When appropriate, the fuel log allows direct comparison between aircraft, even between two or more dissimilar types.

Let's look at our fuel log for turbine aircraft first and then the one for piston aircraft.

The B/CA fuel log shown in Figure 1 is configured for any turbine, fixed-wing aircraft. The vertical axis is divided into trip segments with a trip summary on the bottom line. The log has room for eight separate trip segments, although few trips will work out to exactly that number. Some

FUEL

B/CA Fuel Log—Turbine Aircraft

Aircraft Type: _____ T.O. Gross Weight: _____ Date: _____ Trip # _____

	Segment	Performance Data	Dist.	Time	B.O.	G.S. NM x 60 Min.	FF B.O. x 60 Min.	SR Dist. B.O.	Remarks	% B.O.	NM/%
Climb	–TOC	Spd. Sched. / Wind Comp.									
Cruise	TOC–	Alt. / IAS/Mach / TAS / SAT									
		Alt. / IAS/Mach / TAS / SAT									
		Alt. / IAS/Mach / TAS / SAT									
		Alt. / IAS/Mach / TAS / SAT									
		Alt. / IAS/Mach / TAS / SAT									
	–POD	Alt. / IAS/Mach / TAS / SAT									
Descent	POD–	Spd. Sched. / Wind Comp.									
Summary											

Figure 1

may occasionally require more room, but all trips will lend themselves to at least three segments:

· From point of departure to Top Of Climb (TOC).
· From TOC to Point Of Descent (POD).
· From POD to landing.

Longer flights can easily be subdivided in any convenient manner, although there are valid statistical reasons for keeping the segment distances reasonably constant when possible.

The horizontal axis is subdivided 11 ways, beginning with a list of the trip segments. Moving to the right, the respective columns are:

· *Performance Data*—The essential performance data applicable to the segment. During climb and descent, only the speed schedule and a wind component are necessary. In cruise, altitude, indicated airspeed, Mach number, true airspeed and static air temperature are recorded for proper comparison with other flights.

· *Distance*—Planned mileage for the segment is noted above the diagonal prior to flight with actual distances penciled in during the trip. In most cases there will be no changes aside from some adjustments to compensate for displaced TOC and POD.

· *Time*—Planned time for the segment is written in over the diagonal, actual time under it.

296

· *B.O. (Burnout)*—Planned burnout is again above the diagonal and actual segment fuel consumption under it.

· *Groundspeed*—This is an average groundspeed based on NM ÷ Min. × 60 for each segment. Cockpit groundspeed displays should not be used because they give only an instantaneous reading.

· *Fuel Flow*—This is an average fuel flow based on B.O. ÷ Min. × 60 for each segment. Cockpit fuel flow meters are unnecessary and even when present should not be used. Refer to the totalizer or quantity gauges.

· *Specific Range*—SR is computed for each segment by the formula Dist. ÷ B.O. We use segment distance traveled instead of airspeed, and segment burnout instead of fuel flow, to achieve a smooth average for the leg. At any given moment in the trip SR can be calculated using GS÷FF which is best for real-time altitude or route changes. Thirty miles on 100 pounds, for instance, is just easier to visualize than 0.30 miles on one pound. Move the decimal anywhere you like for your own operation. Wherever you place that decimal, specific range is the most significant figure you will record.

· *Remarks*—A place to note deviations from planned altitudes or routes, or anything that would affect specific range.

· *% B.O. (% of Burnout)*—This figure is calculated by dividing the total burnout into the segment burnout and multiplying by 100. Actual trip figures cannot be calculated until the trip is terminated and actual total burnout has been determined. Percent of burnout is a useful figure for comparing dissimilar aircraft.

· *NM/%*—A measure of the number of nautical miles traveled for each one percent of total fuel consumed. Divide segment distance in NMs by percent of burnout from previous column. This figure also cannot be calculated until the trip has ended and until the % B.O. figures are complete. NM/% is simply another method of comparison that can be useful with dissimilar airplanes. Both of these percent value columns are placed at the extreme right after the Remarks section to separate them from data that can be recorded and calculated in flight.

Notice that information is recorded in an order that flows from one calculation to the next. You will certainly want a small calculator for the arithmetic, but there is no need for anything more elaborate.

Figure 2 shows the results of our example flight. This one was flown in a DC-8 from New York to Las Vegas. Burnouts and fuel flows are multiples of those seen in most corporate jets and turboprops, of course, but the principle and the analysis is valid for any turbine aircraft regardless of size. In this case we multiplied SR by 1000 to achieve a more easily comprehended value.

As you can see, the filled-in log indicates some rather typical deviations from the flight plan. Mileage to the TOC point was over the plan due to an ATC altitude restriction noted in the Remarks section. For some unexplain-

	Segment	Performance Data	Dist.	Time	B.O.	G.S. NM x 60 Min.	FF B.O. x 60 Min.	SR Dist. B.O.	Remarks	% B.O.	NM %
		B/CA Fuel Log—Turbine Aircraft Aircraft Type: DC-8-6 T.O. Gross Weight: 237,100 Date: 4/14/77 Trip # 3									
Climb	JFK-TOC	Spd. Sched. 25°/30°/.78 Wind Comp. -20	169/190	:25/:29	9.8/9.6	406/393	23,520/9,862	17.26/19.79	5 min. ATC holddown at 33,000	17.5/17.1	9.7/11.1
Cruise	TOC-AIR	Alt. 350 IAS/Mach .80 TAS 465 SAT +3	183/162	:24/:20	4.9/3.7	457/486	12,250/11,100	37.31/43.78	Distance adjusted for late arrival at TOC	8.7/6.6	21.0/24.5
	AIR-CAP	Alt. 350/390 IAS/Mach .80 TAS 457 SAT -2	407	:56/:58	10.9/11.9	436/421	11,679/12,310	37.33/34.20	Climb to 39,000	19.4/21.2	21.0/19.2
	CAP-MKC	Alt. 390 IAS/Mach .81 TAS 470 SAT +1	233	:34/:33	6.0/6.5	411/424	10,588/11,818	38.82/35.88		10.7/11.6	21.8/20.1
	MKC-LAA	Alt. 390 IAS/Mach .80 TAS 461 SAT +2	386	:55/:55	9.4/10.3	421/421	10,255/11,236	41.05/37.47		16.8/18.4	23.0/21.0
	LAA-FMN	Alt. 390 IAS/Mach .80 TAS 460 SAT +1	272	:41/:39	6.7/7.0	398/418	9,805/10,769	40.59/38.82	Climb to 410 A/C WX Descend to 390	11.9/12.5	22.9/21.8
	FMN-POD	Alt. 390 IAS/Mach .80 TAS 457 SAT -2	226/184	:35/:27	5.7/5.3	387/409	9,771/11,778	39.61/34.73	Distance adjusted for early descent requested by ATC	10.2/9.4	22.2/19.6
Descent	POD-LAS	Spd. Sched. .80/330 Wind Comp. -25	124/166	:24/:34	2.7/4.3	310/219	6,750/7,588	45.93/28.86	Early speed reduction for spacing	4.8/7.7	25.8/21.6
Summary	JFK-LAS		2000	4:54/4:55	56.1/58.6	408/407	11,449/11,919	35.44/34.15		100.0/104.5	20.0/19.1

Figure 2

able reason, segment burnout to TOC was below plan, despite the increase of 21 miles and four minutes. The reason is impossible to explain with certainty in retrospect, but could be due to inaccurate fuel gauging, erroneous gross weight calculations or any of a dozen errors. Whatever the reason, keeping this log would surely result in some pattern developing over several trips that could well lead to a tailored climb schedule for maximum efficiency.

Notice that a late arrival at TOC necessitated a revision to the first cruise segment distance from TOC to AIR. This minor record-keeping change is necessary for accurate calculations, but has negligible impact on the important results of SR. On this leg groundspeed was 29 knots above planned and fuel flow was disproportionately low, so that the SR is significantly above the planned figure.

The leg from AIR to CAP included a step climb to 39,000 feet, which had been planned and accounted for in the preliminary figures. The two-minute time loss on that leg was probably due to excess headwinds. Notice that time has no direct effect on SR, so there has to be some other explanation for the decrease in that telltale figure.

The clue is an excess fuel flow rate that increased segment burnout. Very likely that high fuel flow in this instance was the result of an early and over-weight arrival at 39,000 so that the airplane was not operating at the optimum Mach for LRC. Some fuel savings may have been realized if the crew had requested a block of altitudes to allow a slow drift-up, or an intermediate altitude until gross weight was down to the max for 39,000.

During the next leg, from CAP to MKC, the crew allowed the Mach number to increase considerably above that for LRC. Operating at this faster but less efficient speed they gained one minute and increased segment burnout by 500 pounds. Notice again that time (groundspeed) does not affect SR directly. Only burnout matters.

When segment time is affected by en-route winds. SR will be changed by the altered segment burnout. It is burnout, not time, that adds or detracts from SR. In our example the speed increase on this leg from CAP to MKC was achieved at the expense of fuel flow, so segment burnout was increased and SR suffered considerably.

The leg from MKC to LAA is precisely within the planned time (groundspeed), but burnout was greater than planned due to a continued high fuel flow rate. In this case the problem was again speed. The crew should have reduced Mach to conform to a LRC profile because as an airplane's weight decreases that one, single angle of attack for optimum LRC occurs at progressively lower speeds. By maintaining Mach 0.80 this crew steadily drifted away from that optimum angle of attack. Since the flight was planned for LRC, the deviation detracted from SR.

Between LAA and FMN the crew climbed to 41,000 feet to top some weather and then descended back to 39,000. Although they picked up two minutes, there was a net increase in burnout from the climb itself and, to some extent, from that brief off-optimum-altitude operation. It is even possible that the two-minute gain was achieved in a high-speed descent back to FL390 at the expense of some added fuel consumption. At the bottom line, SR was down from a planned 40.59 to an actual 38.82. The message here may be that a climb to top adverse weather should be carefully weighed against a lateral diversion for minimizing burnout.

Basically there are two things that will increase burnout:

· Adverse winds or ATC deviations, which increase the total air miles without affecting fuel flow rate.

· Operating circumstances or procedures such as airspeed, air temperature or altitude that increase segment burnout because of excess flow rates. These are the things that allow for substantial analysis and improvement. In all cases, specific range is the only conclusion.

As this trip neared LAS, ATC requested an early descent so that actual POD was 166 nm out instead of the planned 124. Notice that the FMN to POD segment data had to be adjusted for this mileage change. Notice also that the early descent cost 1600 pounds of fuel and devastated the SR for that segment. More careful analysis shows that total actual burnout was 2500 pounds above flight plan and that 64 percent of that overage is accounted for by the 1600 pounds lost in descent. A more aggressive crew may have been able to negotiate a more satisfactory descent point with Los Angeles Center.

The Flight Summary shows that total time was within one minute, but that excess fuel consumption reduced SR from 35.64 to 34.15, a loss of 1.49 nm/each 1000 pounds of fuel consumed. Further analysis shows that planned burnout was exceeded by 4.5 percent and that each 1 percent of that consumption yielded 0.9 nm less than anticipated. In other words, this trip burned enough excess fuel to carry the airplane 90 miles farther (0.9 miles per each 1 percent).

B/CA's fuel log for turbine aircraft is designed to show you how much fuel you are using and where it is going so that operational procedures can be modified and fine tuned for total efficiency. Be careful not to focus on any single segment at the expense of others. Each separate element of the trip should contribute to minimizing *total* trip specific range.

Procedures which repeatedly produce superior SR should be written into the operations manual and mandated for those operations where maximum efficiency has priority. Pilots should be encouraged to experiment with new fuel-saving procedures and to share the results with others in the department. After the fuel log has been in use for several weeks, spend some time analyzing the returns and begin to develop your own optimum trip profile. You will find that this backlog of precise and segmented information allows for very accurate analysis. The possibilities are numerous.

If you operate a single airplane or single airplane type, you can make direct comparisons in all categories. Departments operating more than one type can benefit from a comparison in two ways:

· Direct comparison will permit accurate assessment of the SR differential on selected stage lengths.

· Relative analysis using the % B.O. and NM/%, allows for some interesting comparisons between two different airplane types. If, for instance, the Lear 25 consistently uses a greater percent of total burnout than the Lear 24 to reach cruise altitude, it may be time to reassess the climb profile being used for the 25. Absolute parallels cannot be expected due to airframe and engine distinctions, but percentage similarities can be useful and informative.

For piston aircraft operators, building a meaningful record of fuel burns is rather difficult. That's because the manufacturers have fallen down in their job of providing the proper instrumentation for smaller aircraft. Most of these aircraft have extremely poor gauging systems and no fuel flow instrumentation at all. We recommend that you consider adding one of the several fuel flow devices to your aircraft so you can more quickly get a feel for how various changes in technique are affecting the total fuel burn or specific range.

In the absence of such a device, there are other techniques that can be used to assist you in determining how your fuel conservation efforts are paying off.

The obvious one is to top off the tanks at the end of each flight and read the total burn on your fuel charge slip. The problems with that are, first, linemen don't always top off a tank precisely the same way and, second, it's counter-productive to fuel efficiency to always fill up. A better idea is to "stick" the tanks during the period you are establishing the optimum trip profiles for a piston aircraft. When gauging the tanks in this manner, try to load and park the aircraft so that its ground altitude will be the same each time.

Our fuel log for piston aircraft assumes you will use some such method for determining fuel burns on each flight. The format of the piston aircraft log (Figure 3) is quite different from the one for turbines because in the absence of adequate gauging systems, time, true airspeed and air miles traveled must be recorded. What you want to do is build a history of trends rather than the precise picture that is possible with the better instrumented turbines.

Figure 3

B/CA Fuel Log—Piston Aircraft			
Trip: _____ Date: _____			
	Climb	Cruise	Descent
Dept. Wt.			
RPM			
MP			
Alt.			
OAT			
Time			
IAS			
TAS			
*Grd. Spd.			
Dist. (G)			
*Dist. (A)			
*Wind			

Summary		Remarks
Dist. (G)		
Dist. (A)		
Time		
Avg. TAS		
Burn		
Lbs./Hr.		
SR (G)		
SR (A)		

FUEL

The entries to be made on the log are straightforward except for those with a star in the upper portion and on all entries in the Summary section. A sample log in Figure 4 is for a flight from Dallas to Memphis in a Cessna 182. RPM and MP (manifold pressure) in the cruise segment are recorded in two values because they were reduced en route to conserve fuel, as noted in the remarks box. Altitudes are for the airports and cruise segment. All times are in minutes.

Groundspeeds were computed (distance divided by time, times 60) because an average is wanted, not the instantaneous and momentary reading from the DME. The entry "Dist. (G)" refers to ground distance. The "Dist. (A)" refers to the air distance traveled and is computed by multiplying the *average* TAS times the en route time and dividing by 60. The wind is the actual headwind/tailwind component and is found by subtracting TAS from the groundspeed.

The log has provision for only one cruise segment because it keeps the workload down—and that's how most flights in piston aircraft are conducted anyway. For a multi-segment flight involving changes in altitude, additional logs should be used and the step climbs recorded with each new altitude segment. If a large power change is made, another log should be used as well to record the new TAS and the accompanying computation for

Figure 4

B/CA Fuel Log—Piston Aircraft			
Trip: DAL – MEM Date: 2/16/77			
	Climb	Cruise	Descent
Dept. Wt.	2280		
RPM	2450	2250/2200	2200
MP	24/22	22/20	18/13
Alt.	568/7000	7000	7000/332
OAT	21°/17°	16°	17°/24°
Time	17 min.	154 min.	10
IAS	95 K	117	125
TAS	95/108	134	143/125
*Grd. Spd.	95.3	140.3	138
Dist. (G)	27	360	23
*Dist. (A)	28.8	343.9	22.3
*Wind	−6	+6	+4

Summary		Remarks	
Dist. (G)	440	MP to 21" after one hour. RPM to 2200 and MP to 20" at two hours.	
Dist. (A)	395		
Time	181 min.		
Avg. TAS	131 K *		
Burn	231		
Lbs./Hr.	76.6 *		
SR (G)	1.77		
SR (A)	1.71 *		

air distance traveled. A major change in OAT or the wind may also necessitate using an additional log sheet.

At the end of the trip, or even several days later, the Summary can be computed. The entry "Avg. TAS" refers to average true airspeed and is found by dividing the air distance (the sum of "Dist. A" in the top section) by the total trip time and multiplying that by 60. Specific range (miles per pound) is computed for the ground distance—SR(G)—and the air distance —SR(A).

The numbers in the Summary with a star beside them are the important ones. To make the log really meaningful, 15 or more trips flown in your usual way should be recorded. From that data, averages for Avg. TAS, Lbs./Hr. and SR(A) should be computed. Then begin trying various fuel conservation procedures. Compare the new results for the three parameters with your averages. You can even graph them for better results.

The object is to keep Avg. TAS as constant as possible while achieving a reduction in Lbs./Hr. and an increase in SR(A). While doing that, be careful that you don't get fooled by unusual winds. You should, in fact, throw out data recorded in wind components of greater than 10 knots or when any input—such as wind, OAT, altitude—is so erratic the Summary data is rendered suspect. In any event, remember that a headwind costs you more fuel than the same tailwind saves.

This is a crude approach to record keeping for piston aircraft, but we don't apologize for it. If the manufacturers would install accurate fuel quantity gauges on all piston aircraft, the same log used for the turbines would suffice. Without that information, flights cannot be segmented and so must be analyzed as a whole as indicated by our log.

Fuel conservation is a lonely, frustrating job. It demands scrupulous maintenance standards, detailed operational planning and careful record keeping. When you do get it all together, you will know your flight manual, your airplane and your own capabilities as never before.

Perfection in fuel conservation is probably not possible. Improvement is, and it's becoming more and more critical that we achieve it.

Enough Fuel Is Not Enough

38

by Dan Manningham

Ten years ago aviation fuel problems were largely confined to water contamination and proper octane selection. Now—thanks to the forces of geopolitics, more critical engine specifications, shortages and distribution problems—aviation fuel has become a complex subject with increasing implications for the pilot.

One element that bears emphasis is that you, as pilot-in-command, are responsible for your fuel load. The lineman may pump too much or too little —into any available orifice and out of the nearest truck—but you have to live with it and you carry the legal responsibility for getting the required quantity and quality.

Aviation gasoline (avgas) is a truly unique product that bears only casual resemblance to automotive gasoline (mogas). Avgas is a precise blend of paraffins, aromatics, naphthenes, olefins, tetraethyl lead (TEL) and dyes that conforms to rigid international standards. Its octane rating and lead content are indelibly color coded as follows:

· *Red*—80/87 octane with 0.5 milliliters of lead per gallon.
· *Blue*—100/130 LL (low lead) with two milliliters of lead per gallon.
· *Green*—100/130 with three to four milliliters of lead per gallon.
· *Purple*—115/145 with 4.6 milliliters of lead per gallon.

Octane is nothing more than resistance to detonation and you need at least the minimum octane for the engine in question. Higher octane fuel will always perform well and will not, as a famous myth insists, burn your valves. A higher octane fuel may, however, cause lead fouling of spark plugs. (But that can be minimized by careful leaning.)

Automotive gasoline (mogas) is entirely different. It's octane rating is determined through different testing procedures. It's composition varies widely with locale and there is no single standard. Despite the experiences of others, B/CA believes it is absolutely unsuited for use in aviation for at least the following reasons:

Mogas octane ratings will almost certainly be too low for the airplanes used in business aviation.

Mogas can have a higher vapor pressure because it is not refined for use at altitude. That higher vapor pressure may well cause vapor locks.

Lead additives in mogas contain extra chlorine and bromine which are highly corrosive.

You may not like to burn 100-octane low-lead in your 80-octane engine, but it is far superior than any automotive gasoline you can buy.

Jet fuels come from the so-called middle-distillates of the refining process along with diesel fuel and heating oil. Jet fuel availability and price have been hit doubly hard in recent years by the fuel shortage and by newer, more stringent specifications that limit the total petroleum fraction available for jet fuel. Newer, relaxed standards are currently under study that would increase the fraction by lifting freeze-point levels. Such higher freeze points have real significance for business and commercial aviation, particularly in light of the increased range and altitude capabilities of newer airplanes.

The freeze point of jet fuel ranges from about −40°C. to −60°C. depending on its composition. This freeze point has nothing to do with water contamination and is not affected or prevented by fuel heaters or Prist, which are intended to cope only with water (ice) crystals. At some critical temperature, jet fuel becomes mushy, like soft wax, and will not flow. If it gets cold enough, it will just sit in the tank like jello while the boost pumps cavitate and the engines flame out.

You must know the freeze point of your fuel for any long duration, high-altitude flight and avoid that tank temperature by descending to a warmer altitude if necessary. Jet fuel freeze could become a serious threat in the future.

Two common problems shared by avgas and jet fuel users are: contamination and mixing. Contamination is invariably a water problem and easily avoided by careful sump draining. Remember, though, that it is best to drain fuel sumps *before* fuel is added, rather than immediately after, because the mixing action will stir up any water on the tank bottom and leave it in suspension for a considerable time.

Mixing avgas and jet fuel is a more insidious problem that poses at least two serious possibilities.

First, mixing jet fuel into avgas is a recurring problem in piston-powered aircraft that seems to be aggravated by "turbocharged" decals. Some line personnel just don't know the difference between turbocharged and turboprop. At least one instance of putting jet fuel into a turbo Navajo has occurred. The Navajo is an airplane that happens to closely resemble its turboprop brother, the Cheyenne.

Any blend of jet fuel and avgas will have a dangerously low-octane

305

rating. Depending on the ratios involved, damage will range from minor to catastrophic. Never fly with *any* amount of jet fuel in your avgas.

Second, there's a danger from putting avgas into jet fuel in a turbine-powered aircraft. Virtually all turbine engines will run all right on avgas or jet/avgas mixtures, but there is a dangerous side effect. The vapors from this combination can be exceptionally explosive. Kerosine has a high flash point, which results in the vapors in a jet fuel tank being too lean to explode. Avgas has a low flash point so that its vapors are too rich to explode. When you mix the two, there is a crossover point at which the air-fuel mixture is optimum for burning and any suggestion of a spark will trigger an explosion. The flight manual may allow you to burn some amount of avgas in your turbine engine, but be aware that the mixture can be dangerous in the tank.

It would be nice if we could assume that aviation fuel is an innocuous, helpful fluid. Unfortunately, that assumption can be dangerous. And the prospect is that things will get worse before they get better.

Rich, Lean and In-Between

by Dan Manningham

The art and science of leaning piston engines is one of the better kept secrets of aviation despite repeated emphasis in magazine articles and owners' manuals. There seems to be a collective mental block that prevents most pilots from ever developing real knowledge and skill in fuel mixture management. It can be especially frustrating if you fly a wide assortment of piston-engine airplanes, but proper mixture management should be easy for those who confine their activities to one or two of these aircraft. The principles involved are common to all reciprocating engines.

Air is roughly 21 percent oxygen and 78 percent nitrogen, with a smattering of other inert gases. When fuel is burned with air in the cylinders, the oxygen and gasoline react to create the heat of combustion. This heat is absorbed by the inert and created gases which expand and push on the piston. Mixture is critical to the efficiency of this heat expansion process.

When a chemist burns gasoline and air in a laboratory environment, he finds that the ideal mixture is an air-to-fuel ratio of 15:1 by weight. In other words, with a mixture of one pound of fuel to 15 pounds of air, the combustion process will exactly consume all fuel and all oxygen. This so-called stoichiometric mixture releases the greatest possible amount of heat energy and produces the highest combustive temperatures. But, surprisingly, this 15:1 mixture is of little use in engines.

As the mixture is enriched from 15:1 in the cylinders of an engine, the combustion temperature is reduced, but the power increases progressively to a ratio of about 12:1. This interesting contradiction (more power with less heat) takes place for two reasons. The total heat released by combustion decreases only slightly within this mixture range (15:1 to 12:1), but the vapor formed by excess fuel adds to the total mass of the expanding charge in the cylinder.

That extra fuel vapor accelerates the burning process so that the fuel's available energy is released more rapidly. Thus the 12:1 mixture ratio provides optimum power-production conditions of heat, mass and flame propagation and is referred to as the *best power* mixture ratio.

The *best economy* fuel/air ratio, however, is obtained by setting the mixture for the stoichiometric ratio (the highest obtainable EGT) and then *leaning* a prescribed amount. This leaning reduces temperature, power and fuel flow until, at a ratio of approximately 16:1 or 17:1, the piston engine is producing the most horsepower per unit of fuel. Big radial engines were often leaned to this setting for their maximum efficiency.

In either case, best power or best economy, you must start from the stoichiometric mixture point and that takes accurate CHT or EGT information. Naturally, EGT is more sensitive and can allow you to check each cylinder separately—a very desirable procedure since individual EGT temperatures may vary widely due to uneven intake distribution.

Most horizontally opposed engines are leaned to the stoichiometric ratio and then enriched to best power by reference to some prescribed temperature drop. It sounds counter-productive to ignore best economy in smaller engines, but other considerations such as mass charge, valve wear and lead fouling often take precedence over theory.

If you fly a piston-engine airplane and want to operate for best economy commensurate with long engine life, there are several points to consider:

It is not possible to efficiently lean an engine without good EGT information. The stoichiometric mixture is always at max EGT and is the only possible reference point for accurate leaning. If you don't have an EGT now, seriously consider an installation that allows individual monitoring of each cylinder.

The engine manufacturer's recommendations provide an excellent point of departure, so read everything you can find written about your particular engine and airplane. Write to all the manufacturers involved and conscientiously develop a precise leaning procedure. Even if you think you know how, review your ideas for basic soundness. Bear in mind, however, that for some mystical reason the experts often lean deeper than their own recommendations.

Remember that leaning can be just as important for very low power operations, such as taxing and descent, as it is at cruise because the worst lead fouling occurs at those low temperatures.

Really excellent mixture control is a fine art, requiring much more information than you are likely to pick up in the airport coffee shop. On the other hand, good mixture control is a satisfying skill that can save both fuel and engines.

Another Look at Leaning   **40**

Sure you know about leaning piston engines. After all, you've been doing it for years and have yet to burn up an engine. Your regular attention to leaning has saved you a few bucks on fuel bills and stretched out your range on trips on which you needed every foot per drop.

But with avgas shortages upon us—real, political or whatever—all of us must wring even more miles out of our allotted pounds of fuel. Good leaning techniques coupled with careful cruise control and navigation is one of the surest ways to take some of the squeeze out of your personal fuel crunch.

First let's review some of the stuff you had to learn about the theory of leaning when you first studied for your commercial certificate. It may come in handy as you are establishing new operating techniques to cope with the fuel shortages.

Engine designers have determined that the ideal mixture of fuel and air for complete combustion is 14.6 parts of air to one part of fuel, by weight —not volume. Another way of expressing the fuel to air ratio is in terms of the decimal fraction of fuel mixed with air, or 0.067 in this case. Theoretically, all of the air and all of the fuel are consumed at this mixture. As the fuel to air ratio increases or decreases from 0.067, combustion becomes less efficient and temperatures of the burning mixture, and thus the exhaust gases, decrease.

Power, temperature and specific fuel consumption for a typical general aviation piston engine are plotted in Figure 1. Notice that best power for a given cylinder-intake airflow is on the rich side of peak temperature and best specific fuel consumption is on the lean side of peak. So, theoretically, if you wanted maximum speed, you'd lean to peak, then enrichen the mixture to a fuel-air ratio of about 0.080. Conversely, if you wanted to squeeze every mile out of every pound of fuel, you'd lean beyond peak temperature to a fuel-air ratio of about 0.060, the best economy setting.

Well, the theory is fine, but neither Lycoming nor Continental *officially* recommends leaning beyond peak temperature for most operations. Continental has this to say about leaning: "If the engine is equipped with an EGT indicator, lean out until peak exhaust temperature is reached, then enrichen mixture until temperature is reduced at least 50 degrees on naturally

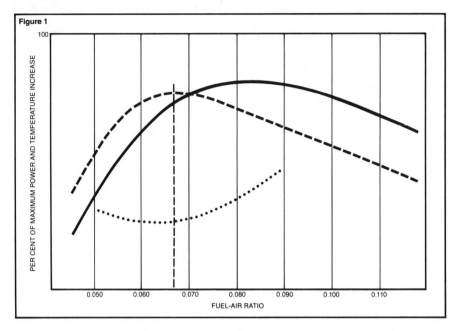

These curves demonstrate that best power falls slightly on the rich side of peak temperature and best specific fuel consumption is realized on the lean side of peak. However, piston-engine manufacturers are hesitant to recommend operation on the lean side of peak EGT.

aspirated engines and 75 degrees on turbosupercharged engines." Continental then adds this warning: "Proper mixture control is of vital importance, because an excessively lean mixture creates a potentially dangerous situation in that it could lead to detonation. This, in turn, imposes unusual piston load and temperature conditions that can result in burned pistons, scored cylinders and broken or stuck piston rings. Use this economy feature with caution. Fuel costs less than a new engine."

It seems pretty clear from that statement that officially—and again we emphasize *officially*—Continental does not want its engines run at peak EGT, let alone on the lean side of peak where the theorists tell us best specific fuel consumption occurs.

Lycoming *will* allow operation of its engines at peak EGT, and in some cases a little leaner than peak, but only (and it's a big ONLY) if the engine is being operated below 75 percent power in the case of direct drive engines or 65 percent power in the case of geared and turbosupercharged engines.

Lycoming engineers admit that a flight crew might get slightly better specifics out of an engine run up to 10 degrees leaner than peak. But the Lycoming folks caution operators against this practice because "on smaller

310

engines it's really a matter of splitting hairs. The instrumentation isn't that good and you run the danger of getting into a detonation problem. Additionally, the pilot will observe a decrease in power with leaning beyond peak and he might be tempted to set up a power setting of say 75 percent then lean it back to 65 percent. This is definitely bad for the engine. We can't stress this point enough."

A glance at the temperature curve in Figure 1 legitimately raises the question, "What difference does it make to the engine whether you are on the rich or lean side of peak as long as the temperatures are below peak?" The problem here is not the absolute temperature but the by-products of combustion. If you run on the rich side, you end up with unburned fuel. If you run on the lean side, you end up with unburned air and thus unburned oxygen. This oxidized atmosphere flowing across the exhaust valves— *under certain conditions*—can lead to valve stem erosion. There is controversy on the possible consequences of this. The fact of the matter is that at temperatures associated with high-cruise powers an oxidized atmosphere can lead to "necking" of the valve stem. In extreme instances that might result in a swallowed valve. But the normal expectation is that the valve would go to overhaul and then have to be replaced, leading to an increased overhaul cost.

All of that theory and official advice is great, but it really doesn't give us much more to work with in getting maximum miles per pound than we had before. The preceding techniques are based on compromises between fuel economy and speed—and in some instances between fuel economy and possible product liability problems. The manufacturers are currently working at great speed to come up with revised procedures that will tip the compromise scale more toward miles per pound. As they do you can expect to receive specific information from the manufacturer of your aircraft.

In the meantime, B/CA is going to crawl out on a limb and suggest an interim technique that will get you more miles per pound at minimum risk to your engine.

Since temperature is the key villain, one can suppose that at some low-power setting there just isn't enough fire in the combustion chambers to do any real harm no matter how you lean. For engines in business category aircraft—*being operated below 10,000 feet*—that power setting is about 55 percent. If you run on the lean side of peak at around 55 percent, you will create an oxidizing atmosphere over the exhaust valves, but the temperature will be too low for it to cause a significant erosion problem. Therefore, you can lean below peak—or, for carbureted engines, until the engine begins to quiver and then enrichen just enough to smooth it out—and you will be as close to the bottom of the specific consumption curve in Figure 1 as it's possible to get with your engine and your instrumentation. We fully expect that will be the basic advice that eventually comes from the

FUEL

manufacturers, but it'll be specific for each airframe/engine combination.

To recap: At altitudes below 10,000 feet, set up 55 percent power, then lean back all you want. As long as the engine is running smoothly, you aren't hurting it. You will note a drop-off in indicated speed below the peak-power mixture. But you will be squeezing every possible ounce of energy from each pound of fuel burned.

One warning is in order, however. Powerplants on the pressurized piston twins are designed for medium power outputs (55 to 65 percent) at altitude. Power settings below 55 percent are inefficient and can be harmful to the engine. The inefficiency comes from the fact that reduced power settings require higher angles of attack for level flight and the higher angles of attack increase the airplane's position on the drag curve, thus increasing specific fuel consumption. The engine damage possibility comes from the fact that cooling air flow is reduced both by the decreased airspeed and the higher angles of attack. So it is possible to overtemperature an engine at altitude even at the lower power settings. For that reason, at this time we cannot safely recommend a low power setting and maximum leaning above 10,000 feet. You altitude flyers will have to wait for official word from the manufacturers before you can achieve best possible miles per pound.

Low Fuel Warning Lights: Concern or Panic? 41

by L. P. Teer

All professional pilots have experienced that momentary anxiety at seeing a cockpit warning light suddenly illuminate while inflight. When you consider that an illuminated warning light is announcing that some irregularity is occurring in one of the aircraft's systems, it really can be a cause for anxiety.

Some warning lights can be more ominous than others, but none can be more terrifying than the light that says, "You are low on fuel." One of the aircraft's engines can fail; fires can occur and be extinguished; systems can malfunction or be deactivated, and the aircraft would be in no immediate danger. But when an aircraft runs out of fuel, there is only one, very obvious and often tragic result.

In order to respond properly, it is most important to understand just exactly what that "Low Fuel" warning light really is telling you. If it is saying, "You are about to run out of fuel," that *would* be cause for panic. But, if it is merely saying, "You have 45 minutes of fuel remaining," then it is *not* cause for panic, but only for concern. Depending on the type aircraft, its altitude and power setting, a distance of as much as 400 miles could still be flown on that remaining fuel, if the situation is properly handled.

Most of today's sophisticated, multi-engine aircraft are equipped with some type of low-fuel quantity warning system. Some are independent of the primary fuel quantity indicating systems. Others are not, and work in concert with fuel quantity gauge indication. Few warning systems are actuated by the fuel quantity indicator; most are tripped by an independent fuel tank sensor. Generally, low-fuel quantity warning systems indicate a condition in which the fuel in a tank has depleted to some designed quantity *in gallons* and not in pounds. This is an important distinction.

A gallon of aviation kerosine weighs 6.7 pounds under standard (ISA) conditions, but on a warm day it may weigh 6.0 pounds. On a cold day fuel may weigh 7.5 pounds. Why the difference? If a gallon container full of kerosine were heated, the kerosine would expand and overflow like full wing tanks overflow on the ramp in the heat of the afternoon. Conversely, kerosine contracts and thus increases its density when cooled. Thus, that gallon container can hold a greater mass of cold kerosine than it can of warm kerosine.

If you take off on a hot day with full tanks and cruise at high altitude long enough for the fuel to cool to ambient temperature, then your full unused fuel tank (if you have one) will have less fuel in gallons than when you started. However, it will still contain the same mass.

Since an internal combustion engine senses fuel mass and not fuel volume, a gallon of cold kerosine provides more energy to an engine than does a gallon of warm kerosine because of the greater mass (or density) of cold kerosine. Filling the tanks at Keflavik, Iceland, for example, will give the aircraft a greater flight endurance than would filling up at warmer Phoenix, Arizona. Thus, a given volume (number of gallons) of cold fuel will get an aircraft farther than the same volume of warm fuel.

The most probable occasion for a low-fuel warning light to illuminate is near the conclusion of a long-range flight when for some atmospheric or operational reason, more fuel was consumed than planned. A jet aircraft would have been at altitude long enough so that its fuel temperature would have dropped to about -56 degrees C. If that aircraft were a G-II and *both* low-fuel level warning lights illuminated, it would mean that 100 gallons remained in each of its two fuel tanks. That 200 gallons at -56 degrees C. would weigh approximately 1,500 pounds. (If the fuel were warm, say $+10$ degrees C., that 200 gallons would weigh 1,200 pounds.) The G-II's total weight with so little fuel would now be less than 40,000 pounds. At 43,000 feet with the engines reset to maximum specific range power, flight time remaining would be 56 minutes for a distance of 345 nm. If the G-II were over New York City, for example, at 43,000 feet (its best range altitude) and its two fuel low level warning lights illuminated, it still could be flown to and landed at cities such as Norfolk and Richmond, Virginia; Pittsburgh; Cleveland; Toronto; Montreal and Quebec City.

This may astonish some veteran G-II pilots who are accustomed to seeing sizeable fuel flows. However, it is important to realize that when a G-II is so light the required power settings and fuel flows are very low at either maximum range or maximum endurance power settings.

Let's look at a JetStar at 37,000 feet (its best range altitude). Four low sump level warning lights illuminate simultaneously near the conclusion of a long flight. The fuel quantity remaining at the ambient temperature (assuming a normal lapse rate) would be approximately 1,300 pounds. Using maximum range power settings, the flight time remaining would be about 42 minutes for a distance of 280 nm.

LOW-FUEL WARNING LIGHTS:

If the "Low Fuel" warning lights on these aircraft illuminated at a low altitude, such as 10,000 feet, their flight endurances would be less than at the higher altitudes. But endurance would still not be so limited as to justify panic. Suppose the G-II fuel low level lights illuminated at 10,000 feet, the aircraft still would have enough fuel for 34 minutes or 150 nm with proper power settings.

The JetStar, in these same circumstances, would have an endurance of 31 minutes for a distance of 84 nm, with proper power settings.

All aircraft flight manuals contain maximum flight endurance information, but it takes time to get the manual, find the chart, analyze it and determine the proper parameters. However, if this information were tabulated and kept with the aircraft's emergency procedures, then it would be readily available if "Low Fuel" lights ever came on.

This figure represents an example of the maximum endurance breakdown of a typical corporate aircraft. Several tables will have to be prepared to cover the most likely low gross weights that you will be at when the low fuel warning comes on. These tables will give you the power settings, in terms of fuel flow and KTAS to produce the most range and the maximum endurance. Plans for landing can be made accordingly, with a minimum of fuel, time and tension.

In summary, if your "Low Fuel" warning lights illuminate this is the course of action to follow:

(1) Don't panic. You probably have more fuel (and thus more time) than you think.

(2) Use your tabulated maximum range and endurance chart. Find the best power setting and adjust the engines accordingly.

(3) Note your remaining endurance flight time and distance. Plan for an airport that is comfortably within that distance.

(4) Maintain your altitude as long as possible. When the airport is in view or you're in the airport traffic area, make a rapid (but safe) descent into the traffic pattern.

(5) Descend as close to a zero thrust, zero drag setting on the engines as possible.

The purpose of this article is in no way to be interpreted as encouraging attempts to stretch your fuel supply. The policies, procedures and regulations of the aircraft manufacturer, the government and the pilot's good judgment should be complied with.

The purpose of this article instead is to encourage pilots to become more familiar with the capabilities of the aircraft they operate so that when irregularities, such as "Low Fuel" warnings occur, they can handle them with maximum efficiency and minimum concern.

PROBLEMS

Among hangar conversationalists, the prime topic is probably trouble. Problems ranging from the small and silly to full-blown emergencies are an inevitable adjunct to an aviation career, and it has often been said that when the big problems arise, a pilot starts earning his pay. Fortunately, real troubles aloft are not common, which in itself can be the source of a problem, for the very infrequency of serious problems in modern aviation creates the threat of complacency, which must be positively resisted. The opposite of complacency is preparation, of knowing positively what to do when an emergency occurs. Such knowledge spurs alertness; it can mean survival.

If one were to make a master list of potential aviation problems, marked similarities would appear among the items. Specific procedures may vary, but human reactions and the airborne environment create a broad area of commonality. This chapter will highlight a few notable problems. You will not learn the solution to every inflight problem here, but the following ten selections will, we hope, stimulate the kind of thinking that will enable you to remember or work out what to do when it comes time to dry those sweaty palms.

Emergencies

42

by Robert N. Buck

What is an emergency? Probably anything that happens which makes you scared, mouth dry, adrenalin pumping and the big apple in your throat.

For some this happens easily; for others things have to be pretty desperate to get them in that shape.

Which tells us that some emergencies aren't emergencies at all—they are only to certain people.

There are slow emergencies and fast ones. A slow one is when you have an hour of fuel left and the nearest place that isn't zero-zero in fog is an hour and a half away. A fast emergency is when you have just taken off, are over a stand of trees at 100 feet and the engine quits.

The thing about most emergencies is that fast action isn't necessary so long as the airspeed is proper. The complexities of most emergencies require a certain amount of analysis before you try to correct them. Fast action without this analysis doesn't cure problems—it only creates more.

Fortunately, emergencies don't occur very often. I know lots of people who have never had an engine failure, and most of us have never had a fire. I've had two, one in a Connie right after takeoff from Frankfurt, Germany. The bells rang and red lights came on, so I had the copilot tell the tower we were landing immediately. Tower started its litany about downwind, number two to land, etc.

"Tell that silly sumabitch," I said, "that we're on fire and we'll be back on the ground in 60 seconds and to get everybody else the hell out of the way!" He told 'em, we landed and that was that.

It was a turbine failure in the exhaust-recovery system of that horrible Turbo Compound piston engine we had in late Connies; DC-7s had them too. We got it out without any damage except to a few engine knickknacks and the parts that had a hole knocked in them.

Number two was a Piper Comanche, and, while not big, it was scary. I was just west of Pittsburgh with son Rob at 8000 feet. There were snow showers below, with ceilings and visibilities from poor to lousy. Gradually, in that unbelieving way, smoke started coming back into the cabin. For a couple of minutes we swallowed hard and dry. It smelled electrical, so I knocked off the master switch, and shortly the smoke began to subside and in a little while was gone. To try to find what was wrong, we shut off all radios and turned the master back on: no smoke. So then we started a process of elimination and turned the radios on one at a time. The second one to go on, a navcom, started the smoke again, so off it went. The smoke went with it. So that stayed off and all others came back on—no problem. The flight proceeded minus one navcom we could easily get along without. On the ground we found that in manufacturing the radio a loose screw had been left inside and it finally bounced itself into position to cause a short, which started the smoke and smell.

But that's a pretty good track record for almost 30,000 hours in airplanes of all sorts. Two fires, and one, only the smoke before a real fire.

The fact we don't have many emergencies is bad in a way, on a couple of counts. One is that we aren't current in handling them, and the other is that we can develop a complacent attitude toward emergencies.

On the airline I've had hundreds of fires, but all in a simulator. It's part of an airline's recurrent training system, and it's excellent.

We might talk about airline training a little and what their pilots think about it. Primarily they train and learn about the things that can go wrong and then what to do about them. You'd think they crash one a minute, but, of course, airlines don't. Their safety record is phenomenal, and training and checking is one big reason why.

Anyone should know how to fly the airplane. This means stick and rudder, the ability to take off and land, do maneuvers, fly an ILS and all the rest. It's like the swing of a good golfer. Being competent, proficient and good at flying is the goal and basis for everything, and especially for taking care of an emergency.

These basics are taken for granted, because if one doesn't do them well eyebrows are raised and job security becomes a problem. What this says is that all of us should never stop trying to improve ourselves in all the basics of knowing how to fly.

Instead of running off somewhere while the airplane's having its 100-hour check or annual, stick around and ask questions, look inside when the tin is all removed . . . being careful not to interfere with the mechanic working on your hourly time! But a little extra cost here is well-spent money.

If you get a chance to visit the airplane's factory, try to catch a coffee break or lunch with the test pilots or sales pilots and pump them about your airplane. These people know a lot more than you'll find in the books. Have a list of questions that have occurred to you from time to time in your mind

319

or written down, so you can ask the men who know. You'll get the questions answered, as well as new ones that will develop during the bull session. It's almost impossible to know all about any airplane, but it's valuable and interesting to make an attempt, a never-ending quest.

The airlines, as I said, do their emergency practice in a slow, relaxed way, for safety reasons as well as for better learning. Too many people have been killed practicing emergencies. It's a known fact that more people have been hurt in simulated forced landings than ever have been in actual ones. People have been killed flying twins with an engine out on training or rating rides, from marginal flying. If an emergency practice session has any danger in it, don't do it!

Now to the point of being current in unusual happenings. As I've said, unusual things don't occur enough to keep us current, so the best insurance is to keep current ourselves. It means to set aside a certain period of time once a year—twice is better, and maybe three times or four—to refresh knowledge of the unusual. The airlines do it twice a year in a simulator or airplane and then have quarterly home-study questions to boot. While general aviation isn't an airline, the airlines have done things that are useful to it, and emergency, unusual and recurrent training is one of the big ones to copy.

Take out that dusty airplane manual and read it over, enough so it doesn't get dusty again, no matter how well you think you know it.

The other big point in all this is that because unusual happenings don't occur very often, we tend, consciously or subconsciously, to think that they never will.

The modern airplane and its engine is a wonderful thing. Engines, like the one in my Skylane, just don't seem to quit, and if they do, more often than not it's because they weren't treated right or, because of poor planning, they were starved for fuel.

Not being treated correctly means things such as not properly fueling and draining tanks to be certain there isn't water or dirt. As I stand around airports just seeing what goes on, I'm appalled to notice how many people drive up, tell 'em to fill the mains, come back after they've had coffee and signed the credit slip, and drive off without checking caps or sumps. I've seen line boys tolerantly half smile at the fussbudgets as I get a ladder and check the caps after they've gassed it. Well, who gives a damn what they think? I don't.

It doesn't hurt to look around inside the cowling for oil leaks each time you gas it, too, even though some modern engines are cowled so tightly that all you can see through the cowl door is the oil cap and the engine name plate. But checking that cap is worth the bother too.

So if we've checked the gas and oil systems, we've made a big start toward preventing engine failures.

Counted among fuel-system problem areas is fuel management in flight, and by that I mean what the gas gauges say versus knowing how much fuel is still in the tanks.

Most little airplane gas gauges are pathetic. They are accurate, generally, when it reads full, although we should look in the tank to be sure. But on anything except full, what they say is just rough information.

A guy ran out of gasoline one mile from the end of the runway at our local airport at Montpelier while landing on a clear, sunny day. Luckily it resulted in only a bashed-in nosewheel and some expensive wrinkles in the fuselage. But how could a guy have guts enough, or be dumb enough, to cut it that fine? It's amazing!

On big airplanes, like 747s, 707s, Citations and others, the fuel gauges are very accurate. They are capacitance types that measure the electrical resistance of the liquid in the tank and from that tell what's in it. It's really a comfort to look at the gauge and know what's in the tank, and I wish they could make them inexpensive enough for all airplanes.

But even with these gauges, the airline crews keep a fuel use record: how much they've burned by the rate per hour versus the time, and that deducted from the amount at the flight start, on a running, current basis.

This is easy to do, and it doesn't take a mathematical genius. Mostly a note on a piece of paper is enough. But time and rate are the important things to know what's left in the tank, and not the indication of a bouncy fuel gauge. Even the good fuel gauges fail now and then, so then where are you without a record?

The only time I ever overflew Paris in a 747 was on a foggy morning, and it was one of the toughest decisions I've ever made, even though a very undramatic one.

I arrived over Paris with 300 passengers at about 0800 hours. It was socked in solid. My alternate, Marseilles. I had pretty good fuel aboard, so I held for it to improve. I went round and round up in the sunshine, on top of a solid white fog bank over Toussuse-le-Noble, near the Palace of Versailles.

After an hour Orly hadn't budged. The visibility wasn't even 100 meters, and our minimum for even a look-see is 200 meters, with 400 meters required for landing.

The situation dragged on. I knew it would open up, everything said it would: low fog cover, clear above, the day young. But as I approached my minimum fuel, I was faced finally with the fact that if I didn't get going I'd be burning into my alternate fuel and not have Marseilles capability. I knew Orly would open up before my fuel ran out—but what if it didn't? There was a 1000-to-1 shot against it, but can you imagine anything worse than a dry-tank 747?

So I peeled off and went to Marseilles. Orly opened up before I landed there. I got fuel—a two-hour chore—and went back to Orly.

I still grind my teeth over that one. Should I have been gutsier and stayed around and landed, or did I do the right thing? Of course it was right —it was safe, and that's what counts—but I screwed up a lot of people and made them late with missed connections and the rest. But as time mellows the decision, I guess it doesn't matter any more to the few delayed.

So going to Marseilles and all the other things we talk about here are part of planning to avoid emergencies. If we plan enough to avoid emergencies, we'll probably have a few, if any—ever.

Occasionally engines do quit from normal quittin' reasons—failed parts, etc. I saw a friend of mine, Warren Doble, have a cam ring break when he was on top of a loop, not far off the ground, right over the airport. Breaking a cam ring stops all the valve action, and that stops the engine—immediately! He did the sweetest rollout and landing, without a ruffle, that you ever saw. Lucky and good.

Engines that can quit brings us to the question of what kind of country one is willing to fly over on one engine, what kind of weather and in the dark or not.

Tough questions. Being old-fashioned enough to have flown airplanes when engines quit a lot more often than they do now, I am probably more conservative than the modern pilot raised on flat opposed engines. The new ones rarely quit, but all that does is raise the odds and make it a better gamble.

So what kind of a gambler are you? I'm a poor one, because I lost too often when engines quit regularly. Now, the modern fellow who has never lost, and has these new good odds to play with, probably will gamble much more than I do, and I can see why. But sometimes even the long odds go against us, and we lose the whole bundle.

Considering that one can lose on a long shot, I'm shaken the way I see people go out across impossible-landing country on one engine: trees, rocky mountains and the kind of terrain where landing is a certain accident.

I fly in mountain areas a lot on one engine, but I don't mind a detour that will keep me over a few places to get down, even if it's quite a few extra miles. And that goes for trees, water and the rest.

Actually, I'm more comfortable over water, because it isn't that bad to land on, unless the seas are running high. Over water I carry life-saving equipment, flotation vest and a raft if it's far. And I make very sure that I'm on a flight plan so somebody knows I'm out there.

Being on a flight plan is good most anywhere we fly, and it's especially true over poor terrain. It doesn't have to be an instrument flight plan—lots of times that just means extra miles. VFR is good enough if conditions warrant it. But having someone know you're out there is very important.

This gets even more important in winter, when it's cold. Where I live in

New England, I file everywhere in the winter, no matter how good the weather. If you land out somewhere and it's below zero, you don't want to have to wait very long for somebody to come by and pick you up!

Along with all this I carry emergency equipment in my airplane. In the Skylane it's a small red nylon knapsack. In it is water—about five quarts except when I'm going to fly desert country, when it's a lot more; also signal flares, signal mirror, a first-aid kit (not a store one, but one put together myself after talking it over with a doctor friend); food concentrates that have indefinite shelf life, like pemmican, bacon bars, tropical chocolate—enough to last me a few days. I have a space blanket, matches, snare, fishing line and some hooks, one of those wirelike saws that wrap around their own handles, and a few other knickknacks. It sounds like a lot, but it's only a package about 15 inches by 14 inches by nine inches and weighs 13 pounds. It sits back in the corner of the baggage compartment and is never removed except for periodic checking and bringing up to date. The water is in tough plastic containers that never leak. In the winter the water in them freezes when it's in a subfreezing hangar or tie-down, but it unfreezes and doesn't bother the containers.

Close to ATC is the question of communications during emergencies. Despite the flying movies Hollywood puts out, it isn't always necessary to grab the mike and yell for help. As a matter of fact, most times the ground adds to the workload.

I've had more than one case, and heard lots more. A guy has an engine failure and tells the ground. Immediately a flood of questions comes back: "What is your position? Which engine is it? What kind of failure?" And on and on, depending on the guy on the ground. These questions seem pretty inane to a pilot who's busy cleaning up his emergency condition and trying to decide if she'll fly OK and if so what's the best next move. Believe me, it isn't the guy on the ground who has the answers. So if you're kind enough to announce your problem, or think you must because you might interfere with ATC, etc., and then a flood of questions come pouring at you, don't be bashful about saying loud and clear, "I'm busy, don't bother me!" If you're too busy to say even that, just ignore the ground.

The modern system seems to breed the idea that we must keep in contact with the ground at all costs. Well, during the first seven years of my flying life I never flew an airplane that had any kind of radio in it. I went coast to coast many times, flew to Cuba, Canada, and Mexico, and, by golly, made it without one squeak of radio!

Of course, today we have a more complex system and there are times we have to use radio, but we use it a lot more than is necessary.

Funny as it seems, our brother pilots are often serious offenders. More than once I've heard an airline pilot say he'd lost an engine out over the ocean and tell Oceanic Control what he wanted to do. Immediately half a dozen wits in other airplanes start calling him, asking if they can help and what is his problem. After the first guy asked him if he needed help, and he said, "No," there wasn't any reason for anyone else to ask again.

We shouldn't have any compunction about asking if we need something, and that goes from big problems like being lost down to little ones like the fact that you just don't understand the clearance that was shot at you fast by an ATC controller imitating a tobacco auctioneer.

But also we shouldn't have any compunctions about not using the radio until it's convenient. As I said in the beginning of all this, FLY THE AIRPLANE. You cannot fly a mike, and it will not keep you from spinning in, put a fire out, get you over the trees with an engine out or anything else.

So when we speak of emergencies we think of communications as something for our help and convenience and, if necessary, to warn others if we're a menace to navigation. But the last thing to worry about is grabbing the mike; grab the airplane first!

To keeping emergencies under control, we must also consider the possibility of electrical and radio failure. We may not have to communicate, but we sure have to navigate if we're on instruments. On the many airplanes with only one alternator, this becomes a real possibility. Airplanes having dual alternators aren't likely to have total failure, but it's possible. Electrical systems are complex and strange things, and events occur to knock them out that engineers never thought of. The 707 electrical system was designed so that it would be impossible to lose the entire system. But someone finally did it. It was mismanagement plus a failure that hadn't been covered in training books. It's in the books now, and again it's impossible to lose it all in a 707 . . . until next time.

Which, simple as it sounds, means: Always have a working flashlight with fresh batteries in the plane. It can be your most important gadget.

With all the wonderful solid-state, battery radios around, it is well worthwhile to have one on which you can at least receive VHF when the ground sends you information after you've done that little "I've got a problem" triangle the *Airmans Information Manual* has listed. How extensive you want this radio to be is your choice, but just to be able to receive VHF is a big step toward making a big emergency a little one.

I've always been a firm believer that one should have a gyro instrument that's independent of the normal power source for the instruments. If, for example, all the instruments are electrical, I like to have at least a Turn and Bank that's vacuum-driven. A battery-powered gyro could do it too. But, whatever, there should be some way to prevent one failure from taking away all ability to fly the airplane on instruments. Can you ima-

324

gine being on instruments with no instruments! That's why I like an alternate source.

That's the way we think about emergencies: proper planning to prevent them, knowledge to help keep an unusual happening from becoming a big emergency and keeping our chance-taking level as low as possible. Like the fellow says, "It takes thousands of nuts to hold an airplane together, but only one to take it apart!"

Aircraft Cabin Fires 43

by Gordon Gilbert

It's not the most common enemy aboard corporate aircraft, but that is why the story of cabin fires needs to be told. Because they are infrequent, flight crews may be prepared for them least.

Professional pilots periodically simulate and train for as many emergency situations as can be expected to occur. Traditionally, they practice and prepare for those that are most critical, such as engine fire, electrical fire, engine out and sudden decompression. It is likely that most operators rarely, if at all, think about going through cabin fire drills.

At first, this thinking seems completely justified. Several of the largest general aviation insurance companies say they have received very few cabin fire damage claims. In addition, the NTSB records for the last few years reveal only a handful of injurious or fatal accidents in general aviation aircraft caused directly by fire in the cabin. It's a different story, though, for the airlines, as we'll see in a moment.

The FAA doesn't seem to be concerned about the problem, although the agency does require that portions of aircraft interiors be flame resistant. Part 23 requirements do not call for having any kind of hand fire extinguisher in the passenger compartment. Aircraft manufacturers don't provide cabin fire or smoke emergency procedures in most owners manuals pertaining to Part 23 aircraft.

There is a history of cabin fires aboard airliners that have caused considerable damage and more than a few injuries. Two cabin fires in particular have occurred recently that point out the need for corporate operators—large and small—to be prepared and protected for such an emergency.

The first and most severe of these events was in the inflight cabin fire aboard a Varig Boeing 707 in July 1973 that resulted in 124 deaths and total destruction of the aircraft. That fire, investigators believe, started in the aircraft's lavatory from a lighted cigarette being thrown in a paper waste container and was fed by combustibles in the aircraft's interior. As a result of this disaster, and reports to the FAA of several more lavatory fires, the FAA issued an AD prohibiting smoking in lavatories equipped with paper or linen waste receptacles.

The second event has to do with an inflight cabin fire caused by the chemical reaction of potentially dangerous articles or cargo. The case in point was the fire aboard a 707 on November 3, 1973 caused by improperly loaded nitric acid. The fire was able to spread because the crew couldn't reach the affected area to extinguish it. This accident, too, has resulted in changes in FARs regarding carrying hazardous materials. The event points up the need for both positive identification of baggage and articles, and supervision of cargo loading.

The National Fire Protection Association has documented 30 cabin fire incidents aboard transport category aircraft from 1948 through 1970 caused by such things as careless disposal of lighted cigarettes, improper oxygen servicing, ignition of cleaning fluids and electrical failures.

The first step in protecting your crew, the boss and his airplane against cabin fire injuries and damage is to start thinking deeply about the what, where and how of your aircraft's systems. The best place to do this, of course, is in the aircraft while it's safely on the ground. Play the "What-If?" game. Ask yourself: What if a fire started in the galley, lavatory, passenger cabin or cockpit? Which way is the smoke likely to drift? Which systems are likely to become inoperative? Which systems will probably continue to function? Which systems should I take off line? Are there any systems in potential fire areas—perhaps under the floor or in side walls—that might add to the fire if they were to burn through, such as fuel lines, hydraulic valves or oxygen? If so, can they be deactivated in a manner that will lessen the danger? While considering what systems, motors, actuators, plumbing and wiring lie behind bulkheads, in the overhead and below the floor, ask yourself what if I lose such and such a system, what redundancy do I have? Or if I take system "A" off line, what precisely do I lose? If I depressurize, will the smoke drift into the cockpit? Note where the outflow valves are located.

Obviously, you can think of even more pertinent questions to ask yourself about your particular airplane. The objective is to get to know your aircraft's systems intimately with fire on your mind. Once this step is achieved, you will have the knowledge to draw up a complete and accurate checklist that will enable you to proceed from item to item without needing to waste valuable minutes playing the "What-If?" game during a real emergency.

Corporate operators of large aircraft have a slight head start over small business aircraft in preventive measures because of more stringent FAR requirements and the fact that large aircraft operators can bear the cost of a custom interior made of the highest-quality materials, many of which are *naturally* resistant to fire.

Small aircraft operators have two strikes against them in the interior aspect. First, a modest budget forces them to be less selective of materials,

Business and Commercial Aviation

INFLIGHT CABIN FIRE OR SMOKE

Emergency Procedures Checklist

At the first sign of fire, smoke or odor:
☐ ATC—Call, "possible cabin fire, descending."
☐ Transponder—Code 7700.
☐ Start emergency or normal descent to at least 12,500 feet.
☐ No smoking—all cigarettes extinguished.
☐ Determine source and location of fire or smoke.
☐ If electrical fire is suspected, inform ATC, and turn electrical system OFF.

CAUTION—Depressurization may occur if electrical system is turned off.

☐ Start extinguishing fire—
  Use CO_2 on electrical fire.
  H_2O on combustibles fire.
  Use Halon 1211 on any fire.
☐ Dump cabin pressure (if necessary).
☐ Oxygen—passengers and crew.

Ideally, B/CA's checklist should be used as a guide in preparing your own formal cabin-fire emergency procedures. These procedures should take the form of a checklist similar to this and inserted into the appropriate place in your flight manual, owners manual or instrument manual.

CAUTION—Do not use supplemental O₂ in presence of open flames.

☐ Smoke goggles—crew and passengers (if necessary).
☐ Call airport of intended landing if the electrical system is on.
☐ Cabin and defog fans—OFF.
☐ Clear smoke—use ram air, cabin air and window vents.

CAUTION—Allowing additional air into the cabin may intensify fire or draw additional smoke into the cockpit.

☐ Executive emergency or precautionary landing—see Emergency Landing Checklist.

---

usually relying on the aircraft manufacturer's standard installation. The most common interiors for the smaller business aircraft consist of synthetics which must be *treated* for fire protection with special chemicals.

At best, the treatment is only temporary—which brings us to the second strike against the smaller operator: Flame-resistant treatments wear off from constant use and frequent cleaning of seats and carpets. Therefore, the first preventive measure against cabin fires for the smaller aircraft operator is to make an appointment to have chairs and carpets retreated for fire protection at least twice a year by an FBO (experienced in the procedure) or the aircraft manufacturer.

Passenger briefings—When operating under FAR Parts 91 (Subpart D), 135 or 135.2, operators are required to give their passengers a preflight briefing.

A tactfully worded briefing should be included in *all* passenger-carrying corporate operations too. But when the boss and other executives are onboard, you'll have to slip into it and choose your words rather carefully in order not to offend anyone. If box lunches are being served, but they are

329

not customarily used, you should get a diplomatic message across not to empty ashtrays or extinguish cigarettes into flammable containers or use styrofoam cups or empty milk cartons as ashtrays. Since aircraft ashtrays are deplorably small anyway, you should provide a container aboard for dumping ashes.

If necessary, you may have to caution an individual passenger against using visible-fluid type cigarette lighters in flight (see FAA Advisory Circular 91–7 for complete details). In any case, if the flight is late at night when the boss and his company are tired or if there are executives on board you know from past experience are careless, you'll have to give a friendly reminder of potential fire hazards.

In single-pilot, cabin-class twins and turboprops, passengers should be informed as to the precise location of the cabin hand fire extinguisher and a quick demonstration on how to get it to operate.

Good housekeeping on the ground—A cabin fire that starts on the ground after landing is potentially more serious than one inflight. In the air, a cabin fire can, in most cases, be spotted and suppressed quickly. A fire that unknowingly starts while the unattended aircraft is on the ground cannot only spread before it is discovered, but could initiate a catastrophe if aircraft refueling is going on at the same time.

B/CA experimented with a single lighted cigarette being left in a box lunch and the results are scary. The fire in the box—full of napkins, cellophane wrappings and other combustibles—smoldered with little visual evidence for *over five minutes* before a flame erupted and the lunch box was completely consumed in seconds. Think about that for a moment. It's very possible that after taxiing in for a fuel stop, everyone will have left the airplane in less than five minutes.

It should be standard procedure to tidy up the aircraft interior thoroughly immediately after shutting down for a brief stop or RON. Check behind and under seats for discarded cigarettes. Remove all discarded lunch boxes and empty ashtrays. Needless to say, give the potty and waste receptacles a check.

As part of your prevention campaign and preplanning for a possible fire onboard, the following five points should be carefully considered.

During flight—Two-pilot operators have an advantage in that a crewmember can go back or look back into the cabin periodically and check for potential fire hazards. He should be on the lookout for odd-ball things too. Take a lesson, for instance, from the following true incident: A company executive on a particularly long flight fell asleep slumped in his chair—safety belt unfastened—but not before he had covered the reading light above his head with a piece of red cellophane to dim the glow. You guessed it. The paper ignited and fell in his lap. Several seconds later he awoke with a start when the flame seared his trousers. As he jumped up brushing the burning cellophane off his lap, he hit his head on the overhead. The pilot not only had to administer first aid for a bruised noggin and a burned thigh, but had to soak the carpet around the board chairman's seat with water to extinguish smoldering embers.

Sizing up your passengers—Most corporate operators transport the same company personnel time after time and thus should have a good idea of who can be counted on to lend assistance if an emergency arises in the cabin. Estimating each passenger's capacity to assist during an emergency is especially important in a cabin-class aircraft flown by one pilot. With no copilot to help out, the guy who sits in the right seat should be the one you figure can be of most help if a cabin fire or any other emergency develops.

Know what's in the baggage compartment—Ascertain that there are no potential fire hazards in the baggage compartment. There's not much you can do about flammable items such as lighter fluid, aerosol cans and toiletries in passenger luggage, of course, but you can watch for fire hazards in the ship's equipment carried in the baggage area and you can load luggage that might have such items in it so that it is not subjected to heat from ducts or lights. Small packages that are sometimes brought aboard the last minute for quick transportation from one company facility to another should be inspected for potential fire hazards or violation of FAR Part 103, Transportation of Dangerous Articles and Magnetized Materials.

Supervising cargo—More and more companies are attempting to take advantage of the complete capability of their aircraft and reduce operational expenses by utilizing some of their fleet for hauling cargo when it's not hauling the boss. Operators moving into this area face an entirely new set of transportation problems, not the least of which is the danger of cabin fire from hazardous materials or improperly loaded cargo. Flight departments or air taxis that are going to get heavily involved in hauling freight should become familiar with FAR Part 103 (recently revised), and get acquainted with an expert in the field. There is a hazards material specialist in each FAA regional office.

Supplemental oxygen considerations—The basic rule in preventing cabin fires in flight from O_2 is to be sure that all flames—from cabin fire or cigarettes—are extinguished before oxygen flow begins.

Unfortunately, the solid-state portable units currently on the market can continue to pose a fire danger even after cigarettes are out. The chemical reaction in solid-state O_2 systems which produces oxygen also produces heat. Consequently, passengers must be cautioned to keep hands, arms and clothing away from the actuators and the mask assembly hose line outlet while oxygen is on and for a period of time after it's off.

NTSB cites a case where three solid-state oxygen canisters came out of their seatback compartments because of the pulling force exerted on the oxygen supply hose. These canisters scorched cushions, burned fingers and reportedly caused a small fire. The preflight inspection, therefore, should include a check to be sure that supplemental oxygen units are securely in place.

Servicing of aircraft oxygen systems has also caused some serious cabin fires.

In the event that all the measures described above, and any others you think of, fail to prevent a cabin blaze, you must have a set of emergency procedures to most effectively cope with the problem. Again, large corporate aircraft operators have an advantage over small aircraft operators. Nearly all FAA Flight Manuals for the big planes include *some* guidance concerning cabin fires, while practically all smaller aircraft—some turboprops included—do not even mention the possibility of a cabin fire. This situation for smaller aircraft may change dramatically if aircraft manufacturers follow GAMA's "specifications for pilot operating manuals." The GAMA guide is an attempt to set an industry standard for general aviation flight manuals. GAMA says procedures shall be provided in aircraft manuals for "coping with cases of smoke and/or fire in the cabin. . . ."

Some procedures for dealing with inflight cabin fires are generally the same regardless of what type business airplane you are flying. But since there are also procedures that are different, depending on the type of aircraft and its systems, we've devised a checklist containing the basic steps that should be followed for nearly all types of business planes. A narrative description follows.

Significant differences in procedures are noted in each item.

(1) At the first sign of flames, smoke or odor, the captain should get on the radio to ATC and tell them he thinks he's got a cabin fire and is descending for landing. Tell ATC you'll get back to them after you assess the situation. While the pilot is on the radio the copilot proceeds through this checklist. (In a single-pilot operation, tell ATC you'll maintain altitude and course on autopilot while you go back to assess the situation.) *Most important of all is to start descending for a landing as soon as practical.*

(2) Attempt to determine and isolate the source of the fire, smoke or odor. If you suspect an electrical fire, get back with ATC and tell them you're switching off the electrical system and will possibly return on line at the bottom of the descent or sooner. Once ATC knows you are going off line, they will clear the airspace below and around you, advise nearby aircraft of your situation and possibly turn up the gain on their primary radar to keep track of you in the absence of your transponder. Caution: In some pressurized aircraft, the cabin will depressurize when the electrical power is turned off.

(We feel compelled to interrupt this checklist for a moment with a suggestion to FAA ATC planners. It seems to us that all this communications between yourself and ATC to explain the nature of the emer-

gency and your intentions is a waste of valuable time—time that you should spend coping with the problem. Therefore, why doesn't the FAA simply designate a one-letter code for operators to use in conjunction with the word "Mayday" to eliminate a lengthy explanation. For instance, a crew with a fire onboard should say simply, "Mayday, Cleveland Center, November 1234 has a Mayday slash Foxtrot." Then instantly kill the electrical system if that is indicated. This would immediately tell controllers (and anyone else listening) that a fire is suspected; the aircraft will start descending; electrical power will probably be switched off, and a precautionary or emergency landing at the nearest suitable airport is planned. In just a split second of time, ATC knows it has to clear the surrounding airspace, turn up its primary radar and possibly locate a suitable airport for the aircraft in distress, notifying the facility manager of the situation so he can be prepared for the aircraft's arrival with suitable equipment.)

(3) Even if the source of the fire is not electrical, caution must be exercised in putting the electrical system fully back on line. Some corporate aircraft, for example, contain seats that are wired for stereo or TV reception. If the fire is in a seat, you want to be certain that the stereo portion of the electrical system remains off line or its CBs pulled before you start squirting water on the flames.

(4) In a two-pilot operation, the copilot should move to the cabin immediately and start assessing the seriousness of the fire, removing smoke and extinguishing flames with the *appropriate* fire extinguisher (see discussion below). *Cabin fires originating inflight must be controlled quickly as possible to prevent major structural damage.*

(5) If a cockpit-to-cabin door is available, it may be used to isolate the smoke source.

(6) "No Smoking" light on. Copilot or trusted right-seat passenger should be in the cabin to insure that cigarettes are extinguished and galley switches are off.

(7) Oxygen—as required for passengers and crew. Most manuals recommend going on 100 percent oxygen for the crew. The copilot or a passenger should assure that occupants are receiving O_2. In the presence of active flames, this procedure is not advisable, of course.

(8) Crew dons smoke goggles if necessary. Smoke goggles are required crew equipment in Part 25 aircraft. We recommend that they also be available to the passengers. Before you have to use this checklist in actual emergency, it would be a good idea to insure that the crew's goggles fit properly, can be worn over eyeglasses and do not restrict the pilot's vision appreciably.

(9) Dump cabin pressure (some aircraft). On others, it is recommended that cabin pressure not be dumped until reaching 15,000 feet or lower.

(10) Call airport of intended landing to appraise them of your situation and ask the tower for ground assistance.

(11) Cabin and defog fans off. With both cabin and cockpit fans off smoke will not circulate through the aircraft.

(12) When depressurized, smoke clearance may be improved by selecting ram or cabin air and opening vents. On some aircraft, ram air should only be chosen if smoke is coming through the air conditioner. Caution: Opening vents in the cockpit could intensify the fire and accumulate smoke in the cockpit rather than drawing it through the cockpit and out the vent.

(13) Execute emergency or precautionary landing as soon as possible at an airport or, if the situation dictates, on the first suitable surface. In preparing for an emergency landing refer to your standard emergency landing checklist.

In any inflight aircraft emergency, there is likely to be a certain amount of initial panic or disorganization by passengers.

As far as your emergency procedures are concerned, you should do what you can to calm passengers—with the help of that guy or gal that you sized-up as being one who could be counted on in an emergency—but aircraft control and attempts to extinguish the fire must come first.

Large corporate aircraft certificated under FAR Part 25 are required to be equipped with an FAA-approved portable hand fire extinguisher. Business aircraft certificated under FAR Part 23 are not required to have an extinguisher onboard, although aircraft manufacturers offer them as options.

An approved aircraft hand extinguisher is any unit which is listed by the Underwriters' Laboratories, Factory Mutual Research Corp., UL of Canada or other nationally recognized fire testing laboratory.

B/CA looked at all the different types of hand extinguishers approved for aircraft cabins and, considering the tradeoffs among their fire-fighting effectiveness, handling ease, toxicity and residue factor, we recommend that two kinds should be carried onboard *all* business and corporate aircraft. Either a carbon dioxide or Halon 1211 extinguisher, plus a water-filled unit.

Before we look at these, let's quickly review the three classes of fires that are likely to occur in aircraft cabins:

(1) Class A—Fires occurring in ordinary combustibles, such as upholstery, plastic, rubber, carpeting, paper and wood.

(2) Class B—Fires occurring in liquids, such as grease, fuel, oil, lighter fluid and various toiletries.

(3) Class C—Fires occurring in electrical systems, such as wiring, motors, actuators, pumps, switches, avionics and entertainment systems.

Now, let's describe the recommended extinguishers:

Carbon dioxide—A CO_2 extinguisher should be mounted in the cockpit.

It is effective on Class B and C fires and CO_2 is "clean." It leaves no messy or harmful residue in the form of powder or dust. CO_2 extinguishers are normally installed by the manufacturer in the Learjet, G-II and JetStar.

Here is the tradeoff: Although it is clean and effective, it has a definite toxicity. In addition, the unwieldly size of even the smallest units available make it awkward to handle and difficult to mount in the cockpit. Incidentally, if you need to use one of the extinguishers in your aircraft to put out an engine induction system fire, grab the CO_2 unit, not the H_2O unit.

Halon 1211—A substitute for CO_2 is Halon. It is an extinguishing agent new to this country, but it has been used extensively for some time by European airlines. Fire prevention experts say that Halon is more effective and easier to use than carbon dioxide and works well on all three classes of fire. Like CO_2 it leaves no residue and has no corrosive effects. There are two kinds of Halon—1211 and 1301. The 1211 agent throws out a spray like CO_2 while 1301 has a vapor spray that is not as easy to direct as 1211. We believe 1211 would be more effective than 1301 in the cockpit. Only a couple of manufacturers offer Halon—notably, Beech Aircraft and Bell Helicopter, each of which equip all their machines with Halon 1301 extinguishers. No manufacturer we've talked to offers 1211.

Water—A water solution extinguisher should be contained in the aircraft cabin because it is the most effective agent for Class A fires. CO_2 and Halon 1211 can be used to smother the flames created by a Class A fire, but if the fire is deep-seated (as in an upholstered chair, for example), the entire area will have to be soaked by the water solution. The tradeoff? Water must be protected by noncorrosive antifreeze where necessary to assure efficient operation.

When we released the trigger after testing one particular extinguisher, leakage occurred through the nozzle. The agent escaping out the leak was detectable only by placing a finger over the nozzle. Therefore, all three types of extinguishers should be recharged immediately after each use, even if they have been only partially emptied.

Here are three extinguishers that have been popular for use in general aviation, but which B/CA feels should definitely not be used in your aircraft:

Dry chemical—These extinguishers contain either sodium bicarbonate or potassium bicarbonate (Purple K). Although they are very effective against Class B and C fires, they leave a residual dust or powder that is a mess to clean up and, more seriously, obstructs vision. They can also cause significant and expensive damage to electronics and environmental control systems. Dry chemical extinguishers are still being manufactured and offered for aircraft installations by some companies, notably Cessna and Piper, but stay away from them. If you've got one in your airplane, get it out. Don't worry, it won't go to waste. You can always use it in the kitchen.

PROBLEMS

Carbon tetrachloride—No longer manufactured or approved, carbon tet extinguishers may be sitting under the seats of some aircraft, installed some time ago. Carbon tet produces poisonous phosgene gas when it comes in contact with hot metals. Over extended periods or in large quantities it can be fatal.

Soda-acid—A combination of bicarbonate soda and sulphuric acid, this type is not manufactured any more nor recommended for use in aircraft cabins for the same reasons as carbon tet. Also, they can be corrosive to the exact components they were designed to extinguish fires on—Class A combustibles.

As we said at the beginning of this article, cabin fires are not the most common enemy aboard corporate aircraft, and their likelihood is diminished even further by proper preventive measures. So the eventuality of such an emergency need not be overstressed—especially if we borrow and apply the famous Boy Scout motto: "Be prepared."

Evacuating Your Passengers

44

by Dan Manningham

On November 12, 1975, a DC-10 encountered large numbers of seagulls during the takeoff roll. As a direct result of bird ingestion, the number-three engine literally exploded and the burning aircraft swerved to a stop on collapsed landing gear.

Despite immediate and widespread fire and despite the fact that several emergency exits were unusable, all 128 occupants evacuated without serious injury.

The amazing success of the DC-10 evacuation is probably due to one basic element: All the passengers were airline employes, most of whom were intimately familiar with evacuation problems and procedures.

Exactly one year later—November 12, 1976—a Falcon 20 crashed at Naples, Florida. The NTSB investigation revealed that the nine passengers encountered "severe difficulties" in evacuating the aircraft because the passengers lacked knowledge of emergency procedures; they were not briefed before departure; and there were no placarded instructions for opening the main cabin door or the two overwing exits.

There was no fire connected with this accident, but if there had been, the results in terms of casualties would have been grim.

The details of the Falcon accident reflect poorly on safety practices in business aviation. As a result, the Safety Board, for the first time in its history, has called for the FAA to spot check business aircraft operators for compliance with passenger briefing, placarding and other regulations in reference to passenger evacuations. But we didn't have to be told by the NTSB that cabin safety procedures and preparedness in business aviation need improving. In the course of researching this article, B/CA editors got a look at a side of business aircraft operation that obviously needs upgrading.

The need for an actual passenger evacuation is rare in business aviation, but it does happen and professionalism demands that the pilot or crew be prepared.

It must be remembered that the situation can arise in any size business aircraft. Although much of what follows may seem to apply only to the bigger turboprops and jets, the businessman pilot with one or more passengers onboard faces much the same problems and should be prepared with much the same training, preplanning and preparations.

Emergency passenger evacuation is, of course, a critical and demanding task that can be properly executed only when both crew and passengers have been trained and prepared. But the special peculiarities of business aircraft operations make evacuation training an uncomfortable task at best. For some flight departments, passenger training has been impossible without alienating the very people for whom the department exists. Nevertheless, training and preparedness must somehow be achieved. The best plan is to divide the problem into its three natural parts and work on each separately.

The aircraft—A successful evacuation begins with a properly prepared and placarded aircraft. First, audit all the storage areas in the cabin and on the flight deck. Visualize what's going to happen in a high G situation.

How many cabinet doors are likely to come open, spilling contents into the aisles and thus preventing easy egress? How many drawers are likely to slide out, blocking the aisle? How many objects at the rear of the cabin are going to become projectiles in a 9-G deceleration?

The answers to all three questions should be none. If you can't honestly give that answer, the situation must be rectified.

Next, audit the evacuation placarding throughout the aircraft. Bring someone in who is totally unfamiliar with business aircraft and have he or she pull and dispose of each emergency exit solely by reference to placards and the passenger briefing card. Then have the subject open the main entrance door, referring only to placards. During the exercise make certain that the test subject identifies all possible exit ports, aided by placarding only. Quite often, the possibility of going out through a baggage door is overlooked.

Finally, make certain that all exits will be clear following a rapid deceleration. In some aircraft, the crew is certain to be blocked in their seats by unsecured baggage from an entrance area storage bay. In others, a dislodged refreshment cabinet will block the main entrance door. In still others, custom interior features actually overlap exit areas.

Crew training—Airlines spend considerable time and money on initial and recurrent evacuation training for their cockpit and cabin crews. Although there are exceptions, that precedent has not been widely imitated in business aviation for several reasons, most notably because trained cabin attendants are so seldom used in business aircraft. Also, there is a reluctance in some flight departments to do or say anything that might alarm the passengers.

But those reasons, justifiable or not, mustn't stop you from preparing your pilots, at least, to act during an emergency evacuation. If you take pride in operating a safe and professional flight department, you cannot ignore specific and repeated crew training for passenger evacuation.

One very obvious area for training is the use and operation of emergency exits. B/CA has talked to pilots from several flight departments who have never actuated the emergency exit on their aircraft, and many more who have done so only once. On some pressurized aircraft the problem is compounded by exits that are particularly difficult to close, so maintenance departments are reluctant to schedule crewmember drills.

Despite any possible difficulties, we believe that every crewmember should operate every exit at least once a year. Anything less is inviting disaster when those exits are needed.

Aside from the benefits of training with emergency exits and insuring proper placarding, there is a continuing need for regular review of the evacuation emergency. The B/CA Emergency Passenger Evacuation Checklist can serve as a mini review and the text of this article itself can be the basis for recurrent evacuation training sessions and discussions.

As a part of the crew training, be creative, be innovative, plan for the worst. Each crew member should have specific duties, but each crew member should be prepared to assume all duties in the event the other is incapacitated.

Have a plan for every possibility; main door jammed, right exit jammed, fire on right exterior, all engine or engines cannot be shut down (that has happened following air carrier crashes), high winds from the left or right, aircraft inverted, a combination of two or more of the above.

Finally, make certain that each crewmember understands that his responsibilities do not end when the last passenger steps through an exit. It may be several minutes—even hours or days—before assistance arrives. Passengers must be protected from a variety of dangers ranging from post-crash fire to being run over in the dark by an arriving ambulance.

Passenger training—As mentioned, in business aviation the evacuation problem may be unique for two distinct reasons: First, there is seldom a cabin attendant onboard; second, the crew may be incapacitated. In short, passengers will quite likely be left to their own devices following an accident.

The most effective solution to that probability is an excellent, well thought out, passenger briefing card.

We have discovered that poorly conceived briefing cards are not rare. Even airline cards suffer from serious shortcomings. For example, of about 30 we've examined (split down the middle between airline and business aircraft cards), five contain specific instructions and illustrate what to do when a passenger has a handful of emergency exit window or door. That's important because in some aircraft, the exit itself will impede evacuation if not discarded or if put in the aisle.

After making certain you have done all possible for the passengers in the form of placards and briefing cards, consider actual training of passengers. That can be a delicate undertaking in business aircraft, but not an impossible one. For a start, the assumption that top company executives don't want to hear about the possibility of an accident may be false. Maybe the chairman has never brought the subject up only because he doesn't want to reveal an inner fear. Schedule a briefing for interested executives and you may be surprised at who leads the contingent to the airport.

If top executives are a genuine problem, or if the problem is that you often have guest passengers onboard, that need not preclude training for junior executives or others who frequently travel in the aircraft. If even one of the several passengers onboard has been trained and drilled, it will quite likely make a big difference in the success of an evacuation. So the more people you can train, the better.

History shows that about one-fourth of all actual passenger evacuations occur under circumstances that allow adequate time for warning and preparation. The remaining three-quarters involve unexpected emergencies requiring immediate and unprepared evacuations. The two are often distinguished by the descriptive terms, "planned" and "unplanned" evacuation. You need to prepare for both.

Procedures for the planned evacuation are built on the assumption that there will be adequate time to brief the passengers and prepare the cabin. In addition, and this is very important, the *degree of success in the planned evacuation will be governed by the degree of preparation and education acquired during training for an unplanned evacuation.*

Planned evacuations often occur as the result of inoperable landing gear, hydraulic failure or some other prelanding problem that compromises landing safety. When you know that a problem exists, you can maximize the evacuation before it even begins. Here are the key points:

Prepare ground personnel—If you even suspect that an evacuation may be necessary after landing, be sure to make that fact very clear to ground personnel and request all available emergency equipment. Let ATC and airport officials know how many people are onboard and if there are any children, elderly or handicapped passengers. This simple coordination will allow ATC and airport personnel to arrange for fire and medical help, plan arrival and departure traffic around your problem and give emergency personnel time to review the specific difficulties associated with your aircraft type.

Prepare the airplane—Consider burning or dumping fuel to reduce landing weight. In all aircraft, consider opening some emergency exits before landing because fuselage damage and deformation may prevent opening them on the ground. (But make certain pressurized aircraft are depressurized before opening exits.) Turn on emergency lighting. Turn off all unnecessary electrical loads.

Prepare the cabin—Successful passenger evacuation can be markedly enhanced by preparing the cabin environment. Stow all folding tables and carefully put away all loose objects. Glasses, cups, magazines, books, pencils and other loose objects will become flying missiles in any difficult landing, contributing to confusion and even impeding the movement of passengers. Aisles should be clear, with all seats moved to their proper takeoff and landing position. Be sure the door separating the passenger cabin from the main entrance is latched open for *all* takeoffs and landings, as required by FARs. (It wasn't in the Falcon 20 mentioned earlier and a small carpet became wedged underneath the door, jamming it in a closed position.)

Proper takeoff and landing seat positions warrant particular emphasis. Without going into details, experiences by B/CA editors aboard corporate aircraft indicate this requirement is routinely neglected during passenger briefings in order not to disturb those who have just sat down and made themselves comfortable.

You should also remove the trim covers from emergency exit handles to eliminate possible confusion.

Prepare the passengers—Passenger preparation begins with the pre-takeoff announcement and/or safety information cards and continues up to the personalized and specific instructions that will be required in the actual preparation for a planned evacuation. Testing and research has consistently shown that well-informed passengers evacuate and survive much better.

As a minimum, specified in 91.99, passengers must have been orally briefed before the flight began on smoking, the use of safety belts, location and means for opening the passenger door and emergency exits; location of survival equipment; ditching procedures (for overwater flights) and the use of supplemental oxygen before the flight began.

According to FARs, an *oral* briefing need not be given "when the pilot in command determines that the passengers are familiar with the contents of the briefing." In that case, "printed cards" may be used that are "pertinent only to the type and model airplane on which it is used."

Ironically, passengers don't tend to panic in an aircraft evacuation. To the contrary, they are more likely to wait calmly for your direction and leadership. In the absence of specific and careful instructions from you, this sort of behavioral inactivity may overcome your passengers, inducing them to calmly remain in the lethal environment of a burning airplane.

When faced with an actual preparation for passenger evacuation, be sure to orally brief your passengers on at least these items:

Comfort and reassurance—It is a psychological fact that confident people perform better. If you reassure your passengers that they can evacuate the airplane safely even in an unusual situation, they will be more likely to respond effectively.

Brace positions—Several brace positions have been developed over the years and they are dependent on seat orientation. For those facing forward, one method is to adjust the seat back to the vertical position and sit well back in the seat. Then bend forward with the head between the legs and grasp an ankle in each hand.

Emergency Passenger Evacuation Checklist

Before Landing

(1) Prepare ground personnel

Request priority handling

Request that emergency equipment be standing by

Report children, handicapped or aged aboard

(2) Prepare the airplane

Dump or burn fuel

Open or unlock emergency and conventional exits if appropriate

Turn on emergency lighting

Reduce electrical load to minimum

(3) Prepare the cabin

Stow folding tables and equipment

Stow loose objects

Clear aisles

Remove emergency exit handle covers

Return seats to required normal takeoff and landing position

(4) Prepare the passengers

Relocate passengers from side-facing seats to fore- or aft-facing seats (if possible)

Reassure and brief passengers (exits, belts, brace)

Assign individual duties

Review exit location and operation

Provide for children, aged, handicapped

Remove glasses, dentures, shoes (if appropriate)

(5) Prepare the cockpit

Stow loose objects

Lock cockpit and cabin/entrance separation door open

Secure flashlight nearby (if appropriate)

Tighten seatbelts and shoulder harnesses

Review individual duties and evacuation routes

After Landing

(1) Position aircraft, set parking brake, shut down

(2) Provide assistance where necessary and evacuate the aircraft

(3) Assemble, account, aid

Aft-facing seats should be erect and the passengers in them should sit erect with arms folded over their chests. If possible, move people out of aft-facing seats. If that's not possible, try to put lighter and shorter passengers in them. They generate less leverage that might break the seat back down.

If it is not possible to move side-facing passengers to other seats, they should brace themselves against any available bulkhead using pillows as a cushion. Side-facing seats are the least desirable for several reasons and should not be occupied for takeoffs or landings unless necessary.

Assign individual duties—You must subtly prepare your passengers to handle their own evacuation because pilots are often seriously injured even when passengers are not. Individual duty assignments are also helpful in minimizing the effects of fear and distress because people who are responsible for other people are less prone to panic behavior. Specific duty tasks may range from opening an exit or exits to assisting a child. The point here is that individual assignment of those duties will facilitate their accomplishment while providing some excellent psychological support.

When assigning duties, try to cover all contingencies. Assign two people to open each exit so that there's a better chance of it getting opened in event one person cannot get the job done for some reason. Also keep one crewmember free of all duties so he can fill in.

Review exit operations—Carefully review the location of *every* emergency exit. Be sure to include baggage doors, overwing exits and even cockpit windows where appropriate. You must presume that some of these potential escape routes will be jammed or blocked either as a result of impact or interior furnishings. Each passenger should focus on the nearest emergency exit, but all passengers should know about all exits. Remember, too, that passengers will need to know how far the drop is to the ground and/or how to slide off the wing.

You must assume that your passengers have no experience whatsoever with the peculiarities of aircraft exit hardware. As has been brought to our attention by an NTSB recommendation, many potentially successful evacuations have been frustrated by the totally unfamiliar handles, motions and pressures associated with aircraft doors. If emergency exit windows are to be discarded, be sure the passengers know that the window will probably have to be turned diagonally in order to throw it out the opening in which it was fitted. Also, caution the passengers of the need to prepare for the heavy weight of the exit once it is dislodged from its fitting.

Passengers subconsciously want to leave through the same door they used when entering, even when the door is blocked by fire, debris or jamming, so this briefing is essential to overcome that fixation.

Provide for children, aged, handicapped—Assign one able adult to

343

care for each child and handicapped person onboard. Have a plan, and a backup plan, for getting them to safety.

Remove hazardous personal objects—Suggest that your passengers remove long, dangling key chains, pens and pencils, eyeglasses unless absolutely necessary, dentures and platform or high-heeled shoes. All of those items should be stowed securely away to prevent missile hazards.

Before you return to the cockpit, review the following essential requirements for your passengers:

· Tighten seatbelts.

· Assume the brace position when the signal is given.

· Wait for the airplane to come to a full stop.

· Understand and mentally rehearse at least one escape route and one alternate.

· Review door and emergency exit opening operations.

When you return to the cockpit be sure that it, too, is prepared. Check that all loose items, including your flight bag and equipment, have been securely stowed. As required by FARs, lock the cockpit-to-cabin door or curtain open so you will have free and ready access to your passengers and exits. Place a flashlight in some secure but readily accessible place and discuss your separate duties and exit routes with other crewmembers if there are any. There won't be time after the landing.

If you have a jump seat passenger, seriously consider asking him to move back into the passenger compartment. If he or she is a crewmember, safety may be enhanced if he or she is back with the passengers. Also, crew egress may be more certain with the jump seat stowed.

If the jump seat passenger remains forward, be certain he's properly belted in so that a flailing body does not jeopardize the crew. (You don't want heads literally knocking together up on the flight deck.)

Following a non-fatal precautionary or emergency landing with some control of the aircraft returned, take time to do things that will optimize the evacuation.

· Position the aircraft so that the prevailing wind will blow any fire away from the primary exits.

· Set the parking brake.

· Shut down all engines and electrical power.

After your cockpit duties are completed, your primary task will be to transfer passengers from the comfort and seeming security of the aircraft to the actual security of the outside. People have been known to remain inside a smoke-filled fuselage rather than step out into the rain. Therefore you must take command of the situation and order your passengers up and out, in the harshest terms if necessary. Tests and accident reports have repeatedly established the fact that the cabin environment is likely to become uninhabitable within approximately 90 seconds due to smoke and fire.

Airline standards require the evacuation of a full aircraft within that time period with half of all exits rendered inoperative. You need to strive for the same minimum capability. Unfortunately for business aircraft operations, this effort can come *only* from preparation and not practice.

During the actual evacuation there will be some confusion and lack of coordination as individuals adjust their thinking from the anticipated to the actual. During this brief period of intense activity you need to know that several things may impede an orderly process. As we've tried to emphasize, the way you have briefed your passengers for an assumed routine flight and the manner in which you prepared them for a planned emergency landing will dictate the degree of problems the following impediments might impose.

· Passengers invariably prefer to leave via the entrance door, even if it is blocked or jammed.

· Passengers are prone to walk forward, even if there is an available exit immediately behind them.

· Particularly distraught passengers may remain frozen in inactivity and silence. You cannot even assume that everyone will try to help himself.

· The old bromide "women and children first" has seldom been employed in real emergencies. Those physically weaker passengers will need extra help.

· Despite your best efforts to explain, passengers may not be able to open the exits.

· Exits are often rendered unserviceable by fuselage deformation or blockage by furnishings so be prepared to use an alternate.

Your single most important role will be to provide positive leadership in a crisis environment. Supervise, improvise, instruct and help to get survivors outside and away from the aircraft. After that it's all downhill.

Detailed emergency landing preparedness is not available, of course, for the unplanned evacuation. Thus the effort by the flight department to include regular crew training, complete preflight passenger briefings on every flight and the assignment of passenger responsibility become your most important allies. Since unplanned evacuations are three times more common and potentially more hazardous, all the requirements discussed apply, plus the following ones:

· If possible, inform ATC that you are evacuating so that the controller can divert other traffic. Once you have shut down the aircraft, it could be an invisible menace on the runway or taxiway, particularly at night.

· Shout to the passengers. A brief and incomplete message is better than none.

PROBLEMS

· Try to position the aircraft so that the prevailing wind will blow any fire away from exit routes.

· Set the parking brake.

· Shut down all engines and electrical power.

· Exercise positive leadership in the cabin to motivate and assist the passengers out and away from the aircraft.

Emergency passenger evacuation is an unusual occurrence, especially in business aviation. But when it does happen, you will be thankful for every bit of training you have taken and all the information you have been able to provide passengers. Flight departments that establish and maintain a specific evacuation program, complete with recurrent exit operation training, appropriate checklists and thorough passenger briefing cards will minimize the risk should that grisly possibility become a reality.

How to Survive a Ditching

45

by Dan Manningham

Two-thirds of the earth's surface is covered by water, most of it cold. Nearly half of the American people cannot swim, and most modern aircraft are very poor floaters. Average wave heights in the Pacific are four to seven feet; they are somewhat less in the Atlantic. As of July 1, 1974, all U.S. Ocean Station Vessels were removed from service. Although it hasn't happened yet, statistics alone will eventually force some corporate aircraft into the water with a load of passengers.

Ironically, the very reliability of turbine equipment, which has largely prevented such incidents in the recent past, has produced a casual attitude toward the real threat of open-ocean ditching.

When you are faced with that stark possibility, your life and the lives of your passengers may very well hang on the training and preparation that can only be done in advance. Specifically, you must prepare for three phases: the initial distress phase, the actual water landing and aircraft evacuation, and survival on the open ocean.

There is no lack of problems that could force you into a ditching situation. Fuel starvation, engine failure, structural damage or even pressurization failure can turn the tables on an otherwise perfect trip. Regardless of its nature, the first indication of serious trouble should prompt you to follow the five "C" rules.

(1) *Confess* your predicament to yourself in order to make an honest, careful evaluation.

(2) *Climb* to the highest suitable altitude to optimize communications and provide a maximum number of options. The exceptions to this climb would be serious, uncontained fire or any other emergency that might require immediate ditching to prevent an uncontrolled crash later.

(3) *Conserve* your fuel supply in every possible way. If you need distance, operate at the speed or angle of attack for maximum specific range. If you just need to buy time, fly at the speed for best endurance. In either

case, if you have a fuel leak, transfer fuel out of the leaking tank(s), even if you have to exceed normal fuel-balancing limitations. During the transfer, operate all engines from the leaking tank as long as practicable to minimize the loss.

(4) *Communicate* your predicament by an urgent or distress message at the first suggestion of serious trouble. If already in contact with someone, maintain communications on that frequency. If you need to establish radio contact, try any of the following emergency frequencies: 121.5 MHz, 243.0 MHz, 500 kHz, 2182 kHz or 8364 kHz.

(5) *Comply* with instructions that are transmitted in return. Naturally you will have to use judgment and discretion in analyzing the free advice offered by merchant vessels and other aircraft, but instructions from the Coast Guard or other official search and rescue groups should be followed precisely.

In the process of establishing communications, don't be afraid to specifically and positively declare an emergency if any doubt exists as to the safety of the aircraft. You can always cancel that emergency later, and no one will think any less of you. Switch the transponder to 7700 and use the voice call "Mayday" until you have positive contact with someone able and willing to inform the appropriate Search and Rescue organization. Tell them at least the following:

· Your *position* or your best estimate of that position. If you are really lost, say so. That in itself is an important piece of information to the people who will have to find you.

· Your intended *course, speed* and *altitude.* That information will establish the search track.

· The *nature of your trouble.* Make it simple and clear. Fire, control failure, engine shutdown or whatever, and skip all the technical details. They just need to know what it is that prompted the emergency call-up so they can effectively utilize the available SAR forces.

· Your *intentions.* You might wish to continue on the original flight plan, change destination or hold where you are. In all cases, make your intentions known, and when you change your intentions, advise others accordingly.

· The *type of assistance* needed. You may reasonably request a fix, a steer, an escort, flotation equipment, medical advice or any other assistance that you deem desirable. Above all, ask. Others are willing and even eager to help.

If you cannot get any radio response, make repeated blind broadcasts giving all the pertinent information, including the frequency used and the fact that you are not receiving. Be persistent. *The most important single thing a pilot with an emergency can accomplish is to let another station know he is in trouble.*

348

When you have checked off the five Cs and satisfactorily completed those preliminary communications, turn your attention to keeping the airplane out of the water and advising the passengers, in that order. Get out the flight manual and go through the applicable emergency procedure on a challenge and respond basis. Discuss the problem and if necessary, improvise. Above all, fly the airplane every minute to prevent some crew-induced irregularity. Even if you are busy, try to squeeze in at least a short announcement to the cabin explaining the problem with the suggestion that all occupants review the emergency procedures card. Later, when time permits, you will need to brief the passengers more carefully and authoritatively.

When you have determined the scope of the problem and established the appropriate communications, make a serious appraisal of your options. Even if a ditching is unavoidable, you will want to make that water landing at the most opportune time in the safest place. If it is nighttime, make every effort to stay aloft until daylight. If the time is close to sunset, carefully weigh the problems of an immediate daylight ditching as opposed to a more calculated and, perhaps, better prepared ditching in the dark. If you are near some substantially warmer water, as you would be in the vicinity of the Gulf Stream, consider that alternative as you would any other. Human survival is considerably enhanced by every single degree of water temperature. And when everything else has been evaluated, you will certainly want to ditch in the area of best possible weather.

During this time, your emergency communications will have been forwarded to the Rescue Coordination Center (RCC), which is the central operations station for all search and rescue activity. RCC is a complete communications center able to contact and control all appropriate SAR facilities. Hot lines between the RCC and the Oceanic Air Traffic Control Center allow a continuous flow of information directly to you. The controlling RCC will take several immediate steps.

In order to confirm and pinpoint your position, the RCC will alert the High Frequency Direction Finding net to take bearings on your HF transmissions. You may be asked to transmit specifically for the HF net, or bearings can be taken from your routine communications. The system is effective between 2000 kHz and 30,000 kHz and furnishes lines of bearing between you and the station. These readings are then classified as to accuracy and forwarded to the HF net control station, where bearings from two or more stations are used to plot a fix. The final information is immediately transmitted to the RCC.

If your location warrants it, the RCC will also request radar positioning from long-range military radar and/or from certain ships at sea.

When your position and track are confirmed, and/or when the situation warrants, the RCC will dispatch an intercept aircraft. Occasionally en-route aircraft may be utilized in this role, but most intercepts will be accomplished by USCG C-130 Hercules, specially equipped for the mission.

The Hercules is a fine airplane, capable of 340 knots at jet altitudes. And in those cases where your speed is substantially greater, the C-130 will perform a maximum coverage intercept, which involves a 180-degree turn prior to actual intercept to place him on your track and ahead of you. When you overtake him and pull away, surveillance will be assumed by another aircraft. Although unable to land on water, the Hercules provides several invaluable services. This sophisticated aircraft can provide exhaustive navigational and communication services, weather information, visual inspection and air-droppable survival and flotation equipment.

During the intercept, the C-130 may request that you take ADF bearings on his airborne homing transmitter. The normal frequency is 522 kHz, but he will confirm that as well as the identification to be used. When the distance closes to VHF range, he will begin homing on your VHF voice transmissions until he can see you on radar. Be sure to keep the transponder on 7700 for maximum conspicuity. When the intercept is completed, the biggest problem of all—search—will be eliminated.

You don't have to be in imminent danger to request an intercept. The service is automatically provided by the Coast Guard when it is aware that a distressed aircraft is operating on less than 75 percent power.

If you are not in a position that allows an airborne intercept, the RCC will attempt to divert a surface vessel when ditching appears likely. The Coast Guard maintains a computer track of ships from over 60 nations that participate in the Automated Merchant Vessel Report System (AMVER). The computer can quickly provide the predicted positions of these ships on demand, and the pertinent information is forwarded to the RCC over prearranged communications circuits. One very useful readout from the AMVER program is called a Trackline Surface Picture. This SURPIC shows a list of the ships positioned along your trackline and can even include such information as the availability of a doctor. The RCC will call up that information as a matter of course when it receives the initial distress message. That data can then be transmitted to you if you request it. When plotted on the chart, you would have a running summary of where the nearest surface vessel is located. In more urgent cases, the RCC will select the most appropriate ship and alert it to your problem.

Ships can be of enormous value when a ditching is imminent. They will supply weather and sea condition information. They can provide a communications link, and their value in the actual rescue phase is beyond measure.

Direct communication between aircraft and ships requires some special knowledge. Merchant ships do not have capability on the usual aeronautical frequencies, although many can communicate by voice in the 2000 kHz band. Normal emergency calling would be on 2182 kHz, even though few ships maintain a listening watch on that frequency. You must ask the RCC to alert the ship or ships to establish a watch on 2182. This is the only frequency that is compatible for use between most aircraft and merchant vessels.

ADF homing is the best method for effecting a surface vessel rendezvous. Most ships can provide homing signals in the 400-kHz band, with 410 kHz used for standardization purposes. Once again, you will have to ask the RCC to request homing signals from the ship; the RCC will verify the frequency and identification to be used. Visual aids will be provided by deck and search lights at night and black smoke during daylight hours.

The actual water landing, when it happens, will require careful planning and considerable skill. Your first task is to evaluate the sea conditions and determine the best ditch heading. If you are in contact with the RCC or an intercept aircraft, they will brief you on conditions and even compute the most advantageous ditch heading. Without that information you have to do your own figuring.

The open ocean surface is in a constant state of change as the waves and swells from different influences override each other. At landing speeds in the vicinity of 100 knots, watery billows are almost as effective as granite in damaging an airframe. For that reason, it is extremely dangerous to land into the wind without regard to the sea conditions. In fact, depending on circumstances, you may not want to land into the wind at all.

Swells are the large undulations of the ocean's surface caused by distant disturbances. Individual swells appear to be regular and smooth, with considerable distance between the rounded crests. They are usually the long-term after-effects of distant storm systems. *Waves* are the choppy roughness caused by local winds. They are more irregular, more crested and of much shorter period and duration.

At any given location, the ocean surface will be influenced by the swell system of some distant storm and the waves generated by local winds. In some cases more than one swell system may be present. When there are swells of any magnitude, your best ditch heading will be parallel to the swell as long as winds are not over 25 knots. Crosswind touchdowns are not nearly so critical in the absence of narrow, hard-surface runways, and the airframe will probably ride through any local chop.

As you descend through about 2000 feet, the primary swell system will be distinguished as a pattern of differing light intensities on the surface. If you maintain a constant heading and watch the surface pattern for a few seconds, the direction of swell motion can be determined. Note the direction because the primary swells will disappear from view below about 1500 feet.

Below 500 to 800 feet, the secondary or local waves will become apparent and white streaks perpendicular to the white caps will indicate the wind direction.

Once you have noted the directions of the two systems and estimated the surface wind, you can compute the appropriate ditch heading using the following guidelines in order of priority for winds under 25 knots.

· Land parallel to the primary.
· Land down the secondary.
· Land into the wind.

When the wind exceeds 35 knots, safety dictates a landing into, rather than parallel to, the primary swells. Generally, with winds of that magnitude, the swells will be from the same direction as the wind so that the markedly reduced groundspeed negates the inherent hazard of landing perpendicular to the swell. When you must land into the swell system, it is paramount that you touch down on the back side of the swell to prevent the nose from digging in. If that happens, the airplane will very likely suffer catastrophic damage.

When the wind is between 25 and 35 knots, it may be necessary to select an intermediate heading. In that instance you would simply modify the parallel-to-the-swell landing with an angle into the wind *and* into the swell to compromise the crosswind while avoiding a landing directly into the swells. Although research is skimpy, there is good reason to believe that low-wing landplanes can tolerate sizeable crosswind components. If the swell system is large, and if there is any question, accept more crosswind in order to stay parallel to the swells.

Finally, if everything else fails, just fly over the water at low altitude on various compass headings. The course that appears the smoothest will usually be the best ditch heading.

When time permits, you will want to carefully prepare the cabin and passengers for the actual ditching and evacuation. All loose items should be gathered up and securely stowed to reduce the "missile" hazard imposed by the very rapid deceleration associated with even the best water landings. Books, briefcases, galley equipment and packages can be piled in the biffy or any other secure place. Folding tables should be stowed away and all interior doors locked open to prevent jamming. Rafts and other survival equipment ought to be relocated close to exits and dispersed so that launching can be accomplished from more than one location in the very likely event of inoperable exits.

Be careful when moving those rafts and have a razor blade or knife handy. It is not at all difficult to inadvertently inflate a raft inside the aircraft with dire results. The noise alone is startling and when it inflates in that confined space, it will very effectively block large portions of the cabin, severely hindering and maybe even preventing an evacuation. The only solution, in that case, is to deflate the raft with a massive knife hole or razor blade slash, which naturally destroys the usefulness of the raft. Because of this threat and others as well, operators should have two or more of the smaller rafts aboard rather than a single large one. Finally, cabin lights should be turned on fully, and even emergency lighting systems can be manually activated to assure maximum illumination.

When the cabin is properly organized, brief the passengers on every aspect of the landing and evacuation. Advise them to put on any extra clothing they may have because even warm water is chilling after prolonged exposure. They should clearly understand the importance of tight seat belts, and they must be briefed on some effective brace position if they are to survive the water impact.

Several brace positions have been defined over the years, and most airlines settle on one or another because all the regular passenger cabin seats face in the same direction—forward. But it is difficult to prescribe one position for forward-, aft- and side-facing seats common in corporate aircraft. One method for those facing forward is to adjust the back to the vertical position and sit well back in the seat. Bend forward with head between legs and grasp an ankle in each hand. Aft-facing seats should be fully reclined with the passenger's arms folded over his chest. Passengers sitting in side-facing seats should brace themselves against the bulkhead using pillows as a cushion. If possible, move passengers from side-facing seats to forward- or aft-facing ones. You should determine some prearranged signal from the cockpit so that passengers can assume the brace about one minute prior to water contact. Any prolonged period in that uncomfortable position is unnecessary and will contribute to light-headed disorientation when they must stand up and proceed to the exits.

Passengers should also understand that the airplane may very well skip or bounce once or twice before coming to rest. Without that knowledge, they might relax the brace or even unfasten their seatbelts before the airplane comes to a full stop.

Pass out the life jackets and assist each individual in donning and fastening them properly. If your jackets are the type that have two separate flotation chambers, have the passengers inflate one now and the other when they are in the water and clear of the wreckage. Single-chamber vests are better inflated outside the aircraft because they substantially reduce mobility when fully inflated and may make it difficult to get through emergency window exits. If the vests are equipped with lights, have them switched on at once. Those little lights are designed for the critical task of locating other people in the water during darkness and will be of little or no use afterwards.

Before you return to the cockpit, review the highlights for your passengers:

· Tighten seat belts.

353

· Assume the brace position when the signal is given.

· Wait for the airplane to come to a full stop.

· Understand and mentally rehearse at least one escape route and one alternate.

· Review raft launching and inflation procedures.

· Review life vest inflation.

· Turn all flashlights on.

Now it's time to prepare yourself and the aircraft for the water landing. Put on your own life vest and leave it uninflated. Lock your seat in the most comfortable position and really cinch down on the seat belt and shoulder harness. Check that all loose items including your flight bag and equipment have been securely stowed in back and that the cockpit-to-cabin door is locked open. Place a flashlight in some secure but easily accessible location and discuss your separate duties and exit routes with the other crewmembers. There won't be time after the landing.

Get out the flight manual and perform the ditching checklist by challenge and response. In the absence of such a checklist, consider at least the following items:

· Dump fuel to the standpipes to reduce landing weight to a minimum and transform the fuel tanks into flotation chambers.

· Depressurize completely below 10,000 feet, and if possible, close outflow valves to minimize flooding and increase flotation time.

· Set the heading bug on the HSI to the ditch heading.

· Turn on all cabin and cockpit lights to aid in the evacuation and even consider using all exterior lights. Every bit of illumination will be of assistance to search and rescue forces, and some exterior lights may even aid in the evacuation.

· Pull the landing-gear warning horn circuit breaker. You should definitely leave the gear up for ditching, and the horn would certainly be distracting in those last crucial minutes.

· Make one last check with the intercept aircraft, surface vessel or other rescue unit to be sure they understand your intentions and have prepared themselves. If there is no on-scene vehicle, review your situation for the RCC and, if necessary, broadcast that information in the blind.

Once the airplane and occupants have been prepared, turn to the ditch heading and begin a gradual letdown while extending the flaps fully. When close to the water, increase power and just hold the airplane in the air at about 1.1 V$_s$. If landing parallel to the swells, keep the wings level with the water surface rather than the horizon. When a smooth patch of water appears ahead, cut the power and touch down at minimum possible speed. The trick is to keep from dropping too far on the one hand while preventing a skip off of the water surface on the other. As in any other landing, fly the airplane right to touchdown and maintain control as long as possible. In this instance you may wish to grip the controls gingerly to avoid injury from the rapid and massive deflections that will surely occur as the control surfaces make water contact.

· When the airplane stops, pull all the engine fire handles and move quickly to evacuate.

Controlled ditchings are actually less hazardous than they seem. Very few people are killed or injured by the water landing itself. Most fatalities are the result of failure to evacuate the airplane or board the raft.

As soon as the airplane comes to a stop, you will be the captain of a rapidly sinking ship with several confused passengers. Your primary task is to transfer those people from the comfort and seeming security of the airplane to the actual security of the survival rafts. Flotation time may be only a minute or two, so haste is important. You must take absolute command of the situation and order your passengers up and out in the harshest terms if necessary. *Positive leadership may be the single most important element in any aircraft evacuation.*

Proceed directly to the cabin to supervise the evacuation. Rafts should be secured to the aircraft interior by a lanyard provided for this purpose and then pushed out the exit as the inflation handle is pulled. When using over-wing exits, secure the lanyard, carry the raft onto the wing and inflate it there. Be prepared to give the inflation handle an aggressive tug. Most rafts require a pull of at least 20 pounds to start the inflation. That lanyard is vitally important. On the open ocean, prevailing winds could blow a survival raft out of reach before it is fully inflated. The raft *must* be attached to the aircraft or it will be irretrievably lost. After the raft is loaded, the lanyard can be cut with a knife that is normally part of raft equipment. If the airplane sinks, the lanyard on most rafts is designed to break under moderate strain.

As soon as it is inflated, transfer the passengers directly from the door or wing into the raft. This "dry" evacuation is not a luxury. It is a survival priority to prevent individual swimmers from becoming separated and lost and to facilitate the actual raft entry. Take care to launch the raft away from jagged metal or debris, which could puncture and rip the raft material.

Survivors should be evacuated directly into the water only in those cases where the aircraft is sinking rapidly or where other circumstances absolutely prohibit direct entry to a raft. If that happens, throw the raft into the water—it will float even in a hard container without being inflated—and follow it with a crewmember or able swimmer to inflate it and help others in. The second crewmember should stay on the wing to insure that passengers follow immediately, inflating their life jackets fully just prior to entering the water. All swimmers should stay as close together and to the raft as possible, holding hands if necessary. When the raft is inflated, get everyone inside using one helper in the raft to pull, and one in the water to push. Once inside, survivors are best placed opposite the boarding station to eliminate congestion and balance the load. When everyone is in, make a careful head count and search the water for any missing. If there are survivors in the water, do not jump in to go after them unless it is absolutely necessary; in that case, tie a lifeline (provided with most rafts) to yourself before leaving the raft.

When you welcomed your passengers aboard the airplane for this trip, you were a genial host and servant. Sitting in that raft on the open ocean, you must be a good-natured but absolute dictator. There is a great deal to be done, and you must direct and delegate that work in a decisive and authoritative manner. In the eyes of the passengers, you are the expert. Capitalize on that opinion and begin at once to coordinate those activities that will maximize your survival chances. If you are too badly injured to exert such leadership, designate some natural leader to assume those responsibilities and tell everyone that he is the boss.

Begin by preparing that miniature vessel for the rigors of the open ocean. Distribute all personnel evenly around the edge and make sure that no one sits up on the inflated sides. That position destabilizes the raft and makes a precarious seat from which it is easy to fall overboard.

Deploy the sea anchor at once. That little cloth bucket that drags along underwater does two very nice things. It markedly stabilizes the raft to prevent capsizing and motion discomfort. And it minimizes wind drift, which would rapidly blow you away from the ditching (and searching) area.

Break out the hand pump to fully inflate the boarding station, canopy, center floor compartment and buoyancy chambers. Check the raft for leaks and make repairs as necessary. Now inspect each other's life vests and use the oral inflation tubes to top off the inflation.

When the raft and its occupants are inspected and secure, inventory that precious survival equipment on which your very lives will depend. Each separate item should be located and individually secured to the raft. These are the things that will allow you to complete your last two responsibilities: to endure and to make yourself as conspicuous as possible.

Use the first-aid materials in your survival kit to treat any injuries. If seasickness medication is available, distribute it at once and insist that *everyone* use it, even though they may not feel nauseous. Seasickness is almost a guaranteed result of open-ocean survival. And when it starts, it seriously dehydrates the body, attracts sharks and, worst of all, impairs the very will to live.

Although water-activated ELTs are available with most rafts, you should have an ELT available in the aircraft to take with you in case the one with the raft is lost. If you have a radio beacon, read the instructions and activate it immediately to provide SAR forces with a fix on your position. If you have reason to believe that those forces are nearby, use one nighttime flare or daytime smoke, as appropriate, to indicate your precise position. In sunlight, assign someone to sweep the horizon in a steady pattern with a signaling mirror or any other reflective surface. These devices are remarkably effective and are visible up to 40 miles away on the surface and more than that to an aircraft.

If it is still daylight and not close to sunset, spread dye marker in the water and carefully rinse out the container for later use as a rain water receptacle. If it is late or dark, save the dye marker for the next day. Dye marker is extremely visible, especially to search aircraft, which can easily miss a life raft in rolling seas.

In brief, you will want to assay every possible means of making yourself conspicuous. Delegate the individual tasks to others in the raft to keep their attention and hopes up, but maintain a close central authority over the total action.

Establish a 24-hour watch. Those on duty should understand their specific responsibilities to watch for aircraft and ships, operate the signal equipment at prescribed intervals and observe and maintain the raft in a seaworthy condition. If it rains, they will need to awaken the others to assist in collecting the water and so all can drink their fill while the rain lasts.

Sunburn is a significant problem in the ocean's reflected glare, so be sure to stay covered up and to use the protective cream in your survival kit.

Dehydration will be even worse. That sun will bake the moisture out of your body at an alarming rate. To minimize that problem, keep your clothes wet with salt water, but under no circumstances should anyone leave the raft. Aside from the dangers of separation and drowning, there is the real problem of sharks.

Despite the current sensationalism on this subject, sharks do present a distinct threat to survivors in many areas in which you would be likely to ditch. Sharks are scavengers that feed on live, healthy animals, the sick or injured, and even those that have been long dead. They feed at all times of the day and night with peaks at dawn and dusk.

When a potential rescue vehicle is sighted, utilize every available device to make your position known. If you have a VHF handi-talkie, select 123.1 MHz, the on-scene emergency voice frequency, and attempt to communicate directly. Certainly use the flares, smoke, mirrors, lights and dye markers, as appropriate, to attract attention. Do not assume that you have been found because you can see a plane or ship, however close. Even when it is perfectly obvious that you have been sighted, continue signaling to guide the rescue forces directly to your position with a minimum of lost time.

The actual rescue, when it comes, may be the most critical time of your entire survival experience. The relief and exhilaration will induce you to

Business and Commercial Aviation

DITCHING PROCEDURES

Communicate (121.5 MHz, 243.0 MHz, 500 kHz, 2182 kHz, 8364 kHz).
Set transponder to 7700.

☐ Determine options

☐ Plan water landing:
    (1) Evaluate sea and wind conditions.
    (2) Determine best ditch heading.

☐ Prepare cabin and passengers:
    (1) Stow and secure loose items.
    (2) Locate rafts and survival equipment.
    (3) Turn lights up to maximum intensity.
    (4) Brief passengers.
    (5) Pass out life vests.

☐ Prepare yourself and crew:
    (1) Secure cockpit items.
    (2) Lock cockpit-to-cabin door in open position.
    (3) Don life vest.
    (4) Secure seatbelt and shoulder harness.
    (5) Secure flashlight nearby.
    (6) Discuss duties and exit routes with crew.

☐ Ditching checklist:
    (1) Dump fuel.
    (2) Depressurize below 10,000 feet.
    (3) Set heading bug to ditch heading.
    (4) Turn on all lights.
    (5) Silence gear warning system.
    (6) Communicate intentions again.

☐ Ditching:
    (1) Set flaps to recommended setting.
    (2) Hold minimum speed for wind conditions.
    (3) Touch down slightly tail low.
    (4) Maintain control as long as possible.
    (5) Pull fire handles and evacuate.

take unnecessary chances at a time when your physical condition has deteriorated far more than you think. Stay out of the water and let the rescuers come to you. Don't attempt to climb ship's ladders or cargo nets without assistance. Above all, follow the instructions of the rescuers themselves. Just relax and let them do the work. Your job is finished.

Ditching and ocean survival is a once-in-a-lifetime experience. Those who have come back did so, in large measure because of mental and physical readiness, which was accomplished long before the fact. Ingenuity, resourcefulness and luck will all help. Training and preparation will save your life.

Inflight Medical Emergencies

46

by Richard N. Aarons

There's an implied contract between a business pilot and his passenger, an understood intention on the pilot's part to deliver the passenger to his destination with dispatch, safety and comfort. In carrying this out the pilot normally needs only to be concerned with the airplane, ATC system and weather. But occasionally another factor enters the equation—the medical emergency. It can range from simple airsickness to catastrophic heart attack or stroke. In any event, the medical emergency must be dealt with quickly and competently.

Fortunately, the pilot has a lot going for him during a medical emergency. Help is everywhere—ATC facilities will expedite your flight to any destination; the Arinc communications net will patch you through to ground medical facilities; airline crews will ask their dispatch offices to lend a hand—all you have to do is ask.

But when do you ask? When does a passenger's illness necessitate immediate landing? What can be done for the patient in the meantime?

The answers don't come easily.

The airlines have been faced with this problem for years and have developed workable procedures for handling inflight medical emergencies. Their procedure begins with the cabin crew who must first assess the emergency situation. *Assess* is the key word here because the cabin and cockpit crews must determine immediately if the flight should be continued or if extraordinary measures must be taken to preserve the life of the passenger. Obviously, any severe illness or trauma must be dealt with as an emergency.

We'll talk about some specific problems later, but assume for the moment that an airline crew decides an emergency situation exists. Typically, the captain will call his company dispatch office and explain the nature of the illness or trauma. Company dispatch will locate the nearest suitable airport for a landing—taking into consideration weather, ground equipment and availability of medical services—and redirect the flight to that destination. Dispatch will also notify local authorities and see that an ambulance and a medical team meets the flight.

This system should work for the corporate or business pilot as well, with the exception that something must be found to perform the function of the airlines' flight dispatch services. That can be ATC, Arinc, FBOs or even another passenger using an air to ground telephone.

Remember first that a medical emergency is like any other inflight emergency. *Tell someone about it.* The earlier you notify ATC that you may have to divert, the sooner they can start clearing airspace for you. Don't be afraid to ask the ATC folks for non-ATC type help. At any given moment, there's at least one guy sitting around in the IFR room with nothing to do. He can get on the phone and check out ground medical facilities for you.

B/CA made a quick poll of the major FBOs around the country. All we checked said their customer service agents (the guys who answer Unicom or Arinc calls) are prepared to make calls for you to see that appropriate equipment is standing by. Flight Service Stations and airlines will do the same. Many major Air Force bases have 24-hour medical services available on the airport. Under normal circumstances, civilian aircraft may not use military facilities, but in an emergency, the military will help out.

Keep in mind too that many major airline terminals have full time medical staffs on the airport. In a pinch, ATC can find out for you.

If you've got an air to ground telephone aboard, and are in range of a ground station, getting medical advice is easy. You can call the patient's physician directly and ask his advice. Or if he's not available, certainly the ground station can place a call to the emergency room at a nearby hospital.

There's no end of help available in a medical emergency if you can establish communications to the ground. But before the emergency crops up you should have a plan.

We said earlier that *assessment* of the situation is the key to handling the medical emergency. The airlines accomplish this by seeing that their cabin crews are trained in first aid. In a corporate operation, the flight crew should have recurrent first-aid training too, and none's better than that offered by your local Red Cross. These courses are given in community adult education programs or as a separate service of your local Red Cross chapter. In some circumstances, arrangements can be made for a concentrated course at your facility. Details are available from your local Red Cross office.

In the meantime, you need a list right now of emergencies serious enough to require immediate medical attention. There are dozens of factors to consider when assessing the seriousness of a medical emergency. But the basic rule is: *If in doubt, get the passenger to competent medical aid*

361

Business and Commercial Aviation

PASSENGER/FLIGHT CREW

Medical Emergency Procedures

☐ Assess situation.
☐ Assign crewmember or passenger to render first aid and to stay with the patient.

    1. Loosen the patient's tie, shirt and belt.
    2. If not breathing, apply artificial respiration.
    3. If having breathing difficulty, or in case of suspected heart
    attack, administer oxygen.
    4. Keep patient immobile, preferably reclining.
    5. If unconscious, search the patient for medical card or tag and
    follow applicable instructions.

☐ Notify ATC of medical emergency and if diversion is required, ask that an ambulance and medical crew meet the aircraft and that a hospital be notified of suspected medical problem.
☐ Notify company of medical emergency and intentions.

    ATC, Arinc, FBOs or airline company radios can work up direct phone
    patch or relay with physician if necessary.

☐ Descend or bring cabin altitude to sea level gently.
☐ Suspected death: Continue to administer oxygen and land immediately. Ask ATC to have local authorities and ambulance standing by.
☐ Company doctor:_____

             Name   Phone

Any medical emergency checklist must be tailored to the needs of your own operations and its passengers. Your checklist should include at least these items.

immediately. Here's a list of conditions which dictate an immediate diversion for medical attention:
- Severe chest, head or abdominal pain.
- Respiratory difficulty.
- Unconsciousness.
- Heavy bleeding (internal or external from any cause).
- Metabolic problems associated with known diabetes.

Severe trauma is rare in general aviation inflight emergencies, but a bout with unexpected severe turbulence can produce fractures, head and internal injuries or scalding from hot water and coffee. More often, however, the corporate flight crew will be faced with non-traumatic medical conditions—heart attack, stroke (apoplexy), epileptic convulsions, unconsciousness (from many causes), choking from foreign bodies in the throat or air passages, appendicitis, and drug or food poisoning. All of these conditions require quick medical aid.

Your first-aid course should deal with each of these conditions in detail. (Make sure the instructor is prepared to place emphasis on the recognition and first-aid treatment of these conditions.)

There is one first-aid consideration that the flight crew should always keep in mind. The human body functions best at sea level pressure and with at least sea level oxygen. Whenever a passenger shows evidence of respiratory problems or any of the symptoms of heart attack, stroke or shock, get him on oxygen and get the cabin to sea level. (In the case of unconsciousness, make sure the patient is on his side to keep air passages clear. Never leave a patient on oxygen unattended. The mask may have to be removed quickly if the patient vomits.)

Your first-aid training will cover appropriate measures for most inflight medical emergencies you can meet. We'll talk only of one here—heart attack. Symptoms vary greatly, but certain signs are fairly common:
- Shortness of breath.
- Pain varying in intensity from mild to severe, most often centered in the chest.
- Perspiration caused by the pain.
- Bluish color of the lips and fingernails (from oxygen starvation).
- Swelling of the extremities.

If the passenger has been under medical care for a heart condition, he may have medication with him. Assist in any way possible to have him take that medication. Get him on oxygen; get the cabin pressure to sea level as quickly as possible, and start heading for the nearest airport where an ambulance and medical team can meet the aircraft. Be sure ATC knows that you suspect heart attack and that the ground facilities will be equipped to deal with the emergency. Make sure the passenger is recumbent and do not allow him to move around the cabin.

The corporate flight crew has one thing going for it that airline flight crews do not. Corporate flight crews generally know their passengers and therefore can anticipate possible medical emergencies and be prepared to meet them.

If one of your regular passengers has a serious medical problem that could crop up inflight, you should know about it. Getting that information can be touchy but there are several avenues to try. Large companies often have their own medical departments. When this is the case, it is entirely appropriate for the chief pilot to check with the company doctor informally to see if the doctor is aware of any special medical problems among the regular passengers that flight crews should be aware of.

Other companies ask regular passengers to fill out forms which list their food, beverage and accommodations preferences, and subtly inquire into any special medical problems that might appear inflight. In smaller companies the chief pilot may be able to compile this information from talks with the appropriate secretaries.

It is especially important to have this information on overseas flights where medical attention may be difficult to get on short notice. If a passenger has a heart pacemaker, you may want to avoid military installations that bristle with radar antennas, and you certainly wouldn't want to take him into a FBO passenger lounge that has microwave ovens.

Passengers with known heart and metabolic diseases often carry medications that are absolutely vital. These medications should always be carried in the aircraft medical kit. Of course, you'll need the passenger's cooperation in obtaining prescription drugs.

You should also have the phone numbers (home, office and answering service) of the doctors of regular passengers with serious medical problems —especially in the case of known heart conditions. A diversion and ambulance ride could be saved if the patient (or crew) could talk to a doctor familiar with the case—another reason the air to ground telephone is important equipment for business aircraft.

Obviously, each aircraft must be equipped with a first-aid kit and the crew must know how to use it. We recommend two—one, normally kept sealed, containing the rarely needed severe trauma treatment items, the other stocked with items to treat minor illnesses, small cuts and burns.

The latter kit should also contain any special medicines needed by regular passengers. The contents of the trauma kit should be inspected every six months and resealed. Keep the kit up-to-date not only in terms of the shelf life of its contents but also in terms of new techniques in first-aid. For example, many older first-aid kits contain burn bandages impregnated with petroleum jelly. Today burn experts prefer dry sterile bandages. The flight crew can't be expected to keep entirely abreast on the latest techniques of trauma management, but it can certainly receive annual recurrent first-aid training and make sure that the contents of the first-aid kit reflects any important changes in the initial emergency treatment of trauma.

There is one pitfall in updating your first-aid kit that should be kept in mind. The Vietnam war brought many new treatments in first-aid for traumatic injuries, but most of these techniques are designed for ground implementation. For example, the pneumatic splint has been widely publicized. It's an airbag which slips over the broken appendage and inflates to immobilize the limb. It works great on the ground but could be dangerous to the aircraft passenger. If the bag is inflated at a relatively low cabin altitude, it will end up over-inflated as cabin altitude increases. This can be uncomfortable for the patient and could be dangerous if the splint applied enough pressure to the appendage to cut off the blood supply. Conversely, as cabin altitude decreases, the splint can collapse allowing movement of the fracture. So as a general rule, avoid any first-aid device that is sensitive to pressure changes. This includes medications in spray cans.

Your day-to-day, first-aid kit should contain the first-aid items found in the typical household medicine chest including non-prescription pain killers, antiseptics, adhesive bandages and anti-diarrheal preparations. It's a good idea to keep a running inventory on the contents of this kit. The stuff has a tendency to go pretty fast.

At one time or another you may end up in the very unhappy situation of having a passenger die onboard. In that event the crew is on its own. There are no simple guidelines, but here are a few things to think about.

· Unless you have the extraordinarily good luck to have a physician onboard, someone has to take the responsibility of deciding that the passenger is in fact dead if you make any other decision than to land immediately. Some conditions of stroke and unconsciousness (from other causes) so nearly resemble death that even the doctors can't be sure without good electronic equipment. (We've all heard stories about "dead" people being shipped off to the hospital morgue only to be shipped back to the ward again quite alive.) So if you've got any doubt at all about the morbidity of the passenger, get him to medical aid immediately and let the professionals worry about pronouncing him dead and your company worry about cutting through red tape to get the body home.

· If there is no doubt about death, then the company and the passenger's relatives will surely appreciate the return of the body to home base. But keep in mind that you could run afoul of local laws if you make a fuel stop on the way back and fail to notify authorities that a dead person is aboard. We've heard some lawyers point out that it's best if the passenger dies on the last leg of the trip. (Remember the problems the Secret Service had trying to get John Kennedy out of Dallas?)

In handling medical emergencies, the corporate pilot must be a combination of Steve Canyon, Joyce Brothers and Jim Kildare. It's a tough act, but thoughtful preparation will go a long way when an onboard crisis develops.

The decisions the flight crew must make in a medical emergency often do not lend themselves to inclusion in the department's operations manual —what to do with a death onboard, for instance. But there certainly should be informal guidelines freely discussed in crew briefing sessions.

Summing it up then, here's a flight department checklist for medical emergency preparedness.

(1) Initial and recurrent first-aid training for every flight crewmember.

(2) Preparation and regular inspection of aircraft first-aid kits—both the heavy trauma kit and the day-to-day medicine box.

(3) Passenger data file on regular flight department customers including (a) known serious medical conditions, (b) required medicine list, (c) doctors' names and phone numbers.

(4) Inclusion in the operations manual of a list which names company personnel who should be notified immediately in case of a diversion for a medical emergency.

(5) Installation of an air-ground telephone to improve the crew's ability to communicate with the proper emergency contacts on the ground.

Lifesaving Techniques for Flight Crews 47

by Dan Manningham

Unconsciousness and death are a grisly business. There is little anyone can do about death, but immediate and professional attention in instances of unconsciousness can save a life. In the remote confines of an airplane aloft, it poses a critical lifesaving challenge that will almost assuredly fall to the flight crew. Naturally they cannot perform miracles, but there are three proven first-aid techniques every professional pilot should know.

Artificial respiration or emergency ventilation is, by definition, any procedure for causing air to flow into and out of a person's lungs when natural breathing is inadequate. Techniques have changed significantly over the past 25 years, but experts are now unanimous in endorsing the mouth-to-mouth method for virtually all instances of arrested breathing. The older manual methods are recommended only for those cases in which mouth-to-mouth is not possible, such as in the case of massive facial injury.

The human body cannot store oxygen. It needs a continuous fresh supply to carry on the life process. Every cell requires that basic chemical element extracted by the lungs and transported by blood, and brain tissue is the most sensitive of all to oxygen starvation. After four to six minutes without oxygen, the brain will probably be damaged to the extent that, even if breathing is resumed, the victim might never recover consciousness.

As you can see, speed is essential. The symptoms of a respiratory emergency are basic:

· Breathing is arrested or severely impaired.
· Consciousness is lost.
· The victim's tongue, lips and fingernails assume a blue coloring.
· Choking or gasping may be present.

When confronted with these symptoms, and especially if they are in combination, begin artificial respiration at once. The average person will die in six minutes or less and some of that time will have passed before you even discover the problem. The procedure is very straightforward.

PROBLEMS

First roll the victim on his back in a location that will allow you to kneel alongside the head. The procedure can be performed in almost any position, but when possible, the supine position is beneficial for both rescuer and victim.

Wipe any visible foreign matter from the victim's mouth to prevent it from being inhaled by the victim. Open the mouth and quickly extract any matter you can see while being careful not to inadvertently drive it deeper into the throat area.

With the victim on his back, if possible, and the mouth cleared, tilt the head back so that the chin is pointing upward. This is best accomplished by lifting the neck with one hand while rotating the head back with the other hand on the forehead (Figure 1). This simple head motion opens the airway by lifting the tongue from the back of the throat. Breathing may resume spontaneously without any further action.

If voluntary breathing is not resumed, hold the head back with a continuous lifting pressure under the neck, but be careful not to break the victim's neck. Now pinch the nostrils shut with the thumb and index finger of the hand that is pressing on the forehead; this will prevent leakage of air when the victim's lungs are inflated by your blowing into his mouth. Take a deep breath, seal your mouth securely around the victim's and blow forcefully. As you blow, watch his chest rise and stop blowing when it is expanded. Raise your head and turn it to the side so as to observe the chest fall and

Figure 1

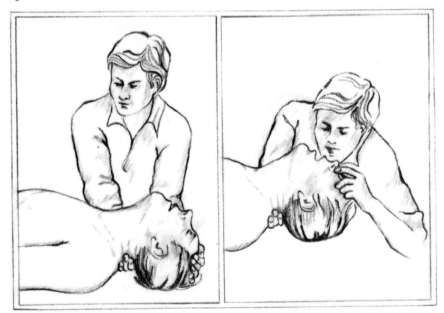

hear the exhalation. Avoid rebreathing the patient's exhaled air. Repeat the cycle at least 12 times per minute.

Ambient air contains 21 percent oxygen, and the normal tidal volume of a resting adult is 500 to 1000 cubic centimeters. Mouth-to-mouth ventilation can provide up to 2000 cubic centimeters of exhaled air per breath and that air will retain 16 percent oxygen. When properly executed, mouth-to-mouth respiration can provide a greater volume of air and oxygen than the victim would receive by normal breathing. In most cases, recovery is rapid.

Drug overdose, carbon monoxide poisoning or electric shock may require prolonged artificial respiration, and the procedure should always be continued until:

· Victim breathes for himself, or
· He is dead beyond any doubt.

When a victim revives he should be treated for shock, including rest and warm coverings.

Supplemental oxygen, when available, would be most desirable as soon as the patient resumes breathing. You should consider diverting to the nearest suitable airport and request that an ambulance meet the airplane. Don't be afraid to declare an emergency.

Choking on food ranks as the sixth most common cause of accidental death. Typically, a large unchewed piece of food, called a bolus, is inadvertently sucked into the windpipe in the process of eating. This physical obstruction to the airway cannot be dislodged by the victim's own efforts and without help he will rapidly die of strangulation. This is not a rare occurrence.

Due to its repeated occurrence in restaurants and the illusive resemblance to a heart attack, the phenomenon has acquired the name of café coronary. Diagnosis is not difficult:

· Café coronary is limited to eating situations.
· The victim will be unable to speak because his windpipe is blocked.
· He will be trying to breathe and will certainly choke and struggle and clutch at his neck.
· Pulse will be normal or faster.

Dr. Henry J. Heimlich of the University of Cincinnati College of Medicine has developed a technique to dislodge the bolus and restore spontaneous breathing. Reasoning that food can only be drawn into the windpipe while the lungs are expanding, Dr. Heimlich concluded that there is always some air in the lungs. His technique involves a sudden forceful compression of the abdomen to force air out of the lungs and eject the offending bolus like the cork of a pop gun. In fact, the procedure is called the "pop method" of first aid for café coronary.

Figure 2 illustrates the preferred position for executing the pop procedure. Stand behind the victim and put both arms around him just above the

369

Figure 2

belt line and beneath the rib cage. Your hands must be positioned beneath the rib cage to avoid puncturing the lungs with a rib. Allow his head, arms and upper body to hang forward. Grasp your own right wrist with your left hand and rapidly press into the victim's abdomen with a strong, sharp squeeze. This action compresses the lungs, forcing the bolus out under the resulting air pressure.

If there is not enough room to stand up, as in many aircraft, or if the victim is lying down, it is not necessary to pick him up. When the victim is lying face down, the rescuer straddles the buttocks and reaches under the body with both arms to exert the same squeeze. If he is on his back, sit astride him and suddenly press with both hands into the abdominal region.

In both reclining cases a second person should be prepared to remove the ejected food from the victim's mouth. In nearly all cases breathing will resume spontaneously, but you may have to use artificial respiration if the

370

victim has strangled for a prolonged period. As in all emergency cases, treat for shock and have an ambulance waiting at your intended landing point.

When the heart stops beating, the circulation of blood is immediately curtailed. Death occurs within a very few minutes as critical areas of the brain succumb to oxygen starvation. The symptoms are obvious:

· Pulse is absent immediately. You can best check that at the carotid arteries along the sides of the neck near the Adam's apple.

· The pupils of the eyes will dilate fully open within a minute.

· Breathing may be slow, gasping or absent.

· The patient assumes a lifeless appearance with pale, clammy, bluish skin.

· The patient is normally able to speak and will have chest pains that radiate into the left arm or neck.

It is essential in such cases of cardiac arrest to restore the flow of blood so as to distribute that critical oxygen supply. Blood circulation can be mechanically restored and maintained on an emergency basis by a simple procedure called external heart compression.

The heart is located between the breastbone (sternum) and the spine. When a person is lying on his back, pressure on the lower half of the sternum compresses the heart between that bone and the spine. Such compression squeezes blood out of the heart's chambers (ventricles) through the pulmonary circuit, where it gathers oxygen, and through the arteries for general distribution. When external pressure is relaxed, the ventricles dilate and draw returning blood out of the veins. Repeated compression cycles create a forward movement of blood sufficient to sustain and even restore life although it is only 25 to 35 percent as efficient as normal circulation.

The first step is to verify cardiac arrest. Feel for pulse at the carotid artery with the middle and index finger (Figure 3). Feel only one side at a time so as not to shut off the flow of blood to the brain. If there is no pulse, begin the external heart compression.

Place the patient on a solid surface, preferably the floor, but any flat, solid object will do. This firm undersurface is absolutely essential for effective heart compression. Kneel to one side of the patient's chest and locate the lower half of the breastbone, which will be the compression site. Place the heel of one hand on the compression site, then rotate the hand toward the little finger until the heel is parallel to the midline of the chest. This position assures that the force will be applied to the sternum and not to the more fragile ribs. Now place the other hand on the back of the compression hand and extend all your fingers upward to keep them off the rib cage (Figure 4). All the compression force must be on the sternum in order to prevent damage to ribs and internal organs.

371

PROBLEMS

Figure 3

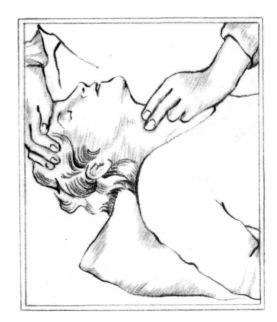

Figure 4

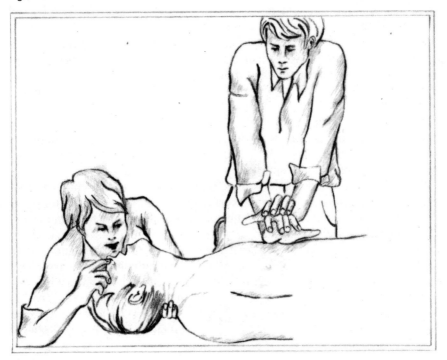

Check that your arms are at right angles to the sternum and that your body is positioned directly opposite the compression point.

Now push forcefully down onto the chest, using the arms as levers and your body weight for force. As you push, rock your body upward so that your shoulders are directly over the patient's sternum when the maximum force is being delivered. That downward thrust should be in a smooth, deliberate motion with enough force, about 80 to 120 pounds (which you can judge from the proportion of your own weight being applied) to depress the sternum one and one-half to two inches. Allow one-half second for the downward thrust and then withdraw your hand pressure quickly. Allow another half second for refilling of the ventricles and repeat the cycle once every second.

Concentrate on a steady, rhythmic 60-per-minute cycle with smooth, forceful compression followed by a quick release and a half-second pause. Keep both hands together and in contact with the sternum to avoid pounding the chest. The work is much more strenuous than you might imagine, but when properly executed, external heart compression will produce a discernible pulse and a blood pressure of 100 or more. There should be no break in the rhythm and heart compression should continue for a substantial time until the victim is either revived or obviously and irrevocably dead. In an airplane, that will very likely mean until you land and the ambulance crew can take over. As in other emergencies, the pilot will want to advise ATC and consider declaring an emergency.

In most emergency cases of arrested breathing or heart attack, it is necessary to apply both artificial ventilation and artificial circulation. Cardiopulmonary resuscitation, or CPR for short, is a combination of artificial respiration and external heart compression that provides oxygen *and* circulation for the patient whose vital signs have stopped. The procedures are the same as described previously, but they must be coordinated to be effective.

If there is only one rescuer, he begins the mouth-to-mouth ventilation and continues for four breaths. He then depresses the sternum 15 times in approximately 12 seconds. This cycle is repeated until help is available. The workload for one man is tremendous, and you may not be physically able to continue for very long, but even a brief coordinated effort may suffice to revive the patient.

When two rescuers are available, one performs the mouth-to-mouth respiration, while the other applies external heart compression. A normal compression frequency of 60 per minute is established and the lungs are then inflated on every fifth compression release. It takes some coordination and practice to precisely fit the ventilation between compression strokes, but it can be done and the procedure is extremely effective when performed by two skillful operators.

CHECKLIST FOR CARDIOPULMONARY RESUSCITATION

Artificial Respiration:

(1) Diagnose the problem.

(2) Remove foreign matter from mouth and throat.

(3) Hyperextend the neck.

(4) Pinch patient's nose closed.

(5) Seal your mouth over patient's and blow enough force to expand his chest.

(6) Lift your head to observe the chest fall and hear the exhalation.

(7) Repeat 12 times per minute.

External Heart Compression

(1) Check for pulse at carotid artery.

(2) Position heel of compression hand on patient's midsternum.

(3) Using both hands, compress the sternum one and one-half to two inches using 80 to 120 pounds of force.

(4) Repeat 60 times per minute.

Cardiopulmonary Resuscitation

One rescuer: Alternately ventilate four times in 20 seconds and compress 12 times in 15 seconds.

Two rescuers: Coordinate ventilation and compression so that patient's lungs are inflated after every fifth compression.

Cardiopulmonary resuscitation is an established and respected technique and there is a wealth of material available for the uninitiated. Films, literature and even speakers are often available from local power companies, telephone companies, and fire and police departments. We found them to be willing and even eager to share their experience and expertise.

As we said in the beginning, unconsciousness and death are a fearsome prospect, especially in the close confines of an airplane. These emergency techniques will allow you to be far more than another anxious spectator. They may very well save a life.

Deep Stall

48

by Dan Manningham

The prototype aircraft, a swept-wing, T-tail, aft-engine transport, was engaged in a series of test flights to assess stability and handling characteristics during approach to and recovery from stalls, with the CG in varying positions. On the fifth stall of the subject flight, at 16,000 feet, the aircraft sank into a high angle-of-attack situation and continued to descend at a high vertical speed and in a substantially horizontal attitude until it struck the ground. At impact it had very little forward speed.

The probable cause? During the stall the aircraft entered a stable stalled condition, from which recovery was impossible. Call it what you like: super stall, deep stall, stable stall. The phenomenon is widely misunderstood, even though several light and medium business jet aircraft include design characteristics that are conducive to this awesome phenomenon.

Deep stall is essentially a condition in which very large angles of attack develop after a stall. Locked-in deep stall (sometimes called stable stall) can develop if elevator effectiveness is not sufficient to compensate for the pitch-up tendency of the aircraft in the post-stall regime. In that case, the aircraft diverges to really excessive angles of attack and sinks into an ever more downward-inclining flight path as the wings progressively lose lift. Ultimately, the angle of attack approaches 90 degrees as the aircraft stabilizes in a vertical descent in a nearly level attitude. In that regime none of the flight controls have even the slightest effect, and recovery is simply not possible.

You might think that such a possibility would be in violation of some FAR, but that is not the case. Certification stall requirements are not very comprehensive. They require adequate stall warning, unmistakable stall identification and a clean drop of the nose at the stall. If those characteristics cannot be incorporated in the basic aerodynamic design of the wings, horizontal surfaces and fuselage, they can be simulated with horns, stick shakers and stick pushers at some speed prior to the actual stall. This type of pre-stall protection can cover even the ugliest stall problem and is often used to satisfy existing regulations. Unfortunately, the pure stall quality may be treacherous in the extreme, and in the event of failure of these stall prevention devices, or turbulence-induced aerodynamic stall, the pilot could be faced with stability and control responses that contradict everything he has learned.

It may be impossible to determine the actual stall characteristics of your airplane; they may be unknown even to the manufacturer. If they are potentially troublesome, he will avoid the problem by providing artificial warning and recovery systems that actuate at some speed above the true stall. In fact, stick shakers and stick pushers are nearly conclusive evidence that the certificating agency felt that the true natural stall might be less than docile. Below those stall speeds (or above those critical angles of attack), there is a no man's land from which recovery may be impossible.

Several elements contribute to poor stall qualities—some are a function of design and some are operational. Let us consider them.

Swept Wings. Swept wings provide one specific benefit—they delay the critical Mach number to enable aircraft to fly closer to the speed of sound. However, in some instances this speed gain is offset by several adverse characteristics, such as Dutch roll, spiral instability and control problems near the stalling regime. Wings designed with more than a minimum of sweepback have naturally high lift coefficients at the tips. As a result, the tips tend to stall first, shifting the center of lift forward and producing a pitch-up moment from the unbalanced lift distribution. In some cases, when the angle of attack is high enough, flow separation will begin at the ailerons. When that happens, the ailerons float upward and contribute an added pitching moment to an already unstable situation. The final result is a reverse of the normal positive longitudinal stability. At some critical angle of attack, the nose begins to pitch up by itself, very possibly against any elevator correction.

There are several ways to minimize or even reverse this pitch divergence. Some designers utilize washout so that the tips operate at an angle of attack lower than that of the rest of the wing. With enough washout, the tip will stall either at the same time as or after the root, providing pitch-down, or at least reduced pitch-up. Washout is effective in modifying early tip stall, but it greatly detracts from wing efficiency in cruise, so engineers are naturally reluctant to use more than the minimum.

The Russians have made a lot of noise about the wing design of their Ilyushin-62 airliner. Those swept wings have a sort of sawtooth on the leading edge at about the mid-span point that supposedly prevents early tip stall and provides for acceptable stall qualities without artificial warning or control.

Some designs incorporate fences to prevent an outward, spanwise airflow, which also destroys lift at the wing tips as angle of attack approaches the stall. There are, in fact, a whole bag of tricks to suppress this raw pitch-up tendency and get an inboard section stalled first. Nevertheless,

376

even when the initial separation occurs inboard, the tips may later become fully stalled before the roots. When that happens, it is entirely possible to encounter pitch-up by simply penetrating the stall area too deeply.

T-Tail. Efficient flight, especially at high subsonic speeds, requires that drag be reduced to an absolute minimum. One significant source of drag is the horizontal tail section. It conventionally operates in the area of disturbed air off the fuselage and wing roots. This reduces its effectiveness, which in turn demands an otherwise unnecessarily large tail area with consequent drag penalties.

When the horizontal tail section is repositioned so as to remove it from the area of disturbed air, it can be made significantly smaller. A smaller area means less drag. Less drag means added performance. As a result, the T-tail is a popular feature with aircraft designers, who are now beginning to use it even on turboprop and light single-engine aircraft. While the high tail reduces drag, however, it can also introduce very serious problems near the stall regime.

Conventional aircraft, as you will recall from your early ground school sessions, possess combined dynamic and aerodynamic pitching moments that naturally cause the nose to "fall through" at the stall. Dynamically, airplanes are nose-heavy; that is, they are designed so that the CG is always forward of the center of lift. Thus, *dynamically,* airplanes want to dive. To offset nose-heaviness, horizontal surfaces at the tail push *down* to maintain an aerodynamic equilibrium. As the speed drops off, the aerodynamic effectiveness of horizontal surfaces, including the elevators, diminishes, and the dynamic nose-heaviness takes over. As a further guarantee that the nose will drop just prior to the stall, low-mounted horizontal tail surfaces are immersed in wing wake (Figure 1). This reduces their effectiveness so as to naturally prevent any deep penetration beyond stalling angles of attack. Should a deep stall develop, the low tail is again in an area of clear airflow (Figure 2) and becomes effective in pushing the nose down.

T-tail aircraft, especially those with swept wings, may very well reverse those conventional (and desirable) stalling characteristics. At or near the stall, high-mounted elevators are still operating in clean air with full effectiveness (Figure 3), which, in some instances, makes it possible to pull the nose up far beyond the stall into an unknown and possibly dangerous regime. After the nose comes up, a critically high angle of attack develops, and the high tail finally dips into the low-energy turbulent wake off the fuselage and wing roots. This severely degrades the elevators' effectiveness at the worst possible time, so it may no longer be able to counteract the extreme nose-up pitch (Figure 4).

Variable-incidence stabilizers seriously complicate the recovery problem. Those trimmable tail planes are normally fitted with a small elevator designed to operate only as a short-term angle-of-attack regulator. Sus-

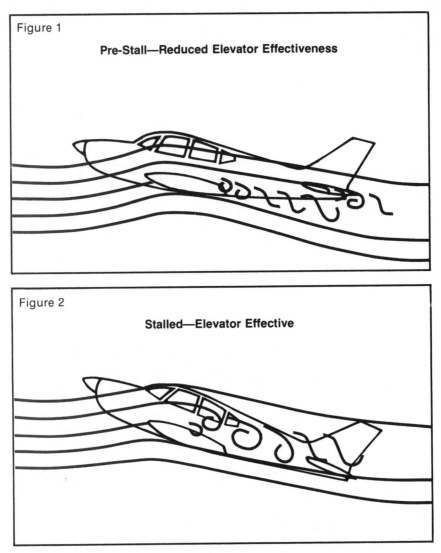

Figure 1

Pre-Stall—Reduced Elevator Effectiveness

Figure 2

Stalled—Elevator Effective

At the stalling point, the low-mounted tail plane moves out of the disturbed air of the wing wake into the clean flow below—a desirable characteristic because effectiveness is restored in the nose-down direction.

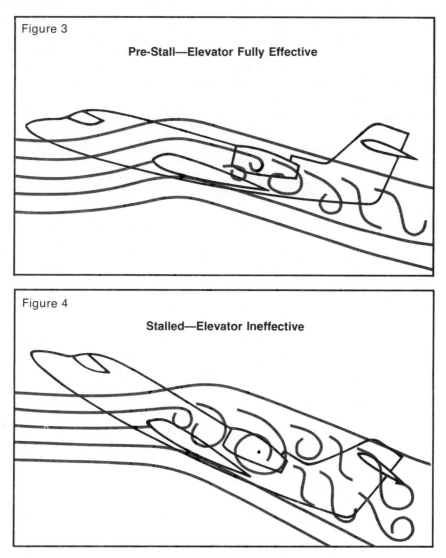

Figure 3

Pre-Stall—Elevator Fully Effective

Figure 4

Stalled—Elevator Ineffective

As the nose comes up on T-tailed aircraft, the tail plane dips into the wing wake turbulence, critically reducing the elevator's effectiveness. Now a real threat of deep stall exists because unwanted nose-up pitch may no longer be counteracted.

tained corrections are reserved for the stabilizer itself. Near the stall, where really gross pitch changes are often required, the elevator just may not be large enough. At such extreme sustained angles, the wings very rapidly shed whatever lift they may have been producing, and the airplane settles into a steep descent that further increases the angle of attack while reducing tail effectiveness to zero. It sounds grim and it is.

Aft-Mounted Engines. Aft-mounted engines solve a lot of problems. They lower VMC by reducing asymmetrical yaw during engine-out operation. They allow the wing to be aerodynamically optimized without the restrictions imposed by powerplant considerations. They may eliminate the danger of foreign object ingestion and reduce aircraft cabin noise. As you can imagine, however, those advantages are not achieved without some trade-off.

Engines attached to the rear fuselage obviously shift the CG well aft, relative to the fuselage. In order to keep the center of lift aft of that CG, the wings must be set well aft, which in turn leaves a long overhanging fuselage in front. That long forward fuselage is troublesome for two reasons. First, in the instance of large pitch changes, the inertial forces associated with sheer length tend to generate an overswing beyond the desired pitch adjustment, which can induce or aggravate the pitch-up that can lead to a deep stall. Secondly, far above the stalling incidence, when the wings have shed most or all of their lift, that forward fuselage, which is also a very fat airfoil, will continue to generate lift with a nose-up component.

Rear engines raise several other serious stability and control considerations. The mass of fuel lines, control linkages and systems plumbing is very evenly distributed along the fuselage, which increases yawing inertia and contributes to a flat-spin potential. In addition, the even weight distribution may also result in the CG being *aft* of whatever lift components remain at extreme angles of attack. Finally, the rear-mounted engines are in a perfect position to blank out the tail at extreme angles of attack when the wing wake is too steep to do so.

Perhaps the most serious operational consideration over which the pilot has some degree of control is the matter of aircraft loading. As the CG moves aft, the threat of deep stall is decidedly increased. Rearward CGs degrade the elevator's nose-down pitch authority and reduce the natural pitch-down tendency. Swept-wing aircraft are often very close to maximum allowable aft CG when operating with full fuel and no payload, as on dead-head or ferry trips. In one recent B-727 accident that appears to have involved a deep stall, the subject aircraft was operating on a ferry trip with the CG beyond aft limits because some required ballast was never loaded. When it is possible to do so, load your aircraft so as to achieve a CG comfortably forward of the rearmost limit.

One other operational consideration applies to training flights that include stall practice. If the necessary speed reduction is performed too rapidly, and/or the aircraft is in accelerated flight, it is possible to inadvertently penetrate into the post-stall regime, an area that is almost unexplored and certainly dangerous. The greater your rate of speed decay, the less time you will have between stall warning and actual stall, or between stall and deep stall. That margin can be as little as three or four knots, so a slow entry provides the best protection. Even if the airplane did have stability reversal, a competent pilot could probably control it if the entry were made slowly enough.

So, then, those are the elements that contribute to the possibility of a deep stall. Even if your airplane has all the worst features, however, it is most unlikely that you'll ever have to face that awesome maneuver as long as you keep the airspeed up, the stabilizer trimmed and the load within limits. Nevertheless, it is foolish to ignore the possibility, so let's look at how the whole grisly business might develop.

Deep stall by definition must begin with a stall, which naturally presumes excessive angle of attack. There are several ways to get there: slowing down while holding altitude, holding a constant rate of climb with progressively increasing pitch angle, steepening a turn as the airspeed bleeds off. Also, there is always the risk of a gust-induced angle-of-attack increase brought about by strong wind shear. However it may happen, the initial excessive angle of attack is the first element in the chain of events.

If the airplane has a longitudinal stability problem, the stage is really set for disaster because, beyond the true stall, pitch divergence may make it impossible to adequately control the nose-up action. In that event, the airplane will self-induce a penetration into the post-stall area deep enough to reach the crossover point. At the crossover, the reduction in lift from the stalled areas of the wing exceeds the increase in lift from the unstalled areas. Beyond crossover, the airplane settles rapidly.

Now the bottom falls out as the airplane sinks into an ever steepening downward flight path, despite the nose-high attitude. This settling motion rapidly increases the angle of attack, and any remaining elevator effectiveness is seriously compromised as the wing wake begins to envelop the high tail. Even if you manage to rotate the nose 10 or 15 degrees downward, the settling will very likely increase the angle of attack faster than you can reduce it with pitch change.

Now you are settling, nose high, wings probably level, tail at least partially blanked out, with the airspeed decreasing far below stalling values. The angle of attack continues to increase to nearly 90 degrees as the airplane sinks into an almost vertical descent. The nose may fall toward level as the forward fuselage sheds any lift it may have been producing, and the airframe stabilizes into a flight path normally reserved for falling bricks. There may be some rotation in the yaw axis, but that slow turning is an academic peculiarity and will not contribute to a recovery. The airplane will not be in a flat spin; it may not rotate at all. It will be in a stabilized stall.

Since none of the flight controls were designed to work at angles of attack approaching 90 degrees, recovery from deep stall is impossible by any conventional means. The engines will be of little or no help because the gross angle of airflow across the intakes will cause deep compressor stalls and extreme loss of thrust, if indeed any thrust at all is available. Rather than sit and await their doom, the crew can try a number of things. If the aircraft has a drag chute, deploying it could cause the tail to be lifted enough to break the stall. Dropping the gear and running the flaps out could conceivably cause a pitch down, and even getting the passengers forward, if there is time, might help. We have discussed deep stall recovery techniques with one of the few men who has walked away from one. In fact, Walt Hensleigh, director of flying operations for Lockheed-Georgia, has recovered from two. The first time, the airplane popped out when a flight-test engineer ran forward to help another crewmember jettison the door. Later, during an FAA certification flight in the same program, the FAA pilot coaxed the airplane into a deep stall, but Hensleigh was ready with his hand on the spin-chute handle. When it deployed, the airplane snapped right out. These recoveries occurred, however, during flight tests with experienced crews onboard. It must be emphasized that, once a deep stall is entered in an operational situation, the likelihood of recovery is extremely remote.

As you can see, deep stall, especially locked-in deep stall, is a horror show. Manufacturers are naturally reluctant to discuss it since they have complied with all legal requirements and since pilots are most unlikely to ever encounter the problem. Still, if ignorance is bliss and knowledge is survival, then it is in the interest of safety to understand the possibility and prevention of even so rare a phenomenon.

Jet Upset 49

by Dan Manningham

In the early 1960s, several heavy airline jets were inadvertently involved in steep, high-speed dives. Major studies of the problem were initiated at that time, and those studies uncovered a pattern of events which gave birth to the term "jet upset."

Upset, or loss of control, is a potential hazard in any aircraft, although jet transports have operational and design characteristics that can exacerbate the basic problem. Specifically, there are four factors that contribute to the upset *potential* of jets.

· They routinely operate at high altitudes, with exposure to restricted speed ranges, reduced maneuvering capability and transonic instability.

· They have much higher momentum than do propeller types due to higher speeds and higher weight/volume ratio. This momentum, when combined with tremendous thrust and minimal drag, creates a massive overspeed potential.

· At the high Mach numbers associated with high-altitude overspeed excursions, unique stability and control problems develop that can combine to inhibit recovery from a steep descent.

· Swept-wing, high-tail airplanes are especially likely to have low-speed and/or high-angle-of-attack stability problems.

It is difficult to determine how closely airline experience relates to the typical business or executive operation. In fact there have been few, if any, serious upsets in corporate jet aircraft, although the possibility grows with the sheer number of aircraft and with the introduction of larger airplanes into corporate fleets. Knowledge is safety, however, and so corporate crews must be aware of the potential, however remote, plus when and under what conditions an upset is most likely to occur, how to avoid it and how to recover from it.

Of 15 reported airline jet upsets from 1959 through 1967, seven occurred during low-altitude climb and eight occurred during high-altitude cruise or cruise-climb. Those eight occurring at cruise altitudes fall in two distinct categories. Three seem to have been the result of turbulence-induced loss of control, and five were precipitated by autopilot problems. All resulted in steep dives from which recovery was complicated by the accumulative effects of extreme speed and consequent control problems.

One classic case occurred in a Boeing 720 at FL380 while attempting to top a thunderstorm over O'Neill, Nebraska. During cruise-climb the aircraft encountered turbulence, which pitched the nose up through 15 degrees with the yoke forward against the stops. The original report by the crew is awesome:

"The nose of the airplane continued to rise beyond the usable range of the artificial horizon, estimated in excess of 60 degrees and possibly vertical. No significant altitude changes were recalled up to this time; however, at the top of the nose-up attitude, the stars became visible. During a series of sustained negative G forces, the fuel-boost pump low-pressure lights came on; flight bags rose vertically; and the captain's maps and papers floated in front of the instrument panel.

"No stabilizer trimming was recalled. No difficulty was experienced with lateral control and the wings were level each time the nose came through the horizon.

"During the final pushover, to get the nose down and hold airspeed, the nose went down until the word 'Dive' appeared on the horizon instrument. The aircraft accelerated to about 300 knots and experienced severe buffets twice before reaching FL340. The aircraft then nosed over into the main dive. The airspeed went to 400-plus knots. At FL250, wings level, nose down about 35 degrees and over 400 KIAS, the elevator was solid and stabilizer trim inoperative. The copilot added a slight amount of power and the nose appeared to pitch up from thrust. More thrust was added and the dive rounded out at 14,000 feet. The captain believes the nose was coming up and the recovery could have been made without addition of thrust. Stabilizer trim functioned normally after level flight was regained."

The dive lasted 55 seconds at an average descent rate of 21,000 fpm. Maximum IAS readable on the flight recorder tape was 450 knots, although the stylus deflected to a point that would interpolate to 480 knots. Four-hundred and eighty knots IAS is equivalent to 1.2 Mach at FL300, 1.1 Mach at FL250 and just slightly above 1.0 Mach at FL200.

It would appear that this crew may have experienced a near-disastrous combination of several of the worst aspects of jet handling qualities.

At FL380, this B-720 would have been operating in a very narrowly restricted speed range where any significant reduction in speed or increase in G loading could precipitate a stall. That in itself is not unusual nor even very dangerous. What may not be fully understood is the static longitudinal instability that causes a "pitch-up" tendency at high angles of attack in many jet types.

In a condition of static longitudinal stability, an increase in the coefficient of lift will produce a consequent downward pitching moment. (See Figure

1). In other words, as the coefficient of lift (the horizontal line in Figure 1) increases at the approach to a stall, the downward pitching moment (vertical line) increases proportionately. Eventually, of course, the airfoil stalls and the nose falls through, even against a full-up elevator position. At least that's what's supposed to happen.

Actually there are several design characteristics that can contribute to marked instability at or near the stall. In the unstable condition, the curve reverses as in Figure 2, indicating an unstable pitching moment. Beyond some point in the coefficient of lift line, any further increase in angle of attack produces nose-up pitching moments, which tend to bring about further increases in angle of attack, and so on. That phenomenon is called "pitch-up," and it can have any of several causes.

Wings designed with a large degree of sweepback and taper normally have very high lift coefficients at the tip. In that case, the tip tends to stall first; the center of lift shifts forward; and the airplane pitches up from that unbalanced lift distribution. This is not a factor in any current-production corporate jets, but inboard wing leading-edge devices may complicate the problem, when extended, by preserving lift on inboard sections after the rest of the wing is stalled. Likewise, a flexible wing can be a contributor to pitch-up, but again it's doubtful whether any of the current business jets have enough flex for that to be a factor.

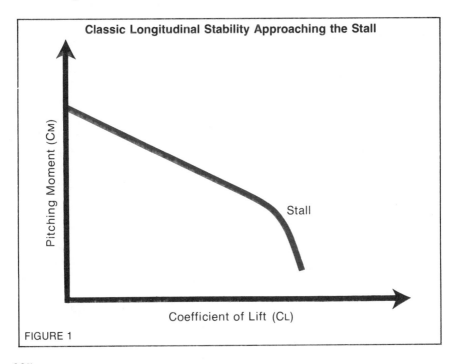

FIGURE 1

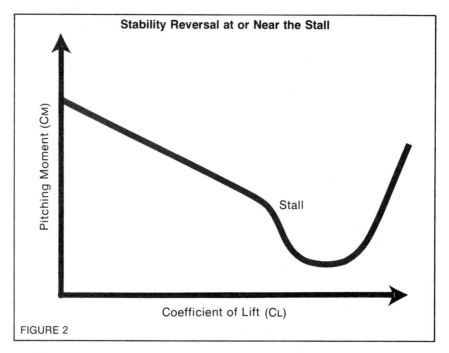

Stability Reversal at or Near the Stall

Pitching Moment (Cm)

Stall

Coefficient of Lift (CL)

FIGURE 2

Another source of pitch-up can be downwash at the horizontal tail. Since downwash decreases the angle of attack (and thus the downward push) of the tail, any increase in downwash with pitch angle is destabilizing. Certain configurations with low aspect ratios (short, stubby wings) have a problem with the horizontal tail actually entering the wing wake at high angles of attack. Some configurations with serious pitch instability may even be subject to deep stall.

Strong downwash can also be produced on high tails by fuselage-generated vortices at high angles of attack; the fuselage can further contribute to pitch-up by its own CL curve. At high angles of attack, the lift generated by the forward fuselage may increase with incidence well past the wing stall, intensifying the pitch-up caused by other factors.

Pitch-up may be the result of an airplane configuration that demonstrates otherwise desirable and even docile flying qualities. It is only associated with high angles of attack, although it's good to remember that high angles of attack do not necessarily require high pitch angles, especially in severe turbulence. Naturally aircraft manufacturers don't like to discuss that, and it is seldom, if ever, covered in training. Unfortunately, however, your kitten may be a real tiger above some critical angle of attack.

The B-720 in our example was climbing in a very restricted speed range in an area of thunderstorms. In other words, the airplane was at a high angle of attack, close to stall and subject to strong wind shear. The airplane configuration included highly swept and tapered wings, further accentuated by their flexibility, which would tend to unload the tips in gusts. If the aircraft encountered an updraft in this circumstance, the gust-induced angle of attack may well have precipitated a stall and driven the airplane into an area of pitch instability. The elevator simply didn't have the authority to counteract that pitch-up.

Elevators are an important part of this upset story, maybe the most important. Most airliners and several business jets are designed with a large trimmable stabilizer and a relatively small elevator. This feature allows for extended CG ranges, minimum drag and pitch control over a large speed range, but at the expense of elevator effectiveness. Simply stated, this primary longitudinal control becomes a short-term angle of attack regulator for brief-period pitch maneuvering and speed control. Stabilizer trim is required for any large or long-term corrections. In effect, traditional elevator authority is seriously degraded, especially in any out-of-trim condition. One degree of stabilizer mistrim commonly requires up to three degrees of elevator displacement.

If the airplane has a pitch-up tendency, the elevator may not have sufficient authority to counteract that instability and may still be quite legal because stability and control standards are only applicable to the certified operating envelope. If the airplane is unstable at the stall, it is simply fitted with a stick shaker or pusher activated just before the area of stability reversal. In normal flight there is plenty of warning. But in heavy turbulence at low speed, gust-induced angles of attack could easily drive the airplane into that unstable regime. Even then recovery would be quite simple if the elevator were big enough. Unfortunately, if the airplane is not certified for operation at that angle of attack, there is no requirement for elevator effectiveness. It's a never-never land of possible nightmare responses and ineffective controls.

Let's return for a moment to that 720 at FL380. Following its initial gross pitch excursion, the B-720 rounded over with strong negative Gs, and the nose dropped until the word "Dive" appeared on the AH. That's at least 30 degrees, and probably closer to 45 degrees, nose down.

The crew could not recall trimming the stabilizer, although others in similar circumstances have abused the trim and aggravated the recovery. In several reported cases of pitch-up due to strong wind shear, the crew has utilized massive nose-down trim in an effort to control the aircraft. Often, that trim takes effect just about the time the airplane moves from an updraft to a downdraft. When that happens, the nose pitches down from the accumulative effect of stabilizer setting and gust reversal. Now headed down at a steep angle, the speed rapidly builds and the crew pulls "back-stick" to round out, but they are in the never-never land at the high-speed end. Two separate factors are working to prevent their recovery.

(1) The stabilizer has been trimmed for airplane nose down and the crew is now opposing that trim with back elevator. Unfortunately, the anemic little elevator, designed for fine corrections in normal flight, cannot nearly overcome the effect of the enormous stabilizer trimmed nose down. (2) The stabilizer won't move because forces from the elevator displacement are large enough to stall the trim motors. One control is ineffective; the other is locked out. The only way to correct that lockout is by releasing back pressure until the stabilizer jackscrews are unloaded, then carefully introducing just enough stabilizer trim to recover level flight without pulling excessive Gs.

It takes almost superhuman presence of mind, but there is no other way to recover sufficient control power. To make matters worse, the airplane may accelerate into a Mach regime in which longitudinal control is seriously degraded.

Above some critical Mach number, shock waves on the tail so disturb the flow pattern that elevator effectiveness per unit of displacement may be reduced by 50 percent or more. One airline-type jet suffers a 45 percent loss in elevator effectiveness when Mach is increased from 0.85 to 0.87. At the same time, maximum elevator available is often reduced by the gross mistrim, and some types may be subject to structural deflection or bending of the stabilizer, which further detracts from, or even cancels, what little elevator control is left.

At extreme speeds you may be able to displace the elevator only a fraction of the normal throw, and that reduced movement will produce even less effect than it would in normal flight. There is not much you can do about this reduced elevator effect at high speed except to hang on until the Mach number drops at around 20,000 feet. As elevator effectiveness returns, there should be a progressive recovery.

It is not clear whether the B-720 over O'Neill suffered from a gross mistrim, but it does seem clear that the trim mechanism was stalled so that the pilots were unable to utilize the stabilizer. Certainly the elevator effectiveness would have been significantly reduced by the aircraft's penetration into speeds of at least 1.0 Mach.

Lest you get the wrong impression, let us emphasize that jet upset is by no means a high-altitude phenomenon. In fact, low- to medium-altitude upsets are probably more common and more disastrous. Of the 15 aforementioned upsets, 10 were unrelated to equipment malfunction. Of those 10, seven occurred between 2000 and 19,000 feet; five aircraft crashed or broke up in the air; and two were damaged during the pullout.

Several common factors stand out. Six of the seven were climbing. All were in moderate to heavy turbulence. All entered steep dives. All were damaged or totalled. Invariably, upsets were confined to the pitching plane. That fact alone created something of a controversy, which has never been resolved.

Captain Paul Soderlind has published several papers on jet upset that have become the standard, accepted documents on the subject. Captain Soderlind places primary emphasis on the static stability of the aircraft and the pitch indications available to pilots. His theory goes like this:

All airplanes are always statically stable. Therefore, they will always weathervane into a gust as indicated in Figure 3. If, for example, the airplane is struck by gust 8 in the diagram, it will pitch down but actually go up. That contradiction to normal aircraft response produces conflicting pitch information, which is misinterpreted by the pilot. In effect, Soderlind says that pilots rely too much on altitude and airspeed as pitch indicators. When the aircraft pitches down in an updraft, they are apt to ignore the AH and push steeper into a dive, abuse the trim and precipitate an upset. In fact, he suggests that pilots ought to cover the airspeed indicator, altimeter and VSI while penetrating turbulence so they will not be distracted from attitude instrumentation.

Opposed to that theory stands Jack Clark, senior captain for a major trunk carrier. Clark has spent more than 20 years on upset research and is convinced that jet transports often have serious stability problems, particularly with reference to pitch-up. His scenario for a typical upset begins with that same gust:

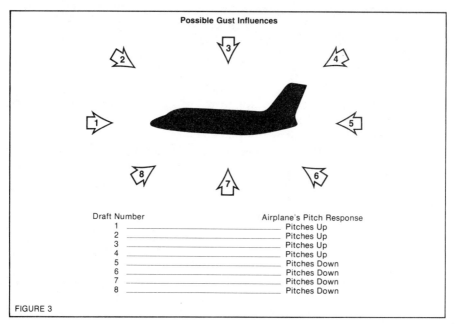

Possible Gust Influences

Draft Number	Airplane's Pitch Response
1	Pitches Up
2	Pitches Up
3	Pitches Up
4	Pitches Up
5	Pitches Down
6	Pitches Down
7	Pitches Down
8	Pitches Down

FIGURE 3

PROBLEMS

Using 8 from Soderlind's diagram again, Clark says that upon entering the updraft, the nose pitches *up;* the aircraft experiences heavy positive G; and the airspeed decreases. As the updraft continues, the gust-induced angle of attack may precipitate tip-stall and further pitch-up, for which the pilots compensate with full elevator and nose-down stabilizer. The aircraft now progresses beyond the updraft into the associated downdraft where the nose and the flight path start down. The stabilizer nears its nose-down limit as the airplane falls into that same steep dive.

Wind shear may be the key to the stability debate. Naturally the airplane will seek equilibrium when speed or angle of attack are changed, but those phugoids are the design response to longer-term displacements rather than to severe turbulence. In extreme cases of wind shear such as you might expect near thunderstorm or mountain wave conditions, there could hardly be sufficient static stability to pivot the airplane into precipitous and turbulent gusts in the fashion suggested by Captain Soderlind. That degree of stability would simply not be controllable and might even be self-destructive.

On the contrary, it seems entirely possible that such strong, local shear could easily buffet the aircraft into almost any attitude, without respect for the longer-period restoring moments of static stability. That displacement could then trigger any of the high incidence or high-speed stability problems that lead to gross upset.

Despite the theoretical disagreements, there is remarkable consensus on the techniques involved in upset avoidance and recovery. Those techniques have been widely circulated in the airline industry for at least eight years and may well be responsible for significantly reducing the incidence of jet upset.

There are four primary recommendations for avoiding jet upset. They are:

· *Avoid areas of known turbulence.* Routinely check severe weather and turbulence forecasts for your intended route and studiously avoid the worst areas, even at the expense of added flight time or an extra fuel stop. ATC is still dragging its feet on the subject of controller-supplied weather information, so keep your own radar in peak condition and resolve any questions you might have on equipment operation or image interpretation.

One of your best tools is the real-time information available from other pilots and controllers, so don't be afraid to ask. Along with asking, of course, you must also not be bashful about telling. When you encounter turbulence, tell the world about it. Others on the frequency will be alerted and—in those instances in which the turbulence had been reported previously—your information will remind the sector controller to keep issuing precautions to other aircraft.

If turbulence cannot be avoided, make every effort to penetrate it at an altitude which allows adequate maneuvering speed margins. Also try to have the aircraft at its optimum weight and CG for turbulent air penetrations. The CG is especially important because it can have a significant effect on pitch controllability. The primary thing is, give yourself all the advantages possible when encountering a situation that could lead to an upset.

· *Use recommended penetration speeds.* These speeds are a compromise of two main considerations: The recommended figure must be high enough to protect against a gust-induced stall and low enough to avoid excessive structural loads. One of Captain Soderlind's most significant contributions to the jet upset problem was a restudy of turbulence penetration speeds. His findings led to across-the-board speed increases for one simple reason. Slower speeds provided inadequate protection from gust-induced stall, which proved to be far more serious than structural considerations. Jets hang together very well at speeds substantially above V_{MO}/M_{MO}. If anything, stay on the fast side.

When penetrating turbulence, trim for the penetration speed and set the throttles to maintain altitude. Then leave the trim alone and cautiously use thrust to correct for extreme airspeed excursions. Do not chase the IAS needle and especially avoid airspeed corrections with pitch.

· *Fly attitude.* Keep the wings level and maintain the desired pitch attitude. In aircraft that do have a pitch-up tendency, avoid penetrating turbulence in a climb since that added angle of attack will reduce the stall margin. Use prompt but moderate control inputs to correct attitude changes. *Avoid large control movements.* Allow the altitude to vary if necessary. Absolutely avoid the use of stabilizer trim.

· *Consider using the autopilot.* Since the solution to jet upset is attitude flying, the autopilot may well be able to perform that task better than hand flying. Disconnect the altitude hold feature to prevent the autopilot from introducing large amounts of trim, and just monitor the operation. Note the stabilizer trim position and watch for any large deviation. Be alert for inadvertent disconnect, especially if your installation includes an automatic cutoff circuit (ACO). If you don't use the autopilot, at least engage the yaw damper.

What about recovery from upset? You'll certainly be busy, but it can be done.

· When, and if, the nose pitches up uncontrollably, avoid the use of stabilizer trim. Hold in a full elevator correction and sit tight. When you ride out of the updraft, the nose will start down and the airplane will still be trimmed for level flight.

· After the nose comes down, allow adequate time for IAS to build before attempting to level off so that any threat of a stall will be completely eliminated. If you have not trimmed nose down, you should not need to retrim nose up.

391

· If you do end up in a steep dive, get the spoilers fully out to minimize the speed. Reduce thrust to idle (except for airplanes like the B-737 or B-707, in which the low-thrust-line engines contribute a substantial pitch-up moment).

If at high speed, apply determined back pressure to the yoke until you are just into the buffet at high Mach number or until you estimate a one-G increment at high IAS. When the speed stops increasing, hold what you have and the airplane will come around to level flight. Ease off the stick force as the nose comes up and be prepared to push as it comes to the horizon. Use elevator only until the airplane is level at the original trim speed.

Contrary to what was said above about the use of trim, if *in a stabilized dive* and the speed increase cannot be arrested with elevator, you may need to use a judicious amount of stabilizer trim. At such speeds, that big slab will be fantastically effective, so don't overdo it. If the trim won't move, release back pressure until it will. Remember that the heavy control forces will tend to mask actual G forces, so be careful to stay within structural limits on the pullout. Remember, too, that normal elevator effectiveness will return as the Mach number drops at about 20,000 feet.

You should also be prepared for surges in power, compressor stalls when at high angles of attack and even loss of an engine in the heavy turbulence. Although not directly a part of the pitch-up phenomenon, these engine anomalies can be counter-productive to remaining calm, so you should be prepared to accept them. Take care of the attitude first and worry about the engines second.

Your airplane may not have swept wings, a variable-incidence tailplane or static longitudinal instability at low speeds. Unfortunately, loss of control is not confined to any specific configuration. Given the right circumstances, any of us could end up reading "Dive" on the AH while watching the airspeed run out of sight.

Jet upset is a grisly and awesome phenomenon that has claimed several aircraft. Happily, the improved statistics of recent years may well be the result of increased understanding and the improved techniques discussed above.

How to Avoid the V$_{MC}$-Related Accident

50

by Stanley N. Grayson

Why is it that accidents related to or caused by V$_{MC}$ continue to make their mark in aviation accident statistics? In spite of millions of words in classrooms and cockpits throughout the world, twin-engine pilots continue to get into trouble at the low-speed, engine-out, limit control condition. What is there about this condition that makes it so hazardous? Even experienced pilots sometimes fall prey. Why can't we avoid becoming trapped in this corner of the flight envelope? Should we continue to train in this corner, or train around it? Is the information we give the pilot about V$_{MC}$ the right kind? If so, why do we have so much evidence of misunderstanding about it? It is hoped that this article on V$_{MC}$ will answer these questions and more.

V$_{MC}$ is defined by regulatory requirement (FAR 23.149, "Minimum Control Speed") as "the minimum *calibrated* airspeed at which, when any engine is suddenly made inoperative, it is possible to *recover* control of the airplane with that engine still inoperative and maintain straight flight, either with zero yaw, or at the option of the applicant, with an angle of bank of not more than 5°."

V$_{MC}$ may not exceed 1.2 V$_{SI}$ with:
· Takeoff or maximum available power on each engine;
· The rearmost allowable CG;
· Flaps in the takeoff position;
· Landing gear retracted; and
· The propeller of the inoperative engine windmilling, with the propeller speed or pitch control in the takeoff position; or feathered, if the airplane has an auto-feathering device.

"At V$_{MC}$, the rudder forces required to maintain control may not exceed the limitations of paragraph 23.143, and it may not be necessary to throttle the remaining engines. During recovery, the airplane may not assume any dangerous attitude, or require exceptional piloting skill, alertness, or strength, to prevent a heading change of more than 20°."

Sounds simple and straightforward enough, doesn't it? Well, it isn't. It is a technological web of compromise. In their desire to make a complicated condition simple and easily tested, establish a minimum level of safety, standardize test procedures and present the pilot with just one number to remember, the authorities have arrived at the above definition, essentially unchanged in the last 30 years or more. By its very longevity, it must be considered one of the better written regulations. But if it's so good, why do we still have those VMC, VMC/stall, VMC/stall/spin accidents in such propensity?

Let's evaluate the above regulation and compare it with the real world:

VMC is defined in terms of *calibrated* airspeed (CAS) while the pilot flies by *indicated* airspeed (IAS). Since the airspeed system is allowed to have a five-knot error at 1.3 VSI and *no specified limit error* below 1.3 VSI, the airspeed error at the occurrence of VMC can be quite large. This does not consider additional errors that may creep into the airspeed reading due to erroneous indicators, high body attitudes, slipstream effects or yaw effects. It is the rare pilot who knows enough and cares enough to analyze his calibration curves to find out where he stands with his own airplane and indicators. Luckily, however, the typical light twin has an airspeed system error of only about three knots at near stall speeds in straight, steady, level flight, so the problem is not as great as it may seem.

The regulation talks of "recovering" control after the engine chop. This is a slight misnomer, for the test pilot never really loses control of the vehicle. If he does, the airplane flunked that test point and he must try again at a higher speed. The test pilot "babies up" on the limit control condition (VMC) by conducting both static and dynamic tests at safer, higher speeds and works his way down to VMC. The test pilot must delay control application for one full second after recognition of engine failure to account for the average pilot. "Recognition" is a difficult and argumentative measurement, so let's not get into that. Just rest assured that the test pilot rams full opposite rudder as soon as he can legally do so. VMC designs the rudder on multi-engine airplanes.

The regulation allows a 5° bank angle into the good engine. This lets the ailerons help the rudder in controlling the asymmetric yawing moment, in effect, lessening the rudder design requirement. You also are allowed a 20° heading change during the recovery, a concession to the dynamic nature of the test and to account in some way for the mandated one-second time delay for the average pilot.

"VMC *may not* exceed 1.2 VSI" is governmentese for "VMC *shall not* exceed 1.2 VSI." VMC and VSI are both in terms of calibrated airspeed, and VSI is the stall speed at takeoff weight, gear up, takeoff flaps, and *forward* CG, even though VMC is tested at *aft* CG. This is one of those little "built-in" wrinkles in the regulations, and allows VMC to be slightly higher than if the aft CG stall speed was used. (To our knowledge, no FAA region has interpreted this ruling to include light-weight takeoff, which would reduce the maximum allowable value of VMC still further.)

The regulation limits rudder forces to 150 pounds during the test, the typical airplane requiring very near the limit. FAR 23.143 allows temporary forces of 75 pounds, 60 pounds and 150 pounds for pitch, roll and yaw, respectively. Prolonged forces are 10, 5, and 20 pounds.

The regulation prohibits dangerous attitudes in the *recovery*, but does not address the unusual (if not dangerous) attitudes extant at VMC *entry* in today's aircraft, which generally have a high thrust-to-weight ratio.

Nothing is mentioned about airplane performance. All the regulation guarantees is that the wings will be level at impact 20° off the runway heading. This assumes you have average alertness, skill, strength and use full opposite rudder quickly and effectively. That's not much hill for a stepper, is it? "Skill and alertness" are basically judgment items in spite of several attempts to quantify them by different institutions.

Now that we have evaluated the government's viewpoint on the subject and discussed some of its pitfalls, let's dissect VMC from a technical viewpoint, remembering that it is the critical design condition for multi-engine airplanes with laterally positioned engines. "Push-Pull" centerline thrust installations are excused from this classroom.

The yawing moment created by asymmetric power, T × ly is illustrated by Figure 1. It must be offset by an opposing yawing moment, F × lx, created by deflection of the rudder. For positive control, the yawing moment of the rudder must be greater than the asymmetric yaw.

When all this is put in coefficient form (engineering terms), the resultant plot looks something like Figure 2. Notice that the yawing moment coefficient, CN, is constant for a fully deflected rudder, but the rudder *power* required goes up as speed decreases. If the other engine were failed, essentially the same curve would result, but CN would be negative.

From the Figure, point "A" denotes VMC, and all speeds below that are out of control by definition. If this speed is too high, or the rudder forces too high, then the rudder must be made larger, or boosted controls must be used, or power must be reduced to bring everything back into proper balance.

That is the story in a nutshell, but let's throw in a few acorns, for the above textbook theory has a few bumps in real life:

· The thrust output is not constant, going up and down like a yo-yo with temperature, altitude and power setting. So really, position "A" in Figure 1 represents only one condition in a whole family of curves. But supposedly it is the most critical (highest power) condition. It is the only number published in most flight manuals.

· We don't know if the airplane would have a positive climb gradient at

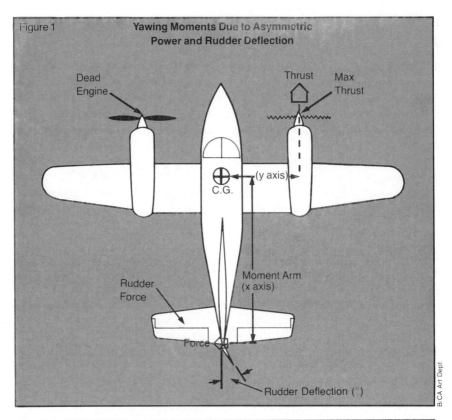

Figure 1

Yawing Moments Due to Asymmetric Power and Rudder Deflection

Dead Engine

Thrust

Max Thrust

(y axis)

C.G.

Moment Arm (x axis)

Rudder Force

Force

Rudder Deflection (°)

B/CA Art Dept.

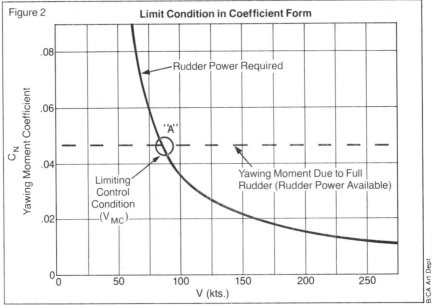

Figure 2

Limit Condition in Coefficient Form

C_N Yawing Moment Coefficient

.08

.06

.04

.02

0

Rudder Power Required

"A"

Limiting Control Condition (V_{MC})

Yawing Moment Due to Full Rudder (Rudder Power Available)

0   50   100   150   200   250

V (kts.)

B/CA Art Dept.

point "A" with an engine out and fully deflected rudder. In many cases, it will not.

· As the airspeed gets slower, the rudder power required gets extremely sensitive, and a five-knot error in the airspeed system in the wrong direction could put you on the short end of control.

· The location of the stall speed relative to point "A" is another control consideration, for if the airplane is stalled just at VMC attainment, you've got a real handful from a control standpoint. Of course, this is highly dependent on the stall characteristics. An airplane with good stall characteristics can be readily controlled even at VMC, but in one with poor stall characteristics, look out!

Also, VMC is always at low speed, near the stall, at high coefficients of lift, where large aileron deflections combined with the resultant roll and the inclination of the lift vectors create yawing moments that add to the asymmetric yaw. In sum, mixing stalls, roll and high amounts of asymmetric yaw are inductive toward spins. The FAA uses this to promote conducting spin tests on twin-engine airplanes, but the negative affects that spin test requirements would have on airplane design can be avoided by providing good stall characteristics, plenty of rudder power and good training.

· The windmilling drag of the dead engine is a function of blade angle, rpm, engine rotational inertia, airspeed and angle of attack. Normally, the windmilling drag is ignored in computations, but certain installations produce high drag, thereby increasing the rudder power requirements still more.

Also, the failure is always considered to be the engine itself—what if a propeller goes into reverse pitch while the engine is running? VMC just went up a bunch! A corollary to this is the story about the four-engine turboprop that ingested birds on takeoff, losing two engines on one side of the airplane. The rudder power was inadequate to handle this much yawing moment—the airplane being below two-engine VMC—and the aircraft went out of control and crashed. Determination of two-engine-out VMC on four-engine airplanes is not a requirement of the FARs.

Let's now look at some peculiarities caused by the propeller rotational direction. From Figure 3, the most critical asymmetric yaw is shown for three twin-engine configurations. The reason the centerline thrust vector shifts around is due to a phenomenon called "P" factor; for example, the downgoing propeller blade has a higher angle of attack relative to the actual direction of the airflow through the prop, therefore a higher C_L than the upgoing blade when the airplane is at high angles of attack. This moves the center of thrust to the right on aircraft with clockwise turning engines (3a) when viewed from the rear. The highest asymmetric yaw occurs on this configuration when the left engine fails. On aircraft with counter-clockwise turning engines, a right engine failure is most critical (3b). With counter-

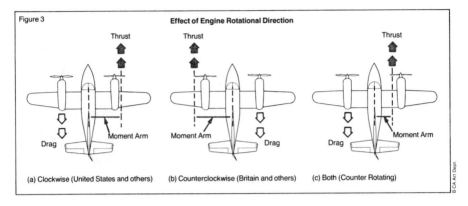

Figure 3

Effect of Engine Rotational Direction

(a) Clockwise (United States and others) (b) Counterclockwise (Britain and others) (c) Both (Counter Rotating)

rotating propellers; for example, one CW on the left and one CCW on the right, the asymmetric yaw is greatly reduced and it is immaterial which engine fails for asymmetric yaw is the same, left or right, all other factors being equal (3c).

Another very critical factor affecting VMC is the affect of altitude on the power available from the operating engine. As altitude increases, power available from a nonturbocharged engine *decreases* and this decrease in power results in a corresponding decrease in asymmetric forces and therefore a decrease in VMC. Thus there is an infinite number of speeds at which VMC may occur.

Now think about what happens as the weight of the aircraft varies, flap positions are changed, the CG is shifted or the rigging is adjusted. Each of those things affects the stall speed. So here we are in an airplane with a constantly changing stall speed and a constantly changing VMC. Yet we must be extremely cautious to never, *ever*, let the two occur simultaneously. The control problems at the point at which the Vs and VMC curves cross are likely to be severe, beyond the capability of almost any pilot.

But, the minimum control speed as a function of power setting normally will not be found in the handbook, so there is no readily available way for the poor pilot to ferret out the dangerous intersections of those stall and VMC curves. A test required by the FAA that basically investigates this problem is one engine-inoperative stall characteristics with 75 percent maximum continuous power on the operating engine. This investigates the handling of the airplane when VMC and stall are very close together, even though they may not be overlapping each other.

Psychologically, then, what have we presented to the pilot when we give him VMC based on the highest engine power? Not much help, that's what.

Certainly, if the pilot always stays above the published VMC, there is little that can happen to him in the way of control difficulty (engine out). Most manufacturers are now relying on a new number, VSSE, safe single-engine speed. This is a speed above VMC, apparently selected by the manufacturer based on his own data. This is fine, but what is wrong with providing a chart of VMC as a function of horsepower? It's easy to come by and would provide the pilot with one more piece of information that, if used intelligently, could help him avoid the Vs-VMC overlap problem. This would be especially good for instructors during training operations.

This brings us to the crux of this presentation. It is a good bet that the vast majority of accidents related to VMC occur during the training situation. In other words, we are trying to prevent accidents by giving demonstrations of accidents. The result has been that too many very experienced pilots have been involved in the VMC accidents in airplanes that were not troublesome from a controllability viewpoint. It is clear that these happen for one or more of the following reasons:

- Complacency or overconfidence on the part of the instructor.
- Too much reliance on aileron, not enough on rudder.
- "The other guy's got it" syndrome.
- *Too much reliance on aileron, not enough on rudder.*
- Seat adjusted improperly to reach full rudder.
- *Too much aileron, not enough rudder.*
- Being "timid" on the controls in order to appear a "smooth" pilot, or failing to apply the full rudder force necessary. A rudder push of 150 pounds is a lot more than you think.
- *Too much aileron, not enough rudder.*
- Vague understanding of adverse yaw, sideslip affects on low-speed operations.
- *Too much aileron, not enough rudder.*
- Repeated operation in a critical control condition.
- *Too much aileron, not enough rudder.*
- Anticipating which engine will be cut.
- *Too much aileron, not enough rudder.*
- Wrong engine, switch, feather control and so forth actuated.
- *Too much aileron, not enough rudder.*
- False sense of security about airplane performance.
- *Too much aileron, not enough rudder.*

If you get the feeling we think most pilots have forgotten (or never knew) what the rudder is for, you're right. Too many pilots "steer" the airplane with aileron while their feet are resting comfortably on the floor. They also "baby" the airplane a distracting amount instead of aggressively making it do what they want it to do. If you do not command the airplane, it will command you, especially engine out. It's guaranteed you will be hip deep in trouble if you don't learn to use the rudder—authoritatively, promptly and defensively. A timid rudder application during a real engine failure will result in a wipeout—probably yours.

PROBLEMS

In regard to horsepower, the current light twin is a different feline from the cat that existed a generation ago. Thrust-to-weight ratios have doubled, which means flight path angles have also doubled. Pour the throttle to both engines on a typical twin today—and hold an airspeed near V_{MC}—and you'll find yourself looking at 30° or more pitch attitude. The instructor who dynamically chops an engine on a green student at that point is asking for trouble. Years ago, an engine chop at V_{MC} was more manageable, but it was dangerous even then. The new thrust-to-weight ratios make it imperative that a way be found to train around making the full-blown V_{MC} demonstration. That will be considered blasphemy by many, but the accident statistics speak for themselves. Instructors repeatedly take students to the limit control condition and too often a disaster results.

One last word on the engine-out condition. Some handbooks have single-engine go-around procedures in the emergency section. Some of these imply that the go-around can be initiated at any time, any height and with the gear and flaps extended. However, the truth is no performance chart exists for single-engine performance with the gear and flaps hanging. Therefore, when you are operating in that situation you are in an area of unknown performance, and you quite likely cannot make a successful go-around.

An example is taken from the flight manual of a well-known light-twin turboprop that has a single-engine go-around procedure. From the balked landing (two engine) climb chart, 2000 feet altitude, ISA + 20°C, 8200 pounds weight, we find that the rate of climb equals 1350 fpm. From the engine power charts we find the shaft horsepower available. Reducing that for an 80 percent efficient propeller (assumed) we find the thrust horsepower available. Through some mathematical trickery, learned at great expense, the drag is found to be the equivalent of 482 thrust horsepower at the recommended speed.

But alas, the full takeoff power available with one engine out is only 436 thrust horsepower. This does not count the drag of a windmilling propeller or the yaw drag due to asymmetry. So our unsuspecting pilot puts full power on at 50 feet to initiate a go-around and finds himself still sinking. He can't pull the gear up because he's afraid he will belly it in and he knows better than to pull up the flaps at such a precarious altitude, so he pulls the nose up, approaching V_{MC}. A half mile or so down the runway, our pilot is faced with landing as is or losing flight control. In essence, he lost control when he initiated the go-around.

The moral of this story is: Do not attempt a single-engine go-around unless you have sufficient altitude to get the gear and flaps up and attain a condition of known performance. This usually takes 300 to 400 feet terrain clearance.

At the beginning of this article, some questions were asked that, by now, you probably can answer from the text already presented. Several steps could be taken by the industry and the FAA that would greatly reduce VMC-related accidents, while improving the flying qualities of the typical airplane. These are:

· Change the low airspeed accuracy standards from $\pm$ five knots to $\pm$ four knots, which is essentially the same error allowed years ago when it was expressed in the former statute mile unit as $\pm$ five mph.

· Apply the above airspeed accuracy standards down to 1.2 VSI in the takeoff and cruise configurations, and down to 1.2 VSO in the landing configuration. These steps would assure accuracy nearer the critical control speed. System variations due to weight, attitude, power setting, asymmetric power and yaw should be investigated during flight test and described to the pilot in the flight manual. This, we think, is a reasonable request; anything that biases the airspeed, the pilot should know about.

· Standardize all charts, placards and airspeed indicators into knots and degrees Celcius (Centigrade). Ban airspeed indicators marked in two units of speed. (Nuts, sales—it's knots.)

· Reduce the maximum allowable VMC from 1.2 VSI to 1.15 VSI and do away with the 5° bank angle concession. VSI should be at takeoff weight and flaps, *forward* CG. All this would result in more powerful rudders.

· Reduce the maximum allowable rudder force from 150 pounds to 135 pounds. This would enhance the probability of full rudder application by the average pilot.

· Provide a chart of VMC as a function of horsepower, shaft horsepower, or thrust, as appropriate, for the range of altitudes and temperatures the aircraft is certificated to operate in.

· Provide docile stall characteristics.

· Do not go looking for trouble by conducting training at VMC. Stay 5

GLOSSARY OF TERMS
CL—Lift Coefficent
CN—Yawing moment coefficent
CCW—Counter clockwise
CW—Clockwise
F—Force
1x—Moment arm, x axis
1y—Moment arm, y axis
T—Thrust
VMC—Minimum Control Speed
Vs—Stall Speed, no particular configuration
Vsi—Stall Speed, specified configuration
Vso—Stall Speed, Landing Configuration
Vsse—Safe signal engine speed
W—Weight

to 10 knots above the actual critical control case. If Vs and VMC are near one another, change the asymmetric yaw situation to separate them.

· Drill students on use of the rudder. It is not just a device to keep the ball in the center. It is the yaw control. Use it!

· Record the altitude lost in transitioning from 1.3 Vso (gear and flaps down, maximum landing weight) to 1.2 VsI (gear and flaps up, one engine inoperative). The power on the operating engine should be the maximum continuous power appropriate for ISA + 20° conditions at 2000 feet altitude. This number should be published in the flight manual as a barometer of airplane go-around capability.

Many will think the above is just the raving of a frustrated rulemaker, but the things outlined would improve engine-out safety, increase the capability of the pilot to control the airplane and reduce confusion due to non-standardized charts. Some of these suggestions could be done voluntarily by manufacturers or instructors and implemented almost immediately.

The increased rudder power could, and should, come along on the next airplane design, for that's what this whole thing boils down to—*we need more rudder.*

After the Accident 51

by Dan Manningham

Accidents are trouble. Even when damage is minimal and no one is injured, the paperwork alone is enough to ruin your whole day. There are so many people with divergent interests and responsibilities who will want to know what happened. You can become confused and say things you shouldn't have or leave unsaid and unreported, facts that would've made the ordeal much less traumatic. Small amounts of planning now can save a lot of grief later, so let's look at the pilot's administrative problems following an aircraft accident or incident.

The sole federal agency responsible for aircraft accident investigation is the NTSB. (In most non-fatal general aviation accidents, however, the NTSB will delegate investigative procedures to the local FAA field office.) When the dust has settled and the basic problems of survival have been cared for, you will have at least three specific responsibilities to the NTSB:

(1) Immediate notification that an accident has happened.

(2) Preservation and protection of the wreckage.

(3) Written report of the accident at a later date.

When you are involved in any reportable event, those three acts constitute your minimum administrative responsibility to the government, but you also have an immediate responsibility to your company and, in the case of a businessman pilot, to your associates. To make certain everything is properly covered, you should draw up a plan now.

All of the information pertaining to aircraft accidents should be organized beforehand into a comprehensive company policy and distributed to the appropriate personnel. Procedures should insure that:

(1) The NTSB has been notified.

(2) Key executives of the company are notified that the aircraft has been involved in an accident, the extent of injuries to passengers, and what arrangements have been made for their continuation of the trip if appropriate.

(3) Company's public relations department is briefed and prepared to handle inquiries.

(4) Company's legal counsel is advised of the basic facts.

(5) Insurance agency or department is contacted directly and advised of the basic facts.

(6) Next-of-kin of each person on the aircraft is called.

(7) Switchboard operators and answering services understand whom to contact and are supplied with the home telephone numbers of key personnel.

Part 430 of the NTSB regulations is the key to what constitutes a reportable happening. Essentially you must report all accidents, and some incidents, when they involve civil aircraft registered in the United States regardless of where the accident may happen. Similarly, you must report accidents and some incidents to foreign civil aircraft when such events occur on American soil.

NTSB regulation 430.2 provides these definitions: *"Aircraft accident* means an occurrence associated with the operation of an aircraft which takes place between the time any person boards the aircraft with the intention of flight until such time as all such persons have disembarked, in which any person suffers death or serious injury as a result of being in or upon the aircraft or by direct contact with the aircraft or anything attached thereto, or the aircraft receives substantial damage.

"*Fatal injury* means any injury which results in death within seven days.

"*Operator* means any person who causes or authorizes the operation of an aircraft, such as the owner, lessee, or bailee of an aircraft.

"*Serious injury* means any injury which (1) requires hospitalization for more than 48 hours, commencing within seven days from the date the injury was received; (2) results in a fracture of any bone (except simple fractures of fingers, toes, or nose); (3) involves lacerations which cause severe hemorrhages, nerve, muscle or tendon damage; (4) involves injury to any internal organ, or (5) involves second or third degree burns, or any burns affecting more than five percent of the body surface.

"*Substantial damage:*

"(1) Except as provided in subparagraph (2) of this paragraph, substantial damage means damage or structural failure which adversely affects the structural strength, performance or flight characteristics of the aircraft, and which would normally require major repair or replacement of the affected component.

"(2) Engine failure, damage limited to an engine, bent fairings or cowling, dented skin, small punctured holes in the skin or fabric, ground damage to rotor or propeller blades, damage to landing gear, wheels, tires, flaps, engine accessories, brakes, or wing tips are not considered 'substantial damage' for the purpose of this part."

Notice that you don't have to be flying or even taxiing in order to have a reportable accident. Notice too that fatalities are counted through the seventh day after the accident.

Don't make any guesses about when a report is required, but get familiar with these definitions because they are the key to what constitutes a reportable accident. When you are involved in a reportable event, you must initiate the contact with the NTSB and you must use the quickest possible means.

Part 430.5 covers the initial notification: "The operator of an aircraft shall immediately, and by the most expeditious means available, notify the nearest NTSB Bureau of Aviation Safety Field Office when:

"(a) An aircraft accident or any of the following listed incidents occur:

"(1) Flight control system malfunction or failure;

"(2) Inability of any required flight crewmember to perform his normal flight duties as a result of injury or illness;

"(3) Turbine engine rotor failures excluding compressor blades and turbine buckets;

"(4) Inflight fire;

"(5) Aircraft collide in flight.

"(b) An aircraft is overdue and is believed to have been involved in an accident."

Again, you need to be familiar with the regulations because the "incidents" listed above must be reported with the same urgency as the "accidents" defined earlier. And all must be reported with speed, which leaves you three options:

(1) A telephone call to the nearest NTSB office.

(2) A telegram to the nearest NTSB office.

(3) Notification to the FAA (a FSS or the closest FAA facility of any type) which will in turn notify the NTSB.

This first notification to the Board must include the following specific information:

"(1) Type, nationality and registration marks of the aircraft;

"(2) Name of owner and (name of) operator of the aircraft;

"(3) Name of the pilot-in-command;

"(4) Date and time of the accident;

"(5) Last point of departure and point of (next) intended landing of the aircraft;

"(6) Position of the aircraft with reference to some easily defined geographical point;

"(7) Number of persons aboard, number killed and number seriously injured;

"(8) Nature of the accident including weather and the extent of damage to the aircraft so far as is known;

Business and Commercial Aviation

FLIGHT CREW AIRCRAFT ACCIDENT/INCIDENT NOTIFICATION CHECKLIST

Priority Procedures

FIRST—NTSB/FAA Notified ☐
SECOND—Company Notified ☐
THIRD—Passengers arrange for accommodations or continued transportation as appropriate ☐
FOURTH—Wreckage; arrange for protection and removal after NTSB clearance ☐

NTSB/FAA Initial Notification
(NTSB Part 430.6)

1. Aircraft Type_____N Number_____
2. Aircraft Nationality_____
3. Aircraft Operator_____
4. Aircraft Owner_____
5. Pilot-in-Command_____
6. Accident/Incident_____Time_____
7. Last Departure Point_____
8. Next Intended Landing Point_____
9. Aircraft/Wreckage Position_____
10. Number Persons Aboard: Crew_____Passengers_____
11. Number Injuries_____Number Fatalities_____
12. Weather: VFR_____IFR_____Vis_____Wind_____Ceil_____
13. Extent of Damage_____
14. Dangerous Articles Aboard_____
15. Type of Flight: Cargo_____Tng._____Pass._____
16. Name of NTSB or FAA agent called_____

Company Notification Checklist
(Home Phone Numbers)

1. Chief Pilot (_____) ☐
2. Chairman of Board (_____) ☐
3. President (_____) ☐
4. Chief of Maintenance (_____) ☐
5. P.R. Department (_____) ☐
6. Company Attorney (_____) ☐
7. Company Insurance (_____ ☐
8. Company Answering Service Briefed ☐
9. Other Key Personnel:
  Title_____ (_____) ☐
  Title_____ (_____) ☐
  Title_____ (_____) ☐
10. Next of Kin Notified, If Appropriate_____ ☐

"(9) A description of any explosives, radioactive materials or other dangerous articles carried."

As you can see, the process is simple enough. Just a phone call to the nearest NTSB or FAA office with the appropriate information. This notice should include only the basic facts without any discussion of the possible cause. You may be asked to make a statement, but you have every right to decline until you have recovered from the trauma of the accident.

If police or press are present, it is appropriate, and even desirable, to supply basic information, but resist the temptation to speculate about the cause of the accident. No one, and perhaps least of all the pilot involved, is in a position to accurately define the probable cause without substantial investigation and research. Simple information about number of passengers, aircraft registration and flight plan will satisfy most law enforcement officials and newsmen. Be courteous and specific, but above all be brief.

Until the NTSB representatives arrive and take charge, you have the responsibility to protect the wreckage along with any mail, cargo or records, to the best of your ability. Part 430.10 explains:

"(a) The operator of an aircraft is responsible for preserving to the extent possible any aircraft wreckage, cargo and mail aboard the aircraft, and all records, including tapes of flight recorders and voice recorders, pertaining to the operation and maintenance of the aircraft and to the airmen involved . . . until the Board takes custody thereof or a release is granted.

"(b) Prior to the time the Board or its authorized representative takes custody of aircraft wreckage, mail or cargo, such wreckage, mail and cargo may be disturbed or moved only to the extent necessary:

"(1) To remove persons injured or trapped;

"(2) To protect the wreckage from further damage, or

"(3) To protect the public from injury.

"(c) Where it is necessary to disturb or move aircraft wreckage, mail or cargo, sketches, descriptive notes and photographs shall be made, if possible, of the accident locale including original position and condition of the wreckage and any significant impact marks.

"(d) The operator of an aircraft involved in an accident or incident shall retain all records and reports, including all internal documents and memoranda dealing with the accident or incident, until authorized by the Board to the contrary."

A company aircraft accident policy and checklist should be written specifically for each person who would have any role during an aircraft accident situation. Your checklist, with the phone numbers filled in, should look like this and be kept in your Jepp manual. Once each item on the list has been taken care of after an accident or incident you can be certain that you have fulfilled your immediate obligations to the government, your passengers and your company.

Our suggestion is to just let the whole sorry mess lie undisturbed and enlist the help of local police to keep away vandals and souvenir hunters. If you must hire a guard, your insurance company will almost certainly accept that as a justifiable expense. When accident investigators arrive, it's their bailiwick until they specifically state otherwise, and you will need a written release from them to move or alter the airplane or its contents.

After you have notified the NTSB and provided for suitable protection of the wreckage, your immediate responsibility to the U.S. government has been fulfilled, but there are several things you may want to do before leaving.

Any information you are able to record will be of substantial help to the accident investigators in determining the probable cause. This same information may also be invaluable in any subsequent liability claims. You must not disturb or move any part of the wreckage, but a careful notation of control and switch positions and fluid levels is certainly in order. And a brief assessment of outside factors such as ice on the airframe or runway and general weather conditions may add materially to the subsequent investigation.

If possible make arrangements for a comprehensive set of photographs of the wreckage and the surrounding area. Be sure to obtain names and addresses of any eyewitnesses and don't forget tower personnel if the accident occurred on or near a controlled airport. Arrange for medical examination of passengers and crew, whether injured or not, and request a doctor's report on each one.

When you do finally wrap up all the loose ends at the scene of the accident, make one more stop on the way home. Gather your crew in a quiet corner somewhere (not in a bar), unwind and discuss the whole episode from beginning to end. Write down a clear, concise chronology, listing everything that happened whether it seems important or not. Stick to the facts; such as times, places, altitudes, speeds, temperatures and pressures. Don't quit until you can all agree on a simple, but complete sequence of events. When everyone is satisfied, make a copy for each crewmember and a few extras for the file.

This little drill will serve to enhance your recall, resolve misunderstandings and fill in the blanks that naturally result from emotional trauma.

Some years ago, a B/CA staff editor helped evacuate an airplane which had an unexplained massive fire on the right wing while taxiing. The entire incident, including passenger evacuation, was all over in less than two minutes, but it took three crewmembers several hours to accurately reconstruct the sequence of radio transmissions, warning bells and cockpit reactions. The chronology generated by this session was invaluable in the subsequent NTSB hearing and was well received by everyone concerned.

Your last responsibility to the NTSB (barring any hearings) is to file a report within 10 days after the accident. Part 430.15 outlines the procedure:

"(a) *Reports.* The operator of an aircraft shall file a report as provided in paragraph (c) of this section on NTSB Form 6120.1 or 6120.2 (for aircraft under and over 12,500 pounds respectively):

"(1) Within 10 days after an accident for which notification is required by 430.5(a) or when after seven days, an overdue aircraft is still missing.

"(2) A report on an incident for which notification is required by 430.5(a) shall be filed only as requested by an authorized representative of the NTSB.

"(b) *Crewmember statement.* Each crewmember, if physically able at the time the report is submitted, shall attach thereto a statement setting forth the facts, conditions and circumstances relating to the accident or incident as they appear to him to the best of his knowledge and belief. If the crewmember is incapacitated, he shall submit the statement as soon as he is physically able.

"(c) *Where to file the reports.* The operator of an aircraft shall file with the Field Office of the NTSB nearest the accident or incident of any report required by this section."

The forms themselves are available at any NTSB office and you will find them well organized and easy to complete. And bear in mind that this agency does not issue violations, so there is every reason to be open and honest. The Safety Board is interested solely in aviation safety.

The FAA has the responsibility to issue violations when and if they are warranted. In the case of an accident or incident, it is possible for the FAA to issue a violation up to several months after the fact, based on information from the NTSB investigation. If this happens, you will have to deal with the FAA directly in regard to any alleged violation, but if punitive action is taken you may request a review by the NTSB which functions on the first level of appeal in all such cases.

Now is the time to prepare for an accident. Read the regulations and get started on a company policy. Coordinate with the applicable departments, your insurance agent and legal counsel so that everyone is in agreement. When you are satisfied with the result, make sure that each person involved has a copy and understands it. After that, review the whole thing annually.

Finally, draw up a checklist for flight crews so that each pilot can carry a copy in his flight bag, and be sure to brief new pilots as part of the company training course. When disaster strikes, everyone will react more intelligently if they are adequately prepared.

A Final Word

We have concluded this book on a rather somber note because the very thing which separates the serious pilot from the aeronautical dilettante is his knowledge that flying is more than blue sky and smooth air. More important, he craves the knowledge that will allow him to cope with those very real hazards.

You see, the serious pilot flies professionally whether or not he is actually paid, because professionalism is a frame of mind, a basic attitude toward aviation quite apart from position or status. Every pursuit has its small core of purists who are motivated by a personal demand for excellence. The pursuit of flying is no different. This book is dedicated to such pilots.

We hope that these pages have helped you to improve your proficiency and preparedness. We know that your enhanced sense of confidence and pleasure will be communicated to your passengers. In the final analysis, well placed confidence, all-around, is the most valuable result of staying current.